Press Silence in Postcolonial Zimbabwe

This book focuses on news silence in Zimbabwe, taking as a point of departure the (in)famous blank spaces (whiteouts) which newspapers published to protest official censorship policy imposed by the Rhodesian government from the mid-1960s to the end of that decade.

Based on archived news content, the author investigates the cause(s) of the disappearance of blank spaces in Zimbabwe's newspapers and establishes whether and how the blank spaces may have been continued by stealth and proposes a model of doing journalism where news is inclusive, just and less productive of blank spaces. The author explores the broader ramifications of news silences, tacit or covert on society's sense of the world and their place in it. The book questions whether and how news media continued with the practice of epistemic deletions and continue to draw on the colonial archive for conceptual maps with which to define and interpret contemporary postcolonial realities and challenges in Zimbabwe.

This book will be of interest to scholars, researchers and academics researching the press in contemporary Africa, critical media analysis, media and society studies, and news as discourse.

Zvenyika Eckson Mugari is Deputy Dean of the Faculty of Social Sciences and Lecturer in the Media and Society Studies Department at the Midlands State University, Zimbabwe. He also holds a Post-Doctoral Research Fellowship with the Centre for Diversity Studies, University of the Witwatersrand, South Africa.

Routledge Contemporary Africa

Press Silence in Postcolonial Zimbabwe
News whiteouts, Journalism and Power
Zvenyika E. Mugari

Urban Planning in Rapidly Growing Cities
Developing Addis Ababa
Mintesnot G. Woldeamanuel

Regional Development Poles and the Transformation of African Economies
Benaiah Yongo-Bure

Nature, Environment and Activism in Nigerian Literature
Sule E. Egya

Corporate Social Responsibility and Law in Africa
Theories, Issues and Practices
Nojeem A. Amodu

Greening Industrialization in Sub-Saharan Africa
Ralph Luken and Edward Clarence-Smith

Health and Care in Old Age in Africa
Edited by Pranitha Maharaj

Rethinking African Agriculture
How Non-Agrarian Factors Shape Peasant Livelihoods
Edited by Goran Hyden, Kazuhiko Sugimura and Tadasu Tsuruta

For more information about this series, please visit: https://www.routledge.com/Routledge-Contemporary-Africa/book-series/RCAFR

Press Silence in Postcolonial Zimbabwe

News Whiteouts, Journalism and Power

Zvenyika Eckson Mugari

LONDON AND NEW YORK

First published 2020
by Routledge
2 Park Square, Milton Park, Abingdon, Oxon OX14 4RN

and by Routledge
605 Third Avenue, New York, NY 10017

Routledge is an imprint of the Taylor & Francis Group, an informa business

First issued in paperback 2021

© 2020 Zvenyika E. Mugari

The right of Zvenyika E. Mugari to be identified as author of this work has been asserted by him in accordance with sections 77 and 78 of the Copyright, Designs and Patents Act 1988.

All rights reserved. No part of this book may be reprinted or reproduced or utilised in any form or by any electronic, mechanical, or other means, now known or hereafter invented, including photocopying and recording, or in any information storage or retrieval system, without permission in writing from the publishers.

Trademark notice: Product or corporate names may be trademarks or registered trademarks, and are used only for identification and explanation without intent to infringe.

Publisher's Note
The publisher has gone to great lengths to ensure the quality of this reprint but points out that some imperfections in the original copies may be apparent.

British Library Cataloguing-in-Publication Data
A catalogue record for this book is available from the British Library

Library of Congress Cataloging-in-Publication Data
A catalog record has been requested for this book

ISBN 13: 978-0-367-25225-0 (hbk)
ISBN 13: 978-1-03-223789-3 (pbk)
ISBN 13: 978-0-429-28841-8 (ebk)

Typeset in Baskerville
by Taylor & Francis Books

Contents

	List of illustrations	vi
	Acknowledgements	ix
1	Colonial foundations of press silence in Zimbabwe	1
2	Colonial press and intersecting loci of silencing	23
3	News whiteouts under UDI and after	41
4	News silence on forced removals in colonial Rhodesia	68
5	*The Daily News* and 'telling the land story like it is'	109
6	*The Herald* and patriotic news on the land issue	158
7	Operation Restore (colonial) Order	207
8	'Operation Restore Legacy' in post-Mugabe era	239
9	Do-it-yourself (DIY) news and the emancipatory promise	276
	Index	300

Illustrations

Figures

1.1	The *Rhodesia Herald* reports 'The Mashona Rising' 24 June 1896. The killed listing was decidedly white. Reprinted by permission. National Archives of Zimbabwe	6
2.1	Relief map of Zimbabwe	29
2.2	Map of Zimbabwe, highlighting the relocations of Chiefs Ruya and Gobo to Silobela and Chief Huchu to Charama	30
3.1a and b	Blank spaces became a common feature in *The Rhodesia Herald* (left) and the *Central African Examiner* (right). National Archives of Zimbabwe	46
3.2	Google aerial map of Harare showing proximity of newsrooms to their main news sources (centres of elite power).	55
3.3	The Zapiro cartoon depicting embedded journalism. © 2003 Zapiro. Originally published in *Mail* and *Guardian*. Republished with permission	59
3.4	Whiteness as a news value before and after independence. Reprinted with permission: *The Herald*	61
4.1	Map of Rhodesia showing status of land segregation by 1969 before the passing into law of the Land Tenure Act of 1969. Source: Parker, 1972	73
4.2	Chief Rekayi Tangwena dressed in his traditional chiefly regalia leads children of his people to the mountains where their parents are hiding after their villages had been demolished. Republished with permission. National Archives of Zimbabwe	91
5.1	Cartoon by Tony Namate depicting oppression of the poor, before and after independence. Source: Reprinted by permission from *The Daily News*	114
5.2	The power hierarchy to name in a typical farm invasion story at *The Daily News*	123
5.3	Front page of *The Daily News* on 5 April 2000. Source: Reprinted by permission from *The Daily News*	125

List of illustrations   vii

5.4	A typical letters to the editor page of *The Daily News* 13 April 2000. Reprinted by permission from *The Daily News*	130
5.5	A full page devoted to a white farmers' account of events at his farm. Reprinted with permission from *The Daily News*	138
5.6	Close to a full page dedicated to memorialising forced evictions of white farmers. Reprinted with permission from *The Daily News*	144
5.7	A typical leader page of *The Daily News* Reprinted with permission from *The Daily News*	147
6.1a and b	Comparable headlines in the two newspapers. Reproduced with permission from *The Daily News* and *The Herald*	163
6.2	*The Herald* leader page 6 March 2000, cartoon caricature of farm invasions. Republished with permission from *The Herald*	170
6.3a and b	Front pages of *The Herald* reporting the killing of white farmers in clashes with war veterans on 17 and 19 April 2000. Reprinted with permission from *The Herald*	175
6.4	An example of how the plight of the farm workers caught up in the milieu of land occupations was seldom narrated in newspapers. Reprinted with permission from *The Herald*	184
6.5	*The Herald* early reporting on farm occupations used delegitimising language, e.g. 'farm invasions' 'invading … farm', including accompanying photographs of axe-wielding mobs on the march to invade the next farm. Reprinted with permission from *The Herald*	192
7.1	Notice of official Launch of Operation Murambatsvina. Reprinted with permission from *The Herald*	214
7.2	The hierarchy of primary definition on the Operation Murambatsvina story at *The Herald*	220
8.1a and b	*The Herald* front page and *The Daily News* front page on the 14 November 2017. Reprinted with permission	243
8.2a and b	Exit Mugabe; Enter Mnangagwa. Reprinted with permission from *The Herald*	248
8.3a and b	*Daily News* headlines marking Mugabe's exit as the beginning of a new era in Zimbabwe. Reprinted with permission from *The Daily News*	250
8.4a and b	Different headlines, the same event: *The Herald* implicates the MDC while *The Daily News* blames military heavy-handedness for the August 2018 post-election violence. Reproduced courtesy of *The Herald* and *The Daily News*	252
8.5a and b	*The Herald* front page increasingly becomes very predictable, carrying the President's picture or his name in the lead headline. Reprinted with permission from *The Herald*	261
9.1	Front page of the last edition of *The Central African Examiner* of December 1965. Courtesy of the National Archives of Zimbabwe	286

viii *List of illustrations*

Tables

1.1	Cecil John Rhodes masked his stake in the RPP through proxies	11
5.1	Zimpapers as alma mater for most journalists in Zimbabwe. Source: Saunders, 1999	116
5.2	*The Daily News* issues of August 2002: Analysis of stories/articles on FTLRP	132
5.3	Language of legitimation and delegitimation of the FTLRP in *The Herald* and *The Daily News*	141
6.1	News story headlines 'critical' of the land reform programme	162
6.2	Headline stories on farm invasions in *The Herald*, March 2000	171
7.1	Officialdom in news sourcing at *The Herald*	216
8.1	Reasons for the dismissal of *The Herald*'s editor	257

Boxes

5.1	Fast Track Land Reform Programme timeline	118
5.2	Typical news headlines in *The Daily News*	119

Acknowledgements

I would like to thank the Midlands State University, my home institution, for granting me a sabbatical leave that enabled me to take up the Postdoctoral Fellowship at the University of the Witwatersrand where I was able to give my undivided attention to the task of coming up with this book.

I also wish to extend my heartfelt thanks to Professor Melissa Steyn, the Director at the Wits Center for Critical Diversity Studies, who was my host for the year-long Postdoctoral Fellowship, from August 2018 to July 2019. Mellissa, as she is affectionately called at the Center, is the humblest person I have known, and thanks to that quality in her, which made my stay at Wits very comfortable and most memorable. She read and made the most critical conceptual interventions at the very formative stages of writing the proposal for this monograph. William Mpofu, Researcher at the Centre, deserves special mention for availing his time and patiently listening and engaging me on different themes of this work during our evening retreats as we relaxed over drinks on many a Friday afternoon at the 'Pig'. To him I owe the critical decolonial inflection in some chapters of this book. Alice Wabule, a special friend and my office mate, the Postdoctoral office would have been a very lonely affair without her. To the rest of my friends and 'partners in crime' at the office – Faith Lazarous, Haley McEwen, Precious Mzite, Gillian Jena, Rudo Muzite, Kudzai Vanyoro, Mbali Mazibuko – your kindness and thoughtfulness will be forever cherished.

My most heartfelt gratitude goes to the editorial staff and management of *The Herald* and the *Daily News* for providing unconditional access to their respective newsrooms for my research and for copyright permissions to reproduce pages of past issues of their newspapers as well as pictures and cartoons in this book. Thanks to staff and management of the National Archives of Zimbabwe and Mr Jonathan Zapiro for granting me permission to reproduce pictures and cartoons retrieved from their archives.

A special thank you to Professor Chipo Hungwe, Dean of Social Sciences, for your support throughout. Many thanks too go to my colleagues in the Department of Media and Society Studies: Nhamo Mhiripiri, Peter Mandava, Elikana Shoko, Caven Masuku, Patience Mushuku, (mukomana weGokwe) Lyton Ncube, (musharukwa weKanye) Albert Chibuwe, Tariro Ndawana, Nyasha Mapuwei, Beauty Muromo, Oswalled Ureke, Painos Moyo and Tichafa Mushangwe. You provided the much-needed homely and collegial environment for this work.

x *Acknowledgements*

Last but not least, I am grateful to my family who were the main source of inspiration for my embarking on this project. Without their support and encouragement, it would have been near impossible for me to see this project through. My wife Sipikelelo, your name says it all. Thanks for persevering during many months of my being away from home. To my daughters Kiki, Yananiso and Shelo and Ray my son, most excellent children, it's I who takes after your example. I dedicate this book to you and to my mother Otillia with love and gratitude.

1 Colonial foundations of press silence in Zimbabwe

Introduction

Zimbabwe's colonial encounter with Europeans and her insertion into the modern global geo-political order happened to her towards the end of the nineteenth century by proxy (it can be argued) mediated by South Africa. This is not to understate an earlier history of contact between indigenous inhabitants of the territory we now call Zimbabwe with European traders of Portuguese extraction who visited the Mwenemutapa capital from their established seaports along the Mozambican coast. That earlier historical encounter, about which much has already been documented in Zimbabwe's historiography (Randles 1979), has its legitimate place as a chapter in the history of Zimbabwe. The subject of the early pre-colonial period, however, falls outside the scope of this study. The concern here is with the news and how the press invokes news values to account for and institutionalise epistemic exclusion and silencing of alternative ways of knowing and in the process aid and abate wittingly or otherwise the maintenance and repair of systems of domination in society. This chapter provides a brief outline of the historical link between the press and the governing authority from when the first newspaper was published in Zimbabwe to the present. It also traces how the dual parentage of government and the press in modern-day Zimbabwe to South Africa.

The historical origin of newspaper production in and about occurrences in the land between the Limpopo and the Zambezi rivers is intricately linked to the founding of this territory as a British colony in 1890, with the first newspaper under the title *Mashonaland Herald* and *Zambesian Times* being published on 27 June 1891 (Gale, 1962), only a year after Cecil John Rhodes' British South Africa Company (BSAC) had taken occupation of the territory. The publishers of this newspaper were The Argus Printing & Publishing Company Ltd., a subsidiary of the Argus Company of South Africa based in Cape Town and Johannesburg, a newspaper conglomerate with very strong links with Rhodes' BSAC. In fact, historical record has it that the Argus Company came to set up in Salisbury on invitation by Rhodes. It is therefore instructive to note that right from its inception the press was viewed as an important if not indispensable part of the colonial enterprise. The façade of separation between those who owned and produced the

2 *Foundations of press silence in Zimbabwe*

press and those who ran the colonial establishment politically was kept in place and maintained throughout the colonial period on the tacit assumption that this arrangement guaranteed and safeguarded the press's editorial autonomy, so critical for the credibility and believability of its news offerings. The BSAC and the Cape Argus had many points of intersection historically and economically as they expanded their operations across the Limpopo into new-found territory. The coincidence of mind and economic interests was clearly encapsulated in the editorial charter of all newspaper publications of the Rhodesia Printing and Publishing Company, as the Argus' Rhodesian subsidiary company was known. In those early years of company rule, the line of separation between the press and the BSAC was indeed thin and blurred, evidenced by the fact that *The Rhodesia Herald* conflated its role as an impartial chronicler of events and being the colonial authority's mouthpiece as it saw no contradiction in printing the *British South Africa Company Government Gazette*, as a supplement to *The Rhodesia Herald*. It also did not find participation in and benefiting from Rhodes' largesse, by way of allocations of large tracts of prime land expropriated from Africans, problematic and compromising of its watchdog role.

In the beginning was communication

The coming of the Pioneer Column in 1890 did not mark the beginning of communication in Zimbabwe even among the small number of white settlers who soon dispersed in all directions from Fort Salisbury, much less so, for the African population who lived in all of the country. People were communicating. It would be to make a huge claim to assume that the way of life of the nascent multi-racial community altered in any significant way with the publication of the first newspaper to be published in Zimbabwe under the name *The Mashonaland Herald and Zambezian Times* by William Ernest Fairbridge, agent of the South African Argus Newspapers company, in Salisbury on 27 June 1891 (Gale, 1962). The celebration of this event has continued to distract from any serious scholarly attempt to engage with the study of communication generally, especially of the larger population of Zimbabwe who have continued to live their lives untouched by the press, those who live outside of the media circuits. The erroneous assumption that those without a press have no means of communication among themselves, partly explains why the very well organised Mashona rebellion of 1896–1897 caught the white settler community in the then Rhodesia flatfooted. Surprisingly, there has been no serious attempt made to systematically study the organisation of an intricate system of communication that was behind that uprising mediated by human agents. No system of modern technicised exchange of information could match it in potency. This is not to romanticise the oral-based communication over other more modern technology based forms of communication. It, too, had its own flaws. For example, it is doubtful that hierarchically organised as it was around spirit mediums as the messengers of *Mwari* [1] could have been immune to abuse by those who wielded almost unchecked power over the form and content of that message in a way that produced silencing of its own.

The other weakness derived from its reliance on human oral messaging, where the original messages were prone to being altered in the telling as the signal fires lit on top of kopjes and chain-letter messages of the Mwari cult passed from village to village. Once the human agents (the masvikiros) 'spirit mediums', with Mkwati at the command centre from whence Mwari spoke the word at the sacred shrine of Mabweadziva in Matonjeni, it had to be relayed through the spirit mediums of Kaguvi, the Mhondoro of central Mashonaland and other regional spirit mediums or Mhondoros such as Nehanda Nyakasikana of Mazoe and Goronga of Lomagundi areas (Ranger, 1967). Once this network of trusted spirit mediums who formed its central nervous system were taken out, the communication system that had sustained the revolt withered away, and so ended the first Chimurenga. Post-facto reconstruction of a coherent account of how the guerrilla messaging techniques behind the Shona rebellion worked is near impossible from the colonial news archive. This is partly due to histriography's focus on individual personalities and its valorisation of the written record and documentary evidence.

That history is often involved in the production of the past in the service of the present hegemon and that it interprets that past in terms of the dominant thought patterns and prejudices of the time is evident in the debate that ensued between Beach and Ranger over the historical significance of the First Chimurenga in the history of Zimbabwe. Beach, writing from a colonial locus of articulation, premises his whole counter-Rangerian thesis on the inferiority of the African, more specifically the Shona whose capacity to organise was held in question. From that point of departure, he then goes on to argue that innocent, scattered and without a unitary state as the Shona were, they could not have been in a position to muster the organisational capacity to spearhead a centralised system of war planning and execution necessary in an uprising against white settlers. His account, however, becomes self-contradictory on many points when it makes the acknowledgement of how war spoils were discovered at the mediums of Kaguvi and Nehanda's strongholds, a detail which should have suggested to any observer that the two must have played key roles as coordinators who had authority over how the war spoils were to be distributed. As a good historian of empire, Beach finds no contradiction in terms, in that the colonial administration in its wisdom particularly targeted chief Mashayan'ombe and that even after killing him would neither rest nor declare that the war was over, until they had arrested, tried and executed the spirit mediums Charwe (Nehanda) and Gumboreshumba (Kaguvi) and the fact that the uprising was declared to have ended after that (Ranger, 1967; Beach, 1979; Beach, 1998).

Historiography, like other objectivist knowledge systems such as mainstream journalism, is simply unconscious of the limitations imposed by its own methods in that the evidence (documentary and oral evidence obtained from trial records and accounts of interested eye witnesses) on which it bases its inductive and deductive reasoning to explain who was and who was not responsible for what during the uprising cannot wash. But what history is silent about or leaves unsaid may be far more important in promoting certain myths rather than others in a

4   Foundations of press silence in Zimbabwe

manner that sustains and stabilises hegemonic structures of oppression and unequal power relations. What even complicated matters was the incapacity of the English jurisprudence to ascertain beyond reasonable doubt who it was they had on trial, the medium Charwe or the Nehanda Spirit that possessed her, since it is also recorded that Charwe during her trial would appear to go into and out of a trance and behave in the most unpredictable manner. 'The Nehanda medium, however, began to dance, to laugh and to talk so that the warders were obliged to tie her hands and watch her continually' (Ranger, 1967: 309). Even more complicated would be how to decide if at the time of issuing the order to kill Native Commissioner Pollard, indeed the order came from Charwe the person or from Nehanda the Spirit, speaking through Charwe, which was actually most likely to have been the case, given the authority and force the message had on those who carried out the order. The decidability of this case becomes even trickier if one factored the religious system of the indigenous people centred on the belief of an almighty god 'Mwari to whom respect is due' (Wilson and Reynolds, 1972: 32). It needed to be acknowledged that the African god did not have a written word nor was there a mediating technology. God communicated directly with the people through a network of human priests and priestesses or spirit mediums present in every region and inter-generationally. In this case the spirit mediums who issued the orders and those who carried them out were not the authors of the messages, they were only vessels through which the divine will had to be operationalised. Such an argument is raised by Beach in a post-facto defence of the innocence of Charwe, the Nehanda spirit medium who was tried, convicted with the murder of Pollard and sentenced to death by public execution. The pillar of his argument though is to dismiss the notion that the Shona could have had any significant influence on the uprising implied in Ranger's thesis. According to him only the Ndebele could have had such organisational capacity. While he accuses others of allowing themselves to be influenced by popular opinion about a Shona-instigated revolt in Mashonaland, he is blind to the influence of widely shared racist prejudices against the Shona according to which the Shona were viewed as a childlike 'race' in need of white protection against the more warlike Matebele. A typical Shona according to white legend was an easy-going fellow with no mind of his own and prone to manipulation (see the story of the Tangwena resistance to forced removal in Chapter 4 of the book). 'The African is above all a merry fellow who loves life and laughter. His laughter shakes his whole body and takes possession of all his senses. He loves to chatter with his fellows and the noisier the gathering, the happier he is' (Wilson and Reynolds, 1972: 32).

The racist stereotypes of a contended African so prevalent in the colonial press were responsible for the perfect surprise and the devastation that marked the beginning of the Mashonaland uprising. The press silence about growing discontent among the Africans with some of the more oppressive policies of the colonial (mal) administration had lulled white settlers with a false sense of security. It had also blinded them to true capabilities of African organisation, internal coherence and communication, which the apparent fragmentation of Shona chiefdoms belied.

Foundations of press silence in Zimbabwe   5

That there existed a system and a network of effective communication connecting dispersed Shona communities could be inferred from the simultaneity and seeming spontaneity of killings of white people in different regions under different chiefly jurisdictions across most parts of Mashonaland in June 1896. The communication strategy also involved acts of sabotage and disabling of the enemy's communication systems by targeting for destruction telegraphic posts, the killing of telegraphic operators and cutting of the lines of telegraph. The Alice Mine battle in Mazoe was an illustrative case of a pervading consciousness, on both sides, of the effectivity of undercutting lines of communications as a war strategy.

Here was a system of communication whose strength lay in a dispersed network of dedicated messenger/mediums who left no written record of how they operated or of the content of the messages they relayed. It was due to the arrogance of white ignorance that *The Rhodesia Herald*'s reporters were caught unawares when the Mashonaland uprising erupted on 16 June 1896 and inflicted many casualties among the settler community. The Rhodesian press silence on how the proverbial shoe of colonial subjugation was pinching on the African foot was probably responsible for the *Herald*'s tangential reporting on 17 June 1896 when the colony was literally burning. Gale recorded the disgraceful failure of the Rhodesian press in the following terms:

> The unpreparedness of the (white) people of Mashonaland for the Mashona rising when it broke out with the devastating suddenness on June 16, 1896, is indicated by the issue of the Rhodesia Herald published the following day. Lonely prospectors and miners had been murdered, the Norton family, who farmed on the banks of the Hunyani river … had been frightfully butchered, the flame of rebellion was racing from kraal to kraal, but there is not a hint of this in the issue of June 17. (Gale, 1962: 27)

The newspaper's editorial orientation prioritised news by and about the white settler community, blunting and blinding its capacity to gauge the growing resentment among the black subject population. Even in the subsequent editions of *The Herald*, beginning with its 24 June 1896 edition, the paper true to its editorial charter interprets the events since the previous week in terms of white fears and opinions of the evolving crisis which the paper describes as the 'Mashonaland uprising' and later as the 'rebellion'. The crisis remained top of *The Rhodesia Herald*'s news agenda throughout the remainder of 1896 up to the end of 1897 with the capture, trial and execution of Nehanda and Kagubi as the main instigators of the uprising.

The organisational build-up among Africans that culminated in the tragic 'surprise killings' of many white people in different parts of Mashonaland beginning on the evening of 15 June 1896 was missed by *The Herald*. Some historians later questioned the basis for describing political events and developments in Mashonaland, beginning June 1896 as a rebellion, dismissing it as a view largely based on white fear and prejudice and not on any substantively expressed understanding of the developments by Africans responsible for instigating the events (Dawson, 2011). Beach is highly sceptical of the veracity of the Shona rebellion narrative which

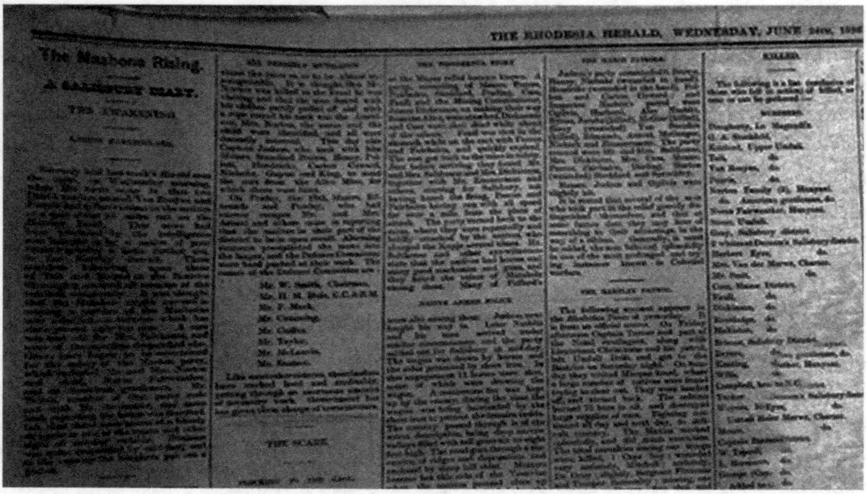

6 *Foundations of press silence in Zimbabwe*

Figure 1.1 The *Rhodesia Herald* reports 'The Mashona Rising' 24 June 1896. The killed listing was decidedly white. Reprinted by permission. National Archives of Zimbabwe.

white colonial newspapers ran and which historians such as Terrence Ranger engage with in their writing. Such a historical narrative was premised on the assumption of the existence of a highly organised and united Shona society prior to the uprising. 'The Shona … however, had enjoyed no such political unity since the 1840s, or, it seems, before then. How, then, had they achieved such a feat of political organization by June 1896?' opines Beach (1979: 398).

However, as soon as it became established fact that the Mashonaland uprising was in full swing, we are told, 'the Herald adopted a highly responsible attitude and showed an understanding of the difficulties facing the authorities … When the Natal Volunteers and the Imperial forces arrived, the paper sent a special correspondent with them on their punitive sorties and his reports were published in full' (Gale, 1962: 49). In fact, during the whole campaign to put down the rebellion, the colonial press establishment viewed its function as one of not only to give the news but also to keep morale alive among the settler community in the face of adversity. 'The newspapers' war correspondents (*embeds*) played their part as defenders and thus came under military discipline in addition to being newspaper correspondents' (Gale, 1962: 47).

The colonial press did not take its lessons then, nor had it learnt any lessons close to a hundred years later, on the dangers to society of its selective silences. Julie Frederikse, in her study *None but ourselves: Masses vs media in the making of Zimbabwe*, illustrates the fallacy of putting great store in the assumed power of the press, which led to white Rhodesians being utterly surprised to see the Patriotic Front parties emerging winners in the 1980 elections. They had taken for a given the assumption that the Africans were not capable of holding views and opinions of their own. 'The

Foundations of press silence in Zimbabwe   7

mass media had never asked for their views' (Frederikse, 1982: ix). Little did they know that the Africans who had been targets of a sustained campaign of white media silence, relied on another system of communication of which the regime knew very little or nothing.

It was Ralph Ellison the writer of the 20th century fictional America in the prologue to his classic story of the invisible man who encapsulated the tragic consequences both to the invisible other and to itself of a civilisation whose means of sight rendered a segment of society invisible by simply refusing to notice. The invisible man's complaint:

> When they approach me they see only my surroundings, themselves or fig-ments of their imagination, indeed, everything and anything except me ... That invisibility to which I refer occurs because of a peculiar disposition of the eyes of those with whom I come into contact. A matter of the construc-tion of their inner eyes, those eyes with which they look through their physi-cal eyes upon reality. (Ellison, 2016: 3)

The inner eyes in the quote above may be viewed as an appropriate metaphor for the way mainstream professional journalism tends to 'see' and report the postcolonial condition of those who fall outside of a gangster class of the inheritors of colonial privilege. 'The news spoke to us, and continues to do so, in 'the language of conquest and domination ... it is the mask which hides the loss of so many stories, all those stories of diverse, native communities we will never hear' (hooks, 2014: 168).

South Africa has played a historically significant role as the gateway to the interior of Africa for European imperial expansion. Ever since the first Portuguese fleet of ships successfully circumnavigated the southernmost tip of the continent of Africa on 12 March 1488 in their search for a sea route to the East and subsequent occupation and development of the Cape of Good Hope first by the Dutch and subsequently by the British, winds of change continued to blow from that part of the continent with life changing consequences for people many miles into the heart of Africa. As shall be fully discussed in the following chapter, the significance of South Africa was inscribed in the very name of the transnational corporation to first set up shop in the land between the Zambezi and the Limpopo. In the name British South Africa Company (BSAC) is a clear acknowledgement of South Africa's intermediary role in the colonisation of Zimbabwe in 1890. Many other European South African-based companies were to follow the BSAC's pioneering example. One such company to follow hard on the BASC's heels in 1891 was the Cape Argus, a media conglomerate which saw opportunity for growing its business in the newly established British colony north of the Limpopo.

The colonising press

It is interesting how history books on the press in Zimbabwe seem to start and end with *The Herald*. One of the reasons of course is that though there existed other newspapers some of which even predate it, *The Herald* managed to outlive

8 *Foundations of press silence in Zimbabwe*

them all and has remained the leading newspaper in the country to date. For example, historical sources such as the Rhodesiana indicate that such publications as the *Tuli Times* were in circulation at Fort Tuli when Cecil John Rhodes visited the Fort by July 1891 (Garlake, 1966: 41). Another publication that predated *The Herald* was the *Nugget* which is recorded as the first newspaper to be established barely two months after Rhodes's Pioneer Column occupied Mashonaland, and published at Fort Victoria (now Masvingo) in 1890. Most of these early publications were handwritten or cyclostyle-produced. An important feature of early settler history is how newspaper businesses were started at every fort established as the nuclei for future European cities and towns, so that by 1895 such centres as Fort Victoria (Masvingo), Salisbury (Harare), Umtali (Mutare), Gwelo (Gweru) and Bulawayo were producing newspapers of their own to cater for information needs of white mining prospectors and farmers in their vicinity. At this point Africans were just onlookers and silent bystanders who found the press an irrelevance. Lack of the requisite literacy skills among Africans in the early days of colonial Rhodesia made the press to remain, for quite some time, a major marker of racial difference between blacks and whites, apart from skin colour. *The Rhodesia Herald* was to remain stuck in this foundational mode of white exclusivity in spite of the rise in literacy levels among Africans until the end of white rule.

The white-oriented press 'was directly an outpost of the South African white press, just as the colony of Rhodesia itself was largely a product of one of South Africa's prominent politicians and businessmen, Cecil Rhodes, who himself had links with the Argus Press' (Dombo, 2019: 186). The link with South Africa ran deeper than this early penetration of the new territory across the Limpopo by a South African media company. Doris Lessing talks about how in spite of all protestations to the contrary, colonial society in Rhodesia from the beginning modelled itself along the South African example in about every aspect. She argues: 'briefly then, Southern Rhodesia has modelled itself on the Union: a law passed down south is always passed within a year or so in Southern Rhodesia, under a different name. the Land Apportionment Act is the basis of Southern Rhodesia policy as the Group Areas Act is in the Union' (Lessing, 1968: 125).

During the early years of colonial settlement, the white editors of *The Herald* and its sister papers were not persuaded about the need for the press to balance African opinion with white opinion on issues that were of interest to the Africans for the obvious practical reason that very few Africans if any were literate enough in the European language to be able to read and understand what was in the press anywhere. But, even as time passed and more and more Africans got educated and were able to benefit from reading the press, it was unfortunate that the old press establishment did not reflect this in its content; there were still too many impediments to the possibilities of capturing an African voice. The following two chapters present a detailed discussion of some of the obstacles that lay in the way of an African voice finding its way into the mainstream press in colonial Rhodesia. In this section we confine ourselves to discussing the South African origins of much of the print capital and how its interlocking political economy interests structured the emerging patterns of newspaper silences on African views and opinions.

Foundations of press silence in Zimbabwe 9

The early press came to Zimbabwe from across the Limpopo, riding on Rhodes's vision of painting most of Africa British red, from Cape to Cairo. It represented the earliest expression of the beginnings of a truly African transnational media conglomerate. Truly African in the sense that the parent or holding company, the Argus Printing and Publishing Company was domiciled in an African country, South Africa. Gale (1962) traces the career of the oldest newspaper to be published in Zimbabwe, *The Herald*, formerly known as *The Rhodesia Herald*. In that historical account Gale details Rhodes' octopus-like interlocking economic and political interests that lay the foundations of a white monopoly press in colonial Rhodesia.

> With his direct interest in the Argus Printing and Publishing Company and his appreciation of the value of a newspaper to any community, it was natural that he should turn to the Argus Company to provide this facility for his Northern colonists. The Board of the Argus Company had for some time discussed its participation in Rhodes's great venture and had intimated its willingness to establish a business in Mashonaland when, on May 25, 1891, the Chartered Company agreed 'to offer no facilities to any other firm'.
> (Gale, 1962: 3)

Although there emerged competitor newspapers from time to time, most of them either simply folded after a short while of publishing, or were simply bought over or swallowed by the media conglomerate, the Rhodesia Printing and Publishing Company to establish itself as a monopoly press at that early stage of the development of the commercial press in the then British colony of Sothern Rhodesia. Notable among such early small newspapers to meet with this fate include the *Advertiser* based at the eastern border city of Mutare, *The Rhodesian Times and Financial News* owned and published by a syndicate of private citizens who had formed the Salisbury Printing and Publishing Company based in Salisbury and the *Nugget*, another Harare-based publication. Gale (1962) gives a detailed chronicle of the nature of competition the RRP publications faced in the newspaper business in the early period of colonial settlement in Rhodesia which came to an end when the editor of the *Herald*'s competitor *The Rhodesian Times* fought and won a protracted legal battle against the colonial administration, but a battle that also left it financially exposed leading to its eventual takeover by the Argus Press in 1905. Whether it was by mere coincidence or by design, the Argus Company within the first decade and half of its establishment in Rhodesia had wiped out any form of competition and established itself as a monopoly press mainly through takeovers of its erstwhile competitors.

Barring its exclusion of African voices (at this stage 'natives' were considered as falling outside of the human), it can be reasonably argued that the media landscape of colonial Rhodesia in the first decade of the colony's establishment was fairly diverse and plural. Archival evidence supports the view that different shades of opinion on issues of the day from all sections of the white society enjoyed a fair chance of finding expression through one or the other of the newspapers of Rhodesia.

10   *Foundations of press silence in Zimbabwe*

That the emergence of the press in the then Rhodesia was part and parcel of the colonising project is often missed by those who unduly criticise *The Rhodesia Herald* for not carrying African opinion at its inception. To make such an accusation is not quite unlike making the suggestion that in order to equalise forces in the battle for Matabeleland for example the invading European armies were supposed to not only give the Ndebele Impis an equal number of the Maxim guns but also train them in their efficient use in battle. So in the early days of establishing a colony, settlers must have been alive to the truism: 'whatever happens, we've got the Maxim and they have not'. The press was just as important, especially in its portrayal of the savagery of Matabele attacks on the Shonas as moral justification for the routing of Bulawayo, the Ndebele capital (Gale, 1958). A friendly press was thus an important arsenal in the British imperial weaponry in Africa. Carrying African views was not part of the objectives of those who started the newspaper in the first place. Its mission was unambiguously and unapologetically stated in the inaugural issue of the newspaper:

> The aims the publishers will keep steadily in view will be to advance to the fullest of their powers the mining and agricultural interests, to discuss and to criticize moderately, but without fear or favour, the topics of the day or hour, and to promote fellowship and unity amongst all classes and sections of the white community (Gale, 1962: 19)

Now, to advance to the fullest the mining and agricultural interests was shorthand for lending full support to the colonial capitalist project whose methods of profit accumulation were anchored on violent mass dispossessions of the native population and driving them into semi-coerced forms of labour exploitation. A lily-livered press prone to raise alarm about ill use of the natives in the enterprise of growing a capitalist society would in fact be undermining to the 'mining and agricultural interests' of the new colony. While the editorial charter promised to pull no punches when it came to discussing and criticising moderately the powers that be, the output and practice on the ground attests to very little realisation of this in actuality. *The Rhodesia Herald* nailed its racial colours to the mast when it announced a commitment to promote 'fellowship and unity amongst all classes and sections of the white community'. No declaration of support for the policy of racial segregation could be clearer than that. Over the years, *The Rhodesia Herald* proved to be the perfect early epitome of embedded journalism. With few and very scattered exceptions of editors who tried to uphold the lofty ideals of editorial autonomy, it actively cultivated and enjoyed a rather cosy relationship with the power bloc of the time up to a point when its editor was accused of having 'joined the conspiracy of silence against the settler community' (Gale, 1962: 8); (Dombo, 2018). The newspaper's support for the Chartered Company in particular and the white settler community more generally may have had a lot do with its parentage. The Rhodesia Printing and Publishing Company (RPP) was a subsidiary of the Cape Argus. Cecil John Rhodes had a stake in both TNCs; the BSAC and the Argus, the parent company of the RPP which exercised no small though indirect influence. At its formation in 1894 the RPP's shareholding structure stood as illustrated in the table below:

Table 1.1 Cecil John Rhodes masked his stake in the RPP through proxies

Name of shareholder	*Details of shareholding*
Argus Company (with a controlling stake)	South African-based newspaper conglomerate in which Rhodes held shares
E.R. Syfret	Rhodes's agent, holding shares on his behalf
John Hays Hamond	Rhodes's American mining engineer

Gale (1962) drops many hints to impute a rather ambiguous relationship between the newspaper organisation and the colonial administration. In spite of how much the paper attempted to maintain healthy neutrality by fending off pressure from the company and ordinary settlers alike, for example, we are told that both the BSAC administration and the settler community held that the newspaper was an instrument of the company. Such an assumption, whether justified or not, was so entrenched that at the creation of the Sanitary Board for Salisbury which would provide the settlers with a platform to have a say in their own affairs, while some members were elected others were nominated as representatives of special interests. And, 'Fairbridge (Editor of the *Rhodesia Herald*) was nominated as a Government member' (Gale, 1962: 20). While a semblance of balance in alignment to different sections of the white community was vigorously pursued, the same was not the case, when it came to deciding between openly supporting white settler interests when these clashed with those of the African population. Thus, instead of being censured for joining the Salisbury Column on its invasion mission of Matabeleland as a volunteer 'in a combined military and journalistic capacity', John William Howard got rewarded with an appointment as first manager of the *Bulawayo Chronicle*. The editor of the *Chronicle* in his inaugural leader, describing Bulawayo and its surrounding areas as 'the erstwhile haunts of the bloodthirst *savage*' (Gale, 1962: 25) (emphasis mine), with reference to Lobengula, was characteristic of the early racist prejudice against the black people of Rhodesia. In fact, it can be argued that for the early colonial press, previous participation in frontier wars against the indigenous peoples was a default requirement for appointment as an employee of the colonial press. Both Francis Dormer and William Ernest Fairbridge had previous experience of one form or another in South African frontier wars before appointment as press men for the Argus Company. In this way they set an early precedent for what was to become routine practice for many journalists at the Rhodesian Printing and Publishing Company many years later when white reporters, with only very few exceptions, did not resist conscription into the Rhodesian Front army on grounds of maintaining professional objectivity in reporting the war.

12 *Foundations of press silence in Zimbabwe*

The 'African' press

In Zimbabwe, unlike in South Africa, no early emergence of an African press by Africans for Africans ever took off the ground until after independence. Some of the contextual factors that may have indirectly contributed to this had to do, first of all, with the late development of a critical mass of a literate African middle class who could constitute a viable newspaper market. Secondly, mainstream Christian missions of various denominations were already catering to the reading needs of the African laity through establishing presses of their own. And finally the establishment of a white-owned press catering to an African readership foreclosed the possibility for an authentically African press which could successfully challenge the oligopolistic newspaper market dominated by RPP and the Paver brothers' project which specifically targeted an African readership. Below I present a more detailed discussion of these and other circumstantial factors that conditioned the emergence and development of an African press before and after independence in Zimbabwe in terms of how that then was also productive of certain forms of silence. The chapter concludes by examining the role of the nationalist press that developed in exile and its contribution in furthering the goals of the liberation struggle. Sylvester Dombo (2018) gives useful insights in his very incisive treatment of the historical development of the so-called independent press from colonial times through to the post-independence era in Zimbabwe.

The missionary press

When it comes to the press there are many ways in which the South African experience provided a sort of blue print for the trajectory of press developments in the then Southern Rhodesia. Christian mission stations pioneered both in spreading literacy among Africans as well as feeding that literacy with the supply of appropriate reading material in the form of bibles, prayer books, hymn books, religious pamphlets, catechism booklets and ultimately periodicals that disseminated mainly church teachings, sermons and doctrine. These periodicals eventually evolved into fully fledged newspapers. All this was done in the name of the church's civilising mission to extend salvation to the African. The missionary press's main objective was to serve as a channel for carrying the voice of the church on important debates about the direction the development of the colonial society should take. Caught in the crucible of the colonial racial conundrum, the church assumed for itself a social vocation and moral obligation to be the voice of the voiceless and protector of the downtrodden – the African. It is important to note that much of the history on the early functioning of the missionary press, both in Zimbabwe and in South Africa, often failed to demonstrate from the content that the publications cannot be regarded as an 'African Press' but a press for Africans. It provided a channel for the church to pronounce itself on issues affecting Africans but not as a channel to enable the African (the church broadly acceded to the view that the African existed in perpetual childhood, seriously in need of white tutelage) to speak his mind freely because he was generally believed to not have any.

At this point, it is important to assess the racial ideology that animated the mind of the church to establish whether it differed at all from white supremacist ideology which formed the lynch pin of colonial administration in Rhodesia. The Roman Catholic collection of pastoral instructions under the title: '*Rhodesia – The Moral Issue*' compiled by one of the last editors of its magazine *Moto* issued over time to address topical issues of the day in the church's attempt to douse flames of racial conflict in colonial Rhodesia would be a good place to start. This presents some useful insights on the intercessional thrust taken by the missionary press targeting an African audience. The church's sentiments on the racial question, as expressed in a pastoral letter titled: 'Purchased People' by the Catholic Bishop of the Diocese of Umtali, Donal Lamont, in 1959 can be summarised as an admonition for the African to accept that he occupied a lower position on 'the hierarchy of being established by the Creator' (Plangger, 1968: 25) and for the white government to exercise their power more responsibly. Unrest in Northern Rhodesia and Nyasaland as Africans there, were pursuing the path of confrontation in pushing for their countries to secede from the Federation formed the context for the issuance of this pastoral instruction.

He chastised the colonising force to assume a more benevolent attitude in dealing with their African subjects always bearing in mind the civilisational chasm that separated them with an altruistic aim of bringing:

> the benefits of their own civilization to an unprivileged people in an undeveloped country; and if in the administration of justice, they are truly impartial and constantly remember that their power is tutelary; and that they act towards the indigenous people as elder brothers in the human family, they can even perform a great work of charity by so colonizing ... Moreover even though as far as growth in civilization is concerned, they may be regarded as 'children', they still have, just as minors can have, 'dominium' rights of ownership. From this it follows that any violent seizure of territory which was at the time inhabited and cultivated by a native tribe ... constitutes unjust aggression. (Plangger, 1968: 31, 29)

He then proceeded to admonish the African to shun what he called false nationalism in the following words:

> the African for instance, must recognize in realistic humility, that however high his thoughts may aspire to complete independence, he is as yet equipped neither academically nor technically nor economically, to assume complete control of what is rapidly becoming a highly complex and industrialised country ... He must remember, too, that in spite of the inequalities which operate against him, he is undoubtedly much better off here than he would be under any other of the colonial system known in Africa, and that he certainly has infinitely more freedom now than he could ever hope to have under communism ... He must not lose confidence, but firmly believe that ... with the assistance of growing numbers of sympathetic and influential Europeans in Rhodesia, he will even more

14   *Foundations of press silence in Zimbabwe*

quickly than he imagines, obtain full social, political and economic opportunity ... If his faith be great enough, he will come to recognize God's plan for him and will see, even in the colonialism which has not been too kind to him, the unsuspecting instrument of Providence, bringing him into the one great family which is the Church, and making possible for him the eternal happiness of Heaven. (Plangger, 1968: 32–33)

The spirit of the sermons above, which betrays a pervasive British colonial paternalism cannot be missed here, counselling patience for the African to wait until the European doles independence to him as a gift in the fullness of time, a view so at odds with the Freirean injunction to the oppressed that, 'freedom is acquired by conquest, not by gift' (Freire, 1970: 47). The sermon conveniently forgets the inevitability of violence at the point of colonial encounter and vitiates against Fanon's claim that 'decolonization is always a violent phenomenon' (Fanon et al., 1963: 2). The spirit in which this sermon was given and coming from white representatives of the church needs to be understood in the context of white privilege which the white priests had access to, too. It is quite revealing of what the church considered as its vocation and the object of its pastoral work including through its press among the natives, namely to focus the African's mind away from carnal gratifications and to strive instead to attain salvation of the soul and heavenly bliss. Its ideal converted and baptized African was one who would be a good subject of government, the submissive type, long-suffering and law-abiding, for whom the very idea of revolting against governmental authority would be something quite alien, a taboo. 'The Church in the colonies is a white man's Church, a foreigners' Church. It does not call the colonized to the ways of God, but to the ways of the white man, to the ways of the master, the ways of the oppressor' (Fanon et al., 1963: 7). The church press was thus conceived of as an instrument with a dual function; to further the objective of civilising the African and spreading literacy which, it was hoped, would ultimately lead the African to the Bible its principal function was to 'call' not to listen to or be the vehicle for African thought and opinion – it therefore participated in silencing the African. The establishment press had sidelined the church's opinion on issues of the day, and the establishment of its own press would provide the church leadership with a channel through which it could make its voice heard by those in government. In certain cases, the missionary press availed itself to government whenever government wished to reach the African constituents with its own messages.

Sylvester Dombo (2018) gives a detailed historical account of how one of the earliest church newspapers in Zimbabwe, *Munyai Washe* established by the Dutch Reformed Church (DRC) at Morgenster Mission in 1913 later entered into a standing arrangement with the colonial government whereby government provided the church with a grant to defray the cost of producing its paper in exchange for space for government announcements through the newspaper which had assumed the title of *Rhodesian Native Quarterly*. In 1926 'the government through the Department of Native Education commissioned the DRC to produce this newspaper for Africans. Under the arrangement the Government paid a grant of 25 pounds, which would cover the costs of publishing each issue, while mission personnel carried out the business of editing and printing the paper' (Dombo, 2018: 8).

By instituting themselves as the authentic knowers and spokesmen for the African, the church inadvertently became participant in the silencing of African voices much along the same lines as the African Chiefs Council were to do when the Rhodesia Front government set them up as a counterweight against claims by the African nationalist leaders to be speaking the mind of the ordinary African. It is a contradiction in terms for anyone to suggest that they can speak on behalf of someone else without negating that other person's humanity in the process. In the following chapters we present examples of how even with the best of intentions the church press under colonial rule and the 'independent' press in post-inde-pendent Zimbabwe somehow participated in undermining the voice of ordinary Africans they claimed to speak for. Chief Jeremiah Chirau, speaking as the Pre-sident of the Chiefs' Council in the Then Rhodesia once made the ridiculous claim that: 'I represent a great silent majority who owe allegiance to the chiefs' (Frederikse, 1982: 125). The important question to ask is; by what means had the silence of the 'silent majority' been secured and why? The actions of both tradi-tional leaders and the church press of installing themselves to speak on behalf of the Africans was totally antithetical to the Freirean philosophy of an emancipatory praxis. He states that: 'but while to say the true word—which is work, which is praxis—is to transform the world, saying that word is not the privilege of some few persons, but the right of everyone. Consequently, no one can say a true word alone—nor can she say it for another, in a prescriptive act which robs others of their words' (Frederikse, 1982: 88).

The church press proved to be largely about the church speaking for and on behalf of the Africans not about letting the Africans speak. Chapter 4, 5, 6 and 7 present some examples of this in respect of the forced removals of the Tangwena and the Hunyani people in 1969–1970 under the Rhodesia Front government and displacements caused under the Mugabe government's fast-track land reform programme from 2000, and the forced evictions of the urban poor under the government's operation Murambatsvina in 2005. It needs to be pointed out, however, that there were vast differences of editorial orientation between news-papers run by different church missions as well as editorial policy shifts within the same publication over time as the papers responded to and were in turn shaped by the evolving history of the country. For example, while there was a great deal of similarity between the Methodist Church's publication, *Umbowo* and the Catholic Church's publication *Moto* in the early years of their establishment, in adopting a pro-white liberal establishment politics which advocated for a gradu-alist approach to political reforms for the inclusion of blacks in government which formed an important pillar of the policy of partnership espoused by colonial authorities as long as the Central African Federation lasted (1953–1963). During that period up to the early years of UDI, the standard menu in the church press addressed to an African readership included 'moralizing campaigns against beer-drinking, laziness and polygamy' (Dombo, 2018: 13). And it must be added that

16 *Foundations of press silence in Zimbabwe*

another regular feature in both *Umbowo* and *Moto* editions published towards the end of the 1950s decade and early 1960s, were regular columns critical of a brand of extremist African nationalist politics and communism with Kwame Nkrumah's Ghana and Patrice Lumumba's Congo being cited as bad examples which right-thinking Africans in Zimbabwe should never contemplate.

The break-up of the Federation and the rise to power of an ultra-conservative right-wing Rhodesia Front party in Rhodesia in 1962 inaugurated an era of adversarial reporting in the church press which escalated to an increasingly confrontational relationship between the missionary press and the government leading to the banning of publications, *Moto* in 1975 and '*Umbowo* ... two years later' (Jones, 2001: 2710).

The change in orientation, some scholars argue, may have been occasioned by the government's closure of the *African Daily News* in 1964, the only daily newspaper edited by African journalists that had provided a platform for the articulation of African nationalist opinion for an African readership. Moto in particular became a thorn on the government's side during Father Michael Traber's editorship of the paper until the process of silencing it was initiated by Traber's deportation. The newspaper had adopted and raised to a very high level the same grassroots brand of journalism that had been introduced by the *African Daily News* before its banning. According to Michael Traber, grassroots journalism refers to a journalism: 'produced by the same people whose concerns they represent, from a position of engagement and direct participation' it adopts 'very different news values from the mass media, introducing "alternative social actors [such as] the poor, the oppressed, the marginalised and indeed the ordinary manual labourer, woman, youth and child as the main subjects of [their] news and features" (Atton, 2002: 16). Chapter 4 discusses examples of how the application of grassroots journalism by *Moto* produced a counter-narrative of mainstream news on forced removals of ordinary African villagers.

The commercial press for Africans

The establishment of a commercial press targeting an African readership did not emerge as early as did a white commercial press for obvious reasons. There was no viable market for such a paper until the few missionary schools had turned out enough numbers of literate Africans, a process which took no less than three decades from occupation. Even when a market for an African press began to appear and its acknowledgement by government was evident in government's half-hearted support for missionary press initiatives to provide 'safe' reading materials for Africans, no local commercially produced newspaper venture took off the ground until in 1931 a former missionary then member of the Rhodesian Parliament F.L. Hadfield started a publication called the *Native Mirror* which published in Shona, Ndebele and English. This publication's independence from government influence was highly questionable given its close association with RPP who printed and distributed it from their *Chronicle* offices and the Native Education Department who bought copies for African schools. Once again, just like in the case of the *Herald*'s

Foundations of press silence in Zimbabwe   17

mission with regards the white community, the *Native Mirror* looked to accomplish the same for Africans. Its purposes were clearly spelt out in Chief Native Commissioner C.I. Carbutt's remarks at its launch, in the following terms: 'The idea to launch the Native Mirror was to inculcate a kind of education "suitable" for the Africans ... take an important place in the education and general advancement of the people for whose benefit it is published' (Dombo, 2018: 12)

So its status as an independent commercial newspaper was quite tenuous until when it was taken over in 1936 by the Paver Brothers, intent on spreading their media empire from South Africa, where they had systemically decimated black owned newspaper businesses to replace them with a white-owned media monopoly under the brand name Bantu Press Company Limited serving a black readership. When it comes to the question of the role that a press with liberal leanings played in silencing particular black voices in colonial Zimbabwean society, it is important to make two points that media historians make about the Paver Brothers and their Bantu world project. Firstly, it is alluded that Paver was a segregationist with liberal leanings. Secondly, while the Bantu Press provided a valuable training ground for black journalists, Bantu Press ensured that 'white editors and journalists were defining the agendas of black news' (Dombo, 2018: 16). By the time Bantu Press comes to Zimbabwe it had established a track record in silencing radical African voices in the South African media space. Limb details how Bantu Press went on an all-out crusade of silencing African owned newspapers in South Africa as follows:

> by 1931 there were nineteen African newspapers, including several linked to Congress. Yet by the mid-1930s, most independent ANC-aligned publications had either collapsed or been taken over by the white-owned media conglomerate Bantu Press. By 1951 the number of African newspapers had declined to seven, all white-owned. (Limb, 2000: 96–97)

The author without alleging white conspiracy to silence African voices lists 'advertising profits, moderating (African) political journalism' as the main logics behind press monopoly drive by white liberals, which fitted in well with 'state efforts to assert political hegemony by encouraging a pliant African middle class' (Limb, 2000: 97). By the time the Bantu world spreads its tentacles across the Limpopo in 1936 no press owned by Africans catering to an African readership had as yet emerged in this new frontier to a level comparable to the South African situation. Thus, when the Paver Brothers established their media empire in Zimbabwe, oriented to an African readership, they were tapping into a virgin market, so to speak, and in that process, preventing an authentically African press from emerging. They acquired the one existing African newspaper, the *Native Mirror* and renamed it *Bantu Mirror*. Just like in the case of the white press it had to take another South African newspaper company to invent an African press targeting an African readership market (Dombo, 2018). This problem of trusting a progressivist white liberal press, appearing to be fighting in the African's corner, was to prove the African's undoing, when the right-wing white government decided to silence even that white liberal owned press, there was little appetite to fight

18   *Foundations of press silence in Zimbabwe*

for the communication rights of Africans in the liberal establishment (see Chapter 3 on the story of the silencing of the *African Daily News*). That is only when the African discovers that he has always been on his own.

During the life of the Central African Federation the Bantu Press publications in the Rhodesias and Nyasaland had played a pivotal public relations function in promoting the policy of racial partnership just like other middle of the ground liberal publications of the time, such as the *Central African Examiner* and publications produced by different missionary establishments. Parker says of the *Daily News* of those days: 'it never made money, and indeed was propped up for some years by a consortium of copper companies at the instigation of Welensky'[2] (Parker, 1972: 124). But, when the Federation dissolved in 1963 and the *African Daily News* began to dabble in African nationalist politics the colonial establishment (an intersection of white press, politics and profit) had no more use of it and did not suffer compunction when government closed it down in August 1964.

Ranger aptly characterises the Southern Rhodesian African society of the post-1930s decades as a nation caught up in the grip of pent up resistance fervour in search of means of self-expression with all the attendant disruptions to the ordered colonial way of life, if left unmanaged. According to Ranger, 'the spectacle of a nation in its birth-throes was obvious to very many people. In the late 1950s and early 1960s, the various traditions of Southern Rhodesian African politics seemed to come together' (Ranger, 1970: 231). African nationalist consciousness was beginning to take shape and was evident in an evolving consensus around the quest for independence from colonial rule. Ranger's very penetrating analysis, though, fails to make the connection between these political developments and the media's role in them. This local context, and spurred on by the winds of political change blowing southwards from north west Africa, after Ghana's attainment of independence in 1957, set the stage for the editorial transformation, in which the *African Daily News*, at the beginning of 1963, now under a new owner, the Thomson Group, morphed from a pro-racial-partnership to a pro-nationalist paper. In the white press, the pressure for change became manifested mainly in the disappearance of the more pejorative language when refereeing to Africans, with such terms as Kaffir and savage disappearing altogether and the term native being replaced by tribesman or simply African. Under the editorship of Eugene Wason, the *African Daily News* pioneered a model of grassroots journalism that gave it a popular appeal with its mostly rural and township based African population. *The Daily News* under the Thomson organisation, unlike under its predecessor owners, the Paver Brothers when it 'had always baulked at the first hurdles'; they refused to recognise that African nationalism was a force to be reckoned with or that the African Public demanded a quality product, set about revolutionising the newspaper. Eugene Wason, its new editor;

> for the first time, aimed the paper directly at the hundreds of thousands of Africans who had flocked to the banner of nationalism. The effect on the Rhodesian public was electric. The circulation of the Daily News, years

Foundations of press silence in Zimbabwe   19

ahead of its time, began to rocket. For 18 months Wason and his merry men reported the African scene as it had never been reported before. Even when Joshua Nkomo was sent to Gonakudzingwa, 450 miles away from Salisbury in the bush ... Wason sent his news editor and a team in a land rover to find the detainees. They came back with news and pictures that made the government's measures a laughing-stock. (Parker, 1972: 125)

It was this brand of 'irreverent journalism' which according to Parker so irked the Rhodesian Front government that it decided on the course of banning the newspaper. The first step was for this irreverent model of journalism to, against all odds, access the nationalist leaders' voice in detention. The next logical and even more dangerous step would be to give voice to that silent majority of African women and children confined to live and die slowly from disease and hunger in the remote tribal trust lands. It had to be stopped short.

African press in exile

Frederikse only refers blithely to the two news publications belonging to the two Patriotic Front liberation movements, ZAPU and ZANU as being produced at their rea bases in Zambia and Mozambique respectively. ZAPU's publication was called the *Zimbabwe Review* and that of ZANU was called *The Zimbabwe News*. An interesting point to note here is how the liberation movements deployed their respective radio stations in exile to good effect in countering the Rhodesia Broadcasting Corporation's war propaganda. This was probably informed by the realisation of the limited levels of literacy among their target audiences in the rural areas where their liberation fighters had established base. This is not to say print literature was altogether abandoned as a propaganda tool. Their use had to be balanced against considerations of portability as carrying a huge consignment of publications introduced practical logistical challenges in the war zone. Thus, instead of carrying bulky newspapers with long treatises on white colonial oppression, theories of liberation among latest news of military operations at the war front illustrated news sheets, posters leaflets were part of the literature guerrillas carried with them for distribution. Both armed wings of the liberation movement appreciated the importance of an information strategy to the successful execution of the war. In her study, Frederikse interviews the media representatives of the two nationalist political parties and here is what they said:

(Abraham Mambuva, ZIPRA political commissar): "And, of course we didn't just come into the country with our guns; we carried so many media tools – pamphlets, magazines, newspapers, cassettes, posters, stickers. And these we distributed to the masses." (Frederikse, 1982; 112)

(Edison Zvobgo, Deputy Secretary, ZANU Publicity and Information Department): "We relied a lot on publications and pamphlets depicting the barbarism of the enemy." (Frederikse, 1982: 112)

20   *Foundations of press silence in Zimbabwe*

Both political parties attributed their winning the propaganda war against the Rhodesian Front's more advanced heavily funded war propaganda machine to penetration and access. Zvobgo is quoted in Frederikse as saying: 'we beat the regime's media campaign largely because their literature could not be effectively circulated throughout the rural areas. They were unable to distribute their propaganda on a personal basis, whereas ours was being distributed door-to-door'. The above comments make two fundamental points about communications media. Firstly, media in this particular case the press were acknowledged on both sides as lethal weapons of war. After the battle of Chinhoi, *The Rhodesia Herald* (6 May 1966) publicised 'the weaponry of the guerillas" media war: photographs of captured "communist" propaganda' (Frederikse, 1982: 111). No sainting of their own media message as 'truer' than that of the regime is attempted here by the guerrillas. Theirs was just as much propaganda as Smith regime's media messages about the war situation were. The only source of strength in their war communication strategy lay in their ability to reach a greater audience which the regime's could not match. Newspapers succeed to the extent that they reach the intended audience, a fact the white Rhodesian press failed to recognise. Circulation mattered.

Cutting the umbilical cord

As has been established above the press in postcolonial Zimbabwe owes its character to a dual ancestry of a press aligned to the state and the dominant economic interests and another that is not, but both with strong historical traces to South African English language liberal press establishment.

At independence the new black government was faced with a dilemma on how to indigenise the media but at the same time continue to exercise some form of influence on this critical ideological state apparatus. It wanted to exert influence on the media without appearing to do exactly what they had criticised in the minority Rhodesian Front government of yesteryear – state manipulation of the press. The independence government also wanted to break ties with apartheid ruled South Africa as a sign of solidarity with the African liberation movements still waging a struggle for black emancipation in that country. Thus, with a grant provided by the Nigerian government the government of Zimbabwe was able to buy the South African Argus out of Zimbabwe's biggest newspaper company and Nathan Shamhuyarira the then Minister of Information and Tourism could boldly announce: 'the South African connection through the Argus Press has finally been severed. Not only will the media be genuinely free in an independent Zimbabwe, the media will also be responsible as well as responsive to the will of the majority' (Jones, 2001: 2774).

To accomplish this, government set up a quasi-independent media institution, the Zimbabwe Mass Media Trust (ZMMT) ostensibly as a protective buffer against threats to the editorial independence of the new media entity that emerged from the ownership reconfiguration of the former Rhodesia Printing and Publishing Company, now Zimpapers 1981 Ltd. whose majority shareholding was now government-held in trust for the Zimbabwean public. Citing Richard

Saunders on how the severance from South African influence on the media was effected at independence, Helge Rønning states:

> The Trust was intended to serve as a vehicle not just for changing the staff and editorial policy of the papers, but also to oversee the transition in the management and operation of the public print media from white minority control to serving the interests of the broad section of Zimbabwean society. It was emphasized by the government that the press should be a free press responsible to the national interest and should in principle be mass-oriented, nationally accessible and nonpartisan in content. (Rønning, 2003: 197–198)

The extent of the independence government's commitment to genuinely reform the media along the lines of decolonisation, deracialisation and democratisation remain questionable to this day as the ensuing analysis shall endeavour to illustrate.

Conclusion

Thus, the colonial press of whatever type, the white press, or the so-called African press of the missionary type or of the commercial type, indeed even the African press in exile had resulted in an arrangement where the African oppressed was given to hold the wrong end of the gun; no matter bent the nozzle how he would, he was destined to end in grief. Bend the nozzle someone indeed did try evidenced by Nathan Shamhuyarira's proclamation of a new era in which the press was to be made 'responsive to the will of the majority' (Jones, 2001: 2774). But, as the following chapters shall endeavour to illustrate, the realisation of the noble goal of enabling the majority to command the weapon, to be in a position to pull the trigger, so to speak, probably still lies in the future.

Notes

1 Mwari was revered by the indigenous black population as the supreme God, creator of every living being, source of life. He communicated with mortals only through a priesthood headed by a high priest and intercessor between Mwari and his people at Mwari's holy shrine at Mabweadziva, alternatively known as Matonjeni, in the Matopo hills. Mwari's messages and commands (to be obeyed under pain of ostracism) were relayed to all the people through a network of loyal regional spirit mediums (oral tradition as documented in Daneel 1970; Ranger 1967; Wilson and Reynolds, 1972).
2 Sir Roy Welenskey was President of the Federation of Rhodesia and Nyasaland from when it was formed in 1953 until its dissolution in 1963.

Bibliography

Atton, C., 2002. *Alternative media*. Sage.
Beach, D.N., 1998. An innocent woman, unjustly accused? Charwe, medium of the Nehanda Mhondoro Spirit, and the 1896–1897 central Shona rising in Zimbabwe. *Hist. Afr.* 25, 27–54.

22 Foundations of press silence in Zimbabwe

Beach, D.N., 1979. 'Chimurenga': The Shona rising of 1896–1897. *J. Afr. Hist.* 20, 395–420.

Daneel, M.L., 1970. *The god of the Matopo Hills: An essay on the Mwari cult in Rhodesia.* Mouton & Co.

Dawson, S., 2011. The first Chimurenga 1896–1897 uprising in Matabeleland and Mashonaland and the continued conflicts in academia. *Constellations* 2, 144–153.

Dombo, S., 2018. African newspapers and the development of the private press in Rhodesia, in: *Private print media: The state and politics in colonial and post-colonial Zimbabwe.* Springer, pp. 21–49.

Dombo, S., 2019. African newspapers limited and the growth of newspapers for Africans in Southern Rhodesia. *Media Hist.* 25, 183–207.

Ellison, R., 2016. *Invisible man.* Penguin.

Fanon, F., Sartre, J.-P., Farrington, C., 1963. *The wretched of the earth.* Grove Press.

Frederikse, J., 1982. *None but ourselves: Masses vs. media in the making of Zimbabwe.* Heinemann.

Freire, P., 2007 [1970]. *Pedagogy of the oppressed* (M.B. Ramos, Trans.). Continuum.

Gale, W., 1962. *History of the Rhodesian printing and publishing company.* Madorn Print.

Gale, W., 1958. *Zambezi Sunrise: How Civilization came to Rhodesia and Nyasaland.* Timmins.

Garlake, P.S., 1966. *Pioneer Forts in Rhodesia, 1890–1897.* Commission for the Protection of Natural and Historical Monuments and Relics.

hooks, b., 2014. *Teaching to transgress.* Routledge.

Jones, D., 2001. *Censorship: A world encyclopedia.* Routledge.

Lessing, D., 1968 [1957]. *Going Home.* Ballantine.

Limb, P., 2000. 'Representing the labouring classes': African workers in the African nationalist press, 1900–1960, in: L. Switzer and M. Adhikari (eds), *South Africa's resistance press: Alternative voices in the last generation under apartheid.* Ohio University Center for International Studies.

Parker, J., 1972. *Rhodesia: Little white island.* Pitman.

Pinto, M., 2009. Silent citizens: On silence and silencing in journalism. Presented at the IAMCR 2009 Conference, International Association for Media and Communication Research (IAMCR), pp. 1–13. Accessed 13 June 2019 from: https://www.academia.edu/3622020/Silent_citizens_On_silence_and_silencing_in_journalism.

Plangger, A.B., 1968. *Rhodesia–the moral issue: Pastoral letters of the Catholic bishops.* Mambo Press.

Randles, W.G.L., 1979. Robert, R.S., (Trans) The Empire of Monomotapa: From the fifteenth to the nineteenth century. Gwelo: Mambo Press

Ranger, T.O., 1967. *Revolt in Southern Rhodesia, 1896–1897: A study in African resistance.* Heinemann.

Ranger, T.O., 1970. *The African voice in Southern Rhodesia, 1898–1930.* Northwestern University Press.

Rønning, H., 2003. *The media in Zimbabwe: The struggle between state and civil society,* in: *Twenty years of independence in Zimbabwe.* Springer, pp. 196–221.

Wilson, D.G., Reynolds, L.H., 1972. *Jumbo guide to Rhodesia.* Wilrey Publications.

2 Colonial press and intersecting loci of silencing

Introduction

The present chapter makes the important connection between racial land segregation in Zimbabwe and presences and absences in the news. It looks at how racial spatialisation of the land into white/black areas, urban/rural intersected with the news episteme in the colonial despoliation, displacement, invisibilisation and incarceration of Africans in compounds defined by race, place, ethnicity and gender throughout the colonial period and after. It discusses how the physical violence that accompanied colonial theft of African people's land and their subsequent subjugation was mirrored and mutually reproduced and reinforced at a symbolic level, by media silence on the plight of the colonised, oppressed and racially discriminated. While physical force was used to literally landlock Africans into poverty, the colonial media establishment reified the adverse effects of colonial dispossession on the African people or at worst largely kept them hidden from public view. This chapter deploys the intersectionality theoretical lens (Crenshaw 1989) to understand on the basis of manifest media content, how urbanity and rurality differentially predisposed blacks and whites to opportunities to appear in the colonial press, and how gender difference further complicated black women's access to economic and social mobility more than their menfolk with knock-on effects on their visibility in the news media. Defenders of journalism and the media as an institution often make lofty claims about its democracy role. They often deploy empirical evidence based on what journalism has said, what it has brought to public attention, exposes of corruption and abuse of power in high places that it has given publicity to, as the basis for deserving the respectable place at the table as the fourth estate of the realm in any functioning democracy. Those scholars that have supported a contrary view of the media and journalism's role as anything but beneficent, have also drawn on what journalism has put out. They would demonstrate on the basis of published content how journalism was responsible for inciting and fomenting ethnic hatred and homophobic and misogynistic treatment of racial, ethnic, gender and sexual minorities. This chapter, without taking away from the important contribution of the critical scholarship described above, seeks rather to place an emphasis on how journalism accomplishes some of its more irremediable harm on some segments of the social

24　*Colonial press and loci of silencing*

formation by way of that of which it is silent about, those things it has been blind to, not by omission but by a combination of factors such as journalism's positionality in the power hierarchy and the methodology at the heart of its claim to professionalism. What (Pinto, 2009) points to as journalism's unselected, 'the unsaid, the withheld, the untold of journalism. The reality that remains in silence, for not being noticed or for being silenced', happens to be at the core of this monograph's discussion, focusing on the colonial news archive in Zimbabwe and journalists' own understanding of how environmental, geo-spatial location of the object of news and socio-cultural dynamics intersect with professional considerations to shape choices and decisions on what passes as news and how they produce news versions of the colonial and postcolonial realities.

The geo and body politics of visibility in the news

It should strike one as rather strange that we should have a chapter dedicated to ruminating on the geography of a country in a book supposedly about journalism and the production of silence. What has the geographical location of people got to do with what comes out in tomorrow's newspaper as news, one may venture to ask. Indeed, it has everything to do with how communities access voice. It has to do with how people's geolocation goes on to structure how the press distributes opportunities to speak differently among different sections of society.

Both in Zimbabwe and South Africa, the removal story was largely a forgotten story; in the few cases when it was reported on, it was framed consistently as a 'good news' story. Forced removals were represented as a development that benefited blacks and for which they were very much grateful. Desmond (1970: 23) cites the South African newspaper the *Star* as reporting that: 'the Bantu people like being moved … The Bantu people like the places where they are being resettled'. The process of uprooting Africans from their ancestral homes and herding them into overcrowded areas of very limited agricultural potential called native reserves (call them labour concentration camps) was foundational to the colonial capitalist order in both Zimbabwe and South Africa right from white settler occupation of these territories. Subsequent colonial administrations continued to build and improve on the basic principle of keeping the races geographically apart. The demographic character of Limehill in Natal, South Africa, which Desmond describes as typical of all such native reserves in that country (colonial Rhodesia was not different), was the absence of able-bodied men for most of the time. Women, children and the aged constituted the largest percentage of the population. The rural areas were set to 'develop into little more than settlements of women and children with the men earning a living in the White towns' (Desmond, 1970). The Phoenix Group (Wood, 1968) an independent think tank based in Harare (Salisbury) in the then Southern Rhodesia concluded that the migrant labour system had the effect of draining off the younger males from the rural household sector with detrimental effects on the economic and social fabric of those areas. This definitive feature of the native reserve has not changed much apart from cosmetic changes to the more racially explicit 'native reserve' to the new racially neutral and sanitised terms such as rural areas or communal areas. These anachronistic relics of colonialism which Africans have become accustomed to accepting as home, have served to lock mainly African women away from public visibility in colonialism's closets, as it were, unknown to the media. This chapter focuses on how the media production process of the news during and after colonial rule was and continues to be structured by power and geography.

The period of concession hunting

The period before 1890 was a period of concession hunting in the interior of Africa. 'The period around the signing of the Rudd Concession was marked by the scramble for treaties, as can be seen with the signing of different treaties between the colonialists and the different Shona chiefs, culminating in the Lippert Concession, for example' (Mupfuvi, 2014). Selolwane discusses at length the many factors that militated against African chiefs' capacity to extract favourable bargains or at least to avoid improvidentially signing away the land of their people to European concession hunters. Firstly, missionaries played no small role in pacifying and softening up the African leaders towards the European negotiators. Missionaries had built trust and good will with the chiefs who took a cue from them as to who among the many European concession seekers were to be trusted and which ones not to be entertained. Examples include Reverent Robert Moffat who had cultivated strong friendship with Mzilikazi, founder of the Ndebele kingdom, and was instrumental in the signing of the Tati treaty in favour of the British. His son after him, John Moffat, helped Rhodes' agent Charles Rudd to obtain Lobengula's signature to a concession on the basis of which a Royal Charter was obtained from the British Crown, mandating Rhodes' British South Africa Company (BSAC) to occupy present-day Zimbabwe. Secondly, the factor that skewed the negotiations in the European bargainers' favour was the fact that those who did the interpretation were whites who had mastered the indigenous language who represented (often exaggeratedly) to the African chiefs the benefits to them of entering into these pacts.

A common practice in the scramble for concessions and treaties with African chiefs and leaders involved, according to (Selolwane, 1980), giving 'the chiefs the impression that the Europeans were doing them some great services which it would be folly not to accept'. The other factor is that there was always bound to be miscommunication and loss of meaning in translation where two parties rooted in different cultural, philosophical and religious orientations were bound to bring different interpretive frameworks to the business of interpreting the import of the phrases included on the paper. Professor Beach in his detailed historical account of Mapondera, one of the most decorated leaders of early resistance to British colonial occupation of Mashonaland, intimates on how some of the so-called concessions were often entered into with individuals not recognised as chiefs by the local community and the terms of agreement referred to territories that stretched far beyond the areas of jurisdiction of the chiefs who signed the documents and in the process often sparking conflicts and territorial disputes among local African chiefs. Beach's description of one such concession entered into

26 Colonial press and loci of silencing

between Frederic Cortney Selous and Mapondera is illustrative of this common pattern and deserves to be quoted in detail:

> The area covered by the grant included not only the whole of Negomo's land but went sixty kilometers south of Nyota to the Mazoe source, and west to the sources of Murowodzi and Garamapudzi and Ruya, thus including most of the territories of Nyachuru, Hwata and Chiweshe. To meet the objection that this was not Mapondera's land it was stated, quite untruthfully, that Hwata had been subject to Negomo in the past. Either Sirewo (Selous) did not tell Mapondera the extent of the concession, which would have been foolish because others could read Mapondera's copy to him, or Mapondera was granting rights in lands that were not his in the south. But none of the lands were his, in any case. Mapondera and Mutemaringa, who was included in the deal, were not independent rulers and had no right whatever to make concessions in Negomo's territory ... Mapondera was not recognized as supreme by the houses of Nyota, let alone by Negomo. (Beach, 1989)

The issues about jurisdiction in the case of the concession negotiated with Mapondera were not an isolated case. In the case of the Rudd Concession too, the European negotiators who were also the drafters of the text of agreement generously defined the geographical area they imputed to be the subject of the agreement without paying due regard to territorial contestations among local chiefs. The process by which European concession seekers extracted African chiefs' signatures to fraudulently concocted concession documents was always fraught with cheating, intrigue, outfoxing, bribery, as well as concealment of true intentions by both parties to the bargain. That the concessions were a big fraud is amply demonstrated by the historical fact that the Europeans were often the first to breach the terms of agreement as once they had a foothold on the country, they immediately resorted to acquiring by use of force what they could not get by fiat (Chakamwe, 2014; Strack and Goodwin, 2009).

Colonial penetration, partition and occupation

The landscapes of societies structured in dominance (Hall, 2018) had to be internally partitioned and redrawn at the point of colonial conquest to give material effect to the racialised social hierarchies of emergent settler colonial capitalism in Rhodesia. In 1894, just a year after the sacking of Bulawayo the capital of the Ndebele kingdom by invading forces of the Pioneer Column under the banner of the British South Africa Police, Cecil John Rhodes, the financier of that colonial expedition into the territory across the Limpopo, was presenting what became famously known as the Glen Grey proposals to the Parliament of the Cape Colony. He preferred to call his proposals the 'Bill for Africa' intimating the possibility for wider use and application in newly annexed territories to the British empire in Africa. The proposals were meant to address what was commonly described in white settler circles as the 'native question' (Denis, 2015), whatever that meant. From that point on, the natives have existed as a question, a problem in a world that was fast becoming white. So since then all kinds of solutions have been devised to deal with the native question in the evolution of the colonial society. The Order in Council of 1893, informed by the goal of protecting British interests which simply meant white settler interests in the colony, established the first principle of racial land segregation by demarcating the Gwai Shangani reserve as the first example of areas in the then British colony of Southern Rhodesia, where Africans whose land had been alienated by whites for their purposes were to relocate. The dispossession and displacement of Africans, which has been dealt with extensively in literature (Arrighi et al., 2010); (Riddell, 1980); (Van Onselen, 1976); (Palmer, 1977); (Phimister, 1988); (Ranger and Ranger, 1985) grew in intensity since colonial occupation up to as late as the 1970s. Chapter 4 presents a case study of the treatment of some of these mass evictions of Africans in the mainstream Rhodesian press.

The partition of Southern Rhodesia between Europeans and Africans as a settler colony had not been fully completed by the end of the 1960s. As has already been pointed out above, the process of colonial segregation of land into areas suitable for European settlement and areas reserved for Africans was an integral part of the process of colonisation right from the beginning. Unlike the Berlin Conference, the partition of the then Rhodesia was not a negotiated settlement among equals. It was unilateral impositions by one race over the conquered and subjugated black other. It did not happen without cooperation and resistance by the native population whose land was expropriated and it has been the subject of much writing and documentation of the history of early European colonial occupation of Zimbabwe (Hulley, 1969; Clements, 1969; Ranger and Ranger, 1985), except that much of that history was authored by the conquerors, members of the Pioneer Column or the first generation of their descendants. The absence of any recorded history from this period by Africans as they suffered dispossession leaves a knowledge gap which no claim of scientificity of historiography can ameliorate. For example, Hulley narrates matter of factly how his father spent months away from home occupied in the business of pegging 'claims for a company, which, anticipating no trouble, was anxious to peg all the ground from Salisbury to Norton, a distance of about 30 miles ... All the work, however, was of no avail, for everything was destroyed during the rebellion' (Hulley, 1969: 67). The brutality by which that rebellion was put down again merits only a flitting description of the public execution of one such African rebel at the gallows at Cecil Square the purpose of which was to instil fear in the African's heart.

The native reserves were especially designed as geographical technologies of oppression, exclusion, marginalisation and exploitation of the African people. They were weaponised to subalternise the black population which was driven into them. They were only better than what (Elkins, 2005) has called Britain's gulag (concentration camps in Kenya used to suppress the Mau Mau uprising) or in any event at least better than Auschwitz. It is also important to give due credit to Rhodes' perceptive 'more humane' system of placing and keeping the African in his 'proper place' in subservience to the master race, because worse things could have happened

28 Colonial press and loci of silencing

and indeed they did in fact happen in King Leopold's Congo Free State (Hochschild, 1998) and in German West Africa now Namibia (Erichsen and Olusoga, 2010), where systemic genocide was perpetrated. The brutal atrocities that accompanied the processes of colonial conquest in Zimbabwe from 1890 through the years of colonial rule would have been appropriately named crimes against humanity had the press not been silent about them. Much of that history can only be reconstructed from piecing together information gleaned from sparse archival records of official documents but not from reading local news reports of the period. The sheer scale of African mass displacement into native reserves which according to (Riddell, 1980) had peaked '283,000' in just about four decades from the late 1920s while in the processes undermining, to a point of decimation, the agricultural economy of the Africans. The upshot of it was that 'through the creation of the African Reserves, the increasing inability of the reserves to provide for the subsistence needs of a growing African population and the consequent steady stream of cheap African *migrant* labour seeking work in the modern sectors of the economy, the structure of the present Rhodesian economy has evolved' (Riddell, 1980: 7). African welfare was not going to be allowed to be a drain on the national fiscus of the colonial capitalist state. Designed along similar lines as the South African homeland system, the native reserve was an enclave which subsisted apart from but articulated with the modern sector (Hall, 2018) by absorbing the social reproduction costs of black migrant labour. The result of land apportionment was the creation of a dual economy with white settlers occupying the commanding heights of the modern sectors of agriculture, mining and manufacturing all connected with a network of telegraph lines, the press, roads and railways to facilitate the development of their mining and agricultural industries, while the bulk of the colony's indigenous population was relegated to impoverished lowveld reserves in far-away places difficult to access for journalists working to a 24-hour news cycle. (Mupfuvi, 2014). Charama tribal trust lands in Gokwe was one such area where nothing newsworthy ever happened.

Memories of a childhood in Charama

But what was the native reserve into which African families were herded together? They can only be better imagined as extended private spheres where the social reproduction of cheap black migrant labour was to take place. In 1970, the Huchu people were resettled in a 'newly opened-up tribal trust land', a sprawling low-lying veld just below the Charama and Mufungwe plateau complex where the descent into the Zambezi escapement begins in Gokwe district formerly known as Sebungwe.

Most of the fertile middle and high veld area of Zimbabwe was declared European land and Africans who previously lived in these areas had to be relocated to the low-lying areas designated native reserves next to game reserves.

An attempt to reflect on one's childhood memories is fraught with many challenges. Memory itself is a very selective process which deploys strategic amnesia to silence inconvenient facts while orchestrating others. If Doris Lessing would say

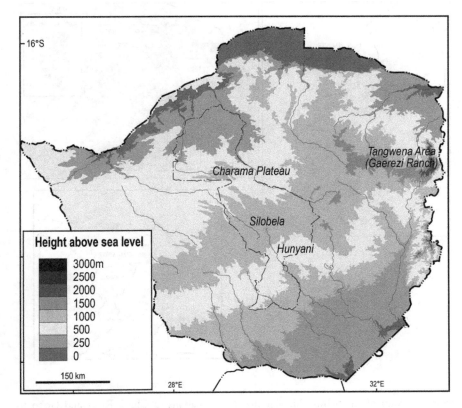

Figure 2.1 Relief map of Zimbabwe

about her own upbringing: 'one cannot be brought up a daughter of a white settler with impunity' (Lessing, 1968: 70), then it is apropos for me to acknowledge here and now, that I too even as I write this monograph, am the discursive product of my unhappy upbringing as the son of a native in an area reserved for natives in colonial Rhodesia of the 1960s and 1970s. My childhood memory of Charama is that it struck me as a thirsty dust bowl whose temperatures in summer were punishingly high. This was the 'fly zone', for, tsetse fly had not yet been brought under control, and our translocation there was part of government's strategy to eventually rid the area of the scourge of tsetse fly (Nyambara, 2002). Upon arrival in the 'new' area, we encamped by the roadside where we amongst our few belongings had been offloaded by the government Isuzu trucks. It was after a day and half travel, for the most part on a dust road, for us to reach our destination from (kumatongo) our former home in a well-watered area near Mvuma, which we knew as Hunyani (see map in Figure 2.2). The tragedy of our changed circumstances was lost to us as young children. It had all been a lot of fun; the long ride, perched on top of an assortment of our belongings; goods, bags of grain, improvised fowl cages of a size

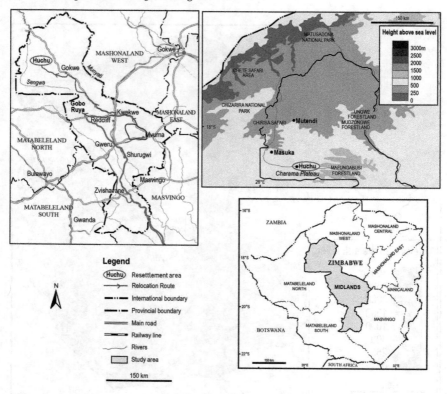

Figure 2.2 Map of Zimbabwe, highlighting the relocations of Chiefs Ruya and Gobo to Silobela and Chief Huchu to Charama.

that carried 4 to 5 fowls inside, water tins, cooking utensils, suitcases among other things loaded onto a train of three Isuzu open trucks. It was a voyage of discovery and we never felt the exhaustion that old people kept harping about. The fact that it took three trucks to remove us was, by our rural standards, a sign that we were not counted among the poor. Other really well-to-do households would take convoys of up to five heavily loaded Isuzu trucks to move. Our middle passage was at least shorter but the rupture with our past no less as complete.

The reality of our desperate circumstances only began to sink home when work began in earnest to construct some sort of shelter before the onset of the rain season, for we had just been left in the open and we spent some days sleeping in the open under a starry sky. The leafy umbrella forest of the *musasa, mutondo* and *mupfuti* trees of Hunyani had given way to sparse, prickly, twiggy, and leafless seemingly lifeless mopane scrub that provided no cover from the searing heat of an October sun. To help us complete the building of huts with alacrity my father had hired two strangers to help with the cutting and hewing of construction materials in the form of poles, thatching grass and string which was obtained from the bark of a local substitute species of tree, to the site allocated for us to build our new home. It was then that we soon discovered that the strangers were not from among the people who had relocated from Hunyani. They were actually local indigenes, people from whom our parents learnt elementary lessons about life in our new reserve. One such lesson was never to use the local *munyera* (corkwood) tree as poles for building a hut because even after cutting it, the *munyera* never dies. It keeps growing, sprouting new shoots that grow into leafy branches. A hut built of *munyera* poles can actually end up growing into a thicket with tree branches jutting in every direction inside and outside the hut. The *munyera* poles are only good for constructing a living fence or a hedge. Other equally important lessons were about what species of wild fruits and berries were edible because we came face to face with a whole gamut of new species of vegetation different from what was familiar in Hunyani.

We also soon discovered that the local people whose Korekore dialect made them sound distinctively different from the way we spoke referred to us as *Madheruka*, a derogatory term to mean those who came to settle and are not originary to the area. Our people, in turn referred to the autochthons as *Mashangwe*, a term they considered deprecating to them (Nyambara, 2002). This is when it dawned on us that the area we were resettled in was not virgin land after all. It had been made vacant specifically for us to be resettled there. Some people who had claims on that area must have suffered loss, their economy disrupted and displaced just as we had also been displaced from Hunyani to make way for European settlers. There was no virgin unclaimed land anywhere in Zimbabwe by 1970. What was only happening was the reduction of areas communities could claim ownership over and their movement and displacement as pieces on a chessboard. The government's claim that there were pockets of virgin and unalienated land were in fact mischievous misrecognition and misunderstanding of existing land use patterns and land tenure among African people. There were lands which were deliberately left in their forest state unfarmed for specific ecological reasons. Some were hunting grounds (*marimuka*) for game meat, others were natural fruit gardens (*machiri*) and they were many for different kinds of wild fruit, wet lands (*matoro*) for gardens etc. The fact that they were not being put under cultivation was generally interpreted as empty virgin lands not belonging to anybody and therefore available for alienation by European settlers. Such was the case with the Charama forest into which we were resettled, semi-arid, prone to drought, most likely left uncultivated by the locals to serve as a hunting forest, teeming with a wide variety of wild fruits and game. The indigenous ecological intelligence of maintaining a sound ecological balance by deliberately avoiding over exploitation of the natural resources was creatively destroyed (Palmer, 1977) and abandoned as primitive and in its place was created a sub-optimal subsistence economic structure which arrested development in the native areas and guaranteed a continuous supply of cheap labour for colonial capitalist accumulation.

In the very first few years of our settling in Charama, our diet changed dramatically. No more cows' milk, for we were not allowed to own or keep cattle. There was lots of game meat, particularly warthog, and vegetables

32   Colonial press and loci of silencing

harvested from the wild on the menu, no 'English' vegetables from the garden. We never raised any gardens; they need a secure and abundant water supply. How we longed to eat sweet cabbage those days! In a short while of our stay, there came hunting companies sweeping through the area combing the forests, gunning down all warthog, antelope and buffalo. For as long as it lasted, those were days of meat plenty. The African employees of these companies would privately barter whole carcasses of whatever game animal for a certain number of bags of grain depending on the species and size of the animal killed. The hunting parties would set up camp at different intervals along the dust road and the boughs of every small bush around would be bent down laden with sliced game meat left to dry out in the sun before it was lorry-transported to we never knew where. In no time, the forest just dried up of any warthog and so also did our plates dry up of any traces of meat and for many months on end, we once more found ourselves eating (sadza) maize meal, with wild vegetables day in and day out.

The other reason for life turning sour especially for us young children in Charama was in the disappearance of familiar place-bound childhood games. There were no rivers or streams where we could go for a pleasurable swim on a hot afternoon or go fishing. The little pleasures that came with tending cattle in the pastures were no more. We boys began to miss even the risky boxing contests which made part of a regular menu of 'entertainment' activities when out herding cattle in Hunyani. We had been stripped of any kind of livestock that needed tending. Instead of play, we had to spend the days helping our parents with the back-breaking work of tilling and cultivating the fields using nothing but the hoe. We had become the perfect substitute for animal draught power, for there was none. This mode of agricultural production naturally translated to meagre harvests each year, not enough to see us through the year to another planting season. We became involved in the serious business of survival too early in our lives and were the generation that had to skip the stage of child's play. We could no longer afford it.

There were years when droughts followed each other in succession, and our area was always favoured by these. Young as we were, we had to spend some days ranging from one to two weeks away from home doing (maricho) cultivating other people's fields in exchange for food. There was this area just on top of the Charama plateau that was favoured by rain and they enjoyed good harvests almost every year, while our area suffered drought. I was to discover, much later, why this was so, our Grade 7 nature study and outdoor world textbook, made us to understand that we happened to be on the leeward side of Charama plateau. That was why. The plateau as seen from Huchu villages forms a ridge of flat topped mountains running along the south of us, from Charama hill on the west to Mufungwe Mountain on the east. This ridge of mountains came to symbolise in my mind a physical barrier that separated us from opportunity. The valley, in which we now lived ever since those government Isuzu trucks dumped us incommunicado, began to give one a sense of being incarcerated in an extended detention camp without trial. I wondered whether living conditions in Charama Tribal Trust Lands (TTLs) were any different from those at Sikombela or

Gonakudzingwa[1]. The inmates of these infamous detention camps got their release at a certain point, though, before national independence. Here we had been thoroughly forgotten, left to our own means to see whether we would live or die. Even the road which had been graded for purpose, by which we had been brought here, slowly fell into disrepair, its sides overgrown with grass and at places, torn with impassable gullies. After a few years stay, what was left of the seven water tanks around which had been sited our villages at 5-kilometre intervals along the road, supplied from one diesel powered borehole, were now history. Only the villages retained their names after the tank numbers but no trace of the water tanks or the water was left. So, if you were to ask someone from the area for their address one would tell you they come from Tank 1 or Tank 6, Charama. This depressing aspect of Charama rural area has not changed much up to today, in spite of independence (see map above). So I still find it quite intriguing how some people in later life have recalled their childhood homes with such fond memory. Doris Lessing's (1968) book: *Going Home* is one such moving account of the sentimental attachment to what she refers to as 'home' where she had spent the youthful most impressionable years of her life. Such were the positive taken for granted childhood attachments to 'home' some of us African children were prevented from cultivating through uprooting and displacements that were common place in the Rhodesia of our childhoods, our loyalties torn between *kumatongo* the areas we were forcibly removed from and the new areas of resettlement.

In no time father, like other men in our villages, simply disappeared from home without needing to consort about it with us children, but mother obviously knew, so we suspected. The man had joined the steady stream of 'African males seeking work in the modern sectors of the economy which were controlled and owned by Europeans and local and foreign-based companies – on white farms, in mines, and in the urban areas' (Riddell, 1980). Then after many months of his absence, a letter addressed in our family name was called out at school assembly by the headmaster. I stepped forward to receive it, took it home to my mother who immediately announced from it with a beaming smile on her face that father had found employment at a European farm, back in Hunyani, the area we had been evicted from, and that we could expect to receive some money to relieve us from hunger as soon as he got paid by the end of month. He did not forget us, although he spent long stretches of time before ever paying us a visit. As years rolled by, father moved from working at the European farm and found employment as a winding gear operator at a chrome mine called Netherburn in Lalapanzi, not far from the farm where he had worked before. We became accustomed to not being with him in the home. Mother, grandmother and grandfather were always there as the adult members of the family until grandpa passed on in 1974. Mother visited father at the average rate of once every year, mostly soon after harvest during the April school holiday, to bring him some of the fresh farm produce from the village. Our situation was not an isolated one; in fact it was the norm in most village households. Any deviation was frowned upon as unAfrican. Weinrich (1979) gives a vivid and graphic representation of the

34 *Colonial press and loci of silencing*

resultant structural modification and social reengineering of the rural African family household characterised by absentee husbands. No self-respecting woman would go to live and raise a family in town where her husband worked. It was unheard of. Such children born and bred in urban areas were always a laughing stock in the villages where they were referred to as *mabhondorokisheni*, a Shona corruption of the English phrase to mean those born in the locations. We in the village, hardened by the coarse life in the village, always thought there was something very unfortunate for anyone to begin their life in town. Such were the slow uneventful (un-newsworthy) days of our lives mired in grinding (Charamian) poverty far away from the hustle and bustle of modernity.

If on the material physiological side, we lived on the verge of growth stunting starvation, our spiritual and informational aspects of life were probably not better either. The geo and body politics of news production just as in the case of modernist Eurocentric epistemologies excluded such places as Charama and the people who lived there as zones unworthy of news. Any encounters with print matter was strictly limited to a worn-out family Bible which no longer had its covers and whose outer pages were gradually peeling off like the rind of some fruit so that early chapters of the book of Genesis and closing pages of the book of Revelations were missing but that wasn't too much of a bother because in any case even those remaining pages looked just intimidatingly too many to finish reading in a lifetime. The smaller Catholic Church catechism and prayer book was a more realistic target if one had an ambition to read a book from cover to cover. As for newspapers, our first glimpse of them was when we saw small pieces of them torn out and used as foil to roll tobacco in, in a do-it-yourself process of manufacturing a village cigarette and then everything would go up in smoke as the elderly menfolk took turns to suck and puff away the smoke by the fireside during the day or at night. We never suspected newspapers had any other useful purpose. Even in the more favoured African living areas closest to modernity such as African townships and compounds near towns and mining centres, as I was to discover much later, the economic value of newspapers for most Africans lay more in their general use as toilet paper or wrapping paper. This is a chapter not present in most history text books on either the march of modernity in Africa or on the diffusion of the press among colonial Africans.

Encounters with the press

It was after progressing through to the higher grades of primary schooling that we had a chance to see what a full newspaper looked like and to even read it. The government supplied every school with *The African Times* free of charge. Every resourceful teacher kept a good supply of these newspapers stashed somewhere in the classroom shelves. But our teacher who taught us in Grades 6 and 7 was even more resourceful. We never got to know how he got some international magazines such as copies of the *Reader's Digest*, and *To The Point*. We put these newspapers to very good academic use. We never read them for their meaning except for such must-read sections as the *Readers Digest's* 'laughter is the best medicine'. Few though they were, it was from their pages, that we harvested a lot of big English words which we called 'vocabulary', for use in embellishing our English compositions by simply scattering about, such newly acquired jawbreakers as 'legendary, solitary, vicissitudes' etc. at strategic intervals throughout the writing, whether it made sense or not, that was something else. The bigger boys put a rich store of such words to good use to confound and impress girls they wrote love letters to. The other reason we found ourselves compelled to read the available newspapers was to improve our general knowledge so we would excel in the General Paper exam at the end of the year. This was the paper in which you could be asked such difficult and ponderous questions as: 'The treaty of Waitangi was signed in 18___' and of course, a clever student was supposed to know and complete the expression; 'Who is the President of Egypt?' to which you were supposed to answer; 'Anwar Sadat'. Or, 'who is the Prime Minister of Israel?' and you were expected to know that it was Golda Meir.

It never ceased to amaze me how a whole self-respecting country could have a woman for a president. So it was always amazing that India, Ceylon and Israel had women for prime ministers, Indira Gandhi, Sirimavo Bandaranaike and Golda Meir. Other imponderables we discovered from these news magazines were that some neighbouring countries to the north of us had African presidents, the likes of Kenneth Kaunda of Zambia, Hastings Kamuzu Banda of Malawi, and Julius Nyerere of Tanzania. Young and impressionable as we were, we always concluded that this must be the work of witchcraft, pure magic. Otherwise how else could one explain it? How comes it, for a woman or an African to be head of government? Ought not government to be in 'responsible' (white) hands? Our own situation was more as it should be. Only white people deserved to be in government and the stories we read in each edition of *The African Times* made this fact explicitly evident. It was folly for any African to ever try to challenge the white man. Its *Letters to Jane Goodheart* column was more helpful in answering many great questions of African young life in Rhodesia. The rest of the other sections, a good sample of which are excellently exhibited in Julie (Frederikse, 1982), carried stories which we never took seriously. News workers in today's Zimbabwe had better take seriously Johan Meiring's caution on the challenges the Rhodesian press faced:

> When you want to communicate with the African tribesman in this country you have a hell of a problem. He doesn't necessarily listen to the radio, or pick up the daily paper – that is the problem. The message, the method of communication is a problem. The pitch is also a problem. It can't just be in English. It also has to be in the vernacular. Plus there is the fact that the African is greatly affected by tribal customs ... We *(media producers)* were on a different wavelength from the black tribesman. (Frederikse, 1982)

36 *Colonial press and loci of silencing*

We never knew the word propaganda, so we never consciously avoided reading the newspapers that came our way either, we just found the whole thing about terrorists rather boring drivel and not consistent with our lived experience, until one day in 1975 three strangers dressed in what didn't look suspicious in any way showed up at our school and they were talking, chatting even being congenial with our teachers. It was not until the teacher told us that they were '*vana vevhu*' (freedom fighters), known as terrorists according to our local newspapers, that we took any notice of them. They were not carrying any guns. They did not look any bit different from our teachers. They were actually a very big mismatch with how we had expected them to look like, basing on the many headlines and pictures of them, we had seen in *The African Times*. They spent quite a few days loitering and just walking about in the villages. Then, one evening, deafening explosions of gunfire rent the peace, which we had always taken for granted and continued late into the night punctuated with searchlight balls of fire which lit up the sky. The following day on our way to school as we went past the village where the shooting incident had happened, we noticed a trail of blood on the dust road. That was the only evidence of what we later learnt was a 'contact' between soldiers and the freedom fighters. There were no fatalities. An information blitzkrieg then started. From a helicopter circling above, day after day, would come a female voice calling out to Sifelani Jubane or Chijokwe, to hand himself over to the police, who would facilitate his return home, so he could be reunited with her, the heart-broken sweetheart he deserted when he went to join the terrorists. From the same helicopters also rained bomb showers of leaflets with graphic details of burned-down villages and gruesome murder of innocent villagers – how terrorists repaid the kindness of those that harboured them without reporting to the police. During this week of intense disturbance, military vehicles, armoured cars and police jeeps, the likes of which we had never seen before, swarmed into our villages with the upshot that Chief Huchu and some members of his counsel were picked up, taken away from us for the crime of 'failing to report the presence of terrorists in his area' (Frederikse, 1982). Chief Huchu was never to return alive even after independence in 1980. Had it not been for that 'contact', who knows, we senior primary school boys and girls might have ended up making what had become a familiar news headline in the next edition of *The African Times* those days: '(so many) School Pupils Abducted by Terrorists at (name of school)'. We would have crossed the border and God permitting, came back alive at independence to rejoin our families. We would now be part of the class that today claims special entitlement to the rulership of Zimbabwe as the guarantors of its independence and therefore 'stockholders' of the country. But that was not to be.

Huchu Primary School where I did my learning and a sister school called Manyepa Primary School, about 20 kilometres away in Chief Sayi's area, were the Mecca and Medina of learning in the world of my childhood. The graduating classes at these schools often held competitive scholastic tests together and one year one school would win and another year the other. I 'finished school' in 1975 after writing and passing my Grade 7 well, by our rural standards, and I now looked forward to one day going to town just like other young village boys to look for employment. I would then have the opportunity, if I wanted, to pick up from where I had left and further my education through correspondence. At school we had seen in *The African Times*, adverts of colleges that offered courses through correspondence. There was the Central African Correspondence College (CACC) or the Rapid Results College (RRC) to choose from. Testimonials abounded of many a young man who had made it in life through studying by correspondence from Rhodesia Junior Certificate (RJC) to the dizzy heights of the General Certificate of Education (GCE) Ordinary level. Once there, what else would an African need. But mine was a typical African childhood in late colonial Rhodesia. There were exceptions of course. African childhoods in African townships had because of their proximity to European areas more opportunities to proceed with their education to higher levels. There were variations even in TTLs. Children who grew up in TTLs close to Christian missionary establishments had better chances than those that were less served by missionaries, as was the case with Charama TTL.

Change in big politics which made news headlines around 1979 and 1980 as Rhodesia morphed into Zimbabwe was responsible for altering the course of my later life. In the *Moto* magazine was the 'Munetsi Says' column; it was of attraction to us mainly because accompanying it captured the kinds of puzzles about life that any young African could have about the many contradictions of life in colonial Rhodesia as seen through the eyes of an innocent child. To reinforce the child's perspective on issues was the accompanying cartoon image of Munetsi in rhombus shorts carrying a typical school book case. As for *The Rhodesia Herald* and the *Chronicle*, we never had sight of these publications in our area. I only came to know of them when at the beginning of 1979 we were 'smuggled' to go and live with our aunt in town as war refugees when conditions had really become very risky for us in the rural area due to the escalation of liberation war. The reasons why these two newspapers, though daily publications and claiming to be national newspapers, had never made it to our rural schools, I only came to know at college as a student of the media. I came to learn that they were newspapers that targeted a white readership, and that at the beginning they were solely available on a subscription basis, and not too many Africans even those who lived and worked in European areas had the wherewithal to afford the subscription cost. So these papers carried white opinion which was of interest to an exclusively white readership.

For many of us rural children, were we to be asked to rank in order of preference which of the three different media platforms that we had access to in the rural areas, among print, radio and cinema which we knew as bioscope, then bioscope would have rated top of the list followed by radio. The criteria for such judgement was of course the entertainment value of the medium. As children, we never suspected that they served any other purpose. It was only much later in life that some of us had to learn that in war-time Rhodesia, those who brought these 'entertainment' media had completely different intentions by them, those of psychological warfare and propaganda manipulation (Frederikse, 1982).

This little detour into the recollections of an African rural childhood goes to demonstrate that beneath the surface of big news headlines about big politics that

38 Colonial press and loci of silencing

clog our information channels, some little life somewhere might actually be getting irreparably damaged if not altogether extinguished unnoticed. The spatial distribution of the Rhodesian population where Africans, particularly women children and the elderly were confined to the tribal trust lands and only those African men whom the whites deemed useful were allowed to live in the European areas had serious ramifications on who had access to appear in the press. This point is often neglected by media analysts who argue that colonial press discriminated against Africans in general and African women in particular. African men lived closer to and even worked for some prominent European men and women who were the subject of much colonial news, and by that proximity had a fair chance of making it into the news even if it was mostly for all the wrong reasons. Thus according to Kaarsholm: racial segregation in the media was made possible because:

> The ideological racism of colonial culture was materially founded in the physical and geographical segregation of town and country and of urban and rural areas within themselves. One direct effect of the colonial conquest was the sharp division of agricultural tracts into white commercial farming regions, on the one hand, and on the other, the African reserves that were re-baptised as Tribal Trust Lands, as well as the construction of towns that were drastically separated into luxurious white suburbs and densely overpopulated African townships. (Kaarsholm, 1989)

Journalists did not need to discriminate between whites and blacks when reporting news; that was geographically inscribed for them in racial land distribution. A 'nose for news', good news opportunities and strictures of a 24-news cycle simply did not happen to direct them to African areas such as Charama TTL that much.

Conclusion

While racial segregation of land distribution and settlement had to be enforced by legislation, for example, there were shops for whites only, schools for whites only and schools for blacks; on the train, there were coaches clearly labelled 'European coaches' and 'African coaches'; this was hardly the case in the pages of newspapers such as *The Rhodesia Herald*. Racial land segregation had already dealt with the task of racial segregation for them by tucking the African population far away, out of their reach. So it is reasonable to say that the front pages of such newspapers as *The Rhodesia Herald* were 'European areas' by designation as land segregation automatically mapped itself out on news layout.

Note

1 Detention camps, where African nationalist leaders (Joshua Nkomo and other ZAPU leaders at Gonakudzingwa and Mugabe and other ZANU leaders at Sikombela) had been detained by the Smith regime, without trial or prospect of release.

References

Arrighi, G., Aschoff, N., Scully, B., 2010. Accumulation by dispossession and its limits: The Southern Africa paradigm revisited. *Stud. Comp. Int. Dev.* 45, 410–438.

Beach, D.N., 1989. *Mapondera: Heroism and history in Northern Zimbabwe, 1840–1904*. Mambo Press.

Clements, F., 1969. *Rhodesia: The course to collision*. Pall Mall Press.

Crenshaw, K., 1989. Demarginalising the intersection of race and sex: A black feminist critique of antidiscrimination doctrine, feminist theory and antiracist politics. University of Chicago Legal Forum; Vol. 1989. Iss. 1, Article 8.

Denis, P., 2015. Abbot Pfanner, the Glen Grey Act and the native question. *South Afr. Hist. J.* 67, 271–292.

Desmond, C., 1970. *The discarded people: An account of African resettlement*. Christian Institute of South Africa.

Elkins, C., 2005. *Britain's gulag: The brutal end of empire in Kenya*. Random House.

Erichsen, C., Olusoga, D., 2010. *The Kaiser's holocaust: Germany's forgotten genocide and the colonial roots of Nazism*. Faber & Faber.

Frederikse, J., 1982. *None but ourselves: Masses vs. media in the making of Zimbabwe*. Heinemann.

Hall, S., 2018. Race, articulation, and societies structured in dominance [1980] in:
D. Morley (ed). *Stuart Hall selected writings: Essential essays, Volume 1: Foundations of cultural studies*. Duke University Press. Accessed 21 February 2019 from: https://read.dukepress.edu/books/book/2554/Essential-Essays-Volume-1Foundations-of-Cultural.

Hochschild, A., 1998. *King Leopold's ghost: A story of greed, terror and heroism in colonial Africa*. Houghton Mifflin.

Hulley, C.M., 1969. *Where lions once roamed*. Pioneer Head.

Kaarsholm, P., 1989. Quiet after the storm: Continuity and change in the cultural and political development of Zimbabwe. *Afr. Lang. Cult.* 2, 175–202.

Lessing, D., 1968 [1957]. *Going home*. Ballantine.

Mupfuvi, B.M., 2014. Land to the people: Peasants and nationalism in the development of land ownership structure in Zimbabwe from pre-colonialism to the Unilateral Declaration of Independence (UDI) period. Accessed 18 February 2019 from: http://usir.salford.ac.uk/id/eprint/32003/1/Final_Copy_PhD_Thesis_Bridget_M_Mupfuvi.pdf.

Nyambara, P.S., 2002. Madheruka and Shangwe: Ethnic identities and the culture of modernity in Gokwe, Northwestern Zimbabwe, 1963–1979. *J. Afr. Hist.* 43, 287–306.

Palmer, R.H., 1977. *Land and racial domination in Rhodesia*. Heinemann Educational.

Phimister, I.R., 1988. *An economic and social history of Zimbabwe, 1890–1948: Capital accumulation and class struggle*. Addison-Wesley Longman.

Pinto, M., 2009. Silent citizens: On silence and silencing in journalism. Presented at the IAMCR 2009 Conference, International Association for Media and Communication Research (IAMCR), pp. 1–13. Accessed 13 June 2019 from: https://www.academia.edu/3622020/Silent_citizens_On_silence_and_silencing_in_journalism.

Ranger, T.O., Ranger, T., 1985. *Peasant consciousness and guerilla war in Zimbabwe: A comparative study*. University of California Press.

Riddell, R., 1980. Zimbabwe's land problem: The central issue. *J. Commonw. Comp. Polit.* 18, 1–13.

Selolwane, O., 1980. Colonization by concession: Capitalist expansion in the Bechuanaland Protectorate, 1885–1950. *Pula Botsw. J. Afr. Stud.* 2, 74–124.

Strack, M., Goodwin, D., 2009. Between the lines: The spirit behind land agreements. Accessed 11 May 2019 from: https://www.irbnet.de/daten/iconda/CIB16645.pdf.

40 *Colonial press and loci of silencing*

Van Onselen, C., 1976. *Chibaro: African mine labour in Southern Rhodesia.* Ravan.

Weinrich, A.K.H., 1979. *Women and racial discrimination in Rhodesia.* United Nations Educational.

Wood, E.W., 1968. The implications of migrant labour for urban social systems in Africa. *Cahiers d'études africaines,* 8, 29, 5–31. Accessed 23 December 2019 from: https://www.persee.fr/doc/cea_0008-0055_1968_num_8_29_3121.

Newspapers

Chakamwe, C., 24 April 2014. The Rudd Concession: A big fraud. *The Patriot.* wwwthepatriot.co.zw/old_posts/the-rudd-concession-a-big-fraud/.

Flora of Zimbabwe. Utilities: List of species vernacular names. wwwzimbabweflora.co.zw/speciesdata/utilities/utility-vernac-species.php.

3 News whiteouts under UDI and after

Introduction

The rise of the Rhodesia Front to political prominence with the election of Ian Douglas Smith as Prime Minister in 1964 and its unilateral declaration of independence (UDI) from Britain on 11 November 1965, marked the beginning of a systematic abandonment of a more liberal politics in dealing with the pro-blacks liberal leanings in the white settler community, that had characterised the previous decade with its policy of racial partnership between whites and blacks. Immediately after the UDI, the Smith government instituted government press censorship as its official policy to curb any liberal leanings and inclinations in the editorial content of newspapers. This chapter uses as its fulcrum and point of departure archived documentary evidence of how the press in colonial Zimbabwe in the early days of the (UDI) attempted, though feebly, to fight back and resist official censorship policy of the regime. Newspaper editors, in protest, went on to publish editions of their newspapers with pages interspaced with whiteouts or blank spaces to mark those stories or portions of them government censors would have taken out. The irony of it was that the blank spaces themselves were white but the news that was uncensored was even whiter in its exclusion of black opinion. Though this practice went on for some time, it was not sustained throughout the period the Smith government remained in power. At some point something had to give and in April 1968 the system of prior censorship ended, at least so it appeared (Windrich, 1979), and newspapers once again became 'normal' publishing with no blank spaces. Those token spaces that represented censored stories became subject of censorship themselves (Chavunduka, 2002) in a process of deletion of the deletions. But how far were the Rhodesian editors prepared to extend the fight to defending their right to publish blank spaces? What sense were readers supposed to make of the fact that their newspapers became full again with no blank spaces? Was this to be taken as a sign that newspapers were now providing their readers with fuller, uncensored and multi-perspectival versions of reality? Or was it a sign of journalism's surrender and acquiescence with being dictated to by the Rhodesian government? This chapter discusses the factors both internal to the news work process itself and some external to the newsroom and more structural that may impinge on the more

42 *News whiteouts under UDI and after*

intractable less visible blank spaces in the news in Zimbabwe since the end of official censorship.

The chapter re-examines the universally accepted conventional wisdom in news production, journalists observe in determining what qualifies as news. Recent scholarship in this area has started to shift discussion away from consideration of news values as fixed qualities immanent in some news events or in some people caught up in events (Harcup and O'neill, 2001; Cottle, 2000; Cotter, 2010; Caple and Bednarek, 2016). Johan Galtung and Mari Holmboe Ruge first defined news values in 1965 as a set of criteria about characteristics intrinsic in some events and absent in others, on the basis of which journalists select what qualified as news. New thinking is beginning to suggest that the so-called news values do not inhere in some events and not in others. They find the proposition that the journalists themselves write the news values into the events they choose to report on to be more consistent with observed journalistic conduct in the field. Either way, what emerges from the debate about the news values in journalistic work is that the process of selection of what to include as news and what to exclude is unavoidably wired into the professional practice of journalism itself, except that when it is done by the journalists themselves it is not ordinarily referred to as censorship although the difference in outcome remains debatable. This chapter discusses the difference between whiteouts imposed by external censors, ordinarily called censorship, and those that come about as a result of the felicitous application of accepted norms of professional journalistic practice.

Government censorship

When the Rhodesia Front (RF) came to power in 1962 it immediately instituted a scorched earth policy 'to silence the press to prevent any dissenting voices being heard from inside or outside Rhodesia' (Windrich, 1975: 524) against Rhodesia Front rule. RF took a poly-pronged approach to bringing the media under firm government control for its own propaganda purposes. Government take-over of broadcasting and outright banning of some newspapers was followed by press censorship of those that were left publishing (Msindo, 2009). African nationalist political parties, ZAPU and ZANU, were banned, their leaders detained and that section of the press that had ventilated African nationalist opinion on politics such as the *African Daily News* was also banned on the same day. 'Consequently, on 26 August 1964, the day on which the African nationalist parties were also banned, the government proclaimed the *Daily News* a prohibited publication in terms of the Law and Order (Maintenance) Act, allegedly because they could not 'permit the much prized ideal of press freedom to be used for spreading subversion' (Windrich, 1975: 532). At this point it may be instructive to recall the spirited fight that *The Rhodesia Herald* put up in defence of the principle of the freedom of the press under circumstances almost similar to the closure of the *African Daily News* the only difference being that though a competitor, the paper involved was a white newspaper. This is what Gale (1962: 62) says about the solidarity of the press then: 'in spite of their editorial differences the two papers had a common loyalty to a fundamental principle of vital concern to them both – the freedom of the Press and when, at a crucial stage of the Boer War, the Times fell foul of the military authorities and was suspended from publication, the *Herald* gave it its full support'. The *Herald* editors then must have understood the implications of state closure of newspapers, that it was tantamount to silencing a community. Contrast this with the lukewarm support given to the *African Daily News* by the establishment press and even more surprisingly by its British based owner the Thompson Group. Windrich points out that:

> with few notable exceptions the press acquiesced in the denigration of their profession and the undermining of their credibility, particularly by publishing all of the Benson-inspired diatribes levelled against them by supporters of the Rhodesian Front. Nor was there much show of professional unity in defence of an independent press. Those who did protest against the banning of the *Daily News* appeared to be more concerned with the dubious legality of the ban (which was a potential threat to their own papers as well) than with the destruction of the only daily publication expressing African aspirations or even African interests. And the fact that the Thomson group did not try to contest the ban was a further blow to the morale of the profession. (Windrich, 1975: 532)

Phillipa Berlyn, who describes herself as freelance journalist, took a position of quiet indifference to the banning of the *African Daily News* as did the most representative organ of journalism in colonial Rhodesia, the Guild which simply did not do enough in defence of the *Daily News* or of the principle of press freedom (Parker, 1972). The white liberal establishment which had all along appeared to advocate the advancement of Africans were a big let down when crunch time came to defend the only newspaper that articulated an African nationalist viewpoint on issues. Berlyn makes this confession which was very revealing of a general white attitude on the silencing of African voices: 'therefore I wept no crocodile tears when the *Daily News* received its coup de grace. Nor, it will be noted, did Lord Thomson make any complaints, once it was made known to him for what purposes the *Daily News* had been used' (Berlyn, 1967: 99). But all this is probably understandable when one puts into perspective the fact that this happened at the height of the Cold War. Here was a newspaper whose editorial policy was slanted in support of the nationalist leaders who had openly espoused a Marxist, communist ideology at odds with the Western liberal ideology most white Rhodesians then left, right or centre as well as the paper's British owners embraced. Opposition to communism was a point around which white Rhodesians agreed even if they differed in many other respects and the *Daily News*'s open support for Joshua Nkomo elicited the old white patriotism and laager mentality.

The *Central African Examiner* which had moved to fill the void left by the closure of the *African Daily News* in providing a voice to African nationalism was hounded out of circulation through censorship so that 'by 1966 this paper had been

44 *News whiteouts under UDI and after*

censored out of existence: 80 percent of its copy was blue penciled' (Jones, 2001: 2710). Some critical white voices were silenced by being deported or forced into exile. The Rhodesia Printing and Publishing Company's publications, such as *The Rhodesia Herald* and the *Sunday Mail* in Harare and the *Chronicle* and the *Sunday News* in Bulawayo, remained as a virtual monopoly press. Competition if any from the Christian missionary press such as the Methodist *Umbowo* published in Mutare and the Catholic *Moto* newspaper published from Gweru was really very negligible. But even these publications which had generally passed as harmless and posed no serious threat to white rule in principle also came face to face with the fact that they too were generally being treated with suspicion by the Rhodesian Front government. Just a day before Prime Minister Ian Douglas Smith declared the Unilateral Independence from Britain (UDI) 'local censorship was actually imposed on the Rhodesian press … Government officials moved into the offices of *The Rhodesia Herald* and the Bulawayo Chronicle and stayed there until censorship was lifted two and a half years later' (Palling, 1979: 45).

According to Malcolm Smith who was editor of *The Rhodesia Herald* then, the first casualties of official censorship at his paper were the press statement by the then Governor of Southern Rhodesia Sir Humphrey Gibbs officially announcing the dismissal of Prime Minister Ian Smith and his colleagues in government for the treasonous action of unilaterally declaring independence from Britain as well as the editorial comment whose tone was generally critical of the UDI. He states that: 'The Governor's message was banned from the following day's paper, as was the leader which was headed "A mortal blow" and began: "The deed has been done, *The Rhodesia Herald* does not acclaim it, or accept that it is rightful or in the interests of Rhodesia"' (Smith, 1969: 61). It is important to note that Malcolm Smith's editorial column became a regular target of the censors ever since they walked into Herald House as Editor Smith had tried to remain true to the newspaper's editorial charter which enjoined the paper to serve the diverse interests of the white community. From its inception *The Rhodesia Herald* had sought to balance competing views and opinions of different sections of the white community. No winds of social and political change had convinced its editors of the need to deviate from this orientation, not even the rise of African nationalist politics and the rise to power of the RF with its extreme right-wing politics would make the newspaper change course. While the Editors were critical of the RF's narrow sectional politics they were oblivious to how the racial toxicity of their own white liberal conservatism naturalised a systemic exclusion of African opinion from the pages of their newspaper. It did not occur to Malcom Smith and his fellow journalists at *The Rhodesia Herald* that before government censors prevented Sir Humphrey' Gibbs expressing himself on the UDI, they had actively, albeit unbeknown to them, silenced many more divergent views on the Rhodesian question through the operation of the 'invisible hand' of editorial selection.

Catering for a wide range of white tastes, *The Rhodesia Herald* especially appealed to the sensibilities and interests of the upper echelons of white society, with its luxury goods advertisements and little features. Up until 1965 the Argus newspapers generally supported the party in power, but fairly

> deliberately spoke out for what white Rhodesians saw as liberal issues. In the Rhodesian context, "liberal" was not used in any broad political sense, but only to denote a position on racial issues. It is argued ... that although there are some significant examples of *The Rhodesia Herald* taking a liberal approach in this sense, this stance was a very limited one. (Cousins, 1991: 4)

In protest at imposed censorship, editors of newspapers published newspapers with blank spaces to mark those stories or sections of stories that had not been passed by the censors.

In certain cases, particularly where large sections of the story were censored, the editors printed whatever was left of the story punctuated with blank spaces to mark where the story had been cut out by the censors. The result was a serious disruption to the intelligibility and flow of the stories affected. This was the only way editors could communicate to the readers that their government was denying them some information. It was a bold decision to take under the circumstances, considering that space is of the utmost importance to any newspaper. The principle is that no space should be put to waste. Every column inch counts. Editors had other options open to them. For example, they could always fill up the blanks with other 'safe' stories, or even fill up the freed-up space with advertising and earn the company more money. But the blank spaces began to assume great symbolic significance to the editors. It acted as an act of defiance on the part of the press and as a source of public embarrassment for the government (see pictures below). It also acted as an open invitation to the fertile imagination of the reading public to supply the missing story through rumour and speculation. Readers, however, had no way of registering their own discontent with government censorship through the newspapers since letters to the editor were not spared by the censors either. So, there was no way readers of *The Rhodesia Herald* could tell how fellow readers elsewhere felt about censorship because any critical sentiment against government policy was itself subject for censorship. In fact, the letters to the editor sections of the newspapers carried the most blankest spaces.

Publication of blank spaces was a form of giving publicity to the story of government censorship. Embarrassed by this publicity, government had put in place measures to stop the publication of blank spaces by February 1966 (Jones, 2001) in a process of double silencing where newspapers were being silenced from telling certain stories and then silenced from informing their readers of the initial silencing – in a deletion of the deletion of sorts.

Some commentators are of the view that it was these extreme measures of government that pushed the press generally and the missionary press in particular into adopting an adversarial position vis-à-vis Rhodesian Front government. The spirited fight against government censorship went on only for some time, at least until those editors who posed the most threat to government had been haunted out of the Rhodesian press, but some of the conditions the press ended up operating in were very compromising of their own claim to a high professional standard. Like the press acquiescence to offering government space for its own propaganda.

Figure 3.1a and b Blank spaces became a common feature in *The Rhodesia Herald* (left) and the *Central African Examiner* (right). National Archives of Zimbabwe.

DR AHRN PALLEY

CENSORS AND THE PRESS

THAT reliable RF barometer, *The Citizen*, explained to us why censorship was necessary: because 'the major newspapers have demonstrated ... that they are highly effective instruments in the political warfare of our times and that they must be treated as such if they come into conflict with the declared will and interests of the majority of the people.' *The Citizen* goes on to explain the criteria which guide the Rhodesian censors. 'The first principle is that the Rhodesian nation has made a decision which cannot be changed short of disaster and this fact must form the basic assumption of anything that is published in Rhodesia. ... Rhodesia is in the process of converting a "de facto" government into a "de jure" government. ... The censors, therefore, refuse to permit inside Rhodesia's borders the publication of any matter which impugns the constitutionality of the new status quo. ... A clear distinction is being drawn, however, between the hard facts which the people of Rhodesia must have if they are to form a clear and coherent picture of their country's situation and hostile propaganda whose only purpose it is to confuse and divide them and undermine their resolution.'

So now we know!

THE CENTRAL AFRICAN EXAMINER   DECEMBER, 196

Figure 3.1a and b Continued

48 *News whiteouts under UDI and after*

It was in response to these taunts that *The Rhodesia Herald* editor offered the prime minister space on a daily basis to put forward the government point of view or, as he put it, to produce a column representing 'what is truth, unbiased and untarnished by human frailty'. Having won this concession, however, Mr van der Byl proceeded to frame the prime minister's acceptance with such restrictions—that the government column must be placed on the front page; that the subject matter (including attacks on the press) must be determined by the government; that the arrangement must be a continuing one and not restricted to any definite period of time. (Windrich, 1975: 529)

More revealing of the feebleness of the resistance put up by editors of the Rhodesian white press against government censorship is John Parker's comment on just how ineffective and misdirected Malcolm Smith's form of gallant fight for the freedom of the press was when he states that:

Malcolm Smith did in fact fight – but not for his right to print the news without fear or favour. He fought for the right to print nothing at all, which I suggest was the wrong battle at the wrong time for the wrong cause. He fought like a tiger to keep the blank spaces in his newspaper caused by the censor's scissors, and to avoid filling up the spaces with other news or leave, as the other newspapers did, 'token spaces'. But neither he nor any other Rhodesian editor found the courage at any time to print the news the censor had removed, or openly to defy the 'laws' by which the regime steadily eroded the prestige and position of the Press. (Parker, 1972: 129)

The idea of distortion by culture jamming or fake news may read like something very novel which only the age of Internet and social media brought about and made possible. Even research literature on the subject has often represented these twin social phenomena as if they had no precedent in history. But the meaning of fake news derives from a visceral claim that what mainstream media present somehow approaches the truth because of its method of sourcing, verification and commitment to objectivity. 'But that was before the *Herald* editor, Malcolm Smith, had discovered that a "semi-professional" cast of letter writers was being "inspired" by the Rhodesian Front to pack the correspondence columns with their contributions' (Windrich, 1975: 527). The effect of this strategy was to create the impression that the RF policies enjoyed wide purchase among the newspaper's readers and by implication by the broader white Rhodesian community. In the post-FTLRP period in Zimbabwe a semi-professional cast of writers to the editor emerged at *The Rhodesia Herald*'s successor, *The Herald*. This time around, however they were packing the 'Letters to the Editor' section with their largely pro-Mugabe and ZANU-PF policy correspondences, but this time writing from the newsroom itself and with the tacit invitation to do so by the editor. A senior reporter at *The Herald* acknowledged that in certain circumstances when they did not receive adequate correspondences from readers, then it was the duty of junior reporters or interns to write such letters.[1] Much more recently, in the post-Mugabe era,[2] President Mnangagwa was reported as having ordered ZANU-PF youths to (*kurakasha*) do through social media, something very similar to what RF political apparatchiks were doing with *The Herald* then – to thrash them on social media through culture jamming.

> In March, Mnangagwa, ever the shrewd strategist, ordered the ZANU-PF youth league to take to social media to serve as online warriors/ thugs "kurakasha" (to hit hard/ batter) the opposition. It's been claimed that ZANU-PF paid unemployed, computer literate supporters to flood social media platforms with attacks and counter-attacks targeted at overwhelming a poorly resourced opposition. The ruling party's varakashi took on Chamisa supporters known as "Nerrorists" (after Chamisa's nickname, Nero) in a series of online propaganda battles.[3]

Between 1985 and 1987 the Gukurahundi atrocities in Matebeleland and some parts of the Midlands province were made that much more possible because of an unacknowledged blanket of press silence that blocked those killings from public view. It is difficult to imagine that the Gukurahundi problem would have still escalated to the levels it did had the Chronicle or The *Herald* been there.

> there was an almost total 'blackout' within Zimbabwe of news on Matabeleland. Foreign journalists were excluded from western Zimbabwe as they had been from 'operational areas' during the liberation war. In 1985 the CCJP received numerous reports of torture involving the Central Intelligence Office (CIO). Amnesty International received similar information and published a report on the matter in November 1985. In response Mugabe dubbed its writers 'Amnesty Lies International' and the report was suppressed in Zimbabwe. The CCJP's own independently published report on CIO activities in Matabeleland led to a serious clash with the Zimbabwean state. The Commission's acting director, Nicholas Ndebele, was arrested under section 5 3 of the Law and Order Maintenance Act and imprisoned in Chikurubi prison. The arresting officers seized a considerable number of documents and files. Charges that Ndebele had supplied sensitive information to enemy countries were eventually dropped (Jones, 2001: 2774).

Just like happened much later under Operation Murambatsvina, it had to take the Catholic Commission for Justice and Peace to conduct an inquiry to unearth the hidden dimensions of Gukurahundi, not journalism even of the investigative type. Journalism as a profession is the most sensitive to external intrusions on its work. It lays great store on what it refers to as editorial autonomy. Any external interference with the work of the journalist is regarded as a serious threat to the freedom of the press. Journalism is however often oblivious to how processes internal to its own mode of operation may result in the same effect it abhors so much when it is forced

50 *News whiteouts under UDI and after*

on them from outside. In the section below we consider some of the ways in which censorship was slowly but surely built into journalism's newswork at the RRP.

Internalised censorship

Official government censorship of the sort that was in operation in colonial Rhodesia under UDI as discussed above was of an extreme sort and its effect was to deny white Rhodesians who were the main target readership of the remaining press, an opportunity to be fully informed about the direction in which the political situation was tending. While this may have been bad enough, the form of censorship that happens daily in the newsroom of which journalism itself is blind has probably far more deleterious and more pervasive outcomes than official press censorship. Malcolm Smith, who was one of the few editors with first-hand experience of how official censorship stifled free expression of *The Rhodesia Herald*, was probably right to suggest that he saw no reason why the Rhodesian government had censored the press, because according to him if the censored items were to be published one day, 'the reading of them *would* make Rhodesians sick. They would learn, if they did not already know, that they had been bluffed for so long by so few for so little purpose' (Smith, 1969: 66). What should be the real cause for disquiet for any reader of Malcolm Smith's insider account of how censorship impacted his work as editor of *The Rhodesia Herald* is the blindness to his paper's systemic exclusion of African opinion on the unfolding events in Rhodesia. He was convinced that unimpeded by official censors 'the press tried to present a fair and balanced picture' (Smith, 1969: 66). So long as the paper was allowed to present a picture that pitted one white opinion against another, that sufficed for Malcolm Smith as 'fair and balanced'. Nowhere does Smith ever intimate that he found the conspicuous absence of African opinion from the pages of his newspaper objectionable. As editor he was in fact complicit in enforcing censorship of African opinion from *The Rhodesia Herald* by upholding a patently racist editorial policy which explicitly stated that it commits to keeping the interests of the white Rhodesian community steadily in focus (Gale, 1962). What this meant is that the editors of the Rhodesia press were the unacknowledged first line of censors before the RF government added another layer of censors.

Journalism does not take kindly to a conception that regards the 'professional' practices by which they achieve more or less comparable outcomes – the articulation of some but not other views as news stories – as censorship. Gate-keeping is the name journalism prefers to call its own system of selection which must not be confused with external censorship. Those journalists who found it difficult to embrace the RF's extreme right-wing political ideology were hounded out of the media, and there were many examples; Malcolm Smith, editor of *The Rhodesia Herald*, John Parker, senior reporter and many others. For those who remained, Windrich (1975) points out, there were fewer options besides playing along and toeing the line set by the Rhodesian Front government.

Actual resistance to official censorship began to wane so that: 'Although it (official censorship) had officially been relaxed in 1968, in practice censorship continued in subtle forms, particularly through self-censorship on the part of citizens and newspapers' (Msindo, 2009: 673). Windrich concurs with the view that official censorship was only lifted in April 1968 when self-censorship had firmly taken over in the newsrooms:

> self-imposed 'censorship' and regular consultation between press and government, the same pressures were exerted on individual journalists and editors, the same attacks on the press continued to come from the Rhodesian Front ... and the same punitive legislation remained to deter any deviation from the van der Byl concept of 'the true interests of Rhodesia. (Windrich, 1975: 533)

Frederikse captures it more succinctly when she maintains that the resistance to censorship by the monopoly press was half-hearted: 'blank spaces continued to appear in the newspapers ... But the protest was token, the Argus publications soon acquiesced to the regime's controls. By the time official censorship ended in 1968, publishers, editors and journalists had assumed the task of self-censorship to such a degree that the departure of the blue pencil teams was a non-event' (Frederikse, 1982: 28).

> For a number of years after UDI the *Herald*, especially, was characterized as being opposed to the Rhodesian Front government. Although there were points on which the newspaper was critical of the government in the period 1963 to about 1969, on the whole the paper followed a path of extreme caution self-censorship, and the editor in the early 1970s, Rhys Meier, was privately approved of by the Rhodesian Front, being thought to be "the greatest editor in the history of this country." ... despite its liberal image, *The Rhodesia Herald* consistently portrayed establishment stereotypes about Africans, and reinforced the assumptions held in common by whites speaking for the UFP and for the RF parties, assumptions that supported the continuation of white domination. (Cousins, 1991: 41)

Other elements within the structure of power were the press and government Information Service. Both of these were important in the transmission of ideas and in helping to formulate a cohesive ideology, speaking both to whites and to blacks, as well as to the outside world on occasion. It has sometimes been suggested that *The Rhodesia Herald* was an independent voice in Southern Rhodesia before the Rhodesian Front's censorship regulations and the government's successful attempts to change that newspaper's editorial staff. This may be true up to a point, but it should be noted that in the 1950s and 1960s *The Rhodesia Herald* maintained the government line for most of the time, and the evidence cited above suggests that the dominant white ideology was to a large extent mediated through its columns. Thus, we have seen that the danger of a politically

52 *News whiteouts under UDI and after*

motivated, extremist group of nationalists was emphasised in leading articles and news stories. There are many examples of pro-government stories, and when the BBC was, according to Whitehead's complaint, showing troops 'stamping out opposition' in African townships, *The Rhodesia Herald* showed the mass of Africans clearly supporting the presence of the troops and police and playing football with them. Similarly, many of the features and stories in *The Rhodesia Herald* reinforced the idea that the mass of Africans were uncivilised, backward and tribal. However well-intentioned, the regular 'Meet the African' column certainly did that. Two of these columns, for example, carried headings: 'The powers of the rain-makers are still sought by tribes', and 'Smoke, fire and drums are still used to send messages'. Even though the text that followed stated that such aspects of life were only a vague recollection to younger generation, the main headlines would have made the largest impact, stayed in the memory longest' (Cousins, 1991: 53).

Professional ideology of newswork

Cotter (2010: 67) calls news values 'one of the most important *practice-based* and *ideological* factors in understanding the focus and shape of news stories and the decisions of journalists' (original emphasis). News values are practice-based in the sense that they inform and guide decisions at every stage of the news production process in newsrooms. Journalists often unconsciously draw on them throughout the news production process from story conceptualisation, news gathering and writing stages. What makes one story ideal to be selected as newsworthy ahead of others is a matter journalists resolve only by applying a taxonomy of news values ordinarily accepted among journalists as a community of practice. They form the basis of interaction between junior reporters and their editors in news diary meetings. Suggestions for story angling, story sourcing and attribution and final placement on the page of the newspaper revolve around them. The story itself is rhetorically structured to make manifest which news values give the story its form and value as a news story. The constructedness of the news story makes it necessary to pro-blematise most of the taken-for-granted assumptions about the self-evident nature of news. One such example is how the term 'news gathering' conveys a simplistic view of the complex process by which journalism creates the final product it calls news. That term suggests that news already exists in its complete form and all the journalist does, is go out there, and guided by a 'nose for news' just gathers the news to package and deliver it to the reader. This reifies and conceals the fact that news does not pre-exist its creation as such by the journalist. Greg Philo cited in (Fowler, 2013: 13) debunks this notion that journalists gather the news, instead, he argues: 'news is not "found" or even "gathered" so much as made. It is a creation of a journalistic process, an artefact, a commodity even.'

The journalist engages in prior research around the story idea, this might involve going to the newspaper's morgue in search of an archive, if one exists, on the subject of the news story and the research may include finding out how other newspapers may have treated the subject in the past. All such information is not only critical in priming the news story and in deciding upon a fresh angle to give it but also in locating the story inter-textually to already existing discourses and interpretive frameworks relevant to the subject. This is then followed by making decisions about which sources to consult, what questions to ask and equally importantly what questions not to ask as a way of framing the ultimate story writing process itself. Source selection itself is contingent upon considerations of their standing as credible sources, ease of access within the limited resources and timelines imposed by the news cycle of the publication. 'News birthing' and not 'news gathering' would be a more apt descriptor of how journalists end up with copious notes from which they go on to write the news story. As McNair (2003: 30) points out: 'news is never a mere recording or reporting of the world "out there" but a synthetic, value laden account which carries within it the dominant assumptions and ideas of the society within which it is produced'. Everyday language use on news production tends to efface the unnaturalness of news.

For the present purposes we limit ourselves to the discussion of just a few of these 'universal' news values, which every journalist is taught to venerate in the Zimbabwean national press. Media scholars, subsequent to the initial formulation of a list of 12 news values by Johann Galtung and Mari Ruge in 1965 (Fowler, 2013), have since revised that original list; in some cases summarising it to a shorter list and in others elaborating and adding new ones to the list (MacShane, 1979; Hartley, 2013; Harcup and O'Neill, 2001; Brighton and Foy, 2007). A comparative analysis of lists of news values in key journalism textbooks used in training colleges in the United States showed little variation in the items listed although they differed significantly on prioritisation. Some news values listed in one textbook were missing in other textbooks. However, the news values of prominence, proximity and timeliness or recency were present across all the textbooks compared (Cotter, 2010), and it is these that we shall confine ourselves to in this chapter. Newsroom practitioners, like their scholarly counterparts, differ on which news values they prioritise and place at the top of the hierarchy depending on exigencies of context, media technology in use and dynamics of the news platform. It is important to reiterate a point media analysts have made about how these news values are not value free, and natural to news. In fact, they are more ideologically effective to the extent that those who use them begin to accept them as natural.

Hartley (2013: 76) makes a distinction between the first eight news values (frequency, threshold, unambiguity, meaningfulness, consonance, unexpectedness, continuity and composition) he considers as 'general conditions' applicable 'to news-selection the world over' and the other four (elite nations, elite persons, personalisation and negativity) that 'are more "culture-bound" the news values underlying selection in news media in the "north-western corner of the world"'. Hartley's analysis is problematic in the sense that it seeks to impose a very context-specific view, obviously obtained from close familiarity with journalism in the Western world as applicable across geographical space and time. It also understates how Western institutions such as the press and parliament were literally transplanted to overseas territories in certain instances with little or no modifications and that some of them have remained tethered to the 'mother countries' after end of formal colonial rule. It does not account for how global asymmetries between media systems in

54 *News whiteouts under UDI and after*

the north-western corner of the world and those elsewhere, some of which have remained their imperfect clones, influence news selection and prioritisation in former colonies such as Zimbabwe. The postcolonial press always addresses a bifurcated audience, a local powerful and globally connected elite and citizens of significant foreign countries, and its news agenda is almost always inflected by considerations of what pictures of the country we are conveying to the outside world over and above concerns of a local readership. Zimbabwe's experience during the UDI era and in the post-fast-track land reform period presents a text book case of how the external orientation of local news stands on its head the logic of universal applicability of news values.

Scholars who study news values have often arrived at them through a process of inferring from manifest news content. By systematically analysing the news discourses, scholars arrive at news values as the constitutive elements behind the news through a process of inductive iteration. But of interest to this monograph is how an assiduous application of the same news values is as much constitutive of silence just as it is of the news itself. Below we deal with each of the three news values referred to above in detail assessing the context of its universalisation, the social implications of its application in news production in postcolonial Zimbabwe.

Prominence or power

It was not a white thing that the editor of *The New York Herald* commissioned Henry Morton Stanley to go into the continent of Africa as a reporter in search of a story not about the privations so rife, Africans were suffering at the hands of Arab or European slavers. A lone white missionary lost in the interior of a huge continent largely unknown to Europeans at that time was the subject of that story. Nothing was to distract him from the single-minded pursuit of that one objective: to 'search for Dr. Livingstone throughout Equatorial Africa'. It was a story, according to Stanley's own admission, the newspaper-owner wanted to get, never mind the cost: 'Mr. Bennett, with a *prodigal generosity*, placed thousands of pounds at Stanley's disposal instructing him to "draw a thousand pounds now, and when you have gone through that, draw another thousand, and when that is spent, draw another thousand, and when you have finished with that draw another thousand and so on, but find Livingstone"' (Gallop, 2004: 132). Nor can it be entirely explained in terms of a Scottish newspaper-owner taking an interest in and seeking to give publicity to activities and achievements of a fellow Scot abroad that inspired James Bennet owner and publisher of *The New York Herald* to commission a reporter to go and get a story on Livingstone. It was probably more of a prominence rather than a white thing that once Stanley met Dr Livingstone at Ujiji that was for him, mission accomplished and he immediately filed his story, the substance of which was 'how I met Dr. Livingston at Ujiji'. The story was not about the many Africans he met on the way going on with the business of their daily existence, nor about his Zanzibari companions and anything that may have been of a life and death importance to them, that would not be of interest for the audience he was writing for – the readers of the *New York Herald* in America or of the *Daily Telegraph* in Britain. If

Stanley had been targeting a different readership then most probably the story would have been pitched differently. Professional journalism would argue that it does not fall within the remit of a journalist to precipitate newsworthy events such as assassinations, mass demonstrations, wars or coups-de-état so they can then go on to cover them for the sake of ingratiating their readers with titillating news. What journalists do, though, is to not just wait perchance events that are newsworthy unfold on their own; rather they stalk individuals, organisations and places with the greatest potential of causing to happen newsworthy occurrences, and everyday there will always be enough supply of these to select from, lest we would have the untenable situation where readers go without their daily paper because there was no story. This factor largely accounts for the seeming homogeneity of news across different newsrooms. Reporters are most likely to be stalking the same prominent individuals, such as government officials, politicians (elite people) and monitoring organisations that are sources of social, political, economic and cultural power such as the parliament, the courts, municipalities, company offices, schools and colleges (elite organisations). These together constitute rich hunting grounds for newshounds and, what is more, they often are located within proximate distances from each other, usually in the capital city. This partially explains why all newspapers which claim to provide national coverage are located in Harare so that they are within convenient distance to the most fertile hunting grounds for 'national' news as is illustrated in the aerial google map of Harare below.

Figure 3.2 Google aerial map of Harare showing proximity of newsrooms to their main news sources (centres of elite power).

56 *News whiteouts under UDI and after*

The green garden crisscrossed with lines in the aerial picture is the Africa Unity Square named in honour and memory of the role the Organization of African Unity (OAU) played in the country's struggle for independence. A helicopter view of the park will soon reveal to a discerning observer the layered histories of the place. Diagonal pathways from each corner as well as foot paths connecting the four cardinal points of the compass intersect around a magnificent water fountain at the centre of the park. The fountain no longer bubbles with water these days. In times past, the walkways used to be framed on either side with beds of well-tended crimson marigolds, daisies, bird of paradise and lilies, all in neat and straight furrows and forever in blossom. In its hay days the thing as a whole represented and still represents a garden replica of the Union Jack etched out on the ground – a reminder of the country's past as a crown colony of Britain. It was called Cecil Square then – named after Cecil John Rhodes, the founder of Rhodesia. It was here, we are told, as destiny would have it, the inexperienced members of the Pioneer Column – in the absence of their more knowledgeable hunter and guide, Frederick Courtney Selous, who had accompanied Leander Starr Jameson on a mission to negotiate a concession with Chief Mutasa – mistook Salisbury Kopje for Mount Hampden, their supposed destination, outspanned and hoisted the Union Jack on 12 September 1890 at this spot and formally inaugurated the 90-year long colonial chapter of Zimbabwe (Gale, 1962). Fort Salisbury was then erected as a symbol of British imperial authority. In its full splendour, the beauty of the square belies a sordid history of the brutal way in which the ideals engraved on the insignia of the BSAC, 'Justice, Freedom, Commerce' were pursued in the early days of occupation. For example, there is no trace left of the fact that where there is the magnificent water fountain at the centre of the square today, was the probable spot where once stood the gallows. Only archival records can reveal that it was at Cecil Square that Louis Andries became the first victim of the death penalty by public execution when he was hanged in 1893, more for the colonial administration's want of a good example to demonstrate to the world its impartial application of the rule of law, in Fairbridge's and other settlers' own estimation of the merits of the case (Gale, 1962). And Andries's was not going to be the first and last case. Hulley gives a vivid description of how in 1895, the first African man ever to be sentenced to death by public hanging in colonial Rhodesia, also met his fate at the gallows, at this very spot for the capital offence of killing a white man. This would send an unmistakable signal of how the administration would deal ruthlessly with instigators of resistance to colonial occupation and its rule of the country.

> Natives from all over the district were told to be at a certain spot, now known as Cecil Square, on a particular date … The gallows, a sordid contraption, was setup in the Square. From dawn on the appointed day, Africans poured in, in their thousands. The atmosphere was taut and there were signs of nervousness everywhere … A great stillness possessed the thousands of

assembled blacks, their eyes on the prisoner and on the white men who had come into their country and who had the audacity to impose their laws on them. (Hulley, 1969: 70)

The purpose was to teach 'the Africans a lesson they were not likely to forget quickly' (Hulley, 1969: 71).

The name had been changed just like happened to the streets that surround the square, at independence in 1980. To the northern side of the square across Nelson Mandela Avenue are three adjacent buildings: Parliament building in the middle, sandwiched on the western side with the Anglican Cathedral of St Mary's, and Defence House on the eastern side. Their front entrances face the square so that the jacaranda trees that form the frills of the square have stood witness to the many displays of pomp and heraldry of power as different Parliaments have entered and exited the House of Parliament over the years since the first parliament of 1923. Along the eastern and southern flanks of the square are the Old Mutual Centre, Barclays Bank and the Meikles Hotel, symbols of the nation's financial and commercial power. Just opposite and overlooking the square along the western side is Herald House, a seven-storey building at the corner of Sam Nujoma and George Silundika Avenue, where *The Herald* has been published daily from Monday to Saturday since 1891. The square designed as a ground replica of the British flag symbolised imperial hegemon as the rallying point and locus around which interests of the state, the church, commerce and the press pulsated, found common ground and coalesced. It is from this 'colonial heart' of Zimbabwe that power continues to throb and radiate outwards to every part of the Zimbabwean body politic. It is from this vantage point that Herald House has stood vigil, an 'honest' sentinel and chronicler of power for more than a century now. Other newspapers too have come, flourished for a while and disappeared to be replaced by yet other newspaper outfits, all attracted and in awe of the spectacle of power at the heart of Zimbabwe. This is all journalism understands by proximity in Zimbabwe. It is essentially proximity to power that lends events with their newsworthiness.

If all of the national newspapers serve for the *Chronicle* and the *Sunday News* which operate from Bulawayo (the second largest city after Harare) cover the 'nation' from within 'earshot' distance from centres of state power as the map of Harare above illustrates, is it any wonder then that the daily authorised versions of Zimbabwean reality, which we are routinely fed by the daily press, are ones which are structured in dominance? The geopolitics of news is shot through with the coloniality of power/knowledge which privileges discursive processes that subalternise and silences those located far away and at the bottom of the socio-political, ethnic, economic and cultural hierarchies (Grosfoguel, 2007).

Proximity or place

Media textbook definitions of proximity as a news value generally understand it as a marker of nearness. But the question that is often left unsettled is; nearness to

58 *News whiteouts under UDI and after*

what or to whom? Where Cotter (2010: 69) understands proximity as referring to 'the extent to which the story has occurred locally or, if it occurred elsewhere, is relevant to readers locally' thus emphasising geographical distance to readers for whom the paper reports, Fowler (2013) on the other hand places emphasis on cultural distance. An occurrence will be judged as newsworthy to the extent that it chimes with what is already culturally familiar to the target readership of a newspaper. Problems, however, arise when this target readership is not clearly defined as is the case with most newspapers that call themselves 'national' such as *The Herald*, the *Daily News* or *NewsDay* in Zimbabwe. The character of the news content is far from representative of the cultural diversity of all people who live across the length and breadth of Zimbabwe. Most of the newspapers have long abandoned any pretence at covering the nation in their reportage or in distribution of their offerings. In character they may pass for community newspapers actually. They are contend to distribute an average of 75% of their daily print runs in the capital, Harare and let the remaining 25% be delivered to the various city centres with no attempt being made to reach the rural areas with their products. Editors cite mainly cost implications as well as lack of the wherewithal to buy newspapers among the rural poor. Judging with the urban-centric and elitist character of much of the news content it may be justified to make the presupposition that reporters at these news outlets apply the news value of proximity guided by their circulation figures and the readers they are able to reach. A senior reporter at *The Herald* summarised the extent of what constitutes 'national' for their newspapers:

> The thing is, it depends on the distribution patterns. They don't go to the rural areas, it's Masvingo town, Mutare town, Rusape town, Harare town, Bulawayo, what not. They assume like urbanites are educated. They are the ones who read. They are the ones who afford a dollar to buy a newspaper. Those are the people we are writing for. (Interview with Maodza, Herald House, December 2013)

So, the application of the above definitions of proximity to mean cultural and geographical closeness to the readership community unambiguously means proximity to the city, in the Zimbabwean context. Reporters in Zimbabwe's national press tend to take Harare as representative of the country as a whole, and once they have Harare covered, for them, that is as good as the whole nation being covered. Where it becomes necessary to get the views of the ordinary people which according to a senior political reporter at *The Herald* rarely happens anyway:

> the challenge now is that ... let's say you doing a vox pop, you go on the *streets*. I'm writing for The *Herald*. If you go on the *streets* and you ask people 'what do you say about the constitution or what do you say about this other development', the views you are likely to get from eh! especially from Harare are anti-policy like anti-editorial policy. You rarely get anything which you

can come here and write because Harare being Harare, is an MDC like dominated thing. So you may collect it but you won't use it. (Interview with Maodza, Herald House, December 2013)

So at *The Herald* it is not just proximity it has to be unpacked so that it is clarified that the closeness is relative to something. It is nearness to power, more specifically, the ruling party, that invests an occurrence with newsworthiness. Two most misleading media terms to have ever been bandied around in the post-Iraq-invasion period to the present are embedded journalism and fake news. They have both been used to signify an aberrant departure from what is normative to mainstream news media.

The journalism that we have ever known in Zimbabwe has always been the embedded type. Where Zapiro satirises the CNN as 'embedded' with the US Army in the cartoon below, one can as easily substitute for the power elite versus the press more generally in postcolonial settings like Zimbabwe. From when Ernest William Fairbridge was dispatched as an agent of the South African Argus to set up a newspaper business at the founding of Rhodesia, it was as an embed of the pioneer column and its invading force of the BSAP and it has remained so for *The Herald* ever since. Which media organisation is not embedded with one power block or another is the question. One may

Figure 3.3 The Zapiro cartoon depicting embedded journalism. © 2003 Zapiro. Originally published in *Mail* and *Guardian*. Republished with permission.

60 *News whiteouts under UDI and after*

argue that this is probably the most cynical view of mainstream media ever expressed. But it is precisely this embeddedness with the power elite that led Galtung and Ruge to surmise the set of news values about which many critical scholars of the media have spilled so much ink. It is precisely the newsworthiness of news that makes it so irrelevant to the lives of more than three-quarters of the population in Zimbabwe. At a media *indaba*, as a discussion forum is ordinarily referred to in Zimbabwe, Geoffrey Nyarota, a veteran Zimbabwean journalist who often flaunts his minority share ownership in Zimpapers 1980 Ltd as a marker of social distinction, bemoaned that he has not received a dividend from the company because the government, the majority shareholder, thinks it did not invest in newspaper business for the money, which *The Herald* could easily make, if it published news which the majority of the citizens are dying to read. Mainstream news' obsession with what it refers to as the breaking news makes it pay a disproportionate attention to that which is exceptional, incidental, affects celebrities and minority elite to the total blacking out of any news about the ordinary, unchanging, systemic, slow but non the less tragic slide into penury of the majority population – here in lies the fickleness if not fakeness of contemporary mainstream news (Wijnberg 2018).

Whiteness

When news is looked at from the locus of colonial conquest and domination then whiteness becomes the unacknowledged organising news value. All other news values pivot around it. Whiteness invests common occurrences with automatic newsworthiness. It is common cause that this news value escaped Western theory's analytic and critical vigilance. European scholars for the reason that the pinching shoe was on another foot developed a deracialised discourse to explain how news under-reported, excluded or de-selected experiences of people of colour. It is ideological that all critical scholarship on the discursivity of news blamed all the other news criteria for the partiality of news (Galtung and Rudge, 1965) except race and racism. The whiteness of news somehow evaded notice and slipped through the cracks. The operation of this news value was so commonsensical that it became invisible to analysts of the media. This is evident in situations where journalists find it to be self-evident that an occurrence involving a white person is inherently newsworthy whereas a similar event involving a black person may go unnoticed journalistically. A cursory look at the content of *The Rhodesia Herald* throughout the colonial period and of *The Herald* during the fast-track land reform programme, decades after formal colonialism had ended, supports the thesis that whiteness might have been the unacknowledged news value that structured the way journalists constructed news as reality in very significant ways (see comparative pictures of *The Herald* front pages below). Chapters 5 and 6 deal with how the discourse of white supremacy was constitutive of news and in turn constituted by news.

Figures 3.4 Whiteness as a news value before and after independence. Reprinted with permission: *The Herald*.

Timeliness or recency

Daily newspapers like *The Herald* and the *Daily News* work to a 24-hour news production cycle. Journalists therefore, come up with news diaries that are synchronous with the time frequency of a news day. Timeliness imposes certain limitations on what may or may not be reported on as news with the result that some occurrences may score highly on other newsworthiness criteria but still be left out because their time reference falls outside the parameters of a news day.

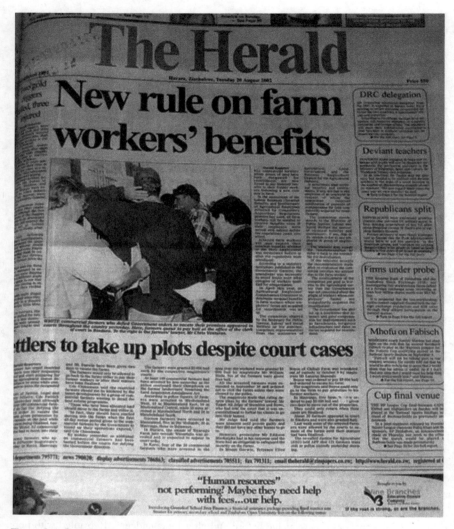

Figures 3.4 Continued

This then manifests itself in the news' characteristic preference for events to processes or steady states that take longer time frames to unfold. Urban life is fast-paced and its temporalities can easily be cut up into daily events and routines that lend themselves to easy reporting as news unlike rural life which is set to longer stretches of time sometimes requiring whole seasons before they can be decided either way. For example, a story on agriculture may need to wait until the rainy season has come to an end before news can report it as a drought year or not. But what newspaper has the patience to wait that long for a story before they can

News whiteouts under UDI and after   63

go to print? Often such conditions as famine take very long drawn-out processes before their more dramatic consequences become pregnant with newsworthiness to warrant journalism's attention.

While Hartley (2013: 80) and some journalists concur that news values are 'neither natural nor neutral' but that they constitute a manmade 'ideological code' most of them stop short of challenging their serious imbrication with power hierarchies along the axes of difference defined by race, class, gender, sex and geographical location. This failure forecloses discussion on news values are not about prominence, proximity and timeliness as they say rather they are about distribution of power and privilege to speak among groups of people on the basis of the colour of one's skin, one's gender and sexual identity. By using the colourless codes, gender non-specific codes of proximity, prominence etc., the very discourse on news values conceals more than it reveals the workings of power through the media. Recent applications of sociolinguistic analysis to the study of media texts have argued that few events that end up on the pages of a newspaper actually come to the attention of journalists laden with news values, rather that journalists in a majority of cases actually write the news values into the story (Bednarek and Caple, 2014). The use of conflict as a criterion for judging newsworthiness of events illustrates this point. Even where there is no armed conflict, journalism often imports a war rhetoric into non-conflictual events and situations to enhance their newsworthiness through mobilising such war topoi as: 'so and so blasted', 'hit back', 'attacked' etc. in news headlines.

Censorship through sourcing

Attribution of voice in news stories is not randomly distributed. Considerations of credibility structure journalists' selection of whom they may or may not source their stories with. Accessibility and credibility are important considerations. Those sources who are easily accessible to the reporter will be most likely to be used and reused in stories by journalists. The ability to cultivate a symbiotic relationship with well-placed sources is a highly valued skill in journalism. Such sources in addition to being easily accessible must also score highly on the credibility threshold. Government officials, politicians and leaders of organised civil society tend to satisfy these criteria and hence the officialdom in most news reports and the absence of ordinary people's voices in news even about themselves. As interviews with *The Herald* reporters below indicate, in news the silent majority will be spoken for (Frederikse 1982).

Resource constraints impose limitations on the possibility and plausibility of broadening access to different sections of society to speak through the press as one journalist commented:

> In doing stories, the challenges that we have are mainly on the resources side. Yah, resources, they are a very big challenge. Here they allow us obviously to go out and get some news but you are only given may be a few days to do that. But for you to have an appreciation of the views of the people from Binga you need to be there for about a week or two, but you are only given

64 *News whiteouts under UDI and after*

may be two days. So, resources are a big challenge, they limit our … you know. There are so many human interest stories out there but because of resources we are failing to get them. We would rather stay here and get a press release without spending anything to get that release and publish. (Interview with Lloyd Gumbo, Herald House, December, 2013)

An intern with a public relations company in Harare corroborated on the reliance of newspapers on what they call news subsidies in the form of press releases from corporate communications and media liaison officers of business entities. The bulk of stories that go under such anonymous bylines as '*The Herald* Reporter', the '*Daily News* Reporter' are often generated from press releases published with very little modification if any.

Another reporter commented on how considerations of cost containment may determine how stories are done, about whom and who may be contacted for comment and by what means:

I normally do the stories that I can do over the phone or just going around calling people doing face to face interviews and I also even do stories using the internet, like the Tsvangirai story, I wrote a story about his marriage, mainly the drama involving his marriage issues. So I was looking at; do we have other presidents in the world who have done the same and I found none. It's like it's something from Mars … (Interview with Abel Dzobo, sub-editor, Herald House, December, 2013)

Elaborating on what gives news its officialdom characteristic one reporter commented thus:

I can just digress a bit, I think you have heard of AIPPA. When you apply for clearance to write a story or to get some facts from somebody in a public body, they say you don't get it from anybody within that public body but they give you the heads of that public body as people who can comment. Their voice is the official voice it may be the most reliable source. People in this case are assumed to be represented by those people what they say is assumed to be in the interest of everyone. So when we write a story and we want to get an official comment, we normally look around for a government official, somebody belonging to a public body who is in a position and in a representative capacity to say 'ah … this happened this did not happen', once that person does that, that's authentic" (Interview with Mr. Chifamba, *The Herald* desk editor on the agriculture desk).

What emerges from the journalists' comments about news sourcing above demonstrates how, as a matter of fact, voices of ordinary people are routinely filtered out and a one-dimensional version of reality as seen through the eyes of holders of power and privilege is presented to the unsuspecting reader as news.

Editorial oversight

The production of news by mainstream news organisations is a highly structured process from beginning to end. The fact that news articles in the newspaper often carry the byline of a particular reporter belies the team effort and collective responsibility that goes into the making of each story that gets published. Media houses large and small have standard procedures that outline the workflow a potential news story passes through from its initial conception as a story idea by the journalist until it is finally assigned to a particular spot on a specific page of a newspaper. First, the reporter discusses his/her story idea with the desk editor to whom they report. It is the task of the desk editor to then compile a summary of all the story ideas from the junior reporters into a news diary for his/her desk which they present for discussion in the morning news diary meeting. The news diary meeting provides a formal mechanism to operationalise the news organisation's gatekeeping process. The news selection process begun when the reporter makes decisions on what events to pursue as potential news story ideas and further refined at the point of discussing them with their desk editor continues but is not finalised in the diary meeting.

The two newspaper organisations (*The Herald* and the *Daily News*) – where the writer spent no less than one and a half months apiece, conducting participant observation for a PhD research project – have institutionalised the diary meeting in significantly different ways. *The Herald* is one of the largest newspaper organisations in Zimbabwe even in terms of the number of its employees. This makes it practically impossible for all reporters to participate in the diary meeting to defend their story ideas. They can only do so by proxy through their desk editors. This often presents few challenges of its own as the intermediary role of the desk editor who can exercise unqualified discretion on what story ideas from their juniors to present, how to present them or even to simply ignore. There is just no way junior reporters can hold their desk editors to account for those story ideas that do not get selected at the diary meeting. A senior reporter at *The Herald* working on the political news desk put the dilemma of junior reporters at *The Herald* this way:

> "Normally there are some stories editors are kind of scared running" as they go for diary, not everyone goes for the diary, for me I would do a round table thing. At the Mirror we would like do a round table thing, you present your diary you argue you argue it you argue it and then its put on the diary. here you present your diary to an individual and that individual takes the story to the conference which is attended by editors which means the chances of that individual killing the story in between is 100%. That individual may never mention it at all and then comes back and says that story was rejected so then very few people follow-up and but why did they reject my story I thought it was a good story. (Interview with Takunda Maodza at Herald House, 21 December 2013).

66 *News whiteouts under UDI and after*

At smaller newsrooms like the *Daily News*, all reporters attend, present and defend their story ideas at the diary meeting in person. This, however, is no guarantee that no story will be killed at this early stage of the editorial process.

Conclusion

It needs to be pointed out, however, that news workers do not deliberately or consciously go out of their way to distort reality in the name of 'adherence to those news values and formal conventions' (McNair, 2003: 81). News stories that get published are like historical monuments that stand erect atop the ashes and rubble of discarded stories, stories that are not. Media analysis that focuses on what news texts leave unsaid, its absences, and disarticulations, leads us to a definition of *The Herald* news as the story of power as told by herself and news in the private press as the story of power as narrated by her significant others.

Notes

1 Interview with Abel Dzobo at Herald House, December, 2013.
2 President Mnangagwa was quoted as having ordered ZANU-PF youths to take their propaganda fight onto the social media platforms and beat their political opponents at their own game by occupying the social media spaces with their own campaign messages. K. Nyavaya, 21 June 2018, 'Social media game changer of 2018 polls'. *Newsday.* https://www.newsday.co.zw/2018/06/social-media-game-changer-of-2018-polls/.
3 The result of Mnangagwa's order was a 'marked upsurge in the use of inflammatory language, and fearmongering as well as the distribution of fake news online. And the violent aftermath of the election that left several people dead played out online even as it played out on the streets.' Jacquelin Kataneksza, 11 November 2018, 'Zimbabwean Twitter is shifting politics'. https://africasacountry.com/2018/10/social-media-and-p olitics-in-zimbabwe/.

References

Bednarek, M., Caple, H., 2014. Why do news values matter? Towards a new methodological framework for analysing news discourse in critical discourse analysis and beyond. *Discourse Soc.* 25, 135–158.

Berlyn, P., 1967. *Rhodesia: Beleaguered country.* Mitre Press.

Brighton, P., Foy, D., 2007. *News values.* Sage.

Caple, H., Bednarek, M., 2016. Rethinking news values: What a discursive approach can tell us about the construction of news discourse and news photography. *Journalism* 17, 435–455.

Chavunduka, M., 2002. The role of media in Zimbabwe, in: Alisa Clapp-Itnyre, Roumeen Islam and Caralee McLiesh (eds), *The right to tell: The role of mass media in economic development.* The World Bank, pp. 281–290.

Cotter, C., 2010. *News talk: Investigating the language of journalism.* Cambridge University Press.

Cottle, S., 2000. Rethinking news access. *Journal. Stud.* 1, 427–448.

Cousins, A., 1991. State, ideology, and power in Rhodesia, 1958–1972. *Int. J. Afr. Hist. Stud.* 24, 35–64.

Fowler, R., 2013. *Language in the news: Discourse and ideology in the press.* Routledge.

Frederikse, J., 1982. *None but ourselves: Masses vs. media in the making of Zimbabwe.* Heinemann.

Gale, W., 1962. *History of the Rhodesian printing and publishing company.* Madorn Print.

Gallop, A., 2004. *Mr. Stanley, I presume?: The life and explorations of Henry Morton Stanley.* The History Press.

Galtung, J. and Ruge, M.H., 1965. The structure of foreign news: The presentation of the Congo, Cuba and Cyprus crises in four Norwegian newspapers. Accessed 13 June 2019 from: https://pdfs.semanticscholar.org/b3b9/29df1fd2aa3ea6ddd7b44448fd409e48ea 0a.pdf?_ga=2.123696523.1252419697.1577439276-1301658245.1567953878.

Grosfoguel, R., 2007. The epistemic decolonial turn: Beyond political-economy paradigms. *Cult. Stud.* 21, 211–223.

Harcup, T., O'Neill, D., 2001. What is news? Galtung and Ruge revisited. *Journal. Stud.* 2, 261–280.

Hartley, J., 2013. *Understanding news.* Routledge.

Hulley, C.M., 1969. *Where lions once roamed.* Pioneer Head.

Jones, D., 2001. *Censorship: A world encyclopedia.* Routledge.

McNair, B., 2003. *News and journalism in the UK.* Routledge.

MacShane, D., 1979. *Using the media: How to deal with the press, television and radio.* Pluto Press.

Msindo, E., 2009. 'Winning hearts and minds': Crisis and propaganda in colonial Zimbabwe, 1962–1970. *J. South. Afr. Stud.* 35, 663–681.

Palling, B., 1979. *Rhodesia's propaganda war.*

Parker, J., 1972. *Rhodesia: Little white island.* Pitman.

Smith, M., 1969. Censorship in Rhodesia: The experience of a Salisbury editor. *Round Table* 59, 60–67.

Wijnberg, R., 2018. The problem with real news—and what we can do about it. http s://medium.com/de-correspondent/the-problem-with-real-news-and-what-we-can-do-a bout-it-f29aca95c2ea.

Windrich, E., 1975. *The Rhodesian problem: A documentary record, 1923–1973.* Routledge.

Windrich, E., 1979. Rhodesian censorship: The role of the media in the making of a one-party state. *Afr. Aff.* 78, 523–534.

4 News silence on forced removals in colonial Rhodesia

Introduction

As already indicated in Chapter 2 above, the early phase of the development of the press in colonial Rhodesia was inextricably linked to the colonial project. Journalism in the colonies was the embedded type, reporting from the vantage point of, and willingly subjecting itself to, the protection and guidance offered by the colonising force. The wars of colonial conquest and dispossession such as the sacking of Bulawayo in 1893 were reported by individuals with a journalist quasi-military role in the Salisbury Column that marched against Lobengula, king of the Ndebele (Gale, 1962). It is therefore not surprising that the dominant narrative of those early colonial encounters between the invading whites and the native population as reported in *The Rhodesia Herald* tended to be one-sided glorifications of the colonising force's courageous exploits in the war against the 'uncouth savages'. The *Bulawayo Chronicle* (a sister paper of *The Rhodesia Herald*) of 11 May 1896 for example, could report events at the end of the Matabele uprising of 1896 along the following lines: 'To the martial strains of the town band, the column under Colonel Napier left the citadel, and boldly started forth into the country lately taken from us by the Matabele.' The phrase 'lately taken from us' in this report clearly shows on whose side of the warring parties, the reporter chose to report from. Absent were narratives of the genocidal dimensions of human slaughter that was inevitable where a military force mounted on horseback and armed with the Maxim gun was pitted against an opposing side whose only strength was in numbers and whose weapon of choice was the assegai.[1] There was a dearth of alternative sources of news both for international newspapers abroad and the Rhodesian Printing and Publishing Company's local newspapers except from the white military commanders who had actively taken part in the military operations.

Many decades later, following the unilateral declaration of independence (UDI) from Britain on 11 November 1965 by the ruling Rhodesia Front party, measures were immediately taken to undo the poly-vocallity in the press and to re-establish the RPP monopoly press status as at the beginning of colonisation of Zimbabwe. A left-leaning liberal press, especially that press which targeted an African readership and which ventilated African nationalist opinion, such as the *African Daily*

News, the *Central African Examiner*, among others, were banned as subversive publications (Dombo, 2018). This effectively made it easy for the state to exercise a significant influence on what was left of the press through a cocktail of measures which included direct censorship as discussed in Chapter 3 above. No other serious alternative newspaper existed in Zimbabwe then, apart from church newspapers like the *Moto* published by the Roman Catholic Church in Gweru, and *Umbowo* published by the Methodist Church in Mutare. Although these targeted an African readership, government generally left them alone probably on the mistaken assumption that they would confine themselves to carrying 'safe' content in service of a Christian pastoral function. That had indeed been the case all along until as Makunike (1998: 33), editor of *Umbowo*, notes: 'as the hitherto popular *African Daily News* had been banned by the government, *Moto* and *Umbowo* had no choice but to fill the new vacuum'. Such was the polarised media context when the forced removal saga of the Tangwena people in Eastern Zimbabwe and the Hunyani people in central Zimbabwe were unfolding, beginning in 1968 and getting to a head in 1969–1970. The government intensified the removals of African communities from European areas following the passing into law of the Land Tenure Act (1969). The present chapter analyses press coverage or lack thereof of the forced removals of these African communities in the establishment press and the church press. It seeks to ascertain how the RPP's *The Rhodesia Herald* managed to continue toeing the editorial line of serving the interests of the white settler community without compromising on the basic tenets of professional news gathering in covering these selected cases of forced removals and how the church press targeting an African readership differed in its own approach to covering the same issues.

When the first newspaper rolled out of the colonial press establishment in 1892 in Zimbabwe, then Rhodesia, it was unmistakably and unapologetically white in its outlook and focus. As an institution, the press did not encumber itself or cloud its vision with such platitudes as seeking to civilise the natives or to bring about edification and salvation for the native's soul who could neither read nor write in their own language, much less so in the white man's. At that early stage of its existence, it certainly did not understand the duty to educate, inform and entertain as also implying extending these information rights to blacks. At this early stage of colonial history, blacks were generally regarded as a sub-human race (Fanon, 1963; Cesaire, 1972) and therefore not yet a rights-bearing specimen of humanity. The duty to spread literacy and numeracy for the cultivation and upliftment of the black population fell outside the press' remit. That task was better left to the Cristian Missionary Society and native administrators. The Rhodesia Printing and Publishing Company's editorial focus on a white readership did not shift over the years even after the growth of a significant educated black middle class in Zimbabwe. This state of affairs would not change in any significant way until attainment of black majority rule in 1980. It would be an oversimplification, however, to present that long history of newspaper production as not having had some variations depending on the different political views and ideological orientations of its many editors who succeeded each other.

Context of land segregation in colonial Rhodesia

Although this study isolates for closer analysis news discourses on forced removals of only two black communities in the then Rhodesia, these were by no means isolated exceptions and therefore atypical. Rather, they were representative cases of a general pattern of white settler attitudes and treatment of Africans begun with the wars of colonial conquest and African dispossession in 1893 onwards and entrenched by law throughout the history of colonial ruled Rhodesia. Many scholars have pointed to similarities and policy convergences in the legal systems of the settler colonies of southern and central Africa. The general pattern being one where land policies tried and tested in the South African context were transplanted onto the Rhodesian colonial frontier, sometimes with very minimal changes and adaptations to suit new conditions and circumstances. In many cases the difference only existed in name. For example, Rhodesia's Land Apportionment Act of 1930 clearly drew its inspiration from the Natives Land Act of 1913 in South Africa, which led to the demarcation of land into racial enclaves which formed the basis of that country's policy of separate development known as apartheid finding its concrete expression in the 1948 constitution. Similarly, Kenya's own colonial land policies that ignited the Mau Mau revolt (1952–1964) had borrowed much from the Rhodesian experience with implementing colonial land segregation. In crafting them, Kenyan colonial authorities followed the same route that Rhodesia had taken, legitimating colonial land policies on the findings and recommendations of a land commission, which incidentally was headed by the same Sir William Morris Carter who had headed a similar land commission earlier-on in Rhodesia (Youé, 2002). Although in the two country cases the objectives and terms of reference of the commissions were somewhat different,[2] the ultimate result was to develop legislation to anchor an unfair demarcation of the land between Africans and Europeans (Kalande, 2008). The result in each case was the mass evictions of thousands of Africans from land which had been declared European and their concentration into areas reserved for them much along similar lines with what had been happening for many decades south of the Limpopo, save for the fact that the authorities in Rhodesia never thought of their policies as the equivalent of apartheid. They preferred to imagine their policies as placing the burden of white trusteeship on white colonists in a relationship of partnership between the races.

The upshot of these very similar land policies was the transformation of freely living indigenous black people of the sub-region into squatters whose tenancy on the land that they had always regarded as theirs became illegal the moment that land was declared European. Existing literature has dealt adequately and exhaustively with the subject of how land was racially segregated in the then Rhodesia leading to a government operation of mass movement and reorganisation of African agriculture conducted over many decades (Riddell, 1978; Palmer, 1977; Phimister, 1988). A subject that has not so fully been investigated is the role that may have been played by ideological institutions, such as the media in, on the one hand, abetting the European land theft on a massive scale and on the other, engineering African consent to this form of racial domination. Furedi (1989: 9) points out:

squatting or labour tenancy was a creation of white settler colonialism in Africa. In the white settler colonies of Kenya, Southern Rhodesia (now Zimbabwe) and South Africa the life of the African population was reorganised around the interests of settlers ... labour tenancy was a relation of serfdom which emerged wherever white farmers with limited capital took land from agricultural peoples.

Given the context and history of the land segregationist policies in Southern Africa the use of the term 'squatter' to refer to the new status that Africans 'acquired' was one of the most important colonial myths in support of white supremacist ideology to give the mistaken notion that Africans were the ones who 'happened' at the white man's farm and were now unwilling to leave when in fact the reverse was more consistent with the fact of the late nineteenth-century European colonial occupation of African land. Robin Palmer exposes as mistaken the notion that the Europeans found the land on which they went on to settle empty and uninhabited by Africans, when he points out that: 'In selecting their land they [white settlers] have naturally been guided by the number of natives located thereon, whose knowledge of the productive powers of the soil must necessarily be the best guide' (Palmer, 1977: 94). Riddell (1978: 7) further argues that 'Most indigenous Africans were not living in what were later called reserves when the Europeans arrived in the country, so the majority had to be moved there'. Thus began the myth that Europeans owned the land on which blacks intruded upon and squatted. This conflictual relationship over land between whites and blacks rooted in the colonial history forms the broader political context within which to make sense of news discourses about the resistance and collaboration to forced removals by the Tangwena people and the Hunyani people in Zimbabwe between 1969 and 1970.

Happening as they did in 1970 around the time the Rhodesia Front Government enacted a new law, the Land Tenure Act of 1969 to finalise the land division of Rhodesia along racial lines for all time (Riddell, 1978), the removals in question were among the last mass removals in more than six decades of an unrelenting systematic process of mass dispossession, alienation and disempowerment of black people in Zimbabwe. This, however, is not to suggest that this form of colonial violence was not met with stiff resistance by individual communities from time to time. The point of the matter, however, is that news (supposedly history's first draft) about such resistance was sparsely reported on if at all in the mainstream press, evidence of the fact that the press of the time was firmly embedded with the colonial establishment. In fact, a completely nuanced history of racial conflict in Zimbabwe could not be reproducible from press records as Frederikse (1982) was to discover as she worked on collecting evidence for her book *None but ourselves: Masses vs. media in the making of Zimbabwe*. The press had all along been unable to witness the colonial events except through the prism of the white colonial interest. The Official Report of Parliamentary Debates of the House of Lords of 23 June 1926 succinctly captures the history behind the contestations over ownership of land as between groups with a vested interest therein of the then Southern Rhodesia, namely the British government, the British South Africa Chartered Company and the 'natives' of Southern Rhodesia

72 *News silence on forced removals in Rhodesia*

which we shall not delve into here. Suffice it to say that the House of Lords warmed up to the provisions and suggestions made by the Morris Carter Land Commission in their report to bring finality to the controversies on land ownership in Rhodesia. The debate in the House of Lords went something along the lines cited below: in the words of one Lord Olivier,[3]

> this report I have read with very great pleasure and satisfaction because it appears to me to be the most broad-minded and liberal document that I have seen emanate from any official source with regard to Southern Rhodesia on the land question ... and, as I have mentioned, it was decided to recommend the principle of absolute segregation and the abrogation of the existing right of natives to purchase land in certain areas.

Although he tended generally to agree with the proposals of the Commission report on the imperative for land segregation in Rhodesia, Lord Olivier, however, found the proposed ratio of land alienation between the two races, white and black of 33.5:1 rather startling.

The Commissioners had justified their proposals for land segregation on a vision of a dual economy as the destiny of Southern Rhodesia where natives would develop a subsistence mode of agricultural production with some from their number being available for labour on the large-scale commercial agriculture in the European sector which would occupy two-thirds of arable land in the country. In response, Lord Buxton, drawing on his past experience as High Commissioner to Southern Rhodesia, felt strongly in favour of the Commission's recommendations that the delimitation of land in Rhodesia between Europeans and natives be finalised once and for all time. He accused those who were critical of some aspects of the Commission's recommendations, of taking a rather extreme native view. He argued:

> I am quite confident that it is in the best interests of Southern Rhodesia, looking to the future, that this question of the delimitation of the native area between the white and black populations should be settled at the very earliest moment before further difficulties arise. If one wanted an argument in favour of that, it is only necessary to look to the Union of South Africa itself, where very unfortunately, in earlier days before the white population became what it is and before the black population was as numerous as it is now, they did not have the opportunity which is given to Southern Rhodesia, in having a delimitation of the territory of the country between black and white, of avoiding the great number of difficulties, which they are now encountering and also the great amount of friction and ill feeling which naturally arise between the two races. (ibid.: 154–155)

The establishment and crystallisation of colonial rule in the then Rhodesia as in many parts of colonial Africa took the form of racial landscaping of space usually involving the displacement of indigenous peoples from their traditional settlements

(Joanne, 2009: 57). The racialised landscape then formed the core text through which discourses of white supremacy over colonised 'Others' were made visible, perniciously ever dramatised and therefore naturalised. One needed to look no farther than the different geographical areas the races occupied in Rhodesia after implementation of the Land Apportionment Act (1930) and they would see writ large the doctrine of white supremacy.

While the map of Rhodesia below encapsulates the unfair land distribution between blacks and whites, it only tells half the story. For example, it is silent on the difference in the productive potential of land between the races. The disparities were further compounded, as Riddell (1980: 3) argues, 'by the differing qualities of the African and European land; the European areas consist of twice as much of the most fertile agricultural land as the African areas'. The bulk of the land reserved for African settlement was located in the poorest agro-ecological zones of the country, poorly watered and prone to draught. The subject of forced removals to create two essentially different nations in one is not something that happened only in 1969 or 1970, nor did it just affect two black communities in the then Rhodesia, the Tangwena and the Hunyani people. It was a massive operation carried out by successive colonial governments in Rhodesia affecting the lives of many indigenous communities throughout the decades from the founding of Rhodesia. What made the Tangwena and the Hunyani removals an interesting textbook case as pointed out earlier is mainly their contemporaneity and therefore comparability and the

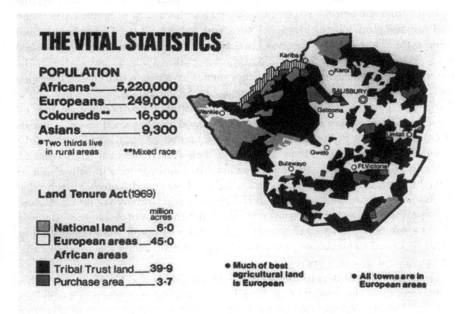

Figure 4.1 Map of Rhodesia showing status of land segregation by 1969 before the passing into law of the Land Tenure Act of 1969. Source: Parker, 1972.

74 News silence on forced removals in Rhodesia

different treatment they received in the local press. The other reason is that they come late and at the crowning and intense moment in the history of struggles about land in the then Rhodesia, happening as they did after the passing into law of the Land Tenure Act of 1969. The sheer numbers to be affected to put to effect the provisions of the act were staggering and therefore likely to generate conflict and media attention to the issues as Daniels points out:

> The institution of 'African Areas' under the Land Apportionment Act affected the African population by crowding them together in areas where it was impossible to earn an adequate livelihood. In many instances, the Rhodesian government had to use direct force in order to resettle Africans in these areas. An outstanding recent case is that involving the Tangwena Tribe. It illustrates the brutal methods employed by the Rhodesian Front government to implement its policies of racial separatism under the Land Apportionment Act. Another example of forced resettlement was the removal in 1967 of 5,000 Africans to the area of Gokwe, which is infested by tse-tsefly, producing debility in cattle and human beings. (International Commission of Jurists, 1976: 13)

Chief Rekayi Tangwena and his people's struggle to remain in their ancestral land on Gaeresi Ranch became a symbol of all Africans' resistance to displacement by Rhodesia Front racist policies. He became an icon of the liberation struggle and his persistent refusal to give in to the demands of the colonial regime to move from the land he regarded as sacred and his ancestral home, earned him and his case so much worldwide acclaim and publicity. One famous myth built around the Tangwena people was how, after their homes had been demolished by government by day, they would come back from their hiding places in the mountains and quickly rebuild temporary shelter by night so that by the following morning the village would be up once again. So famous was the story of the Tangwena people's struggle among the black population of Zimbabwe that all quickly built temporary shelter and slums that later mushroomed on the outskirts of cities and towns in the then Rhodesia were named *zviTangwena* after those the Tangwena people had built in defiance to their forced removal from Gaerezi. Later on he became so involved with the liberation struggle for Zimbabwe that he played a significant role assisting the late Edgar Tekere and Robert Mugabe skip the border into Mozambique and in the recruitment of many young black Zimbabweans to join the armed struggle for the independence of Zimbabwe. Because of this consistent record of resistance against colonial domination of his people, Chief Rekayi Tangwena got a senatorial appointment in the first majority rule government at independence.

The three chiefs of the Hunyani people – Huchu, Ruya and Gobo – on the other hand, were quite the opposite of Rekayi Tangwena in many respects. Though they and their people were affected by the land laws of the then Rhodesia in ways that were similar to the Tangwena case, the three chiefs did not demonstrate spine, they capitulated and cooperated with the regime. Similar co-operation and loyalty to white colonialists during the 1896–1898 African uprisings against colonial occupation had not helped the cause of Chief Huchu's forebear, as the area where he and his people lived in Mteo Forest near Mvuma was alienated for European occupation and they could only remain on the land as rent paying or labour tenants to the new owners of the land (Beach, 1970). Of the three, only chief Huchu has a record of recalcitrance towards the question of his removal from Hunyani but probably finding himself in the minority of one to two his resistance became ineffective. And because of this, he got the worst bargain for himself and the people who were under him as he ended up being resettled in the tsetse fly infested zone, in Charama valley in Gokwe District, where he was not allowed to take any livestock with him. This was quite unlike his counterparts who managed to extract 'better deals' for their people by being offered resettlement in the Silobela reserve which was much nearer to Hunyani compared to Gokwe where Huchu and his people were resettled. These other two chiefs were also allowed to take with them a limited number of heads of livestock per family. Chief Huchu did put up some form of resistance, though, he lacked the sophistication of Rekayi Tangwena. He was the last of the three chiefs to concede to being moved from Hunyani and as a result he and his people ended up having to be resettled in a hot semi-arid area below the Charama plateau in Gokwe, more than 300 kilometres away.

I have very vivid memories of how at the age of 10 I and the members of my family as part of the Huchu 'tribe', found ourselves being bundled up together with our few belongings into Isuzu trucks and driven away on a journey that took a day and a night before we could get to our destination and were offloaded in the middle of the bush with no shelter until adults in the family could put up some huts for us (Chapter 2 has outlined a detailed account of the odyssey of the Huchu people to Charama).

By way of inducement, the white regime had built a fairly beautiful 'chiefly' house for the chief in the new area, a large rectangular building (by our standards) of brick under a zinc roof situated close to the main road and fitted with tap water. However, the chief refused to move into this house in protest and instead built his own huts pretty much similar to those of his people. Chief Stefani Huchu like his counterpart, Chief Rekayi Tangwena, ended up incarcerated for failure to report the presence of 'terrorists' in his area in 1975. We never saw him alive again. Unlike Tangwena, he never got any token of recognition from the independence government for his part in the liberation struggle. For the Huchu people he remains their unsung hero of the struggle against white domination. In the following section I critically analyse and discuss the different ways the forced removals of the Tangwena and the Hunyani people were constructed by the local press. Chief Tangwena and Chief Huchu became symbols of resistance at a time when most chiefs chose to capitulate to pressure from the white settler regime (Frederikse, 1982). Their treatment in the local press was widely different.

Archival evidence shows that Chief Rekayi Tangwena's case enjoyed greater media visibility during the period 1969–1970 owing to a number of factors among which include the fact that he obviously benefited from the sympathy, moral support and advice he got from some sections of the white community through his connections with Guy Clutton-Brock. He also enjoyed close personal contact with leaders in the nationalist movement such as Advocate Herbert Chitepo, Able Muzorewa and a host of others who hailed from his province of Manicaland and who obviously must have offered him material and moral support in the protracted legal battle (Makunike, 1998), as well as sound legal advice on his rights on the land issue. One way in which the Tangwena case owed it to people like Clutton-Brock to get media attention was through a book he wrote and published under the title *Rekayi Tangwena – Let Tangwena be*. The book gave an account of government's failed attempts to forcibly evict the Tangwena people from their ancestral home. Thus, it can be argued that the linkages with the Nyafaru project near Gaerezi, the Cold Comfort Cooperative Farm near Harare, and the white personalities connected to these missionary projects, were instrumental in generating local and international media interest in the Tangwena story. There is a precedent to it in the Limehill case in South Africa as Desmond (1970: 24) points out in his book *The Discarded People* that 'the removal to Limehill was not the first nor the worst of such removals, but it was probably the most widely publicised and the best documented. This was because there were some Whites who were interested in these people and brought their fate to the notice of the public. Otherwise they would have been completely voiceless.'

The Hunyani people, on the other hand, unlike the Tangwena, were far more numerous. The people involved were many times as numerous as the Tangwena. There were three chieftaincies involved under chiefs Huchu, Gobo and Ruya. Their removal was much around the same time as the Tangwena – around the 1969–1970 period. The distances to new areas to which these people were being removed were far greater in comparison to the Bende area first offered to Tangwena. The difference between the area they were coming from and those to which they were being resettled was sharper in the Hunyani case. One of the chiefs and his people were actually removed to an area more than 300 km away in the hotter, drier region of the Zambezi valley, in the tsetse fly belt. Not a single story was to be found about the plight of this people either in the state press or in the existing alternative press of which *Moto* was the foremost. The few stories in the *Moto* newspaper which broke the story of the removal of the Hunyani people concentrated on the other two chiefs resettled in the Silobela area. The state press only published one news story and two or three letters to the editor which referred to the resettlement of people in Silobela.

Thingification, infantilisation of the Tangwena in *The Rhodesia Herald*

'Chief Tangwena disclosed that the government had tried to bribe him. "They say that if I move to Bende I will be paid $25 a month and will be officially recognised as a chief," Chief Tangwena said,' (*Moto*, September 1969: 3). The story above was very revealing of the carrot and stick strategy the regime applied to pressure chiefs to volunteer away their people into subjection to indirect rule by the white colonial authority. Official recognition of his chiefly status was now being offered to him in exchange for signing away his people's claim to the land Gaerezi. Chief Rekayi Tangwena remained faithful to his people and steadfastly resisted all pressure to bow to the colonial regime's order to leave his ancestral home in the Gaerezi area. There were consequences for this recalcitrance on his part.

> They said you are no longer a chief but a self-styled chief, because you are troublesome. They took from me that chain that made one look like a donkey, the Smith used to indicate which of the chiefs were his donkeys so they would not go astray. I didn't mind because I didn't like to appear like a donkey. (Frederikse, 1982: 78)

The Rhodesia Herald's complicity with the white supremacist ideology of the colonial regime was apparent in its overall reportage on the Tangwena controversy as is patently evident in all the 12 stories on the Tangwena issue the newspaper published between August 1969 and August 1970. White ownership and interest in Gaerezi Ranch is presented matter-of-factly as uncontestable, but Tangwena claim to the land is portrayed as unreasonable and nothing more than just that – a mere claim. Another way *The Rhodesia Herald* promoted perceptions of white supremacy and black inferiority in its coverage of the Tangwena story is the way in which the Africans are reported and spoken for rather than being accorded voice in news stories that concerned them directly. The speaking subject in these stories is always white. In some stories the African is treated in a manner that is patronising if not condescending. The African, even in the act of resisting domination is denied agency and treated as not capable of acting on his own initiative. The African's humanity is denied him, as it is imputed in the news narrative that there must be some white godfather behind it all. The African is only a pawn in a grand political strategy of some white trouble makers or communists. To illustrate this point a good starting point would be a story published in *The Rhodesia Herald* of 1969. In a front page story (27 August 1969) *The Rhodesia Herald* dedicates close to three-quarters of the page to the Minister of Internal Affairs, Mr Lance Smith who is supposedly giving the last word on the Tangwena story in Parliament. Below is an excerpt from the story:

EYEBROW, UNDERLINED: Minister gives background to Tangwena Issue
BANNER HEADLINE IN BOLD TYPEFACE: Subversion claim
KICKER: Communists and 'fellow travelers' blamed
LEAD: Much of the activity which had led to the present difficulties with the Tangwena tribe was Communist inspired, and operated by fellow travelers, the Minister of Internal affairs, Mr. Lance Smith, said in Parliament yesterday. The Africans concerned were being ruthlessly exploited by Mr. Guy Clutton-Brock and his associates in an effort to break down the Land Apportionment Act, he said.
BODY: In a statement at the start of yesterday's proceedings, the minister said that in recent weeks various statements had appeared in the Press about the

78 *News silence on forced removals in Rhodesia*

> Tangwena issue, which was in fact a straightforward matter of a land-owner seeking to remove squatters from his land, blown up into a major issue in the local and overseas Press.
>
> The Tangwena had been used by certain subversive elements to undermine the Government, and the present position was part of a plan to challenge the laws of the land, and in particular the Land Apportionment Act, he said.

The story was attributed to *Iana* news agency as part of its Parliamentary Service. Thus by marking the story as originating not from its own reporters the paper hedges against responsibility for the story in spite of the fact that they are still using it and on front page too.

Another technique the paper employs to distance itself from the views contained in the story while still giving it publicity is by putting the phrase 'Communists and fellow travellers' in single quotation marks to indicate that this may not necessarily be a view they shared as a paper. But by placing it on the front page the paper still manages to communicate to the reader that the story is the most important story of the day and that it is worthwhile reading it. The fact that the views are being attributed to a government minister, that it was said in parliament and that there were no contrary views expressed against it implies to the reader this is a view shared by the whole of the Rhodesian white government on the Tangwena issue. Putting out such a one-sided unbalanced story would normally be regarded as propagandistic and flying in the face of basic journalistic principles of right of reply and verification. But this has to be understood against the context of a press cowed by extreme pressure in the form of government surveillance and control of the press that characterised the UDI era under the Rhodesia Front Government.

The main point the two-sentence introductory paragraph establishes is the fact that the real source of problems in the Tangwena issue lies not with the Tangwena themselves. The Tangwena were to be viewed as mere victims of ruthless manipulation by a clique of communists and their sympathisers led by Mr Guy Clutton-Brock. A possible surface reading and interpretation of the minister's remarks is to understand that the minister is exonerating the Tangwena people placing the blame for Tangwena resistance squarely on fellow white men who were guilty of spreading communist influence (itself a foreign and un-African idea) among unsuspecting 'childlike', Africans. In this way the minister could be argued to be absolving Africans of any wrong doing in the Tangwena saga.

At a deeper and more critical level of interpretation the remarks could be read as understating the capacity or rather placing the capacity of Africans to act on their own initiative in doubt thus denying them of agency in this matter in a process Cesaire (1972: 42) calls 'thingification' or reduction of the colonised into objects of white action even in defying the government order to remove from Gaerezi Ranch. The minister frames the issue not as one of black resistance against white government's unjust and oppressive legal system based on race but as one pitting the white government against one section of the white community bent on subverting government authority by instigating a spirit of revolt among the otherwise peace-loving and law-abiding African subjects. This shifts the debate away from whether government should proceed with its plan to forcibly remove the Tangwena people or not. That is beside the point, according to the minister who saw it as 'a straightforward matter of a land-owner seeking to remove squatters from his land'. What only needed to be done was to deal with the communist instigators by removing or neutralising their influence among the innocent child race of 'impressionable' Africans. This the government of Ian Smith was to do two years later when in 1971 it stripped Mr Guy Clutton-Brock of his citizenship and deported him as a 'threat to public safety' (*The Telegraph*, 3 July 2013). The trope of regarding Africans as an underdeveloped category of humanity caught up and imprisoned in a state of perpetual childhood has a long and deeply embedded genealogy in the European colonial imaginary of Africa and Africans. It was a view widely shared in the European civilised circles way before the founding of colonial Rhodesia. Sir Godfrey Huggins expressed a similar paternalistic view which he shared with fellow proponents of the idea of a federation between the Rhodesias and Nyasaland on the white man's burden over Africans when in 1953, he likened his vision of racial amity between blacks and whites as akin to a partnership between a horse and its rider – the white settler of course being the rider and the African the horse.

The reference to 'Communists and fellow travellers' in the story has to be read against the background of the Cold War era politics, where Rhodesia's Ian Smith had proclaimed his UDI as committed to the defence of Western Christian civilisation against the spread of communism. All those who did not agree with government policies were either communists or communist sympathisers and therefore enemies of the state (Frederikse, 1982). The interpretive frame being invoked is one that foregrounded African innocence and naivety. The picture of the African in this instance is consistent with a white racist stereotype of the African as a childlike race, naive and lacking in sophistication and perpetually in need of white guidance of one sort or another. It drew on pre-existing imperialist tropes of colonial Africa as existing in a childhood filial relationship to imperial parenthood of Europe as set out in Cecil John Rhodes' principles in dealing with what he referred to as the native question in his 1894 Glen Grey proposals as cited in Ashcroft (2001: 43) that: 'As to the question of voting, we say that the natives are in a sense citizens, but not altogether citizens - they are still children ... Now I say the natives are children. They are just emerging from barbarism'.

The lenses through which the reality of the struggle of the Tangwena people had to be corrected and adjusted in order to give a perspective that fitted well with existing knowledge and myths about Africans. The story drew on a mythology upon which was justified the domination of black indigenous people by minority whites, a basis for keeping governmental power in 'responsible' white hands for all time in Rhodesia. Tangwena had to be boxed to fit into the minister's preferred stereotype about the African, consistent with that image of an African as the noble savage. The Ministry of Information's booklet and other historical records portrayed a typical African mindset, the central theme of which was that

80 *News silence on forced removals in Rhodesia*

the Africans were generally a contented subject population happily accepting their allotted station under the benign rule of the master race. 'The African loves laughter. His needs are few and simple and when he has satisfied them he is inclined to sit back' (Frederikse, 1982: 16). The cause of the misunderstanding between the Tangwena and the government according to the minister, could therefore not stem from the Tangwena's own initiative, rather it was 'Communist inspired and operated by fellow travelers ... The Africans were being ruthlessly exploited by Mr. Guy Clutton-Brock and his associates'. The racial myth that runs through Mr Smith's argument is the view of Africans as a childlike race incapable of rational choice without a lot of hand-holding and guidance by their white masters. Thus the Tangwena defy the landowner's eviction notice by remaining on the property because they were 'advised', 'counselled' and 'incited' to do so by Mr Keeble, a white farm manager on the adjacent Nyafaru Development Project founded by Mr Guy Clutton-Brock in 1957. In the minister's view, it was white men like Mr Clutton-Brock and his associate Mr Keeble who were abusing these tribesmen as pawns in the main plan, and they have been incited to transgress the law' ... Naturally, there is resistance, but resistance through ignorance, and it is this ignorance that is being used by the infamous machinations of people such as Guy Clutton-Brock and his associates to further their political ambitions' (The Rhodesia Herald 27 August 1969). The emphasis here is on Tangwena as an ignorant people, easy to manipulate. With such characteristics it was unimaginable that they would be able to rise up without incitement by some white people.

Thus this fairly long article in which the minister sets the record straight, as it were, also tends to set the agenda and the reasonable parameters within which future debate on the Tangwena case may possibly unfold. The news story thus achieves two objectives. First, it dismisses Tangwena people's claim over the land in dispute, as frivolous and vexatious as their own occupation of it is described as having taken place at about the same time that whites also came to occupy and possess the land. Second, by representing the African as ignorant and therefore prone to manipulation it forecloses their participation in the debate as they are not likely to articulate any rational arguments on the issues. This probably accounts for the reason the paper seeks and publishes Mr Hanmer, the landowner's and Mr Clutton-Brock's responses to the minister's article in its next day's issue and takes no trouble to seek out and publish Chief Rekayi Tangwena's view on the matter since he, like a child, can only be spoken for. In this way the voice of the colonised other is silenced or relegated to the margins of the news rendering of an aspect of colonial reality. This explains why in what appears to be a follow-up story titled: 'Impossible to cooperate with Tangwena' *The Rhodesia Herald* (28 August 1969: 13) seems to bolster the minister's earlier argument when, Mr Hanmer, the landowner, finds no contradiction in terminology when he uses the terms 'pegging boy' and 'man' to refer to an African employee in:

I was given a 'pegging boy' by the department who had a certain amount of agricultural knowledge. He left hurriedly within a month. Another man was

News silence on forced removals in Rhodesia 81

sent, but he went quicker and left his blankets behind, which he has never come back to claim. Both these men were intimidated into getting off the property as the locals were not going to be told what to do.

The apparent white paternalism was in this way and in other encounters between whites and blacks so systematically inculcated and ingrained in the colonial mindset of both coloniser and colonised, through insistence on a form of address between the two races in a perpetual master–servant relationship where the white man insisted upon being called 'Baas' or 'Mister' if an adult white male and pikinin-baas a white male child, however young, by an African. The African servant was either 'boy' if they were male or 'girl' if female. Accommodation quarters to house their black servants situated at the back of every European homestead were called boy's kya and the man who worked their gardens was 'garden-boy', the house servant was 'house-boy' or 'house-girl', an African male promoted to the rank of foreman who supervised fellow African workers was to be addressed as baas-boy. This was unrelated to their age, being an adult or not was irrelevant (Guvamombe, *The Herald*, 14 March 2013).

In both articles attributed to Minister Lance Smith and landowner William Hanmer, the white people involved are individuated by being respectfully addressed as 'Mr.' each time they are mentioned in the story, but Africans are denied this individuation (Loomba, 1998), and are imagined only as a faceless collectivity, a herd or as a 'tribe' as in the 'Tangwena tribe', 'the Makombi tribe' or just 'the Tangwena'. Where they had to be named as individuals in a story, they were never addressed as 'Mr.' so-and-so. It was either simply 'Kinga, the Tangwena chief who lived in the adjacent Holdenby Tribal Trust Land' or 'one Rekayi Tangwena who had been working for years in many centres of Rhodesia' (*The Rhodesia Herald*, 27 August 1969: 1). The representation of Africans and their land in this and other articles in this newspaper is quite typical of and consistent with what Bill Ashcroft defines as the imperial imaginary of natives and of Africa as in need of European imperial inscription:

> The unformedness of colonial space is the geographic metaphor of the savage mind; both consciousness and space form the childlike innocence which is the natural surface of imperial inscription. This process of inscription is not merely metaphoric, because it is in writing itself that place is constructed out of empty space, and it is in the control of representation and the dissemination of this control in literacy and education that the colonial subject is subdued. (Ashcroft, 2001: 40)

The news as text of empire was thus naturalising imperial inscriptions on both the land and on the African mind. In the minister's interpretation, which *The Rhodesia Herald* reports matter-of-factly in its later instalments on the Tangwena issue is 'a straightforward matter of a land-owner seeking to remove squatters from his land'. That the Tangwena are squatters is made to seem self-evident, therefore there is no need to ask the Tangwena about it. That Mr Hanmer is the farm-owner is also

82 *News silence on forced removals in Rhodesia*

presented as if it were in the nature of things for a white man to be landowner. These facts are presented as lying outside history, incontestable and therefore natural. In Mr Smith's words, 'there were two reasons why the Tangwena must move. The first was that 'it was private land in the European area, and squatter occupation was contrary to Land Apportionment policy'. The eviction of the Tangwena in this case is being legitimated on the grounds of legality. It is a requirement of the Land Apportionment Act. The nominalisation and externalisation of what was otherwise an outcome of a historical process in 'land in the European area' purports that the European has always been there and nothing can be done about it and since the Tangwena are non-European and find themselves in an European area, they automatically become squatters by definition. The reason for their being squatters is to be looked for nowhere beyond the fact that they are Africans. It is immanent in the colour of their skin to be squatters. It is naturalised, and presented as something blacks are born with in a process of ideological legitimation through reification and naturalisation of what is otherwise historical. The second reason given as justification for the removal of the Tangwena was that 'the cultivation methods being used on land which had extremely steep slopes was causing considerable damage from erosion'. Implicit in this second reason as grounds for their eviction are African primitive methods of cultivation which cause land degradation, the Tangwena are too primitive and their treatment as such in this case is therefore merited. Only a man like Mr Hanmer is qualified based on a racialised conservationist-environmentalist discourse where whites automatically qualify as conservers of nature (Hughes, 2010).

Anchoring the page on which the landowner's version of the Tangwena's story appears as the lead story is an article devoted to Guy Clutton-Brock's response to the minister's attack published in an earlier issue of the paper. The article titled, 'Clutton-Brock issues challenge to Minister' extends an opportunity for a view opposed to that of government as represented by the minister, in the paper's own way of achieving balance in its reportage on the Tangwena case, a form of balanced reporting that admits of no African opinion on a matter that directly affects them. When the three stories are taken together as expressions of competing white opinions on the Tangwena case, it becomes very clear whose version is being privileged by the paper and which explanation is being subordinated. The minister, by being privileged to speak first, enjoys the privilege of setting the agenda and parameters for discussion, framing the important issues to which Hanmer the landowner makes additions and elaborations and Clutton-Brock can only respond to the accusations levelled against him. Another thing that becomes apparent is that the debate is a whites-only affair. No African opinion on the matter is relevant here even the Tangwena's. Entrenched racial discrimination becomes all too evident in the news logic that balances white view with opposing white opinion on a subject that affects African interests without the need for seeking an African comment on it. An event affecting Africans becomes newsworthy only by its association with white people. In *The Rhodesia Herald*'s logic, news is the story of whites as agents of history among Africans. Credibility as news sources also coincides with whiteness. Africans, unaided with a generous dose of external influence, are in this way represented as an inferior race incapable of generating their own ideas.

These three articles beginning with the minister's statement clarifying the Tangwena issue, followed by the landowner's own elaboration reinforcing government position and Clutton-Brock's rebuttal and challenge of the minister's statement represent *The Rhodesia Herald*'s own way of 'balanced' reporting on the Tangwena story in a way that seems to bring finality on the debate in government's favour. The three articles all coming within two to three days before expiry of the 31 August deadline when the Tangwena were supposed to have removed from Gaerezi Ranch voluntarily, or risk being forcibly evicted from the area, provide the mental maps by which to understand and interpret future government action on the Tangwena people. So, when on 18 September, government security forces escorting a convoy of graders and bulldozers, descend on Gaerezi to demolish Tangwena villages under the cover of darkness in a dawn surprise attack, and with members of the press having been embargoed from the area, *The Rhodesia Herald*'s largely white readership have been fully psyched-up and softened for this action. Thus, the world had no other picture of events that took place at Tangwena village on the 18 September 1969 apart from that which *The Rhodesia Herald* presented based on evidence gleaned from a safe distance, 30 kilometres away from the site of government operation against the Tangwena people in Gaerezi.

Thus on 18 September when government effected the removal of Tangwena people by force and razzed their village huts to the ground under cover of darkness and the protection of a blanket ban on members of the press from accessing the Gaerezi area, neither *The Rhodesia Herald* nor *Moto* news crews dared defy government imposed curfew to the area. Instead of fighting to have its crew on the ground to witness first-hand the events of 18 September *The Rhodesia Herald* is content to run a broad-berthed political analysis of the likely problems the proposed Land Tenure Act would cause, not for displaced poor people but for the white government, as the headline of the story published (18 September 1969: 11) and attributed to its political correspondent Ian Mills clearly suggested to its readers: 'Land Tenure Act will pose major problems for Government'. This is the story *The Rhodesia Herald* sees fit to carry on the day that the Tangwena village in Gaerezi was literally burning and Land Tenure Act was actually causing problems for affected Africans. The language in this story constructs an image of the colonial authorities as a benign government working against all odds to resolve a land issue arising from 'illegal land occupations' caused by the high 'rate at which the African population was increasing'. An important intimation from this story is the sheer numbers of Africans facing displacement as and when the provisions of the proposed law came to effect. Commenting on the magnitude of the administrative problems the law would entail for government, the writer states that: 'there is already a serious problem facing the authorities as a result of people occupying land illegally in terms of the Land Apportionment Act'. When this story is read in the context of other stories the paper carried on the Tangwena people it is not

84 *News silence on forced removals in Rhodesia*

unreasonable for the reader to infer that the writer refers to the black communities like the Tangwena by 'people occupying land illegally'. Citing from an annual report by the Director of Lands, Mr R.R. Jack, the reporter goes on to add:

> In his report for last year the Director ... said that during the year 3,000 illegal occupants were *rehabilitated* ... Mr. Jack adds that a rough census of those occupying land illegally showed that between 10,000 and 12,000 families needed *rehabilitation*, and the problem needed 'urgent attention'. Taking a conservative estimate of five for an African family, Mr. Jack's disclosures show that at least 50,000 Africans were liable to be moved. (Ibid., 18 September 1969: 11, emphasis mine)

This article in its analysis of the problem removes all doubt as to who the label 'illegal occupants' referred to, between whites and blacks in Rhodesia. The writer without needing to explain it, just switches and substitutes 'illegal occupants' with African families and Africans in need of rehabilitation and being moved. Through common and regular use the paper impresses upon its reader's mind the picture of Africans it so refers to, as people who at some point after the land demarcation occasioned by settler occupation of their land and legally entrenched through promulgation of the Land Apportionment Act of 1930 willingly and in defiance of the law decide to migrate, occupy and settle on European owned land. These are Africans in breach of the law of the land who would otherwise deserve incarceration. But thanks to its benevolence, the white government conscious of its trusteeship and tutelary role towards its African subjects, opted to take the course of rehabilitating rather than gaoling the African population concerned. The irony of it, however, is that the use of the term rehabilitation of the African is actually an euphemism for the dehumanising act of dispossession of Africans of their land and wealth. Coincidentally such rehabilitation was being carried out on the Tangwena people on the very day this story is published. This story masks the white settlers' massive theft and occupation of African land through processes of colonial subjugation of the African people, so that, between whites and blacks white takeover of land was more deserving of the term 'illegal land occupation'. But by some inverted logic of colonial racial division of labour whites are landowners and blacks are squatters by operation of the law, except that the reader is not told how that law came about in the first place let alone whether it is just or unjust.

The day that followed the demolition of Tangwena village and the forced removal of Chief Rekayi Tangwena, on 19 September 1969, the newspaper reading public in the then Rhodesia and the world was denied the story of how the government had actually executed the operation to forcibly remove the Tangwena people from Gaerezi Ranch and how the Tangwena people resisted or submitted to their forced removal. What the world got from *The Rhodesia Herald* (19 September 1969) was a front page story accompanied with an attention-grabbing landscape picture showing the Tangwena, mostly women, in a protest march clashing with the police laid out as follows:

EYEBROW: Police take away self-styled 'chief' (bulleted, in italics and underlined)
MAIN HEADLINE: Tangwena Trouble (Banner large font size)
KICKER: Protest by tribesmen (in italics)
BYLINE: From Brian Charlesworth, Inyanga, Thursday
LEAD: Hundreds of Tangwena tribesmen fled through the mountains east of here when police and Government officers arrived just before dawn to take away their self-styled chief, Rekayi, and a headman, Tsatsi. Several of these tribesmen were put into a police cell at Inyanga this evening, and women into a caged compound. They had been demonstrating outside the office of the District Commissioner, Mr R. Wyatt, and had demanded that their "chief" be returned to them.
BODY: When two or three of the men who had been held resisted searching, the police used their batons. Dogs were used while moving the people from the DC's office to the police station. Newspapers who had heard of the impending move and had driven out towards the Tangwena village before dawn today were stopped by police guarding a bridge over the Gaeresi River and told they would need a permit to go any further.

The operation, conducted in conditions of extreme security, began an hour before dawn this morning. A convoy of trucks drove through Inyanga to a clearing which had been prepared some days ago ...

As the two men were being led quietly to a truck, several women, screaming and crying hurled themselves at the district messengers ... some of the women were kicked and hit and Rekayi's wife, Matadziseyi, had her dress torn.

The rest of the tribe scattered through the mountains some plunging into the Gaeresi River ...

One way to disrupt the plane of interpretation that journalistic norms and conventions seek to impose on the reader acceptable hegemonic reasoning it would be useful to suggest alternative news headlines for the same story on the basis of even those limited semiotic resources the story places before us. These would include the sum total of the linguistic slips that lie buried beneath the rubble of words on the page the pictures and typographical matter. For example, the second sentence in the lead of the story: 'Several of these tribesmen were put into a police cell at Inyanga this evening, and women into a caged compound', drops one very interesting hint which could change the texture of the story and its whole line of argument. The fact that of the crowd that marched in protest to Inyanga District Office the men were all fitted into a police cell, while the women had to be put into a caged compound suggests that women who took part in this protest march far outnumbered the men. They could not fit into a single cell. The fact that way down the story it is mentioned that one of the women Matadzisei, the chief's wife, had her dress torn in a scuffle with a policeman is yet another piece of evidence of how courageous and expressive of their outrage women were in this protest. On the basis of this detailed analysis story headlines that suggest themselves include but may not be limited to the following:

86 *News silence on forced removals in Rhodesia*

Gaeresi women in a protest march to Nyanga;

Woman's dress torn in fight with police in Nyanga;

Matadzisei takes on the police in protest at husband's arrest;

Police terrorise women protestors in Nyanga.

The conventional wisdom by which journalists and editors guide themselves in coming up with news story headlines like the one which was decided upon by *The Rhodesia Herald* on that day would have obviously failed each one of the alternative headlines suggested here for failure to satisfy one important news value. The news value of consonance suggests that a developing story must be easily identifiable as such. A follow-up story must give cues that enable the reader to link it to a past story on which it builds. The news value of prominence when coupled with male prejudice in a partriarchal society would fail the above headlines on the ground that women or Matadzisei the chief's wife would score less than the male who also happens to be chief, Rekayi Tangwena. What this serves to illustrate is that the story that *The Rhodesia Herald* decided to give its readers on 19 September 1969 was not the only story in town. There could potentially be a myriad number of ways of witnessing and interpreting the events that happened in Nyanga that day.

The theme the headline seems to suggest to the reader, which the three-sentence lead also goes on to re-emphasise appears to be that the police, with justification, have had to apply minimum force to remove from the Tangwena people one Rekayi Tangwena, who is not the legitimate chief of the Tangwena people but a usurper and sole cause of trouble. Although this action by the police may have triggered a protest march by the Tangwena 'tribes people', that also has been quelled and contained by the vigilant Rhodesia Police without incident. The use of nominalisation in the headline, 'Tangwena Trouble' elides and conceals the state's or the Tangwena's agency in causing the trouble. But by collocating 'Tangwena' and 'Trouble' the text evokes the imaginary of the Tangwena as somehow blameworthy for visiting the trouble upon themselves. As if to underline this fact, just below the headline is a landscape photograph showing the Tangwena 'tribesmen' being frogmarched in a single file by the police. The important message the picture conveys is one of the invincibility of the Rhodesian police represented here by a white police officer restraining a vicious police dog on a leash and at the same time giving orders to junior police officers controlling and subduing the protesting crowd. The use of extended euphemism acts at two levels in this story. Either the reporter is masterfully being satirical and in the process succeeds in exposing government hypocrisy in claims of a peaceful role of the police in the Tangwena case, but at the same time revealing much of the opposite in stating that the operation was carried out under 'conditions of extreme security' and that villagers scattered through the mountains 'others plunging into the Gaeresi River'. It is difficult to imagine conditions of extreme security that are short of those applicable in a war situation, and the sort of conditions and circumstances that would necessitate some people taking the risk of plunging into a crocodile infested river by way of escape.

News silence on forced removals in Rhodesia 87

At another level of interpretation, this could well be a story that is a product of extreme self-censorship on the part of a paper which is so pliant that it voluntarily does the government's bidding in reporting in a manner that minimised damage to the government's reputation and public image in a manner that does not make the story fall foul of the Law and Order Maintenance Act's provision against causing alarm and despondency. The caption explaining the picture states: 'Police using dogs to move the crowds of the Tangwena tribesmen who gathered outside the Inyanga District Commissioner's office yesterday. They went there to protest at the removal before dawn yesterday of their self-styled 'chief', Rekayi Tangwena, and a headman to the tribe's new lands. The crowd were moved to the police station where they were searched and held. Police used batons when one or two resisted' (*The Rhodesia Herald*, 19 September 1969: 1). The use of such empty signifiers as 'used batons' or 'using dogs' omitting the detail on how these instruments of violence could be used is both paradoxical and open to multiple interpretations. One possible reading may be that by using the indeterminate and neutral verb in police 'used' the story deliberately masks and sanitises police brutality on unarmed demonstrating 'tribes people' both men and women. The report is biased in favour of the police and by extension, in support of government action in this matter. On the other hand the story by employing selective understatement and silence on how the police possibly used dogs to move the crowd and used batons on resisting ones without inflicting bodily pain on those on whom these instruments of terror were used, could alternatively be understood to have been the newspaper's strategy to negotiate and circumvent government censorship but at the same time putting vital information out onto the public domain. Given the restrictive operating environment in the country at the time the paper had to make difficult choices between reporting something, or being prevented from reporting anything at all.

The later reading appears to be corroborated by the paper's decision to use more graphic details of police brutality as shown in the two additional pictures detailing what the reporter described as a scuffle yet they clearly show a mixture of defiance, terror and a sense of outrage on the faces of the demonstrating crowd particularly women as the police details push, shove and use their baton sticks on one or two of them. The caption on one of the pictures read: 'A scuffle breaks out between a policeman and a woman in the crowd of Tangwena, protesting at their self-styled "chief's" removal to new lands yesterday. The photograph was taken near the District Commissioner's Office at Nyanga'. It appears the paper has taken a deliberate decision to let the pictures tell the story with very little commentary. The use of 'self-styled' and the term chief in quotes repeatedly in this and other stories on the Tangwena, by *The Rhodesia Herald* serves to emphasise the illegitimacy of Rekayi Tangwena's claim to the chieftaincy and leadership of his people and by extension his claim to the land from which he and his people are being driven.

The following day in a follow-up story on the Tangwena issue, *The Rhodesia Herald* led with a front page story headline announcing to the world that the Tangwena versus government saga had finally been amicably resolved between

88 News silence on forced removals in Rhodesia

the two parties in favour of government's position, with the bold two-word headline: 'Rekayi Agreement' and to match the previous day's story, this headline too was sandwiched between an eyebrow and a kicker which read: 'Tribe promises to move off Gaeresi Ranch' and 'Police free 160 men' respectively. This story whose layout is very similar to its predecessor of the previous day also carried a landscape aerial photograph of the scenic 'Holdenby Tribal Trust Land', the future home of the Tangwena according to this story which is largely based on official ministry sources and government press releases. The story makes no pretence at balancing the largely official and white opinion expressed, with the views of the black people who are the subject of the story. Instead we are told in the story: 'White residents here seemed to applaud the government action. Hoteliers and others I spoke to said the Tangwena people had been *spoiling* the land, and in any case they had no right to live in a European area'. This patently false one-dimensional story gets proved for what it is only seven days later, when another story, 'Rekayi determined to continue fight' (*The Rhodesia Herald*, 27 September 1969: 1), this time based on a witness from among the Tangwena people themselves refuting the allegation that the Tangwena had agreed to being moved from Gaeresi Ranch to the new reserve. Instead we learn from the story that in fact Rekayi Tangwena and his people have returned and are rebuilding their destroyed homes, and so ends the government's attempts to forcibly remove the Tangwena in 1969. The fight would resume after the end of the new planting season in July the year that followed.

The Rhodesia Herald's presentation of government's second attempt to forcibly evict the Tangwena people from Gaeresi is dressed in legalistic language in a symbolic process that legitimised government position. On 8 July 1970 the paper carried a story on page 3 headlined: 'New bid to move the Tangwena'. In this headline it does not become apparent whether the new bid itself is justified or not, whether the move itself was on the invitation of the Tangwena people. The nominalisation technique exploited here makes the removal sound almost inevitable, or unavoidable. The intro further reinforces the inevitability and the legitimacy of the removal by attributing the intended action to Government in the sentence: 'The Government is to make another attempt to move the Tangwena tribesmen from the European owned land in Inyanga, which the tribe claims as its ancestral home'. This sentence serves to impress it upon the reader's mind who has the claim and who has the fact between the Europeans and the tribesmen. In the phrases 'European owned land' and 'which the tribe claims as its ancestral home', European ownership of the land is a fact beyond question because they own the land while the tribesmen's claim to the land is suspect and questionable because it is they who claim. Rekayi Tangwena, their chief representative in this dispute against government is delegitimated by casting aspersions on his claim to the Tangwena chieftaincy. He is dubbed 'the tribe's self-styled chief'. The tribesmen's loss of livestock in an earlier government attempt to evict them is just as contestable as their claim to the land of Gaeresi because it is presented as a mere allegation in 'livestock which tribesman allege they lost ...'; the idea of livestock which they allege they lost without stating to whom conceals more than it reveals. The meaning would be entirely different for instance if the story had stated the point as follows 'livestock which the tribesmen allege government confiscated' which other sources of information confirm was in fact the case (Frederikse, 1982). It appears everything from title to land, Rekayi Tangwena's claim to chieftaincy, and tribesmen's claimed loss of livestock amount to unfounded claims and allegations unsupported by facts. The tribesmen are presented as habitual liars not to mention the racial overtones in references to European and tribesmen. If the pages of *The Rhodesia Herald* were to be taken as a metaphor for Rhodesia of the 1960s and 1970s then it could reasonably be argued that racial segregation on its pages had been far more perfected and complete with a stricter enforcement of racial purity than through land segregation. Its front pages in particular and other pages that carried political content had long been quietly declared European area onto which African opinion could rarely trespass. The efforts at making Rhodesia into what Parker (1972) in his book calls a 'Little White Island' were thus not just backed by law that legitimised the use of force in removing blacks from white areas but it was ostensibly supported by the entire ideological apparatus of the white press of which *The Rhodesia Herald* was looked upon as the flagship. The exclusion of any African opinion no matter how mildly critical of government policy is itself a marker of the extent to which by 1970 *The Rhodesia Herald* and indeed all Argus publications were willing to apply self-censorship in acquiescence with the Rhodesia Front policies so that its editor by 1968 could be quoted as saying:

> The need for a degree of self-imposed press censorship has always been accepted. Rhodesia's needs come before Government, party, or press. Matters affecting national security or trading against sanctions have always had to be carefully examined to discover whether publication would be harmful to the country's interests. (Frederikse, 1982: 28).

Reporting on forced removals of the Tangwena and the Hunyani people probably was one such instance when a story had a bearing on matters of national security and as such merited careful examination, even censoring, in the eyes of *The Rhodesia Herald* editors. That *The Rhodesia Herald* of the late 1960s to 1970s had adopted an increasingly sympathetic stance towards the Rhodesian government becomes evident in government extending to them a carte blanche franchise to cover and 'freely' report on its activities.

Moto and re-humanisation of the Tangwena

Given the virulence and pervasiveness of racial segregation under Rhodesia Front government of Ian Smith in the late 1960s to early 1970s the reportorial stance taken by the *Moto* newspaper was quite radical in the spirit of giving voice to the voiceless and economically and politically marginalised Africans in the land dispute case pitting Chief Rekayi Tangwena against the white authorities. In story after story that the paper published, it sought the comments and opinions of the

90 *News silence on forced removals in Rhodesia*

Africans on the matter and publicised the African view on the subject. It even gave front page status to such stories clearly demonstrating that the paper was African in its news orientation. In its August 1969 edition it carried a front page story titled: 'Chief won't move. He will defy Govt order' with a picture of the defiant Rekayi Tangwena captioned:"'They are trying to throttle us". Chief Tagwena (below) said emphasising his words with a gesture of his hand. "We would rather be killed than be forced to move from our land"'. Even though the story is not given lead story status, the use of the picture and its caption gives the story a prominence that almost dwarfs the supposed lead 'TWO MEN ON THE MOON' story (*Moto* used the style of using caps to indicate lead story status). The Tangwena story lead is a quote of the chief's words "'This land has been our home for countless years, since long before the first white man came. It is sacred to us," Chief Rekayi ("leave alone" Tangwena told his assembled people at a spirited meeting on July 19 which was attended by a *Moto* reporter.' The story then goes on to give context, chronicling events leading up to this meeting taking place.

The grassroots news paradigm used by the *Moto* was diametrically different from the top-down officialdom characteristic of *The Rhodesia Herald* news. A reporter had to be dispatched to Gaeresi to get the people's version of the story of the government plan to forcibly remove them. The story places emphasis on a counter-hegemonic discourse of a superior claim to the land based on precedence of occupation in 'this land has been our home … since long before the first white man came'. The Tangwena were not basing their title to the land on some piece of paper, but on tradition, because the chief argues: 'our ancestors have passed it on to us, and the D. O. is not one of them'. In addition, the claim of legality of occupation had been upheld by the High Court.

An important way in which *Moto* also debunked the myth of white supremacy was through publishing some of its stories in ChiShona and Isindebele, the first languages of its African readers, 4 out of 12 stories were written in ChiShona. In September 1969 *Moto* gave a very focused attention on the Tangwena issue with three articles including an editorial comment on the Tangwena's resistance to forced removals from Gaerezi. One such story published on the front page of the *Moto*'s September 1969 issue was in Shona titled (Tangwena navanhu vake vaita ndamba) 'Tangwena and his people Defiant' ran in one column below a mugshot picture of the chief with a caption 'Chief Rekayi Tangwena'. It is important to note that *Moto* refers to Rekayi Tangwena as chief, unlike *The Rhodesia Herald* which consistently referred to him in deprecatory terms as: 'self-styled chief'. In the picture the chief was wearing his trade-mark hat woven from what looked like the bark of a Musasa or a Baobab tree adorned with sea shells along the bottom band. This appearance alone marked him out as a defiant rebel chief who was non-conforming with the standard dress of those chiefs who cooperated with and were thus recognised by the government. Other chiefs would normally be dressed in identifying regalia of office which included among other things a red robe, a chain with a half-moon shaped badge and a white pith helmet. In all pictures of him, Tangwena never appeared wearing the chiefly regalia, a clear sign that his chieftaincy was not recognised by government. This story gave a detailed

News silence on forced removals in Rhodesia 91

Figure 4.2 Chief Rekayi Tangwena dressed in his traditional chiefly regalia leads children of his people to the mountains where their parents are hiding after their villages had been demolished. Republished with permission. National Archives of Zimbabwe.

chronology of events leading up to the fallout between the Tangwena people and the government. The *Moto* backed up its argument obviously sympathetic to the Tangwena position on the issue with facts and dates. For example, when it reports that;

> Madzitateguru aTangwena akagara munzvimbo iyi kubva pasichigare ndokuzoti mugore ra-1905, nzvimbo iyi yakapiwa kuCompany yavarungu. Muna

92 *News silence on forced removals in Rhodesia*

1930 kuchitevedzerwa murau weLand Apportionment Act, nzvimbo yekare iyi yakabva yanzi inofanira kugarwa navachena chete. Tangwena navanhu vake akanzi ngavatute vaende." (Tangwena's ancestors lived in this area from time immemorial and then in 1905 this area was given to a European company. In 1930, applying the law under the Land Apportionment Act this old place was declared a European area. Tangwena and his people were then ordered to leave).

The term used in ChiShona translated here as 'from time immemorial' is a signifier of an incontestable title to the land as it is interpreted to mean that the Tangwena were there from when time itself began.

The second story in this issue of *Moto* appears on page 3 with a picture of two grim faced villagers whom *Moto* describes as 'two Tangwena elders intently listening to an instruction of Chief Rekayi'. The reader is also informed that the picture was taken during a meeting at the chief's village. That *Moto* consistently takes sides with the villagers' position is demonstrated by their consistently referring to the land in question as 'the land of their ancestors' as opposed to referring to it as Mr Hanmer's farm.

On the same page as this story is an advert of a recently published book on Chief Tangwena written by Guy Clutton-Brock. The ad read:

> Mr. Guy Clutton-Brock has written a book on Chief Rekayi Tangwena and his people "in the interest of truth and also of compassion" It is entitled "Rekayi Tangwena – Let Tangwena be" The book is an account of the attempt to evict the Tangwena people from their land and mainly reproduces the chief's own words. Chief Tangwena's courage has done a great deal for the country. It is now up to us to support him through our interest in his case.

Below this blurb is an order form for those who would want to purchase the book. The book was published by Mambo Press who happened to be the publishers of the *Moto* newspaper as well.

The fourth article on Tangwena in the same issue was an editorial comment (September 1969: 8) titled 'The power of resistance'. In this article, *Moto* nails its colours on the mast as a newspaper on the Tangwena land dispute by clearly and unambiguously endorsing the courageous stand taken by Chief Rekayi Tangwena against government's efforts to forcibly move him and his people from Gaeresi area.

> Unlike so many other chiefs and leaders of our people today, Chief Rekayi Tangwena has refused to admit that he is powerless. He has been threatened, intimidated, offered bribes. But in the past four years he has stubbornly protected his people's right to their land. Like a noble David he has, in the interests of his tribe, stood up to the Goliath of the Ministry of Internal Affairs and refused to budge, (*Moto*, September 1969: 8).

Moto took a very bold stance in its praise for Tangwena's courageous and principled stand in defence of 'his people's right to their land'. In this article the editor uses a very evocative imagery drawn from the ancient biblical story of little David who courageously stepped forward to fight the Philistine giant Goliath, to symbolise the most unequal struggle pitting Tangwena and his people referred to in this article as 'his tribe' against the unparalleled sophistry and might of the Rhodesia Front Government. In the similitude, Chief Rekayi Tangwena is the David and the Goliath is located somewhere in the Ministry of Internal Affairs. Using that epic battle *Moto* is also by implication making the prediction that Tangwena would, like David, eventually emerge the victor.

On the other hand, the paper's use of the derogatory term 'tribe' to refer to Africans betrays an uncritical racial blindness on the part of those behind this editorial. It is uncritical in the sense that although it would never have occurred to the writer to use the same term when referring to whites it came so natural for him to refer to the Africans as 'tribe'. But this has to be read in the context of an entrenched racist ideology which often reasserted itself in spite of attempts at repressing its manifestation in language. It has to be read against the backdrop of efforts at purging the language of the more blatantly racist terminology evidenced by the disuse and disappearance of such terms as 'natives' to refer to Africans even in government circles. A search on Google Images using the term 'tribe' produced a total of 288 million images all of which presented quaint figures of some barely dressed groups of people invariably people of colour drawn from many parts of the southern hemisphere, largely showing evidence of not having been touched by 'modernity', images of people caught up in a time warp of an ossified traditional mode of existence. What emerges from an analysis of such pictures gives one unmistakable pejorative associations and connotations of the meaning and uses of the word tribe to connote inferiority, primitiveness of the African people as compared to whites.

The timing of the forcible removal of the Tangwena is a clear illustration of government intention to keep the story of forced removals of Africans hidden from the glare of the world press. *Moto* had accurately predicted that nothing dramatic would happen to the Tangwena on 31 August the date by which they were supposed to have moved according to a government proclamation because, the paper argued:

> The representatives of the world press will be waiting and it would be too embarrassing for Mr. Smith and his men to have photographs of what could be a minor 'Sharpeville' splashed across the pages of the world's newspapers. But that does not mean that force will not be used to move these families at a later date - when they are no longer 'in the news'. (*Moto*, September 1969: 8)

Indeed, as *Moto* had predicted, the regime's security forces only swooped down on the unsuspecting hapless Tangwena villagers in a dawn raid when the authorities made sure nobody was watching, members of the press had been barred from the area and from talking to the Tangwena people. Press coverage of the removal of the Tangwena people should be understood against a background of a policy of censorship and information blackout. The most likely brutal and savage attack on

94 *News silence on forced removals in Rhodesia*

a defenceless people was thus hidden away from public glare. The world was denied access to that event, except to censored and highly sanitised versions of it published by government permission in *The Rhodesia Herald* and its sister papers under the Rhodesia Printing and Publishing Company. But the Tangwena story still managed to attract reasonable media attention unlike stories about other African communities facing similar displacements because of the protracted nature of the dispute and its dramas. It had already gone through the courts. Chief Rekayi Tangwena enjoyed the media gravitas also partly because he managed to lead his people in a sustained resistance campaign against brutal state machinery spanning a period of four years. The Tangwena resisted this first attempt at forcibly removing them from what they regarded as their land by birth-right. The November issue of the *Moto* reports, in a front page article titled: 'Tangwena may sue Govt for destruction of huts', the return of the Tangwena people to Gaeresi to rebuild their destroyed homes and to cultivate their fields and grow crops in the new rain season. The lead story on this page titled '10-acre average for each African, 175 acres for each European', appears to stoke the flames of African anger against colonial injustices over land and the story flows along the same grain as the Tangwena story. The third story on this page which seems to also aggravate government's view of *Moto* as bent on fighting government, is a report of the court trial of its editor, for publishing what government regarded as a subversive statement – a cartoon which depicted 'a pair of white hands crushing together small African bodies ... with a caption that read; "The proposed new constitution will ensure that government will be retained in responsible hands"'. This case was to eventually lead to the deportation of Fr. Michael Traber, editor of the *Moto* in an attempt to remove the man who had become a thorn on the government side when it came to criticising its policies in dealing with the Africans.

In 1970 the Moto's attention on the Tangwena case appeared to wane after publication of a bold assertion: 'Tangwena will stay', again on front page of its May 1970 edition. But the Moto had not altogether abandoned its interest in the land issue and forced removals of African people from their land. Its attention had only shifted to a new and breaking story of the removal of the Hunyani people, another much larger African community facing a similar predicament as the Tangwena people. Their land had also been declared European area.

The Rhodesia Herald, and silence on the Hunyani removals

The Rhodesia Herald's policy on reporting forced removals of the Hunyani people can be summarised as one of deliberate silence or disinformation on the matter. The first ever article to appear in the paper making reference to the issue of the removal of the Hunyani people was published under a headline no reader could have suspected that it dealt with the subject of the removal of the Huchu, Ruya and Gobo chiefdoms from Hunyani 'reserve' – an area that stretches from Mvuma in the east to Lalapanzi in the west and bounded by the Mvuma–Kwekwe road on the northern side and Mvuma–Gweru road on the southern side, the area around

News silence on forced removals in Rhodesia 95

Iron Mine Hill, the famous meeting point between the Fort Victoria Column and the Salisbury Column of volunteer BSAC forces en-route to the battle for Bulawayo against the Ndebele in 1893. Right from the initial government meetings with the chiefs to negotiate with them the terms of their removal from Hunyani and their relocation to newly opened African reserves, after the land they lived in had been declared European area under the new Land Tenure Act of 1969 through the actual evictions, *The Rhodesia Herald* had remained mum. It probably saw no reason to carry a story about this massive government operation to move close to 15,000 Africans to new areas in Gokwe and in Silobela. This was a long drawn out and protracted operation that lasted many months and accompanied with no dramatic scenes as those associated with the removal of the Tangwena people. This can be explained in terms of journalistic news values that favour reporting on events rather than processes or status quos.

The first ever story to be published in *The Rhodesia Herald* on the Hunyani removals appeared in its 9 July 1970 edition, many months after the programme had been in full swing. The paper (*The Rhodesia Herald*, 9 July 1970) ran a lead story on front page headlined: 'Civil Servant hits at "men of God"'. This is the only key story to have ever been written by *The Rhodesia Herald* on the subject. The rest that followed were actually letters to the editor reacting to this story. It is thus worth quoting from it at length since it is the paper's centre piece on the Hunyani removals:

HEADLINE: Civil servant hits at 'men of God' (Three deck, Bold and in caps)
BYLINE: Midlands Representative, Que Que, Wednesday
LEAD: The huge task of trying to make changes to improve the African economy is often bedevilled and held back by disruptive elements who appear to be sponsored by the 'men of God', the Secretary of Internal Affairs, Mr. Hostes Nicolle, said here today. Addressing the annual meeting of the Nkone Cattle Club – his listeners included the Minister of Information, Mr. P. K. van der Byle, who is a member – Mr. Nicolle said that, "on occasions it seems that Satan's fork is substituted for the bishop's crozier".
BODY: "We have a tremendous task and one would think that as we are aiming to improve our indigenous population, particularly in the tribal areas, the first people who would assist us in trying to advance these people would be the men of God – not to be in the opposite camp, sabotaging and causing a lot of disruptions in the schemes we are putting forward," he said.

In the Que Que area his Ministry was now resettling Africans on virgin land after moving them from an area which for years had been causing innumerable complaints because of the damage to the natural resources. These people were cooperating and moving readily.

"When the Government contemplated this move I warned them that I thought we would have to use the security forces. As it happens, we have not had to use them for the people are moving voluntarily."
SUB-HEAD: 'Appalled'

"But I am appalled to find that a local paper affiliated to these men of God has seen fit to disparage this movement and it purports to depict the

96 *News silence on forced removals in Rhodesia*

new areas in a very poor light indeed by comparing them with the devastated areas from which these people are moving.

In fact it purports to depict the devastated areas as being the land of milk and honey and the area to which they are being moved as something less than the desert," he said.

These distortions of the truth, said Mr. Nicolle, did not make the task any easier. He was worried about this continual prodding behind the scenes to try to create trouble.

The story carried a mugshot picture of a grinning Secretary for Internal Affairs, Mr Hostes Nicolle who must obviously relish the free publicity he is getting while over-dramatising his patriotic sentiment in the presence of the Minister of Information Mr P.K. van der Byl whom the story reports to have been part of Mr Nicolle's audience. The strongly worded story directed to unspecified 'men of God', turns out to be a thinly veiled attack on the Roman Catholic Church diocese, publishers of *Moto*, for publishing a 'disparaging' story on the removal of the Hunyani people to Silobela.

The story which is an uninterrupted harangue of the 'men of God' by the Secretary for Internal Affairs obfuscates the real motive behind the removal of Africans from Hunyani (to make the area a European area in line with the provisions of the Land Tenure Act) as part of government efforts '*to improve* our indigenous population, particularly in the tribal areas … trying *to advance* these people'. Worth noting is the paternalistic, patronising and condescending use of such language as '*improve* our indigenous people'. The assumption implicit in this statement on the basis of which it is intelligible to *The Rhodesia Herald*'s readers is that Africans were inferior to whites and thus it becomes inevitable that on the white man lay the tremendous responsibility to develop and modernise the Africans. The other reason why the Africans should be removed from this area and resettled in virgin lands is because they are the implicit cause for 'damage to the natural resources' in the area where they have to be moved from. Here the paper appeals to the usual trope of 'primitivism' blaming the 'nigger' for inviting this government action on themselves as if government has now to resort to giving them virgin lands so as for them to again damage and degrade through their primitive methods of farming.

The story is silent on the white government having any other motive than the altruistic intention to 'advance our indigenous people in the tribal areas'. Concealed is the motive to bring into effect the provisions of the new Land Tenure Act, in terms of which the former Hunyani reserve had been declared European land. That selective silence has the effect of excluding from debate the racial basis for the government policy of land division between Europeans and Africans. The terms of reference for discussion thus veer off the real issues of the inevitable disruption this policy was likely to cause on African livelihoods, and the important question of the relatively poorer climatic and agro-ecological zones of the new areas compared to the area they were leaving behind.

Implicit in 'These people were cooperating and moving readily ... the people are moving voluntarily' is the idea of African complicity in their own domination by the whites. If any problems should arise, they are imputed to be the work of instigators from among some sections of the white community and not from 'our contented Africans' themselves. This was a deeply entrenched racist prejudice even some church leaders harboured about Africans as Bishop Donal Lamont's remarks in a pastoral letter show: 'the recent appeal to extremism and to the use of force on the part of some Africans, is probably not of local origin, for it is quite something alien to this patient and peace-loving people ... It is an importation ...' (Plangger, 1968: 26). Africans would put up with anything but for the mischief of some whites like the men of God who had exchanged the crozier for Satan's fork, who were continuously, 'prodding behind the scenes to try to create trouble'.

Just as in the Tangwena case discussed above, the coverage being given here to the removal of the Hunyani people displaces the real issue of the hardships visited on the Africans affected by the racial policy of land segregation and reinterprets it as an issue of some subversive elements among whites who needed to be dealt with to solve the problem. The repertoires of possible courses of action would thus range from the Minister of Information putting in place measures to either completely silence the Catholic paper for publishing such 'distortions' or deport some white editors of the paper, who must be behind the mischief. In fact, as it turned out, both these solutions were already in the process of being effected as the *Moto* editor, Fr. Michael Traber and his deputy editor Anthony Schimtz, had been deported earlier in the year and the paper itself was to be eventually banned from publishing in 1974.

The importance of *The Rhodesia Herald*'s story is first of all in the fact that it was not a story directly reporting on the removal itself nor about Africans' reactions to it. It was a story on a story about removals. It brings into high relief the slipperiness of journalistic 'truth', the *Moto* is accused of depicting 'the new areas in a very poor light indeed and the devastated areas from which these people are moving as being the land of milk and honey'. Such depictions, Mr Nicolle argues, are distortions of the 'truth' which he and probably the government alone somehow 'know' and are best placed to represent. This highlights the contested nature of media representation of reality, particularly relevant in the age of fake news and alternative facts.

The story provoked a robust white debate in which in *The Rhodesia Herald* true to its founding principle of providing coverage to all shades of white opinion, the Catholic Bishop of Gweru diocese, Rt. Rev. Alois Heane, is offered an opportunity to make his own statement responding to this attack in the story published a day after (*The Rhodesia Herald*, 11 July 1970: 2) headlined: 'Catholic Bishop on "men of God" attack'. Below are excerpts of some key paragraphs from the bishop's response:

LEAD: A Government exercise to resettle Africans in the Que Que area was described today as a 'political decision' by the Roman Catholic Bishop of Gwelo, the Rt. Rev. Alois Heane. Replying in a statement to recent comments by the Secretary for Internal Affairs, Mr. Hostes Nicolle, Bishop

Heane said that as a result of these comments 'the operation of moving about 15,000 people from established homes to virgin land some 120 miles away is now bound to receive world-wide attention ...

BODY: He asked what Mr. Nicolle meant when he said that the people moved readily and voluntarily. 'They were not given the choice to move or to stay. Most of them agreed to go to the Exchange Block; others decided to go elsewhere. But leave they had to'.

The bishop said three quarters of the people concerned were Roman Catholics. Their greatest concern was whether the Church and the priest would move with them. The Church decided to move with the people to give them the service they desired.

The officials in charge of the operation were fully aware of the Church's involvement, and must have heaved a sigh of relief' at the co-operation they received, he concluded.

The Church will always be where the people are but to give Christian service, not to play the game of power. This may well be the reason why no security forces were required at Whunyani. We are now meted out the 'gratitude' of the Secretary for Internal Affairs.

Thus, by the bishop's own admission, the church played a not insignificant role in manufacturing African consent to the condition of colonial domination, in softening them up for the white seizure of their land. So effectively did the church play its part, that colonial administrators needed not use security forces to enforce legalised land dispossession of the Hunyani people. What is apparent here is that the church was fully aware of its role in instilling the servility and stoicism with which Africans in Hunyani bore the hardships and privations visited on them by the government policy of land segregation. With tongue-in-cheek, the bishop reminds government authorities of the 'Church's involvement' of which those tasked to carry out the operation were aware, and due to which, it was possible for them to heave 'a sigh of relief' at the co-operation they received'. The bishop's criticism of Mr Nicolle is not on the substance of the policy of removal of Africans from what they regarded as their ancestral land but on his and the Rhodesia Front Government's failure to give due credit to the church for its role in softening Africans into accepting white domination and hegemony without having to use security forces as the state had to do in the Tangwena case the previous year.

Another very startling revelation the Catholic bishop makes in his rebuttal of Mr Nicolle's attack on the 'Men of God' is the fact that there existed a tacit agreement between the white government and the church on the need to avoid doing anything that would potentially draw the world's attention to the forced removals. Bishop Heane thus takes the opportunity to remind Mr Nicolle that he was in breach of the silence contract through his reckless statements the consequence of which 'the operation of moving about 15,000 people from established homes to virgin land some 120 miles away is now bound to receive world-wide attention ...' Press silence was everything to keep these matters out of public view. One Mr J.E.S. Turton, Chief Native Commissioner, once commented about similar African removals way back in 1954 that 'the smooth running of these mass movements, *unnoticed* by the general public, redounds to the credit of the administrative staff' (Lessing, 1968: 127) (emphasis mine).

What is worth noting in the Hunyani as in the Tangwena case is that the real debate through the pages of *The Rhodesia Herald* pitted white opinion against white opinion on white attitudes towards blacks; it did not deal directly with, or question the effects of, the government's land policy on Africans, thus in a way legitimising it. The question is whether *The Rhodesia Herald* reporters found the removals themselves somehow lacking on all points of newsworthiness or it was consistent with what Van Dijk (1998) called the ideological square of mitigating or understating the negative effects of our 'white' actions on the 'black others'. Out of the question too was African perspective on the matter.

The debate later on spills into a wider white public discussion as readers of *The Rhodesia Herald* pick up and comment on the debate through the paper's letters to the editor section. Three letters contributing to this debate were published on July 20, 23, and 25 under the headlines: 'Men of God have helped the African'; 'The devils fork' and 'African faith in Moto', respectively. The articles reveal very interesting insights on the commonly held and widely shared white attitudes, myths and prejudices among the paper's editorial staff and their white readership towards Africans. *The Rhodesia Herald* in all these articles sought no comment from Africans directly affected by the removals nor from any African for that matter. Probably *The Rhodesia Herald*'s own self-censorship on the Hunyani story can only be explained in terms of a deeply held fear by its white editorial staff, of the African's 'undeveloped' critical faculty which inclines him to take indiscriminately every printed word as gospel truth – a fear perfectly well expressed by one of the paper's readers through a letter to the editor (*The Rhodesia Herald*, 25 July 1970: 9) titled 'African faith in Moto' where the writer warns publishers of *Moto* that: '*Moto* has a predominantly African readership. The bishop should in future give consideration to the fact that the Africans labour under the delusion that these reports ARE complete and accurate in every detail'.

So, *The Rhodesia Herald* probably as a measure to guard against its paper straying into African hands and risking misinterpretation and aberrant reading by the African, decided not to write at all and pronounce itself on matters of government policy as it affected Africans. *The Rhodesia Herald*'s conduct on the issue of the removals of the Hunyani people was quite characteristic – a near total blackout of news. Such behaviour was consistent with an elite and ethnocentric news doctrine that guided most professional journalistic work then and now. And it could also be explained in terms of deliberate propaganda policy. Way back in 1961 the Board for Natural Resources in a statement, giving evidence to a Government Select Committee on Resettlement of Natives (NAZ. S2625/29) had warned against practices that entrenched settlement of black labourers on European farms on a permanent basis where:

owners of alienated farms allow their native employees a certain acreage of arable land for cultivation and to give them the right to run a number of head of stock. This in effect is turning a part of every farm and ranch into a private native reserve. The object of the practice to provide a permanent, settled labour force. The Board had then proceeded to advise that: The so-called 'squatter' problem whether in contravention of the Land Apportionment Act or not is, from the board's point of view, one that can adequately be dealt with by means of propaganda

It would be reasonable to surmise that for *The Rhodesia Herald* to give unsolicited and unnecessary publicity on the hardships suffered by 'natives' as a direct consequence of removals from European areas and resettlement in new native reserves would work against the interests of propaganda aimed at resolving the 'black squatter problem'. Another factor that needs to be taken into account when interpreting *The Rhodesia Herald* story on removals is its editorial policy which enjoined it to always keep white interests steadily in sight when doing its work.

The *Moto*'s complicity

Moto, given its pro-African editorial stance, would have naturally been counted on by its African readership to cover developments of interest to and affecting Africans from an African standpoint. The removal of the Hunyani people would naturally have been of huge interest to *Moto*, given that the Roman Catholic Church had as a church very visible presence among the Hunyani communities, having established a thriving mission station complete with a clinic and school at Gobo Mission in this area.

Also given that *Moto* had given wide coverage of the Tangwena case recently, it stood to reason, now that a similarly 'tragic' development had struck home in *Moto*'s own backyard since Hunyani fell under the same diocese, it was reasonable to expect that *Moto* would train its readership and the world's attention to the removal of the Hunyani people. Break the story, yes Moto did in its February 1970 edition with a front page story titled: '12,000 people will be moved from Umvuma'. Concealed in this passive headline is the government's agency in causing the movement of the people from Umvuma which would have been the case if the headline had been written differently as: 'Government to move 12,000 people from Umvuma'. The effect of this syntactic strategy is to shield government from blame for the mass displacements of black people. The technique is further reinforced in the first two sentences of the story:

LEAD: Between 12,000 and 15,000 people will have to leave 'Hunyani Reserve' by August and will be moved to Silobela, some 130 miles away, the chiefs and headmen of the area were told by Ministry of Internal Affairs officials on December 22.

BODY: This is believed to be the biggest resettlement of people that has been taking place in Rhodesia in recent years.

> The area to which they move is roughly the same size as the one they presently occupy. But people doubt if there is as much rain in Silobela as they have enjoyed in Hunyani, where they had excellent crops practically every year and where some 200,000 head of cattle have prospered.

The use of the intransitive modal verb 'will have to leave' and passive form 'will be moved' used in the lead paragraph of the story de-emphasises government agency in the impending movement of the people. And in the second sentence government planned action to forcibly remove the Hunyani people is nominalised into 'the biggest resettlement of people that has been taking place in Rhodesia in recent years' as if it happens of its own accord spontaneously. The effect is to dehistoricise, naturalise and thus render the impending removal even more inevitable. Even the lexical choice of the word 'resettlement' ahead of such alternatives to it as 'forced removal', 'displacement' or 'eviction' tends to invest the story with the more positive connotations of 'resettlement' making the planned government action that much more acceptable. When this story is read against the background of an ever-present threat of government censorship then it may be understandable that the paper had to balance between provoking government anger and the need to put out some vital information to its African readership. That this story is being written in this clearly timid manner at a time when two of the paper's editors had been deported may indicate that a sea-change has happened with the paper's editorial stance.

Moto followed up this initial story with another in their June 1970 edition announcing the mass movement of the Hunyani people with the title 'Gobo people on the move'. Again by putting the victim of government action in the subject position of the sentence the story shifts the responsibility for the action described in the verb and places it on the Gobo people themselves. These two initial stories on the Hunyani removal privilege reporter voice and perspective on the issue and no effort is made to seek out and publicise the affected Africans' own view of the matter in a process just as marginalising as the government act of forcibly removing them.

This was then followed by a much more radically different story giving extensive coverage of the hardships that resettled people were experiencing in the new areas after what the paper described in the headline of the teaser on the front page announcing the story as 'The Forced trek'. The actual story on page 3 had a much more elaborate headline 'Silobela: everything has disappeared' with 'The forced trek from Gobo' as a kicker. Below are excerpts of some key paragraphs from the story:

LEAD: The three chiefs of Hunyani here, Chief Ruya, Chief Gobo and Chief Huchu are being moved by the Government to other areas. Some 2,000 families are affected. They leave seven schools and a clinic in Hunyani and will have 5 schools in Silobela.

BODY: Hunyani area is 47,000 acres; the areas, in Que Que (Silobela) and Gokwe District where people are being moved to are approximately 44,000 acres.

102 *News silence on forced removals in Rhodesia*

The reason for the movement of all the people is that they are "illegally occupying state land in European Areas," according to Mr. Lance Smith's statement in Parliament recently. Hunyani was never national land. It was acquired by a previous government many years ago, but the position today is that it is state European land.

The Government has begun to move the people of Chief Gobo and chief Ruya to Silobela to erect granaries prior to their permanent settlement of the land. It is the famous Tangwena story over again but without a Tangwena.

To move all the people from Hunyani the Government played a wooing game. Like it did with chief Tangwena it is said, the Government offered many things to Hunyani chiefs if they agreed to move. They were promised five schools, boreholes, good roads, free transport to the new areas etc.

This human interest story written in the style of a detailed investigative piece is laid out on three-quarters of page 3 of the newspaper. It is interspaced with two landscape pictures taken, one depicting a cattle sales market day in Hunyani where people are forced to sell their livestock at very low prices, and another taken in Silobela showing men cooperating to erect their shelter in the new area. The pictures provide the frame against which the reader is expected to interpret the meaning of the story. The importance of this news story is further emphasised by another picture depicting women drawing water at a borehole in Silobela plus a teaser advertising it on front page. Both the teaser and caption of the picture announced as follows:

TEASER HEADLINE: The forced trek

BODY: One of our reporters went to Gobo and to Silobela to find out what happens if thousands of people have to leave their homes behind and start afresh at a new place. Read the inside story of the forced trek on page 3.

PICTURE CAPTION: The Hunyani people resettling in the Silobela area are battling for water. Bore holes are the only source of drinking water for both human and animal needs. But Hunyani Reserve, where these people are being driven from has been a land of milk and honey with ever-flowing rivers and green pastures. It is now declared a white area. The Hunyani people will have to be contented with this semi-arid country.

It was this story which so incensed Mr Hostes Nicolle, that he issued his verbal broadside on the 'Men of God' published by *The Rhodesia Herald*, referred to above. The use of terms such as 'the forced trek from Gobo' and the inter-textual reference to '... the famous Tangwena story over again but without a Tangwena' made a bold indictment of government enforced removals as inhuman and racist. The rhetorical strategy of the story in juxtaposing the stark contrast between Hunyani as the 'land of milk and honey' and Silobela as 'semi-arid', from Mr Nicolle's point of view, amounted to an attempt by the paper to incite the Hunyani people, an otherwise contented people into rebelling against government just like the Tangwena had done before them. This naturally elicited a strongly worded rebuke from him which when coupled with the very recent deportation of the *Moto* editor Fr. Michael Traber, must have had a spine-breaking effect on the *Moto*'s operations and thus put paid on Moto publishing any further story on the Hunyani removals. *Moto* soon appeared to lose its earlier fighting spirit to keep the story of the forced removal of Hunyani people alive on its pages.

Another probable reason why *Moto* could not sustain the momentum on its story of forced removal of the Hunyani people was a sense of betrayal that most readers who wrote letters to *Moto* expressed when they openly eulogised Tangwena in comparison to the other chiefs who appeared to cooperate with government and never put up any form of resistance in the fight for their people's rights. Some letters which were openly critical of the Hunyani chiefs' lack of spine included the one published in *Moto*'s July 1970 issue, written in ChiShona and titled: 'Tangwena murume wevamwe varume' (Tangwena is a man among men). In the same issue Rekayi Tangwena himself is quoted as calling the three chiefs Gobo, Ruya and Huchu, cowards and therefore deserving to be driven from their land, in a story headlined 'Vatsungirira kubvisa Rekayi'. In another letter to the editor written in Shona, and published in the November issue of *Moto* titled: 'Vanhu veHunyani reserve' the writer again puts blame on the chiefs for what happened to their people. The writer says:

> Panhau yevanhu veHunyani hatingasvori vachena chete ayiwa. Asi zvikuru madzishe. Deno madzishe ose aifunga savaRekayi Tangwena munoti Rhodesia ingasadai inorugare? Kuna ishe here anotsigirwa nevanhu vake nepamusana peutengesi? (On the issue of the Hunyani people we can't put the blame entirely on whites alone, No, but also the chiefs are partly to blame. If all chiefs thought like Rekayi Tangwena, Rhodesia would be a better country. Is there a chief who gets support from his people for being a sell-out?).

Moto, however, true to its mission as one of the few remaining newspapers for Africans continued to ventilate African opinion on issues that affected its readership one of which was about land segregation. It was the only paper remaining that kept a sustained coverage of the Tangwena story closing that eventful year with a fitting tribute to Chief Rekayi Tangwena for remaining steadfast on the land issue by carrying the 'Tangwena anotizira mumakomo' (Tangwena hides in the mountains) as its lead story with a picture of him looking intently ahead as if at his enemies unflinchingly. The story also carried a supporting picture showing the Tangwena women hiding in the bush.

With regard to the two newspapers considered in this section – *The Rhodesia Herald* and *Moto*, it is important to underline the fact that from their inception, they addressed their messages to different audiences and this had a significant if not determining influence on the content they produced and circulated. 'The production of texts always has at least one eye on the imagined or target consumer and the kinds of text that they prefer to read' (Richardson, 2006: 41). *The Rhodesia Herald* from its establishment in 1891 as the *Mashonaland Herald and Zambesian Times* had dedicated itself to serving information and communication needs of the

104 *News silence on forced removals in Rhodesia*

white settler community. It sought and publicised different and competing shades of white opinion on issues of the day. When it began its life as a printed newspaper on 29 October 1892 *The Rhodesia Herald* had announced as its aim:

> to advance to the fullest of their powers the mining and agricultural interests, to discuss and to criticise moderately, but without fear or favour, the topics of the day or hour, and to promote fellowship and unity among all classes and sections of the white community (Gale, 1962: 19).

This editorial charter meant *The Rhodesia Herald* was, in spite of claims to the contrary, by definition an ethnic community newspaper out to serve interests of a geographically dispersed but ethnically defined community. It remained in this mode right up to the attainment of majority rule in 1980. This editorial orientation then broadly marked the outer limits of the discursive framework within which *The Rhodesia Herald*'s reporters and editors framed their editorial choices when reporting issues in Rhodesia. It was unambiguously white-interests driven, both in terms of manpower and content. Thus, on the basis of its editorial charter, to expect *The Rhodesia Herald* to have carried content that balanced off white opinion against African opinion would be to judge the paper unfairly. It was essentially a community newspaper although the white community it aimed to serve was less defined by geography than by race. *Moto* on the other hand, established itself as a platform for the ventilation of African opinion and was thus regarded as a credible source to turn to if one wanted to gauge African opinion on issues of common concern in the then Rhodesia and sets itself as a counterpoint to the hegemonic white interpretations of events in Rhodesia.

The context within which the press operated in the Rhodesia of the 1970s should be fully appreciated to understand why and how any newspaper of that time covered issues affecting Africans broadly and in particular the racial segregation of land and resultant mass displacements of Africans in the aftermath of the passing of the Land Tenure Act of 1969. The African oriented press had been whittled down to a whisper, after the closing down of such newspapers as *The African Daily News* in 1964 and the *Central African Examiner* later. The remaining church press *Moto* and *Umbowo* were monthly publications and their commitment to raising the African voice on issues could thus easily be drowned in the din of white opinion which enjoyed extensive daily coverage in the Rhodesian Printing and Publishing Company's daily newspapers, *The Rhodesia Herald* and the *Bulawayo Chronicle*. Official state censorship of the period from the declaration of UDI in 1965 to 1968 had firmly introduced a culture of self-censorship to a pliant press by the 1970s. Criticising in retrospect, what he perceived as docility in the official white press of the Argus Company John Parker (a former reporter at *The Rhodesia Herald* who got deported by the white regime for perceived left-leaning liberal views) states that:

> The Rhodesia Press as a whole and individual journalists in particular had done very little to fight for that freedom of the Press about which they so

often wrote so movingly in their leading articles. Malcolm Smith did in fact fight – but not for his right to print the news without fear or favour. He fought for the right to print nothing at all, which I suggest was a wrong battle at the wrong time for the wrong cause. He fought like a tiger to keep the blank spaces in his newspaper caused by the censor's scissors, and to avoid filling up the spaces with other news or leave, as other newspapers did, 'token spaces'. But neither he nor any other Rhodesian editor found the courage at any time to print the news the censor had removed, or openly to defy the 'laws' by which the regime steadily eroded the prestige and position of the Press. (Parker, 1972: 129)

Empirical evidence considered here would seem to suggest as more accurate a view consistent with Van Dijk's (1992) analytic tool of the ideological square in which it is partly theorised that the more negative the effects of elite people and elite nations' actions on social groups, nations and individuals who occupy a lower rung on the social hierarchy, the less likely it is for such an event to make headline news. Galtung and Ruge's thesis was mainly focused on what made it into news rather than on what the news would be silent on. It was based on an analysis of what was actually reported and not on what was left out. It stands to reason then, that where a conflict between the white government and its black subjects over land erupted as happened in the Tangwena case, the white press shied away altogether or toed the Rhodesia Front Government line by reporting the 'official' position as *The Rhodesia Herald* largely did with respect to the removals of the Tangwena and the Hunyani people in 1969–70. Thus silence on African issues defined *The Rhodesia Herald* editorial policy during most of the UDI period. It limited itself to circulating different shades of white opinion on all key issues of colonial policy in Rhodesia. In all but very few instances, *The Rhodesia Herald* used white individuals as sources for their stories thus affording them the opportunity to define and interpret the colonial reality primarily from a white racist perspective. Black forms of knowing were largely suppressed or simply excluded. In all the cases in which *The Rhodesia Herald* reporters found it meet to report on the events related to the forced removals of Africans in the Tangwena and the Hunyani cases cited above, African voices were systematically excluded or edited out of the news text. An important point to note is how the inferioritisation of blacks was materially produced in social practices of which physical and brutal uprooting of indigenous people, economic marginalisation, racial geo-landscaping and symbolic annihilation and displacement of the 'native' subject population formed an important unity. The news text was produced by and was in turn productive of the racist system with which it formed a continuum. By under reporting or maintaining silence on the political processes through which Africans were plunged into poverty by the thousands, the press became complicit in the making of white aristocracy and the manufacture of blackness as representing lack.

Michel Foucault uses the concept of the dispositive to explain 'a kind of "formation', an ensemble of heterogeneous elements whose major function it has been at a

106 News silence on forced removals in Rhodesia

given historical point in time to respond to an urgency"' (Jäger and Maier, 2009: 41). It describes a mobilising force where different elements are connected for a common cause which must be urgently addressed. In the context of this study the colonial situation in Rhodesia of the late 1960s, the urgency to which the concept of the dispositive would probably have applied was the need for entrenching white privilege for all time, in the name of 'retaining government in responsible hands' against the threat of rising African nationalism (*Moto* 10 June 1969). Thus, it is important to note that Foucault, in his theory of the dispositive, is less interested in differentiating between what is discursive or what is non-discursive among the elements that a dispositive as the connecting net, bonds together. The concept gets closer to the ordinary meaning of pre-disposition in so far as it means an orientation towards. Since this study delimits itself to a consideration of an aspect of language use in the form of news texts, my reference here to the concept of the dispositive is confined to the very limited objective of clarifying the non-discursive para-linguistic context within which news about forced removals was produced and the range of epistemic interpretations of the colonial situation it made possible. In this particular context news as the discursive element of the colonial dispositive did not operate in isolation but was located in a network of other elements like the racial geographisation of racial dominance etched on the land itself and other legitimating elements like the legal system that enabled it. The effectivity of the dispositive, it would appear, was premised on the assumption that all elements in the ensemble were well integrated towards the singular objective of addressing the urgency with no room for internal contradiction. White supremacy and racial privilege would, as Van Dijk argues be 'supported or condoned by other group members, sanctioned by the courts, legitimated by laws, enforced by the police, and ideologically sustained and reproduced by the media or textbooks' (Van Dijk, 1993: 255).

Thus the attainment of independence would theoretically mean that a new urgency emerges to replace the old colonial one. Instead of seeking to entrench racial domination, the new urgency would be about decolonisation and deracialisation. This would necessarily entail a transformation of the elements of the old dispositive to make it serve the new urgency. The news as part of the discursive elements of the dispositive would be expected to reflect this change. Whether and how this was the case in the discursive representation of forced displacement of subaltern groups in the mainstream press is the focus of the remaining sections of this book.

A point of consensus between colonial and missionary attitudes towards Africans was in their regard of Africans as an inferior race in need of the civilising encounter with European colonialism. Donal Lamont's defence of rights of indigenous primitive people argues: 'Moreover, even though as far as growth in civilisation is concerned, they may be regarded as "children" they still have, just as minors can have, "dominium" rights of ownership. From this it follows that any violent seizure of territory which was at the time inhabited and cultivated by a native tribe ... constitutes unjust aggression' (Plangger, 1968: 29). Thus the missionary charitable attitude towards the African was premised on no higher moral ground than that of the colonial government whom the church admonished to always 'remember that their power is tutelary, and that they act towards the indigenous people as elder brothers in the human family, they can even perform a great work of charity by so colonising', (Plangger, 1968: 31). In the same pastoral letter Bishop Donal Lamont warned against what he regarded as some of the evils of Western civilisation upon the African that African nationalism ought to be about: 'a refusal to be stripped of their ancient character and turned out in mass production, decharacterised and presented to the world as ersatz Europeans'.

Conclusion

This chapter focused on how *The Rhodesia Herald* representing the white press establishment targeting a white readership, and *Moto*, as the leading missionary press targeting an African readership approached the coverage of the removals of the Tangwena people from Gaeresi Ranch and the Hunyani people from the Central Estates area between 1969 and 1970 in the then Rhodesia. These newspapers and their reportage on these events became part of a larger theatre in which the struggle for control of the hearts and minds of men played themselves out during the colonial era in Zimbabwe. A news text as a genre of writing makes the claim that it constitutes a record of fact about what actually happens in history. In this way it is often far more successful in concealing its ideological vestments than other genres of writing. The above analysis of the two papers' coverage of the Tangwena and Hunyani issues clearly demonstrates how those stories became a site of struggle where a racist ideology was imposed, challenged and at times subverted through hegemonic and counter-hegemonic discursive practices of narration and newsification, much more importantly silencing on events about the Tangwena and Hunyani people. *The Rhodesia Herald*'s stories largely reproduced discourses of a white supremacist ideology of the Rhodesia Front Government by legitimising and naturalising white seizure of black owned land and by displacing the narrative of black resistance as inauthentic and white inspired and instigated in a process of thingification and objectification which denied the African of his humanity. *Moto* on the other hand, subverted this ideology by giving a voice to those in the margins and by privileging a counter-hegemonic perspective on issues and placing the struggles over land in their proper historical perspective. In the next two chapters, I examine any genealogical connections or disruptions of coloniality in the way the press reported mass evictions and forced displacements of both whites and blacks in independent Zimbabwe under the fast track land reform programme in the year 2000, and evictions of urban slum dwellers in 2005 through a government operation purportedly aimed to restore order in Zimbabwe's cities.

Notes

1 The assegai was a short stabbing spear which required the fighter to get to within arm's reach of the opponent in order to strike him down in close combat.
2 Lord Olivier Address to the House of Lords UK, June 1926.
3 Parliamentary Debates of the House of Lords UK, of 23 June 1926: 543.

108 *News silence on forced removals in Rhodesia*

References

Ashcroft, B., 2001. *On post-colonial futures: Transformations of a colonial culture.* A&C Black.

Beach, D.N., 1970. Afrikaner and Shona settlement in the Enkeldoorn area, 1890–1900. *Zambezia* 1, 25–34.

Cesaire, A., 1972. *Discourse on colonialism* (J. Pinkham, Trans.). Monthly Review Press.

Desmond, C., 1970. *The discarded people: An account of African resettlement.* Christian Institute of South Africa.

Dombo, S., 2018. African newspapers and the development of the private press in Rhodesia, in: *Private print media: The state and politics in colonial and post-colonial Zimbabwe.* Springer, pp. 21–49.

Fanon, F., 1963. *The wretched of the earth.* Grove Press.

Frederikse, J., 1982. *None but ourselves: Masses vs. media in the making of Zimbabwe.* Heinemann.

Furedi, F., 1989. *Mau Mau war in perspective.* J. Currey.

Gale, W., 1962. *History of the Rhodesian printing and publishing company.* Madorn Print.

Hughes, D., 2010. *Whiteness in Zimbabwe: Race, landscape, and the problem of belonging.* Springer.

International Commission of Jurists, 1972. *Racial discrimination and repression in Southern Rhodesia.* The Catholic Institute for International Relations, London and International Commission of Jurists. Geneva. Accessed 22 December 2019 from: https://www.icj.org/wp-content/uploads/1976/01/Southern-Rhodesia-Racial-discrimination-and-repression-report-1976-eng.pdf.

Jäger, S., Maier, F., 2009. Theoretical and methodological aspects of Foucauldian critical discourse analysis and dispositive analysis. *Methods Crit. Discourse Anal.* 2, 34–61.

Joanne, S., 2009. *Geographies of postcolonialism: Spaces of power and representation.*

Kalande, W., 2008. Kenyan land disputes in the context of social conflict theories. Presented at the FIG Commission. Accessed 11 May 2019, from:https://www.fig.net/resources/proceedings/2008/verona_am_2008_comm7/papers/13_sept/kalande_paper.pdf.

Lessing, D., 1968. *Going home* (1957). Ballantine.

Loomba, A., 1998. *Colonialism/postcolonialism.* Routledge.

Makunike, E.C., 1998. *I won't call you Sir.* Harare SAPES Books.

Palmer, R.H., 1977. *Land and racial domination in Rhodesia.* Heinemann Educational.

Parker, J., 1972. *Rhodesia: Little white island.* Pitman.

Phimister, I.R., 1988. *An economic and social history of Zimbabwe, 1890–1948: Capital accumulation and class struggle.* Addison-Wesley Longman.

Plangger, A.B., 1968. *Rhodesia–the moral issue: Pastoral letters of the Catholic bishops.* Mambo Press.

Richardson, J., 2006. *Analysing newspapers: An approach from critical discourse analysis.* Palgrave.

Riddell, R.C., 1978. *The land problem in Rhodesia: Alternatives for the future.* Mambo Press.

Riddell, R., 1980. Zimbabwe's land problem: The central issue. *J. Commonw. Comp. Polit.* 18, 1–13.

Van Dijk, T.A., 1992. Discourse and the denial of racism. *Discourse Soc.* 3, 87–118.

Van Dijk, T.A., 1993. Principles of critical discourse analysis. *Discourse Soc.* 4, 249–283.

Van Dijk, T.A., 1998. *Ideology: A multidisciplinary approach.* Sage.

Youé, C., 2002. Black squatters on white farms: Segregation and agrarian change in Kenya, South Africa, and Rhodesia, 1902–1963. *Int. Hist. Rev.* 24, 558–602.

5 *The Daily News* and 'telling the land story like it is'

Introduction

The previous chapter focused on how different newspapers represented and narrated the stories of conflict that arose as black communities responded differently to forced removals from their ancestral lands by the white settler colonial regime between 1968 and 1970. This chapter extends that critical analysis of the news discourse on reverse forced evictions and mass displacements of white commercial farm owners and their black farm workers on a national scale at the instigation of government beginning 2000 in a campaign ostensibly aimed at correcting colonial injustices in land distribution in a programme dubbed the Fast Track Land Reform Programme (FTLRP). The chapter seeks to tease out genealogical lineaments and connections if any between the colonial and the postcolonial narrativisations of forced displacements in a context where political actors have changed and especially where the principal victims of such displacements happen to be former white colonial masters. It examines the prospect that the newspapers under an African editorship were capable of returning ignorance about the adverse effects of government policy on white people. How far can it be argued that change of regime from white to an African one was a significant factor in how journalists at different media houses deployed their reportorial strategies in covering events of socio-political importance as forced evictions from the land? This chapter discusses the extent to which *The Daily News* lived up to its motto of telling it like it is in covering the Fast Track Land Reform Programme.

> I am talking about societies drained of their essence, cultures trampled underfoot, institutions undermined, lands confiscated, religions smashed, magnificent artistic creations destroyed, extraordinary possibilities wiped out. (Cesaire, 1972: 6)

Farm invasions, peaceful demonstrations, land repossession

In the preceding chapter we analysed news articles on the forced removals, in late colonial Rhodesia, of the Tangwena and the Hunyani people. The evictions, characteristic of many similar removals in different parts of Southern, Central

110 *The Daily News and 'telling the land story'*

and Eastern Africa throughout the colonial period, involved forcibly uprooting and relocating indigenous African communities from areas alienated for European settlement in terms of colonial land policies of land segregation based on race. The resultant demographic map of colonial Rhodesia looked like a quilt with large swathes of white farms and estates running across the central high veld with a smattering of black patches along its low lying semi-arid frills. The systemic and sustained land dispossession of black people was discursively re-presented in *The Rhodesia Herald* in a way that largely legitimated them. The colonial dispossessions could not be framed within a human rights violation discourse because somehow by right of colonial conquest the indigenous peoples had no more ownership claim over the land on which they stood. The news treatment of the events privileged white land occupiers over black evictees' perspectives and interpretations of those evictions largely because the journalists who wrote those stories, as John Parker (1972: 66) admits: 'As well as being journalists were also settlers'. The colonial press' silence on (what today would have qualified as crimes against humanity), legalised theft of black people's lands and forced relocations to the most inhospitable areas only fit for habitation by wild animals was not the result of journalism gone awry but rather as a typical outcome of what Malcolm X called the 'white and dangerous press' in the service of empire (Heise, 2018)

The systemic land heist by white colonial settlers spanning a period more than half a century from 1890 to the early 1970s was never imagined as such by the establishment press of the time, as clearly demonstrated in the foregoing chapter. The process according to which, 'more than 100,000 black Zimbabweans were moved, often forcibly, into reserves and inhospitable and tsetse fly-ridden unassigned areas', to make way for white settlers 'in just one decade, 1945–55' was either treated as completely not newsworthy or in those few cases when news reports filtered into newspapers, the reporting somehow did not generate a de-legitimating discourse by naming it as: 'land grabs', 'land invasions' or 'violent land occupations' or 'land seizures' (Hanlon et al., 2012: 36). Such negative epithets did not enjoy pride of place among journalistic circles of the time. That de-legitimating diction had to wait until an appropriate time and context. What then were the changed journalistic circumstances and press reconfigurations in which such epithets and invectives become conscionable in the coverage of white dispossession through compulsory acquisition of 'their farms' for resettlement of landless blacks under a black government-sponsored FTLRP in 2000?

Background to the Fast Track Land Reform Programme

In concluding her book on land and domination in Rhodesia, Robin Palmer (1977: 246) made the following prognostication:

> Land has been and is a major issue of contention … A variety of political solutions now appear to be possible, though none of them is inevitable. What can however be affirmed with certainty is that the most acute and difficult question confronting the first African, or African-dominated, Government of

Rhodesia/Zimbabwe, whatever its ideological hue, will be that of land, bedeviled by its past use as a political and economic weapon by the whites, and by the consequent mythologies to which this has given rise.

The racial geography of land ownership in Zimbabwe had changed little, two decades after the end of white minority rule in 1980. The Lancaster House Constitution had dictated the terms of initial transition to independence, imposing 'substantial limitations and constraints on the legal means and financial resources and political pace of land reform' (Alexander et al., 2003: 4). At the beginning of 2000, government embarked on an agrarian policy it called the Accelerated Land Resettlement or the Fast Track Land Reform Programme (FTLRP). What really triggered and precipitated this policy response to what Alexander et al. (2003) referred to as 'Zimbabwe's unfinished business', the perennial land question in Zimbabwe, had remained highly contested.

One school of thought (Selby, 2006; Scarnecchia, 2006; Raftopoulos, 2009; Moretti, 2017) argues that it was a survival strategy by the ruling ZANU-PF party whose political fortunes and relevance hung in the balance as had been clearly demonstrated in the rejection of a government-sponsored draft constitution in a referendum held at the end of 1999. Another school of thought maintains that the timing was purely coincidental, as the repossession of land had always been top priority for the liberation movement now in government and any seeming lethargic approach to the issue in the past was due to constitutional constraints that the Lancaster House Constitution had imposed on the independence government (Moyo and Chambati, 2013; Worby, 2001). Whatever the case might be, the geographical demarcation of Zimbabwe into European areas and African areas had remained the most-difficult-to-undo relic of the country's colonial legacy by year 2000. Whites remained where they had always been at the commanding heights of the country's commercial agricultural sector. Africans, whom colonial governments had herded off into 'native reserves' and kept incommunicado, largely remained there, and independence had done little to free them from these colonial labour 'concentration camps' that turned them out as cheap black migrant labour readily available for employment at white-owned farms, mines and factories (Mugari, 2015).

This system tended to reinforce rather than challenge colonial racist myths and prejudices about white supremacy and affluence and black inferiority and poverty. The difference in agricultural potential between white-owned commercial farms and the reserves also reinforced the myth that whites were hard working and industrious and that blacks were generally lazy and could only be made to labour by necessity or force. The racial difference also seems to come out when one compares the sheer volume of news coverage the resultant displacement of white farmers generated across the media divide – '… oh! "What a protest"' it all amounted to (Hanlon et al., 2012: 209). *The Daily News* in particular led the publicity campaign, against what it was wont to describe as 'the violent and chaotic seizures of white farms'. The farm

112 *The Daily News and 'telling the land story'*

invasions story remained top of *The Daily News*'s news agenda from when the first farm invasions were inaugurated by war veterans in 2000 until the newspaper was forcibly shut down by government in 2003 (Willems 2004). The newspaper did not solely rely on its own staffers to cover the land occupations on the ground, it relied mostly on copy produced by locally based correspondents of Western news agencies such as CNN, Reuters, BBC and Associated Press (AP) as well as by the well-resourced white farmers' representative organisations such as the Commercial Farmers Union (CFU), Justice for Agriculture (JAG) etc.

Palmer's (1977: 58) observation that: 'the native reserves which were created in Rhodesia at the turn of the century are important precisely because they have survived – with a good deal of amendment but recognisably in the same pattern – down to the present', remains very relevant in today's Zimbabwe as the bifurcated land ownership structure continued to bear the hallmarks of the colonial racist architecture many decades after independence. What started off as 'native reserves' in 1894 after the sacking of the Ndebele kingdom in north western Zimbabwe and was extended to the rest of the country in 1896 after the brutal putting down of native rebellion (1896–1897) due to superior fire power of the invading armies of the Pioneer Column, became known as Tribal Trust Lands (TTLs) in 1962. By 1970, the division of the land into European and African areas had been completed and firmly entrenched in the then Rhodesia through use of a combination of force, duplicity and then enforced by legal instruments. On the attainment of independence, the TTLs were christened Communal Areas or simply rural areas. From that time on, in official usage the derogatory 'native reserves' or 'Tribal Trust Lands' were no longer used to name the areas where Africans lived in independent Zimbabwe. The changes in name were not matched with any meaningful structural transformation of racial land segregation as Zimbabwe remained in essence, two countries, two economies two modes of production and two nations in one, with the black subsistence economy and nation tethered in subservience to the white modern capitalist economy and nation. What independence managed to achieve for most Africans was the masking of a colonial structure by a veneer of new toponymic signifiers that overlay a substratum of colonial signifieds and referents. Just as Rhodesia became known as Zimbabwe, Salisbury became Harare, former locations or African townships of Harare, Sakubva, Mutapa, Makokoba and Rimuka became known as the 'western suburbs' or simply 'high density suburbs'. The new toponymic identity did not herald meaningful alteration to the colonial legacy of intergenerational racial indignity Africans inherited. The reserve, from when it was introduced served as a hatchery and incubator for cheap black labour (Mugari, 2015). In *Waiting for the Rain*, the late novelist, Charles Mungoshi immortalised the stark contrast between European farm lands and the TTLs reserved for African settlement, viewed through the bus window as one approached Manyene Tribal Trust Land from the city of Harare past the rolling ranches of Hampshire Estates in the following terms:

The sudden transition from the rolling ranches of Hampshire Estates, with their tall dry grass and the fertile soil under that grass, in to the scorched nothing-between-here-and-the-horizon white lands of Manyene Tribal Trust Land, with the inevitable tattered scarecrow waving a silent dirge in an empty field, makes a funeral intrusion into the bus. (Mungoshi, 1975: 39)

The evocative associations of death, desolateness and despair cannot be mistaken in this rendition of Manyene TTL as a place to which Africans were destined to return when their labour was no longer needed by their European masters in the city, on the mines or on the white-owned agriculturally fertile rolling ranches of Hampshire Estates. This system had become so naturalised by Africans that any serious attempt at changing the status quo could not be imagined as anything but aberrant to the 'natural' order of things. Throughout the 1980s and 1990s the independence government had demonstrated on numerous occasions its intolerance of any form of spontaneous self-resettlement by the poor landless blacks on white commercial farms. Any such action was viewed as illegal squatting and was dealt with accordingly in terms of the law. What happened in Zimbabwe during the first two decades of independence tended to disconfirm Annia Loomba's assertion that:

The race relations that are put into place during colonialism survive long after many of the economic structures underlying them have changed ... the racial stereotypes that we identified earlier still circulate. A complex amalgam of economic and racial factors operates in anchoring the present to the colonial past. (Loomba, 2007: 129)

In the case of Zimbabwe, it was the economic structures that undergird the race relations and underpinned the ideology of white supremacy and black inferiority even though the rhetoric had somewhat shifted. Africans and whites were now 'equal' before the law, in independent Zimbabwe, but continued to inhabit separate economic universes.

At the International Donors Conference held in Harare in 1998 President Robert Mugabe had warned of impending conflict over any further delay in speeding up a managed and organised land resettlement programme:

We must move forward speedily and vigorously otherwise they will resettle themselves in a manner they deem appropriate. Such anarchy will not be helpful to anyone. We therefore trust that the government's efforts for orderly resettlement will receive the necessary donor support.[1]

Unfortunately, Mugabe's warning was not heeded much by representatives of donor countries present at this conference, as can be inferred from the less than expected support given in response. Two years down the line things turned out pretty much along the lines predicted by Mugabe and foreseen at the Donors Conference and the rest was history.

114 *The Daily News and 'telling the land story'*

Zimbabwe's shifting mediascapes

Once the black liberation movement assumed governmental power it had eased itself into the shoes of its colonial predecessor and pursued a policy of reconciliation with its erstwhile enemies. In essence, the independence government did not stop at just trying to reconcile the warring blacks to their former white oppressors. It went further than that. It literally gave a new lease of life to the colonial exploitative and extractive institutional framework which it maintained in place to the continued detriment of formerly excluded black majority. Tony Namate aptly captured the pervasiveness of the colonial culture, the reproduction of dominance and servitude beyond temporalities and spaces of (post)coloniality in Zimbabwe in his cartoon shown below:

Figure 5.1 Cartoon by Tony Namate depicting oppression of the poor, before and after independence. Source: Reprinted by permission from *The Daily News*.

The burden of exploitation and poverty continued to weigh just as heavily on the subaltern's backs after independence as it had done before then. The new class of exploiters was different from the former only in skin colour but the system remained just as exploitative if not worse. This is not to suggest that the meaning of the cartoon could be fixed one way or the other. That its value as a sign would be polysemic and its meaning slippery is almost inevitable. A possible colonial nostalgia could also be read off the figures of the cartoon. The oppression of the dominated figure appears actually more acute after independence as the oppressed bear their burden bare-footed. They cannot afford even broken sandals as under colonial rule. Whatever is left of their colonial inheritance by way of items of clothing is now held together with patches. There are no more banana peels on the ground, a sign that the same load has to be borne under conditions of belt-tightening austerity on the part of the exploited class. Exploitation in the independence era seems to continue unremittingly to affect the same groups it did under white colonial rule. The exploited, after independence must obviously look back with the benefit of hindsight and recall with a sense of nostalgia, that white domination was by comparison more benign. The difference: media then were proscribed under pain of death from bearing witness to the processes and conditions of the under-class; media now operate under no such prohibition. The remaining four chapters of this book address themselves to illustrating why and how. The press' incapacity to cover the oppressed cannot be entirely blamed on government action; part of that incapacity is wired into its DNA as an original sin according to which the poor are not a subject of news. The story of the cartoon above is the story journalism actively silences. The story that the poor of this world haven't benefited from the much-vaunted end of colonialism, that their condition has gotten much worse is a story that, if written at all, points an accusatory finger at the victim. The poor's story also scores so poorly on all factors journalism uses to rate the newsworthiness of events. First, the decline in living conditions of the poor is not an event it is a condition that comes of slow, often invisible workings of impersonal structures. Most importantly, it fails dismally on the points of cultural proximity to journalism's imagined audience, those with the wherewithal to buy both the newspaper and the wares advertised therein. You can take the journalist into the land of the poor for a whole year and they will file no story until a stray government minister or Member of Parliament passes by. When they get desperate for a story they might as well turn to navel gazing and exoticising these strange places. The journalist may walk into a public health facility and witness the poor die of a heart condition gone wrong or of hypertension or of a contagious disease and the story in the following day's paper will be about the unhealthy life-styles of the poor themselves, their unhygienic ways, the viral load etc. In those cases when the journalist happens to be conscious of his watchdog role, he blames it all on a pathological disinclination for democracy and good governance among African politicians in government. The journalist finds no connection between the misery of the poor and the rise in profitability and rate of return on equity for business corporations. Event reporting journalism will not infer from the facts a causal link between the decline in public health delivery system in a country and the macro-economic policies meant to make the country an attractive destination for foreign direct investment – market deregulation, tax holiday packages for corporates etc. It's misgovernance, stupid. Journalism has no capacity to see the work of the invisible hand of a market fundamentalism gone global.

116   *The Daily News and 'telling the land story'*

The Daily News and a counter-hegemonic news agenda: 2000–2002

The Daily News, by its selection of name, had deliberately sought to tether itself to and benefit from the rich counter-hegemonic tradition of the *African Daily News* of the pre-independence period, a paper which had earned its stripes at the crucible of African nationalist struggle against white colonial domination in Zimbabwe (Dombo, 2014). When *The Daily News* started in 1999 not an insignificant number of its staffers had spent the formative years of their career at one of Zimpaper's newsrooms. In fact, the entire editorial leadership of the paper had cut their journalistic teeth at one or other of the government controlled Zimpapers (1980) Limited's newspapers or Ziana as shown in Table 5.1:

Table 5.1 Zimpapers as alma mater for most journalists in Zimbabwe. Source: Saunders, 1999

Name of journalist	Position at The Daily News from 1999	Past position(s) held at Zimpapers
Wilf Mbanga	Founding executive and managing director ANZ	Editor in chief, Community Newspapers Group Founding editor, Ziana (1981–1983)
Geoffrey Nyarota	Founding editor-in-chief	Editor, *The Financial Gazette* (1990–1991) Editor, *The Chronicle* (1983–1989) Editor, *The Manica Post* (1982–1983)
William Saidi	Founding deputy editor	Zimpapers Group Features and Group Foreign editor (1984–1990) Editor, *The Sunday News* (1982–1984)
Davison Maruziva	Founding assistant editor	Reporter, *The Chronicle* (1983–1989)
John Gambanga	News editor	Editor, *The Manica Post* (1992) Features editor, *The Herald* (1987–1992)

An important legacy of *The Herald* on other national newspapers including *The Daily News* is in guaranteeing a pro-elite and anti-poor slant in the news content through usage of English as the de-facto language of 'serious' news and the capital city, Harare, as the most obvious site to report it from on account of its proximity to the seat of governmental power. What is even more important is that *The Herald* also provides a vital symbolic link with Zimbabwe's colonial past, discursively seeking to transcend but also providing at the same time: 'what (Mudimbe, 1988: xi) has called the colonial library—the grand narratives, tribal tropes, distorted images, and 'natural' histories that forged 'the foundations of *news* discourse about Africa' and that, as Mbembe (2001) so vividly demonstrates, remain firmly entrenched in the postcolony? (Apter, 2007: 1). This is not to suggest, however, that the colonial library was a sole and unilateral imposition from above. It was co-produced at the intersection or confluence of contestations between the dominating colonial ideological impositions and the tension between cooperation and resistance by dominated subaltern groups. The newsroom presented the theatre of struggle and historical conjuncture of contradictory tendencies in postcolonial Zimbabwe, post-2000. Thus in an environment where *The Herald* as the leading daily newspaper in Zimbabwe had become a mouthpiece of the ruling party in government, *The Daily News* saw as its vocation to provide ventilation to the alternative story as a counterpoint to the government mouthpiece's version. Thus, in a conflictual situation like that which the farm invasions presented, *The Daily News* naturally found itself aligning with those opposed to the government's position on the issue. It boldly nailed its adversarial colours to the mast with a motto that promised 'Telling it like it is'. *The Daily News* invited its readers to take its story for a fact and guaranteed a 'truer' account of events than that of any other paper in the country. As the selection of stories analysed below demonstrate, 'telling it like it is' was no mean standard for any newspaper to measure up to.

News values and newsroom practices at *The Daily News*

The Daily News's role as a source of alternative interpretations on the prevailing social, economic and political reality in Zimbabwe was cut out for it by the evolving competition for political authority between the ruling ZANU-PF and the newly formed Movement for Democratic Change (MDC), a political party that brought together a coalition of the labour movement, the student union and other activist civic organisations increasingly disillusioned by government's adoption and implementation of neoliberal economic austerity measures under the Economic Structural Adjustment Programme (ESAP) in the 1990s decade (Kagoro, 2003; Laakso, 2003)

The news production process at the re-launched *Daily News* is in many ways similar to and a continuation with the tradition of the paper before it was closed down by government for failing to comply with a legal provision requiring it to register under the new media law, the Access to Information and Protection of Privacy Act of 2002. A typical day at *The Daily News* starts off with a diary meeting chaired either by the editor-in-chief himself or his deputy or by the news editor, in instances when the two top men are busy. The meeting is attended by all reporters and some members of the sub-editors desk. The meeting starts off with a review of the day's paper. Any errors and mistakes are noted and discussed with suggestions given of how such mistakes could have been avoided in the first place. The lead story is particularly analysed and compared with news headlines the rival papers chose to lead with. During such discussions editors have often expressed satisfaction with the performance of the team especially when the story they decided to lead with happened to be close to or similar to that the rival publications would have also chosen as the most important story of the day – evidence of a 'pack journalism mindset' (Matusitz and Breen, 2007). They mainly benchmarked themselves on their lead competitor on the privately owned national dailies market, *Newsday*. They also considered it a mark of excellence to the extent that their news headlines differed from *The Herald* as much as they conceded that the publication was a standard bearer when it came to the professional finesse that *The Herald* was always a good example of.

118 *The Daily News and 'telling the land story'*

In one such meeting the issue of the other independent daily newspaper leading with the same news headline 'word for word' was noted with concern that it could no longer be attributed to sheer coincidence or to the phenomenon of journalists hunting together. The editor had to raise this matter in the diary meeting and he immediately launched an investigation to find out if there was a mole who was leaking *The Daily News* headlines to their competitor and new measures were taken to plug any such leakages. Instances when the paper breaks an exclusive story were also hailed as a mark of high performance and exclusive sources were highly sought after and aggressively pursued because, as the editors often impressed it upon their charges, exclusive headline stories sell the paper. As a way of instilling a sense of collective responsibility for the paper, sub-editors were required as a matter of policy, after layout had been approved by the proof readers, to display on the notice board every completed page as it was expected to appear in the next morning's edition of the paper. It was then everyone's duty to scrutinise the pages and point out any mistakes for correction if they noted any before the paper went to print. This mode of operation inculcated a strong sense of teamwork at *The Daily News* which seemed less evident at bigger newsrooms like Herald House.

Box 5.1 Fast Track Land Reform Programme timeline

Year 2000:

16 February.	War veterans commence farm invasions in protest against the 'no' vote in a constitutional referendum
1 March.	War veterans invade a total of 27 white-owned farms countrywide
3.	Police issue an ultimatum ordering war veterans to end farm siege
4.	war vets defy order to vacate farms
18.	High court rules farm invasions by war veterans illegal and grants CFU relief by ordering war vets to leave occupied farms within 24 hours
20.	War veterans defy court order to vacate commercial farms
3 April.	Police officer shot dead, a Marondera white commercial farmer, Ian Kay attacked and injured at his farm by war veterans
6.	Parliament passes constitutional amendment bill to empower government to acquire land without paying compensation.
13.	Government orders war veterans to leave farms
15.	A Macheke white commercial farmer Stephens shot dead becoming the first white farmer to die in clashes with farm invaders.
18.	A Nyamandlovu white commercial farmer Mr. Martin Olds shot dead

Year 2002:

9 May.   Government issues a 90-day notice of eviction to over 2,000 white commercial farmers whose land had been designated for resettlement of landless blacks.

9 August.   More than 1,600 white commercial farmers leave their farms in compliance with government notice of eviction.

The invasion of white-owned farms retroactively legalised under an intensified government land reform programme FTLRP beginning March 2000 was greeted with a sense of outrage and consternation in both local sections of the press and international press. There was almost unanimity in condemnation of government takeover of land belonging to white farmers for redistribution to landless black Zimbabweans. *The Daily News* was one paper that kept the land issue firmly on top of its news agenda for three years running from 2000. In this section I make close reference to a few typical newspaper articles for analysis and discussion. A point that immediately strikes one as worth noting is the relatively large volume and prominence given to the seizures of white-owned land by war veterans for resettlement of landless blacks compared to land seizures of blacks' ancestral lands by white settlers during colonial rule, considered in the previous chapter. One thing that becomes evident is that takeover of land and forced eviction of incumbents becomes more newsworthy when blacks are perpetrators and whites the victims. Even the pro-state press could not ignore the story of farm invasions and occupation of white farms as it had done in cases where Africans were the victims.

When the farm invasions started in March 2000 *The Daily News* coverage of the phenomenon differed little from that of *The Herald*. At first the objective was just to give publicity to what the paper deemed a very significant political unfolding. The story had all the necessary news ingredients that recommended it to any journalist with a nose for news.

Box 5.2 Typical news headlines in *The Daily News*

Opposition political parties condemn farm invasions (1 March 2000: 3)
CFU says invaders have taken over 40 commercial farms (2 March 2000: 2)
Farm invasions worry EU (2 March 2000: 3)
War vets ordered off farms (3 March 2000: 1)
Farmers to meet war vets (3 March 2000: 6)
War vets defy State orders to vacate farms (6 March 2000: 1)
Hunzvi to tour invaded farms (7 March 2000: 2)
Mugabe urged to stop invasions (15 March 2000: 1)
Business Leaders' Forum condemns farm invasions (16 March 2000: 2)

120   *The Daily News and 'telling the land story'*

The farm invasion story was rarely off the front page of *The Daily News* during the first month of its inception. The reportage of the story at *The Daily News*, moved from a focus on raising alarm, where news reports were concerned with setting the terms of the discourse and indications of the magnitude and scale of the event. It ran headlines such as: 'CFU says invaders have taken over 40 commercial farms' (2 March 2000: 2), delegitimising the farm invasions as illegal, chaotic and violent. And, as it became increasingly clear that war veterans enjoyed government's tacit support and were not going to back down, the paper's focus shifted to a concern with exposing government complicity in a clear case of breakdown of rule of law and human rights violation and finally to underscoring the negative effects on the economy and on the white evicted farmers as well as their black employees.

The Daily News's motto: 'Telling it like it is' made the claim that the news stories it put out were a mirror image of what was actually happening in society. It gave assurances that those readers who wanted to get an unbiased account of reality would be sure to get such untainted accounts of the daily occurrences in Zimbabwe from its news pages. This motto made sense in a context where the Zimbabwean public was increasingly getting disillusioned by what was perceived as heavily biased reports from state media such as the Zimbabwe national broadcaster and *The Herald*. It was to this readership that the newly established newspaper organisation; the Associated Newspapers of Zimbabwe (ANZ), publishers of *The Daily News* sought to address themselves. In their published editorial charter (*The Daily News*, 31 March 2000) the newspaper group had described itself as an independent newspaper organisation that had set for itself very lofty standards of professional and ethical reporting. They had announced that *The Daily News* as their flagship newspaper would pursue an editorial line that would be:

> independent of any political, commercial, or sectional obligations or commitments, and will not represent the interests of any one section of the population at the expense of another. They would strive to ensure there is no discrimination on the basis of race, gender, religion, ethnic group, sexual orientation or any physical attribute. Reports shall be fair, balanced and accurate, and diversity of opinion shall be encouraged.

On the face of it, the statement that the paper would not discriminate disarms any reader and turns off any ground for scepticism. But as it turns out, such testaments of faith when coupled with an unquestioning application of the professional journalism creed in news selection and news gathering would necessarily produce a bias of its own often in favour of the powerful elite and against the poor in society. For a newspaper to not discriminate and turn a blind eye on how racial positionality structures access to voice and positions people differently on the 'universal' hierarchy of credibility as news sources, is tantamount to practising the most insidious form of discrimination. Such a paper cannot claim to occupy higher moral ground than a paper which under colonial rule unabashedly

The Daily News and 'telling the land story'   121

discriminated affordances to voice on grounds of race. The fact that in a post-colonial context, where some blacks have joined the ranks of the affluent and therefore enjoy access to the news is no consolation for the majority of blacks who have remained in poverty and therefore excluded from privileged access to express themselves in the news, the reasons and basis for excluding subaltern views in the news may be different but the effect remains the same. News, by nature, is not about what has been said or what has happened but about who has said what, and editors of the two papers concurred on this point as aptly illustrated in interviews with the editors below:

> As newspapers, we are in business so we look at stories that sell. Prominent politicians on either side sell. For example, if Obama says your president must go, there is a difference between Obama and someone from the street saying your president must go, so the seller there will be Obama not that the pre-sident must go. The issue is not important. So if Biti says whatever he says because Biti is an authority in that area, has been finance minister, he is MDC secretary general and so on. So he has authority. But if one of your students comes here and says Mugabe must go it's not a story, same views exactly. (Interview with Stanley Gama, editor of *The Daily News*, 27/01/2014)

Asked whether one would be justified to charge *The Herald* as an elitist paper carrying stories written from the point of view of the powerful in society, the editor of *The Herald* made the admission that:

> Just like any other paper we can't escape the universal news values. They are universal, you look at the prominence of the person, the prominence of the event, the proximity, the unusualness, human interest aspect, the currency of the event. But we can't escape just like any other publication. I am sure someone would be willing to read about Robert Mugabe, Morgan Tsvan-girai than about some peasant in Muzarabani unless there is something bizarre pertaining to that peasant something unusual or something of human interest. So we can't escape from universal news values. In that respect we are guilty as charged. Also as a newspaper we are in the market to sell news and the audience, the people who buy, want to read about prominent people those are the people who interest them. (Interview with Caesar Zvayi, editor of *The Herald*, 20 February 2014).

The unequal distribution of discoursal power that limits the opportunities for subaltern groups to participate in naming the world they live in is so common-sensical and taken for granted at both *The Daily News* and *The Herald* that it becomes naturalised and unchallenged. And, according to Fairclough (2013: 43) such institutionalised ways of knowledge production become ideological, natur-alised and 'most opaque and may come to be seen as the norms of the institution itself'. The views expressed by the editors of the two papers above are not in any way unique. Jennifer Hasty, in a study of newsroom cultures of Ghanaian

122 The Daily News and 'telling the land story'

newspapers, discovered a very similar pattern when she remarked that 'journalists with the state press recognise official news when it is pronounced by officially qualified sources in specifically qualifying contexts. Without the official qualification, the truth is simply not newsworthy', (Hasty, 2005: 52). In postcolonial settings what this often translates to is a continual subordination of subaltern black perspectives to those of their erstwhile white masters as became the apparent case of the way *The Daily News* covered the FTLRP in the early 2000s.

Thus the editors of the two newspapers make no apologies for the obvious elite bias in their news offerings. Reporters at *The Daily News* generally structure their news gathering activities guided by a tacit acceptance as a universal truism, that news by and about prominent people sells. Economic imperatives play a critical role in the selection of news and news sources at *The Daily News*. They were also critical even in making choices about their location as a paper and the language in which to write. The capital Harare accounts for three-quarters of the paper's daily copy sells and 90% of its advertising revenue according to the paper's editor. But how that triple proximity to its main audience market, to its advertising market and to its 'credible' therefore elite news sources translated to the production of news content as a cultural product whose ethos was also proximate to that of the elite section of the population was generally lost to the practitioners. The news stories selected for close analysis below clearly demonstrate this inbuilt incapacity to reflect reality from subaltern stand points.

HEADLINE: CFU says invaders have taken over 40 commercial farms (2 March 2000: 2)

BYLINE: Staff reporter

LEAD: The Commercial Farmers' Union (CFU) says at least 40 farms belonging to its members have so far been invaded by war veterans throughout the country.

BODY: A spokesman for the CFU said: "We cannot give exact figures, but the information we have is that between 40 to 50 farms have been invaded. The figures are still coming in."

As the invasions continued, some commercial farmers said they now feared for their lives. A farmer whose farm just outside Harare was invaded yesterday said he was surprised the police were watching the ex-combatants engage in illegal activity. "As whites, we now fear for our lives," he said. "It is surprising that the police are not taking any action. This is lawlessness." ...

Wayne Bvudzijena, the police spokesman, would not comment on the invasions. "It's something I cannot comment on," he said.

Augustine Chihuri, the police commissioner, has said the invasions are beyond the police while Chen Chimutengwende, the Minister of Information, Posts and Telecommunications has also said there is no solution to the problem at the moment.

Chenjerai Hunzvi, the chairman of the Zimbabwe National Liberation War Veterans Association has been touring farms, encouraging the ex-combatants to remain on the farms. The war veterans have been invading farms in the past few weeks, saying they are bitter the draft constitution, allowing the government to grab land without paying compensation, had been rejected.

The picture accompanying this story clearly shows who is the subject and object of the camera gaze. The camera shot captures 'women', from the front, as they, 'rush to seize pieces of land on arrival at Sam Levy's Lilfordia Estate'. The cameraman is obviously standing on Sam Levy's farm for him to picture the women approaching the farm and thus is making the camera narrate the invasion of Lilfordia Estate as it would have been seen by the farm owner thus advantaging the farm owner's perspective of the event being recorded.

If one used Hall's hierarchy of primary and secondary definition, then schematically one would have the CFU, the organisation representing white farmers and some individual white farmers themselves occupying the apex of the inverted pyramid, followed by government authorities and at the bottom the war veterans who have not been directly afforded an opportunity to give their own side of the story but are only referred to indirectly as the perpetrators. As the diagram below clearly illustrates, the actual landless rural subaltern are conspicuous by their absence on the primary definition pecking order. They fall outside journalistic standards for credible sources for a news story. Such an inverted pyramid of definitional power in reporting the farm invasion story at *The Daily News*, with few exceptions, would generically look something close to the illustration below:

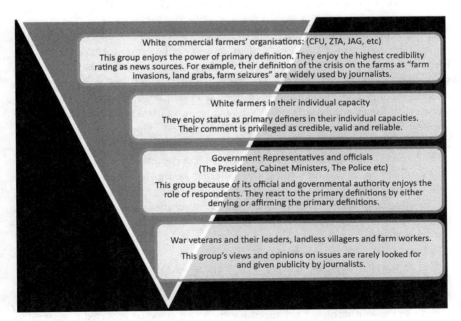

Figure 5.2 The power hierarchy to name in a typical farm invasion story at *The Daily News*.

124 *The Daily News and 'telling the land story'*

Although journalists at *The Daily News* wanted to think of themselves as always speaking on behalf of the underdog and think of their paper as the voice of the voiceless, in reporting the FTLRP, that commitment became narrowly defined to mean actively avoiding to be another government mouthpiece after *The Herald* and all Zimpapers publications. The paper therefore found itself most of the times they reported on the land conflict privileging white commercial farmers' voices on the issue and marginalising the real underdogs in this conflict, the farm workers and rural based landless blacks in whose name the programme was purportedly being implemented. Thus, in essence *The Daily News*'s claim of independence from external influence masked the paper's own ethnocentric biases in the way it reported the land conflict between whites and blacks. The way *The Daily News* (5 April 2000: 1) reported incidents of violence and killings on the farms in April 2000 demonstrates this point:

HEADLINE: Policeman dies in farm violence
BYLINE: Artwell Manyemba
LEAD: A police officer was shot dead yesterday at Chipesa Farm where on the previous day, farmer Ian Kay was severely beaten in violence that threatens to overwhelm the Marondera farming community.
BODY: Police withheld the name of the deceased officer saying her relatives had still not been informed. Kay's neighbour, Rodney Steel, said marauding war veterans have unleashed a reign of terror in the area. They speared to death four cattle and devoured the meat in a display of thuggery, he said. Police have been slow to react to the widespread anarchy, he said ...

Atop this story announcing the death of a police officer as a result of violent eruption at Chipesa Farm is a mug-shot picture showing the upper torso of farmer Kay lying on the ground face up, showing a blood spattered almost lifeless face from the severe beating at the hands of the invading war veterans. An accompanying caption announces: 'Ian Kay, a Marondera farmer who was brutally assaulted by people suspected to be ex-combatants at his Chipesa farm on Monday. Kay is said to have angered the ex-fighters when he failed to meet a deadline to reconstruct shacks belonging to the farm invaders that he had earlier destroyed.'

The layout plan of the story clearly gives secondary status to the death of the police officer by over-dramatising the suffering of the white farmers. The story headline would suggest the picture of the deceased police officer would have been the most appropriate to use with this story, but editors chose the white farmer's face as the more appropriate. Probably the dead body of the police officer was not photogenic enough and did not present as good a picture opportunity as that of a butchered white man's face.

But at another level of analysis it is reasonable to argue on the basis of the news value of proximity to prominent people that the death of the police officer on its own would not have attracted as much audience interest on its own merit.

But its newsworthiness got enhanced if somehow it could be reported in relation to the broader effects similar acts of violence had on prominent elite people like farmer

Figure 5.3 Front page of *The Daily News* on 5 April 2000. Source: Reprinted by permission from *The Daily News*.

126 *The Daily News and 'telling the land story'*

Ian Kay. As an event, the death of the police officer only makes news because of its nearness to what befell the white commercial farmer, Mr Ian Kay. Even as a lead it could not stand without leaning on the more important though less recent violence meted out on Ian Kay, the white farmer. That the police officer's death is comparatively of less news interest to the reporter's imagined readership than the disruptive effects of the eruption of violence on the white farming community, is made more evident in the second paragraph of the story where the police officer's death is given short shrift in just one line before being abandoned in favour of refocusing the story on effects of violence on white farmers. The terminology used by the white source, Rodney Steel, to describe the actions of war veterans on their farms borders on racial slur. He invokes the imagery and symbolism of wild animals when he uses such words and phrases as 'marauding', unleashing 'a reign of terror'; 'devoured the meat'; 'display of thuggery'; and 'widespread anarchy' with reference to the war veterans.

In 2000, however, reportage on the FTLRP was a little more nuanced and not just one dimensional in support of and sympathetic to the white farmers and against Mugabe's land policies. Although on the whole, stories condemning the land invasions easily formed the bulk of *The Daily News*'s reportage on the FTLRP, during the early phase of the programme, attempts were made to balance the stories by giving fair opportunities for comment from both sides of the conflict. In this way *The Daily News* strove to present a balanced view of the land conflict, giving expression to all contesting parties on the issue: government, white farmers, and war veterans leaders. Stories like the one sourced from the UK-based *Guardian* and published in *The Daily News* (Monday 24 April 2000: 12) though condemnatory of Mugabe's land reform programme as racist inspired, also castigates the British government as blameworthy for what was happening in Zimbabwe. The feature story which occupied the centre-spread of the paper on pages 12 and 13 is cited below:

HEADLINE: Britain not well placed to lecture Mugabe

KICKER UNDERLINED: 'Like Jack Straw and William Hague, Mugabe is using racism as a cheap – and not very effective means – of winning votes.'

PULL-QUOTE CENTRED: The recent land seizures mirror the thefts which first enabled the whites to control so much of Zimbabwe's economy. In the 1890s, Cecil John Rhodes and the settlers he led first cheated, and then forcibly dispossessed the Shona and Ndebele.

LEAD: The British establishment is poorly qualified to lecture President Mugabe about racism. The government's condemnation of the murders of two commercial farmers contrast oddly with the blandishments with which it greeted Russian President Vladimir Putin, the killer of thousands of Chechens.

BODY: Just as it revealed that Zimbabwe's white refugees are welcome for "reasons of ancestry" to settle in Britain permanently, it announced that it would expel 3000 Kosovan Albanians.

While the newspapers devoted hundreds of column centimetres to the horrible killings of the two farmers, they scarcely mentioned the equally horrible killing of a black foreman who worked for one of them. The dispute between London and Harare is a dispute between racists.

The Daily News and 'telling the land story' 127

Like Jack Straw and William Hague, Mugabe is using racism as a cheap – and not very effective – means of winning votes

The recent land seizures mirror the thefts which first enabled the whites to control so much of Zimbabwe's economy. In the 1890s, Cecil John Rhodes and the settlers he led first cheated, and then forcibly dispossessed the Shona and Ndebele.

The whites stole their land, their cattle and, through taxation, their labour. When they rebelled against those impositions, the blacks were cruelly suppressed and their leaders were hanged.

From 1930 onwards, blacks were forbidden to own land outside the barren and crowded "reserves".

Today though the laws have changed, the distribution of land has scarcely altered. Zimbabwe's 4500 white farmers occupy 70 percent of the best land, while some seven million blacks still inhabit the old reserves.

Readers write back

The 'Letters to the editor' page provides a point of interface between the readers and the editors of the paper. It also acts as a feedback loop which gives editors a clue as to which stories their readers followed. From time to time each published letter was some form of comment on a story carried in an earlier edition of the paper, as it inter-textually referred back to an issue the paper would have published before. In this regard the letters page provided the connective tissue between new developments and earlier aspects of a developing story like that one on farm invasions. The letter titled: 'There can never be a peaceful invasion', published on 16 March 2000, illustrates this point. This letter would make little sense unless read against a background of an earlier front-page story published in the same paper on 3 March. 2000, headlined: 'War vets ordered off farms'. In that story President Robert Mugabe had been quoted as having said: 'No, we are not going to put a stop to the invasions which are demonstrations, peaceful demonstrations and lawful demonstrations by the ex-combatants'. By pointing out the contradiction in terms in 'peaceful invasion' the letter writer casts a fresh light on the whole issue of trying to represent farm invasions as a peaceful demonstration and thus carries the debate forward.

On 13 April 2000 *The Daily News* published two letters on the same page which clearly demonstrate the paper's policy of encouraging lively and open debate on issues of common interest by giving publicity to views clearly divergent to the paper's own in that way providing an ideal public sphere and true market place of ideas at least on its letters to the editor pages. The two letters of more or less equal length occupy eye-catching positions on the letters page of 13 April 2000. One straddles the top middle section of the page, flanked by short one columnar letters on both sides. The other anchors the page and runs across five out of the six-column page. The top article which obviously is the lead letter is marked out by a double-deck headline with the largest font size and in bold. This layout technique also gives a clue as to the paper's preferred point of view on the land reform issue between the two stridently divergent opinions being articulated in the two letters cited below:

128 *The Daily News and 'telling the land story'*

Letter 1

Headline: Ex-combatants should avoid being manipulated

Body: May I through your popular paper, congratulate first Dzinashe Machingura and Webster Gwauya for coming out in the open as war veterans to show that not all war veterans are in the same league with the likes of Chenjerai "Hitler" Hunzvi and ex-dissident Andrew Ndlovu who perpetrate violence.

Machingura and Gwauya are true heroes who know what they fought for and they need the support of all war veterans and peace loving Zimbabweans. The liberation war was fought to remove the unjust system that prevailed then and it was not fought for a particular race. All the people of Zimbabwe contributed in one way or another to that liberation war.

Ask the ex-combatants who were at the front (not in Poland) and they will relate what role villagers played in the war. Ask the role that other races, including whites, played, in the war. Those of our former guerrillas who operated in urban areas will agree with me that some whites and Indians assisted in one way or another. They cannot now be held to ransom to keep one party in power, when it is crystal clear that change is required. Machingura and Gwauya should ask their former comrades to open their eyes to reality and see that the bush war ended 20 years ago and war against corruption and mismanagement of the economy.

My second congratulations go to Cain Nkala and the ex-combatants in Matebeleland for taking an avenue of negotiating with the white farmers on the land issue. This is a sign of maturity. Keep up your efforts. After all, the whites did not refuse to share the land with landless Zimbabweans.

Our black brothers, our leaders gave each other a number of farms that were meant for the resettlement of the landless. The best idea is to start by repossessing all those farms instead of interrupting production on farms that bring us foreign currency. After all, most of the farms that were given to our big black brothers are not producing anything. Nkala and his colleagues should not allow themselves to be used by politicians for their own selfish ends. The ex-combatants in Matebeleland should be reminded of the 1980s when they were hunted day and night by the Gukurahundi brigade. Today the same people who wanted you dead want you to cause violence and fight the whites.

Signed: Thebula, Bezel Bridge.

Letter 2

Headline: Blacks can be successful commercial farmers

Body: I will be glad if you publish this letter although I believe it's your policy not to publish letters written in support of land redistribution and sharing which, for reasons best known to you, you call, "land grabbing". That term would best apply to the way the land was taken by settlers a long time ago.

The Daily News and 'telling the land story' 129

If your car is stolen and then it takes you months to find it and when you find it should you be called a car grabber? Of course the thief will have reregistered the car using fake documents to make it legally his.

The situation here is you know where your bread is buttered. If Judas could sell Jesus for three pence what could millions do to those who are campaigning for land to remain in the hands of a few whites while the majority blacks eat grass?

Those who are familiar with the rural set-up know the pathetic situation which exist in these areas. People are crammed on unproductive, stony and sandy soil. Yet some of you want this situation to remain forever.

Why should we be condemned to unending suffering? Is it because of the colour of our skin? While planned redistribution of land would be the most ideal approach, it is also a fact that those who hold most of the land would not want to share it through peaceful means.

It is not true that blacks cannot be successful farmers but, what is true is that they have no access to resources such as credit facilities and inputs. After all, who does the donkey work on the farms? Experience is the best teacher. The good farmers of today have come a long way. They were not born good farmers. Let's share the land.

Signed: Martin Chikowore, Chinhoyi

Editor's Response: The Daily News is not at all against land redistribution. All we ask is that the exercise be carried out in a transparent manner for the benefit of all deserving cases. – Editor.

Through its opinion pages and letters from readers pages *The Daily News* proved much more accommodative of differing points of view on the FTLRP.

Most letters pages were organised along the general pattern shown below, with letters expressing very varied opinions on the land issue. This seemingly liberal perspective actually belied the paper's more critical stance against the manner the government implemented the land resettlement programme. This pattern was probably the paper's attempt at more faithfully reflecting and simulating the inchoate opinions of a society increasingly getting divided and polarised along political party lines. The object of the first letter is to highlight the lack of a broad consensus and unanimity among war veterans generally on the subject of land invasion.

There are some highly respectable war veterans out there, whose more impeccable war credentials place them in good stead to challenge the likes of the leader of the ZNLWA Chenjerai 'Hitler' Hunzvi.

The Matabeleland war veterans under Cain Nkala, are said to be taking a different, more 'mature' approach, that of negotiating with the white farmer. This letter deliberately seeks to tribalise the issue of land seizures by representing that there was difference of opinion between the Shonas and the Ndebeles. It rehashes the very emotive and divisive Gukurahundi atrocities allegedly perpetrated by the Shonas against the Ndebeles in the mid-1980s. The uncritical deployment of tribal identity markers such as 'Shonas', and 'Ndebeles' was itself problematic as such ethnic categorisations were themselves colonial inventions remotely related

Figure 5.4 A typical letters to the editor page of *The Daily News* 13 April 2000. Reprinted by permission from *The Daily News*.

to social relations on the ground. Phrases like 'liberation war was fought to remove the evil system then 'the bush war ended 20 years ago' are deliberately very imprecise terms that conceal the centrality of colonialism's very unjust land segregation policies as at the core of the unnamed 'evil system'. 'The bush war' invokes notions of barbarism and cowardice on the part of those who waged the armed struggle against settler colonialism as opposed to heroism and courage often associated with such terms as 'liberation struggle' or 'Chimurenga' which are used to celebrate the guerrilla war that brought independence as a glorious struggle. The letter also deploys rhetorical strategies of inclusivity to recruit the reader in defence of retaining the existing land ownership patterns. Instead of viewing the white farmer as the enemy the focus should be on warring 'against corruption and mismanagement of the economy', a shorthand for pointing an accusatory finger at the black political elite now in government. The blame is shifted from the white farmer whose productive farm 'brings us foreign currency'.

Letter 2, on the other hand, discursively deconstructs the paper's use of terms like 'land grabbing' to refer to the ongoing war veterans and landless villagers led land redistribution exercise. The letter also explodes the taken for granted assumptions that blacks cannot be successful farmers and whites are by nature successful at farming commercially. It locates the genesis of the current land dispute between white farmers and the former freedom fighters in the historical dispossessions and mass evictions of Africans from their ancestral lands by the BSAC's pioneer column beginning in 1890. In the salutation paragraph the writer pleads with the editor to publish his letter in spite of its opinion which was contrary to the paper's own view on the land issue. In making that explicit plea for publication of his letter the writer gives a clue about the editorial decisions and selections and how these possibly colour the reality being reported in line with the paper's ideological leanings and inclinations.

The Daily News and inter-media agenda setting

In 2002 the story of forced evictions of white farmers became a story written abroad for a global audience but also reproduced and read in Zimbabwe. At least 29 articles published in *The Daily News* in August 2002 were on or referred to the FTLRP. These included news stories political feature stories, opinion pieces, editorial comments, and letters to the editor. A total of six articles were written directly by some of the affected white farmers themselves nine came from Reuters London one from the *Washington Times* and seven were letters to the editor written from the diaspora in the geographic north, Canada, Sweden USA, UK (a strong pro-white farmer lobby based abroad). Only four articles are credited to *Daily News* reporters with the remaining four being letters from *The Daily News* ' local African readership or from known members of the opposition MDC party. Table 5.2 is an analysis of *The Daily News* stories on farm occupations and eviction of white farmers in August 2002.

Table 5.2 shows that *The Daily News* somehow gave wider publicity to the affected white farmers' accounts of the developments on commercial farms and

Table 5.2 The Daily News issues of August 2002: Analysis of stories/articles on FTLRP.

Date	Article type	Page	Headline	Author	Race	Country/Town
03/08	Letter to the editor	5	Farming not a mere way of life but an arduous business	Ndagumbuka Amai Nababa	black/Ex-farm worker	Chinhoyi/Zimbabwe
08/08	News	2	Farmers divided over exit package	Takaitei Bote	black/*Daily News* reporter	Harare/Zimbabwe
08/08	News	30	Evicted farmers gather for the final farewell	Reuters	Local Correspondent	Mvurwi – London
08/08	News	30	Farmers vow to fight Mugabe	Chris Chinaka	black/Reuters correspondent	Mvurwi – London
09/08	Letter to the editor	7	Gullible CFU now paying for its ostrich mentality	Charles Frrizel	white	UK
10/08	News	15	Evicted settlers accuse Mugabe of using them	*Daily News* correspondent	black	Masvingo/Zimbabwe
10/08	News	15	Wildlife artist hounded off farm	Chris Chinaka	black/Reuters correspondent	Harare – London
12/08	News	15	Government vows to punish farmers who defy eviction	Reuters	Local correspondent	Harare – London
12/08	News	15	Key dates on the land reform	Reuters		London
13/08	News analysis	6	World media misrepresenting facts about the real tragedy unfolding on the farms	Cathy Buckle	white ex-farmer	Harare/Zimbabwe
17/08	Letter to the editor	5	US must stand up for white farmers regardless of race	Jim Politano	white	Washington
17/08	Letter to the editor	4	Hounded out of a farm for supporting MDC	Kerry Kay	white ex-farmer	Bulawayo/Zimbabwe

17/08	News analysis	4	The Baas is dead, long live the fellow citizen	Fr Oscar Wemtar SJ	white Catholic priest, author of 'Breaking the Silence',	Harare/Zimbabwe
21/08	News feature	19	The death of a dream: a white farmer's story	Larry Norton	white ex-farmer	Harare/Zimbabwe
21/08	News	17	US labels eviction of farmers senseless act	Reuters		London
21/08	News feature	20–21	Mugabe runs out of ideas and money as famine spreads	Delan Walsh	white ex-farmer	Chadereka Zambezi Valley Zimbabwe
22/08	Letter to the editor	7	Whole world is watching disgustedly the racist based theft of farms	M. W. Leahy	white	Ottawa, Canada
23/08	Opinion	11	Farm evictions – a sad chapter in the country's history	Saul Gwakuba Ndlovu	black/Zimbabwean	Zimbabwe
23/08	News	32	Harare accuses US, UK of racism	Reuters		London
24/08	Letter to the editor	5	Racist seizure of white farms similar to Nazi dispossession of Jews	Claes Gylling Malmo	white	Sweden
24/08	Letter to the editor	5	Heroes' day preacher misquoted Bible on God supporting land grab	Thabang Nare	black	Bulawayo/Zimbabwe
24/08	News	26	Blair urged to snub Mugabe	Reuters		London
24/08	News	26	Illegal land seizures set to worsen food crisis, Gasela Warns	Collin Chiwanza	black – *Daily News* reporter	Harare/Zimbabwe

(Continued)

Table 5.2 (Cont.)

Date	Article type	Page	Headline	Author	Race	Country/Town
26/08	News	14	Grace Mugabe grabs choice piece of land	Adrian Blomfield,	white – Washington Times/Zwnwes.com	USA/Online
26/08	News	35	Straw blames Mugabe for impending mass starvation	Reuters		London
28/08	Letter to the editor	7	Mugabe's guts over land issue commendable	Erica		USA
28/08	Letter to the editor	7	Distribute land only to those with a farming background	Rachel		USA
28/08	Letter to the editor	7	Whites are equally Zimbabwean	Rudo	black	Masvingo/Zimbabwe
28/08	Letter to the editor	7	No to ruthless, unfair seizure of farmland!	Kesharibabu		UK
31/08	News	Centre/spread 16–17	Chidyausiku admits fast track land reform in Zimbabwe chaotic	Court Reporter	black – *The Daily News*	Harare/Zimbabwe
31/08	News Feature	Centre/Spread 16–17	The time has come for each and every Zimbabwean to stand up and be counted	Roy Bennet	white – ex-farmer, MDC MP	Chimanimani/ Zimbabwe

The Daily News and 'telling the land story' 135

very little space for alternative accounts of the evolving story of farm occupations. The white farmers' accounts were in that process made to assume the status of 'truth' through repetition and exclusion of alternative interpretations. The sourcing of those news stories was also heavily skewed in favour of white farmers and spokespersons in commercial farmers' organisations such as the Commercial Farmers Union (CFU), the Zimbabwe Tobacco Association (ZTA) and Justice for Agriculture (JAG). The picture one gets is of *The Daily News* playing megaphone role for largely Western opinion on events in Zimbabwe with Western news agencies such as Reuters featuring very prominently as agenda setter for *The Daily News* reporting on FTLRP. The imminent threat to civilisation, the barbarism and savagery of the farm takeovers by landless villagers was recursively lexicalised in the stories with the use of such phrases as: 'marauding war vets', 'thugs on the rampage', 'mayhem', 'chaotic land seizures', 'violent land grab'. Only in very few cases was the voice of the men and women caught in between (the farm worker and the so-called landless black beneficiary) ever given expression. Unlike their white counterparts, the farm workers and the landless villagers lacked the representational and organisational power through which their side of the story could be sourced and narrated. The language used invoked and tended to emphasise the breakdown of the rule of law and disorderly nature of the land redistribution programme if it may be called that at all. It characterised those spearheading it as irrational, primitive and savage and the white farmers as presenting the last line of defence for what Ian Smith, the last prime minister of Rhodesia once called 'western Christian civilisation'.

The only few instances when the unorganised opinions of ordinary people, both victims and beneficiaries of the land revolution then taking place in Zimbabwe, were confined to the 'Letters to the editor' section of the newspaper. Even in such cases the invisible hand of editorial oversight was quite evident as letters sympathetic to the plight of the white farmer in the FTLRP enjoyed wider circulation. An article published in the letters to the editor section of *The Daily News* (3 August 2002) attributed to one African child of a former farm worker demonstrates African complicity in what Mbembe (2001) describes as co-construction of colonial subjectivities. The farm worker expresses gratitude to the white farmer whom he regards as his benefactor and is therefore opposed to the government-sponsored takeover of the white man's farm mainly on the grounds that such action destroyed viable workplaces for many black farm workers who depended on the white farmer for their livelihood. It reads like the white farmer came with land from somewhere and out of his philanthropic magnanimity, created employment for Africans who must have been desperately in need of employment. The article, a letter to the editor (*The Daily News*, Saturday, 3 August 2002), is cited below for closer analysis:

HEADLINE: Farming not a mere way of life but an arduous business
BODY: I am writing this letter so that I can make few very relevant points. I was born on a commercial farm and I was educated at a local farm school. My father was a tractor driver.

136 *The Daily News and 'telling the land story'*

The farmer helped my father to educate my two sisters and myself. We completed secondary school and all achieved good results ... This farmer paid for my entire education. I have sent him letters to keep him and his family aware of my movements and progress in life. I am now a 35 year old successful farm manager.

My point is – this farmer helped me and others to achieve our goals. His farm was a very well-run organisation that employed some 126 permanent workers and their families. My heart cries out for him and his family and all the workers who were so well looked after. My father and mother who are now old and have retired, were evicted and treated like animals ... while these racist blacks destroyed a well-run unit. Who will feed Zimbabwe? I can tell you one thing – it won't be the five million pseudo-war veterans and their squatters.SIGNED: Ndagumbuka Amai nababa, Chinhoyi.

The white farmer in this story is obviously being used metonymically to refer to all white farmers in general as benevolent and the same is arguably true of the farm workers and their children and the mutually beneficial relationship between them. Implicit in the rhetorical question: 'Who will feed Zimbabwe?' are deep-seated assumptions about who between whites and blacks is naturally a better farmer in Zimbabwe. Left alone, blacks (pseudo-war veterans and squatters) cannot farm. Farming becomes a race thing. To be white is to be a commercial farmer and employer. The employer–employee role relationship between white commercial farmers and black farm workers occurs so naturally, matter-of-factly to the writer of this letter. The writer is conscious of his debt of gratitude to the white farmer for his benevolence. The imprint of an ideology of white supremacy and black inferiority is so indelibly inscribed so that it becomes natural that an African like him cannot aspire for more than just to become a better-skilled employee than his forbearers, 'my father was a tractor driver ... I am a successful farm manager'. To do what war veterans were doing, to usurp the white man's role, that of becoming farm owners themselves and employers is to go against nature in the reasoning of the writer of this letter and by extension in the reasoning of the editors who published the article. Farm invasions are unacceptable in the world of this writer, precisely because they destabilise a system of shared meanings and beliefs that structured the colonial world order. The implied inversion of roles which were the bedrock of a colonial and neo-colonial order is the crux of the crisis threatening to bring to an end the world order the writer had ever known and had come to accept as natural. The real Rhodesia, which John Parker (1972) had described as 'Little white island' had now come unstuck.

The privileging of white opinion on the FTLRP was unmistakable as opinion pieces authored by white farmers were often elevated to a status slightly above letters to the editor into featured articles, as many articles attributed to Cathy Buckle and Larry Norton's article below show. Larry Norton aptly captures the prevailing sense of loss among white farmers whose land was being seized by war veterans in his feature article: 'The death of a dream: a white farmer's story' published in *The Daily News*, 21 August 2002.

HEADLINE: The death of a dream: a white farmer's story.

LEAD: I sit in a storage shed in Harare, surrounded by the chaotic elements of our life and home and our piles of possessions, and try to reflect on the past few days. On Thursday 8 August 2002, we evacuated our farm – Dahwye – in Mvurwi, abandoning the home in which three generations of our family had lived for almost half of a century.

BODY: After two years of mayhem we could not stay on. The government sponsored land invasions had begun in March 2000, shortly before our 14-month-old son, Oscar, died from cancer. We were unable to spend his last days on the farm because of the trouble. He died in an apartment in Harare surrounded by refugee farmers from Macheke 75km to the east of the capital, where in April that year David Stevens, a supporter of the main opposition Movement for Democratic Change (MDC) was the first white farmer to be killed. Since that time we have lived through the unparalleled destruction of a country and economy, under the corrupt and dictatorial rule of President Mugabe and his Zanu-PF party. Our farm has been a microcosm of a battlefield. My mother and father came north from South Africa in the 1950s. They worked as managers on various farms and borrowed money to purchase Dahwye in 1957. They nearly went broke, and for a time my father lived in a tent made from fertiliser bags until he opened up a tobacco farm in virgin bush. It was in an area described as Terra Incognita, but he made enough money there to pay off the loan. We returned to Dahwye in the mid-1960s. I was born in 1963 ...

A full page was dedicated to this story, a moving account of how Larry Norton, now an ex-farmer and his family, had witnessed their world come shattering down around them like was the case for hundreds other white farmers who had recently left their farms in compliance with government eviction notices.

The plight of evicted white farmers is so eloquently captured and narrated in Larry's story. In the second sentence of his narrative Larry tells the reader: 'On Thursday, 8 August 2002, we evacuated our farm – Dahwye – in Mvurwi, abandoning the home in which three generations of our family had lived for almost half a century'. The long stretch of time referred to in 'three generations' and 'half a century' used in one sentence has the rhetorical effect of underlining and emphasising the writer's legitimate entitlement to the place which passage of time alone seems to bestow. The theme of entitlement is further strengthened and almost placed on a plane beyond challenge when the writer invokes the right of first discovery as the basis of that entitlement when he goes on to narrate the unparalleled hardships his parents had gone through to acquire and transform what was essentially empty 'virgin bush' into the modern farm that it had become at the point when it was taken away from them. He says: 'It was in an area described on the map as Terra Incognita ...'. If Larry's story is representative and microcosmic, as he claims it is, of the situation with regards how white farmers got the farms from which Mugabe government was now evicting them then indeed theirs is a situation crying out for justice.

Figure 5.5 A full page devoted to a white farmers' account of events at his farm. Reprinted with permission from *The Daily News*.

But history is replete with ethnocentric discursive constructions claiming emptiness of spaces as a convenient excuse to justify colonial occupation of territories already inhabited by indigenous peoples. If by 'terra incognita' is meant unknown then there is the question 'to whom or by whom and according to whose map?' That a place is not known to one or to those that one chooses to associate with may not be adequate proof that such a place is virgin and unclaimed. This only makes sense where African inferiority is accepted as a given. What can be inferred from the tone of this article is the fact that Dahwye would, without the civilising presence of its white owner, almost inevitably regress to its primordial bush state under black stewardship. Norton's white paternalist attitude towards Africans was widely held among the white farming community in Zimbabwe and easily resonated with views attributed to Eddie Cross by Hanlon et al. (2012: 9) ten years later:

> Eddie Cross, the opposition Movement for Democratic Change (MDC) MP and policy coordinator general, said in April 2011 that white farms had been 'invaded and occupied by this rag tag collection of people' who are just 'squatters' and that 'the majority of these farms have become largely defunct, their homesteads and farm buildings derelict and their arable lands have returned to bush.

Thus, when Captain Cook first landed on the shores of Australia in 1770, when in 1855 the Scottish explorer and physician, David Livingstone was first led by his African aides who already new about the smoke that thunders – Mosi-Oa Tunya, which he named after Queen Victoria of England; and when Henry Morton Stanley, the American journalist and explorer first arrived in the Congo in 1877, they all in characteristic European arrogance declared that they had discovered vast empty expanses, Terra Nullius, still in their virgin wild states and therefore in need of the white man's civilising influence. This was in spite of the fact that there were aboriginal races who had lived in these so-called new found lands for many centuries before. In a report he sent to his paper *The New York Herald* Stanley is famously quoted to have described the parts of Africa he had passed through as:

> one wide enormous blank ... an absence which is also a region of imagination and desire, a tabula rasa on which imperialism can fulfil its mission. It is at the same time the uninscribed, a land of fabulous possibility, and a land of the barbarous and sub-human. The unformedness of colonial space is the geographic metaphor of the savage mind; both consciousness and space form the childlike innocence which is the natural surface of imperial inscription. This process of inscription is not merely metaphoric, because it is in writing itself that place is constructed out of empty space, and it is in the control of representation and the dissemination of this control in literacy and education that the colonial subject is subdued. (Ashcroft, 2001: 40)

140   *The Daily News and 'telling the land story'*

Larry Norton's own reminiscence about his lost farm in this article betrays an uncanny similarity of attitude with that of old empire towards both the land and the indigenous people who have always lived on it. By extension, the absence of landless blacks' news accounts of the FTLRP from the pages of *The Daily News*, created empty spaces upon which white inscriptions such as Larry Norton's could be possible. Their articulations were often at the expense of the silencing of the black others. More important than the gaps and questions that Larry's and other white sourced news constructions of reality on the land issue in Zimbabwe, is in what is not discursively represented about it, what news discourse leaves unsaid or their silences (Willems, 2004). The unsaid of news often provides the blank canvas against which that which is explicitly stated may make sense. Larry's story and many such stories that alleged unjust government-sponsored theft of white-owned farms by war veterans make so much sense against an absence or media silence on the massive scandal of white seizure of the same land from blacks when it happened over a period of half a century of settler colonial rule in Zimbabwe. If indeed white settlers had expropriated by force or guile, Zimbabwe's most fertile land from blacks, we would have read it in the news, so the argument goes. Such is the power of news media, 'because', as Bird (2010: 2) argues: 'it purports to describe reality, news is clearly a crucial force in representing and shaping public culture'. What often passes as policy responses to social reality are in actual fact responses to published media versions of that reality. Examples of real policy options in direct response to the feature news story 'The death of a dream' above might include, among other things, suggestions about fair compensation for Larry and his farmer friends for the loss of their farms or reinstatement back onto their farms. Public policies less likely to be made in response to the version of reality painted by the same story, would be policies that seek to address farm workers' needs, rights and entitlements if any appear apparent at all. Least likely even would be policies about any Africans who may have been displaced or prejudiced somehow when that farm was established in the first place so many decades back.

Larry Norton's narrative of suffering and brutality that haunted them from their farm in Mvurwi is also important in so far as it claims to be representative of every white farmer's experience during this time. Other farmers paid the supreme price and this article makes a rather interesting revelation in an intertextual reference to the story that made news headlines in the local as well as international press announcing the murder of David Stevens, the first white farmer to be killed at his Macheke farm. Larry writes: 'David Stevens, a supporter of the main opposition Movement for Democratic Change (MDC) was the first white farmer to be killed'. A closer look at this sentence string raises the question whether Mr Stevens was killed for his being a farmer and white or for his political activism as a supporter of MDC, in politically instigated violence. If indeed his political affiliation was partly responsible for his being targeted by those who killed him, then the story becomes different and the press' reports of his death and the purported reasons can be argued to have been very misleading at least in so far as this very material fact of his political affiliation against the backdrop of the very tense political atmosphere prevailing in the country. The number of deaths, abductions and political intimidation of many MDC supporters during the time had been conveniently de-emphasised, entirely ignored or under-played in favour of his identity as a white farmer as the sole reason for his liquidation.

The nominal phrase: 'The government sponsored land invasions' in the clause 'The government sponsored land invasions had begun in March 2000' at the beginning of this article is only possible and makes sense where certain assumptions are held as given and these are that the land so invaded belongs to the white farmers who currently live on it as of right; that their title to it is not in question; that the government is culpable for the crime of land invasions. It is interesting to note the comparative inflections of meaning the same basic process of a government-sponsored compulsory land acquisition from white commercial farmers to resettle landless blacks acquired through editorial choice of lexical items and language usage as in the 'independent' press represented by *The Daily News* and the state-owned and controlled press, *The Herald* in the table below.

Table 5.3 Language of legitimation and delegitimation of the FTLRP in *The Herald* and *The Daily News*

The Daily News	The Herald
Government backed land invasions	Government-sponsored land repossessions
Invasions of white-owned farms	Land reform/resettlement
Land seizures	Farm occupations
Land grabs	Land acquisitions
Farm invaders/squatters	New farmers

The intended meaning would be different in each of the five pairs of lexical inflections above but in each case the government's responsibility for wrong doing is greatly diminished in *The Herald*, if anything it is actually legitimated. *The Daily News*'s choice of diction, on the other hand, is unambiguous in its criminalisation of government action on the farms.

Whiteness as news value

In the following stories published by *The Daily News* the single most defining news value was white identity of news actors or proximity to whiteness and consonance with existing notions of white ownership of land and property rights.

The Daily News, Thursday, 8 August 2002:

HEADLINE: Farmers divided over exit packages
BYLINE: Takaitei Bote
LEAD: Cracks showed within the Commercial Farmers' Union (CFU) membership yesterday over whether or not farmers should challenge a new labour statutory instrument, which some farmers say is unfair.

142 *The Daily News and 'telling the land story'*

BODY: Speaking during the CFU's 59th annual congress held in Harare yesterday, some of the farmers said statutory instrument 6 (SI 6) promulgated this year for farm workers affected by the compulsory acquisition of commercial farms should be resisted in courts because the terminal benefits suggested were too high and farmers could not afford the packages. This is not the first time that the CFU leadership and farmers have clashed over how to deal with issues related to the land reform programme.

The stance of appeasement adopted by the CFU, which does not want to appear confrontational by taking the government to court, has been rejected by some farmers who have decided to form a new pressure group, Justice for Agriculture (JAG) ...

Farmer after farmer called on the ALB to consider challenging SI 6 because it gave rise to some bogus trade unions which were inciting workers to force their employers to pay packages even in cases where the farmer had not been issued Section 8 orders. The Zimbabwe Federation of Trade Unions (ZFTU) is alleged to be instigating farm workers to force employers to pay them redundancy packages. The ZFTU is alleged to have extorted more than \$3 billion meant for farm workers' exit packages from commercial farmers issued with eviction notices in the past four weeks.

(*The Daily News*, Thursday, 8 August 2002: 30.) Atop this story is a landscape picture of white commercial farmers posing for a farewell photograph at Mutorashanga Country Club.

HEADLINE: Evicted farmers gather for the final farewell

CAPTION: Group of Zimbabwean commercial farmers have their photograph taken at the Mutorashanga Country Club on Tuesday. This is the last time many of them will see each other as they prepare to vacate their farms prior to a deadline set by President Mugabe's government. Mugabe ordered nearly 3000 white farmers to stop all production in June and gave them until tomorrow to vacate their farms to make way for landless peasants.

LEAD: MUTORASHANGA – White farmers gathered on Tuesday for what could be final farewells across Zimbabwe as many prepared to pack their bags to comply with a government deadline to quit their land.

BODY: President Mugabe ordered about 3000 white farmers to stop all production in June and gave them until 10 August to vacate their farms and homes to make way for landless blacks. On Tuesday, 60 farmers in Mutorashanga, 100km north-east of Harare, huddled for a group picture at the local social club and in some cases said their last goodbyes ... Reuters

The Daily News, Thursday, 8 August 2002: 30:

HEADLINE: Farmers vow to fight Mugabe

BYLINE: Chris Chinaka

LEAD: A NEW organisation of embattled white Zimbabwean farmers vowed on Tuesday to fight land seizures more aggressively through the courts - but a top lawyer said President Mugabe would ignore them even if they won.
BODY: Nearly 3000 white farmers, two thirds of the country's total have been served notices to get off their land this weekend, the first major group to face eviction ... Reuters

The Daily News, Friday 9, 2002: 10:

HEADLINE: Farmers paying heavy price for old sins
BODY: Mugabe has a magical spell. It bewilders his fellow African leaders into acquiescent stooges, and much of the west into embarrassed inaction every time. It is this: "My people were wronged by colonialism." Who perpetrated this great wrong? According to Zimbabwe's president, it is the tiny and shrinking band of white commercial farmers, that's who. Hence the Third Chimurenga, or war for land.

The Daily News, Saturday 10 August 2002: 15:

HEADLINE: Wildlife Artist hounded off farm. 'Norton battled tears as he tries to explain what the farm, nestled close to the Great Dyke, meant to him, his wife and their three children'
BYLINE: Chris Chinaka
LEAD: Mvurwi – Larry Norton has shown the best and the worst parts of his life on the Zimbabwean farm he called home until yesterday. Reuters

The Daily News story which it told consistently throughout the latter phases of the FTLRP, from 2002 onwards, was a story of the tragedy of the forced eviction of white farmers told from the standpoint of the evicted white farmers themselves as is clearly evident in the stories cited above. The story literally remained a top story in Zimbabwe's press for close to three years. It became a taken-for-granted feature of the press's news agenda. This agenda for *The Daily News* became a news agenda dictated to it by global news agencies like Reuters. If it was not on front page or the news sections – which was in fact the case most of the time, it was on the letters page or opinion and analysis pages of the papers. How it retained its newsworthiness cannot be fully accounted for in terms of a materialist realist operation of news values alone where the news event itself or the personalities involved have newsworthiness characteristics inherent in themselves which then recommend them to the professionally trained eye of the journalist as newsworthy (Bednarek and Caple, 2014). Such an assumption would expose the news value theory of newsworthiness of events and people as ethnocentric when applied in explaining how the eviction of white farmers was adjudged as newsworthy and the displacement of farm workers was not so newsworthy. The displacement of farm workers as an event shared most of the same features with that of the eviction of white farmers from commercial farms. What it lacked in terms of reference to elite people it more

Farmers vow to fight Mugabe

By Cris Chinaka

A NEW organisation of embattled white Zimbabwean farmers vowed on Tuesday to fight land seizures more aggressively through the courts – but a top lawyer said President Mugabe would ignore them even if they won.

Nearly 3 000 white farmers, two-thirds of the country's total, have been served notices to get off their land this weekend, the first major group to face eviction.

Some say they will go, others say they will defy the land acquisition and eviction orders, and the leader of the new Justice for Agriculture (JAG) group said they should all carry on fighting through the courts.

"We must continue fighting. We are challenging the orders through the courts because we have a very strong case that this whole process is unjust and destructive," chairman David Connolly a conference organised by his fledgling group.

Connolly said JAG was formed in the last few weeks to assert the legal rights of Zimbabwe's commercial farmers because other organisations were in fruitless talks with the government.

These included the long-established Commercial Farmers Union and the Zimbabwe Joint Resettlement Initiative, set up for farmers who offered voluntarily to over parts of their land.

"must not be apologetic about our rights," Connolly said.

"There is a very good chance we will get justice. We want justice, peace and freedom to produce food for the people of Zimbabwe."

Zimbabwe, once the breadbasket of Southern Africa, is now facing severe food shortages, largely due to the disruption of commercial agriculture.

Mugabe, sole ruler since the former Rhodesia gained independence from Britain in 1980, says the land plan will right the wrongs of colonialism.

His critics say the plan was designed to win votes in recent elections and, now, to reward his cronies.

One of the civic rights leaders and opposition figures invited to JAG's meeting said the courts would not be much help.

Eric Matinenga, a top black lawyer, urged the farmers to keep fighting, saying they had a strong legal and moral case which had to be recorded for posterity.

But he said Mugabe's government would not accept any court orders against his land seizure policy.

"I don't have any confidence that any result against the government is going to be obeyed," he said.

Mugabe forced Zimbabwe's top judge, who was white, to retire early last year, saying his rulings against the government's land seizure drive were meant to serve his kith and kin.

Mugabe, 78, has declared that he would never allow the law to be used to defeat his drive for land. – Reuter

Motorist assaulted during hijacking

A motorist last week was seriously assaulted and robbed of his car by a gang of violent hijackers. He was followed into his driveway by the gang who then proceeded to pull him out, strip him of his clothes, beat him up and then drove him in their hurry to escape with the car.

The vehicle was later recovered as it had an antihijack device.

This is an unforgivable crime against an innocent motorist and we would do well to take note. If your car is fitted with such a device, is it worth resisting the attack and subsequently being assaulted? You are going to get the car back anyway but safe one's instinct dictates how you will react. That is why we must discuss these eventualities within the family and agree on how we deal with hijackers. If we are aware at all times and are suspicious of anything, we must NOT go straight to a Police Station or somewhere very public. It is a fact, that if we resist in any way, we will be injured and, in some cases left for dead. AWARENESS is your ONLY PROTECTION.

Anti Hi-jack Trust, Harare.

A GROUP of Zimbabwean commercial farmers have their photograph taken at the Mutorashanga Country Club on Tuesday. This is the last time of them will see each other as they prepare to vacate their farms prior to a deadline set by President Mugabe's government. Mugabe ordered 3 000 white farmers to stop all production in June and gave them until tomorrow to vacate their farms to make way for landless pea – Reuter

Evicted farmers gather for the final farewell

MUTORASHANGA – White farmers gathered on Tuesday for what could be final farewells across Zimbabwe as many prepared to pack their bags to comply with a government deadline to quit their land.

President Mugabe ordered about 3 000 white farmers to stop all production in June and gave them until 10 August to vacate their farms and homes to make way for landless blacks.

On Tuesday, 60 farmers in Mutorashanga, 100km north-east of Harare, huddled for a group picture at the local social club and in some cases said their last goodbyes.

A barley farmer, who declined to be identified, said over 70 percent of the group were leaving, and that the majority would seek a new start in neighbouring countries or overseas.

"The mood around here is generally depressed. Most of us want to stay in Africa. I want to stay, but my government doesn't want me because of my colour," he said.

"There are neighbouring countries around us which have been very responsive and are actually asking us to come. They are opening their door to us."

Mugabe says his "fast-track" land resettlement programme is aimed at correcting imbalances in land ownership created by British colonialism, which left the bulk of Zimbabwe's prime farming land in the hands of minority whites.

Another farmer said while he had not been issued with an eviction notice, he did not see much of a future in Zimbabwe.

"The economics of the whole country is collapsing. It's not viable to farm in this country and I think that is going to be the basis of my decision," he said.

"A lot of farmers – if they do leave Zimbabwe – will never come back, and the expertise of generations that is going to be lost to the country is frightening."

Rootie Braunstein said he was leaving for New Zealand within a week to take up a job as a toolmaker, leaving behind a farm that has churned out 550 tonnes of wheat, 220 tonnes of tobacco, 46 tonnes of paprika and 500 tonnes of maize a year.

"The reality is I now haven't got a place to farm and my business is basically unable to function any more. I've made my applications to the government and made my objections but nobody has listened so I'm going," Braunstein said in an interview.

A lone farm truck briefly pulled off the main Mutorashanga road and the driver said that he was ferrying his employer's furniture from his property.

Critics say the land reform will leave some 350 000 farm workers unemployed.

"A lot of these chaps have with us 20, 30, 40 years and are going to get their (exit) p but they're basically hom one farmer said.

Farmers have been ord pay their workers redun packages.

The government says farm ers can apply for resettlem has encouraged new re farmers to employ some of Zimbabwe, facing its political and economic cr 22 years of independence, h centre of a critical food sh in the Southern African that includes Malawi, Z Lesotho, Swaziland and M bique.

Once a breadbasket, Zin now needs food aid for six million people because of and the invasion of white farms has slashed its staple output. – Reuter

Teachers say 20 percent rise an insul

From Brian Mangwende in Mutare

THE Zimbabwe Teachers' Association (Zimta) and the Progressive Teachers' Union of Zimbabwe (PTUZ), have rejected the 20 percent cost of living adjustment awarded to civil servants by the government.

The teachers' associations said the increment fell well below the inflation rate pegged at over 100 percent.

Takavafira Zhou, PTUZ's president, said his organisation unequivocally rejected the percent... saying "PTUZ unreservedly rejects the recent pathetic and insulting 20 percent cost of living adjustment awarded to us by the government.

"While it is important for us to maintain a united front around issues that confront us, we should not engage in a conspiracy of silence. We must speak out.

"In our view the percentage is nothing but an issue of misrepresentation and the greatest betrayal against teachers in particular and civil servants in general."

He said among others things, PTUZ was demanding a 100 percent cost of living adjustment, a salary increment of between 155-165 percent on a sliding scale and realistic transport and housing allowances.

Ngaite Zimunya, Zimta's provincial executive officer, said the percentage did not meet their demands.

"What happened is that we negotiated with the government for 60 percent cost of living adjustment," he said.

"Then after sometime, the government officials informed Apex, which embraces Zimta, the Public Service Association and the Zimbabwe Nurses Association, that we had been awarded only 20 percent."

"That percentage is not accept... and teachers are not happ it. We will continue to suff do not do something about Asked what action the t would take, Zimunya said: ways wise to keep your car to your chest."

Zhou said while the bus sonnel and armed force awarded hefty pay increases this year, teachers were at t tom of the list.

"The 20 percent therefore short of our minimum requirements, particular in mind, that the inflation...

Figure 5.6 Close to a full page dedicated to memorialising forced evictions of white farmers. Reprinted with permission from *The Daily News*.

than made up in terms of the numbers of those affected. If news values were immanent in the events themselves, then the story of forced displacement of farm workers would have generated an equivalent number of news stories like the eviction of white farmers from the farms. A deeper analysis of the eviction story in this study would tend to support Bednarek and Caple's (2014) thesis that the news values were discursively produced in the process of news writing itself, that they became newsworthy as events in the way they were discursively written and laid out in the newspaper. The editors' selection of such events as fit to print was the cause rather than the effect of the events' newsworthiness. This analysis would tend to recommend a rethinking or revision of Galtung and Rudge's original list of news values to include reference to white people as a marker of newsworthiness in the coverage of events in postcolonial settings.

Another possible explanation may be looked for in theories that attempt to explain the transcendence of racism beyond the end of formal colonialism. That racial inequality would tend to structure as well as inflect many of the activities of such ideological institutions as the press had been aptly predicted by Bishop Donal Lamont in protesting the dispossession and displacement of thousands of Africans as a result of an apartheid system of government in Rhodesia in the 1970s when he warned that:

> Were there to be an African government in this country—and indeed that seems inevitable, and very soon—and if the present laws which have been enacted and applied to create and preserve *white* privilege—if these were retained and applied in reverse against the European, what a protest there would be! (Hanlon et al., 2012: 209), emphasis mine)

The amount of media gravitas and outcry the farm invasions story occasioned goes beyond available journalistic explanations about news values. Indeed, when the volume and regularity of stories on the eviction of white farmers in the press were to be compared with the manner in which the evictions of thousands of Africans from their ancestral lands in colonial Rhodesia were covered, then the racial basis of the differential access to media as tools of self-definition becomes all too evident. The eviction of blacks from their homes when fertile land on which they had lived and raised their families was taken away from them and parcelled out to white settlers under colonial rule was clearly not a big story. But as the white man's eviction is treated with difference, it is given loud visibility as the stories analysed in this section demonstrate. The difference in media treatment of such apparently similar events – evictions and dispossession of thousands of black families in colonial times and evictions of 3000 white farmers by a black government – is often explained away in terms of journalistic application of news judgements based on the prominence of the event and deviation from the norm or unusualness. If such an argument were to be followed to its logical conclusion then it would appear that when policies disadvantage Africans, then the press sees nothing unusual in that but when whites are similarly disadvantaged it is so unusual that it becomes news. A crude equivalence is found in the journalistic

146 *The Daily News and 'telling the land story'*

adage: 'when a dog bites a man that is not news but when a man bites a dog, then that is news'. Thus, the significant thing here is in the press finding the evictions of white farmers such a big story. It is less in why and how the evictions were effected but in journalists' finding it to be newsworthy.

Cathy Buckle's own analysis of the way the farm evictions story had been covered over the period from March 2000 to 2002 brings out the racial biases in the manner the stories were obsessed with the white farmers' plight to the total exclusion of highlighting how their black farm labourers were affected.

The leader page of a newspaper typically expresses the senior editors' opinion on what they consider to be the most important issue of the time. In this particular case of *The Daily News*'s leader page followed a familiar template layout with three different articles that tended to act as a pointer to the most important issue of the day and the paper's position on it:

The three articles, the cartoon across the top middle section of the page, the editorial comment boxed in a column running down the left margin of the page from top to bottom and the opinion piece strategically placed on the attention grabbing space immediately below the cartoon from the middle to the bottom of the page usually formed the template of *The Daily News* leader page. This section of the newspaper is usually dedicated to regular contributors often outsiders and not part of the paper's editorial team. Cathy Buckle, one such regular contributor, happened to be one of the white former commercial farmers affected by the government's land acquisition policies.

Below is an extract from one of her articles:

HEADLINE: World media misrepresenting facts about the real tragedy unfolding on the farms

BYLINE: Cathy Buckle

PULL-QUOTE: The closing down of the majority of Zimbabwe's commercial farms continues to be reported as if it was simply a racial issue and a correction of a colonial imbalance. Report after report talks of 3000 white farmers being evicted from their properties, but say nothing about 300,000 black farm workers also being dispossessed of their homes, jobs and livelihoods.

LEAD: Zimbabwe has once again caught the world's attention with the eviction of 2900 commercial farmers from their properties. But after 29 months of information, what shocking coverage they are giving to this massive human tragedy. News services all over the world continue to misrepresent the facts and I wonder if they know what an enormous disservice they are doing to both Zimbabwe and their worldwide audiences.

BODY: The closing down of the majority of Zimbabwe's commercial farms continues to be reported as if it was simply a racial issue and a correction of a colonial imbalance.

Report after report talks of 3000 white farmers being evicted from their properties, but say nothing about 300,000 black farm workers also being dispossessed of their homes, jobs and livelihoods.

Figure 5.7 A typical leader page of *The Daily News*. Reprinted with permission from *The Daily News*.

148 *The Daily News and 'telling the land story'*

> Film footage shows white farmers loading their furniture and agricultural equipment onto huge trucks, but never give a glimpse of how the farm workers leave.
>
> The cameras do not show the pictures of black men, women and children walking off those farms with their few meagre belongings loaded onto wheel-barrows, in boxes and enamel basins on their heads or tied onto bicycles.
>
> The world's best reporters and political commentators say nothing about where all these people are going to go or how they will survive in a collapsing economy.
>
> They do not point out that these people, too, know nothing but farming.
>
> Over half a million black Zimbabweans are also being dispossessed of their homes and yet the world chooses to focus on 3000 white farmers ...

The cartoon and the editorial comment provided relevant context that reinforced the subject matter being discussed in the article by Cathy Buckle above. The cartoon a satirical commentary on the ruinous effects of Mugabe's land reform programme shows Mugabe driving a tractor marked 'Agriculture'. The tractor was drawing a trailer marked 'Economy' filled with worthless Zimbabwe dollar bills. Mugabe appears to be determinedly driving the 'agriculture tractor' towards the brink clearly marked 'Dead end'. And as he does so the agriculture tractor is spewing dark toxic fumes that seem to choke the economy trailer it is drawing. This cartoon seems to make a statement that Mugabe's agrarian reform policies were irresponsible and were bound to plunge both the agricultural sector and the country's economy with it into the abyss. The only wise course of action for him to take was to stop or even begin to reverse the agricultural reform policies represented in this particular cartoon by the tractor.

The editorial comment under the headline: 'After Heroes speeches it's back to the chaos' draws readers' attention to 'the chaos' that now characterises the Zimbabwean economic life. The use of the definite article 'the' in a way marks the chaos as one with which the reader will already be familiar. The agrarian reform policies have been described as chaotic by most critics of the policy and in reporting about it in many of its news reports the phrase 'chaotic land reform' was an epithet *The Daily News* was wont to use.

Cathy Buckle's article thus picks up and continues this general theme of criticism against Mugabe's land reform policies. The overall aim of this article, it appears, is to establish new moral grounds on the basis of which to discredit the FTLRP. At the surface level of analysis, Cathy Buckle seems to be merely stating that the press had overstated the white farmers' case in the ongoing farm evictions story, and had been totally oblivious of the plight of black farm workers as victims of these displacements. Being a white farmer herself who had also lost a farm under the same exercise, Buckle demonstrates a high sense of magnanimity and empathy to write the way she has done in this article. Her sense of duty and civic obligation towards fellow men makes her rise above considerations of racial difference and mere self-pity to take responsibility to speak for and on behalf of those whom society and the media had silenced and decided to treat as second class citizens or less than human. She pronounces the media guilty of 'misrepresenting facts about the real tragedy unfolding on the farms' by concentrating on how the farm evictions were affecting '3000 white farmers and saying nothing about 300,000 black farm workers ... in the past 29 months'.

A content analysis of news headlines of *The Daily News* during this period clearly supports Buckle's conclusions about the racial bias in the news coverage of the FTLRP redistribution and the farm evictions it occasioned. 'Report after report, as Buckle suggests, showed 'white farmers loading their furniture and agricultural equipment onto huge trucks, but never a glimpse of how the farm workers leave'. The story Buckle tells here is one about the story the press never told, never reported on the farm evictions issue. Buckle is merely pointing out the obvious when she says: 'film footage never showed the farm worker ... the cameras never showed the pictures of black men, women and children walking off those farms with their few meagre belongings ... the world's best reporters ... said nothing about ... farm workers'. What Cathy Buckle probably did not know is that it was not due to lack of professionalism or to malware in the journalistic establishment in Zimbabwe that our best reporters did not report on the tragic consequences of the FTLRP on black farm workers. Mainstream professional journalism anywhere in the world was by nature wired to turn a blind eye or to look away when actions of power tend to hurt the powerless. Were the story to be told, it would have been to expect too much to hope that the reporter would have also tried to throw some light on how it had been possible that 'black men, women and children walked off those farms with their few meagre belongings' while their opposite number among white folk loaded 'their furniture and agricultural equipment onto huge trucks'. What she does not tell us in her own report is how this is at all possible and why in a newspaper run by an almost entirely black editorial team and in a self-respecting black country which has been independent for more than two decades. At another level of analysis this story may be betraying white paternalism towards blacks. The story might be also suggesting to fellow white men that the black men's welfare is the white man's burden.

The focus of this study is to find out how it is possible for the media to so under-represent facts about the reality of the eviction story as Buckle seems to allege in this article, especially when blacks happen to be the victims. First the division of labour on the farm happens along racial lines. The farm owner is white while the farm worker is black. The white farmer is obviously rich while his black farm worker is poor, evidenced by film footage of the white evictee loading his furniture and agricultural equipment onto 'huge trucks' while his black farm worker makes off on foot for an unknown destination with 'meagre belongings' on his head. According to Cathy Buckle, the media's ethnocentric obsession with narrating the farm eviction from a white angle, tends to crowd out the real tragedy of the farm eviction story from the stand point of the black farm worker. To what extent are interpretive frames applied by *The Daily News* in picturing the issues around the farm eviction story continuous with a colonial archive? How are alternative ways of knowing the farm eviction story trivialised, excluded, suppressed and repressed in *The Daily News* story on farm evictions? One of the

150 *The Daily News and 'telling the land story'*

techniques at work here as in the land conflict story earlier in colonial Zimbabwe, is the use of a race-based hierarchy of credibility as news sources. Whites in Zimbabwe and abroad, including white farmers themselves, enjoy wide access as news sources on *The Daily News*. For example, Mr Larry Norton, Mr Roy Bennet, Delan Walsh, Cathy Buckle, David Mills and Charles Frizzel are among some of the former white farmers given access to write and define the problem of farm evictions from their own stand points. Their views of the nature of the problem are further reinforced by comments and views from white elite organisations such as the Zimbabwe Commercial Farmers Union (ZCFU) and the Zimbabwe Tobacco Farmers Association (ZTFA), whose views and opinions on the ongoing farm evictions are sought after and given wide publicity by the newspaper in story after story on farm occupations and evictions of white farmers since March 2000. This is not to suggest that what these stories reported about the land issue was untrue, except to say that it could not have been ideologically innocent.

At another level of division of labour in the production of news as forms of knowledge in the service of power, *The Daily News* of the period 2000 to 2002 presents a unique case of the global north providing the lenses through which to 'know' and make sense of southern realities such as the land reform programme in Zimbabwe. Thirteen of the major stories on the farm evictions were sourced from Reuters, the UK-based *Observer*, the UK *Guardian*, the *Washington Times* and these articles play a key role in setting the agenda as well as providing the framework within which journalists and reporters at *The Daily News* went on to imagine local realities of the land reform programme in a manner that privileged certain interpretations of those events and not others. The agenda setting architecture for the newsification of Zimbabwe's FTLRP at *The Daily News* could be conceptualised as forming an hierarchical continuum with Reuters and other Western news agencies occupying the apex, followed by the local white farming community and a global network of sympathisers who dominated the reader commentary and opinion sections of the newspaper. At the bottom rung of this knowledge production architecture, were the newspapers' own reporters whose important role was mainly in gate keeping, through news selection and extractive, mining of raw facts for processing in the production chain of news as knowledge on the land reform programme in Zimbabwe.

The white perspective on and narrativisation of the FTLRP as becomes increasingly evident through the pages of *The Daily News* is founded on certain common sense assumptions about who the owners of the land were in Zimbabwe between whites and blacks, about when history began in Zimbabwe and those assumptions are simply that history begins with colonial inscriptions and racial geographisation of the land. In story after story, whites are presented as the owners of the farms where the role and identity of blacks is cut out for them as either farm workers or squatters. Whites are the farm owners and blacks are the landless peasants, squatters, or land grabbers. In one story carried in *The Daily News* but attributed to Reuters, Key dates in the land reform saga' for instance only begin after 2000, quite contrary to what even Eurocentric historiography on the land question in Zimbabwe teaches us (Ranger, 1970; Palmer, 1977; Van Onselen, 1976; Riddell, 1978).

The story which shares the same page with another story on farm evictions illustrated with two landscape pictures of distraught white farmers reminiscing about the past or pondering an uncertain future is cited below for further illustration of the dehistoricisation of the FTLRP story in *The Daily News*.

HEADLINE: Key dates in the land reform saga

LEAD: Nearly 3000 white farmers were ordered to abandon their farms by midnight last Thursday and make way for landless blacks or risk jail under President Robert Mugabe's controversial land reforms. Here are key dates in the evolution of the thorny land question.

BODY: 2000 January-February – Zimbabweans reject in a referendum a draft constitution that Mugabe critics say would have entrenched him in power. Thousands of independence war veterans, backed by the government, invade hundreds of white owned farms, saying the land was illegally seized during British colonial rule.

10 March – A private poll – which Mugabe's government dismissed as "rubbish" – says that few Zimbabweans back Mugabe's land seizures while 74 percent blame Mugabe's government for failing to resolve the issue.

19 April – The High Court convicts war veterans leader Chenjerai Hunzvi of contempt for inciting farm invasions after they had been declared illegal.

The story goes on to chronicle events leading up to the present farm evictions involving 3,000 white farmers. But what is pertinent in this article is the choice the writer makes in citing the year 2000 as marking the start of land conflict in Zimbabwe. Such historisisation deliberately ignores and writes the liberation struggle out of the story of land conflict in Zimbabwe. It writes off as insignificant the structural violence of land segregation in Zimbabwe. To report that: 'Thousands of independence war veterans, backed by the government, invade hundreds of white owned farms, saying the land was illegally seized during British colonial rule' is to dismiss the claim that the land that is now the subject of dispute was indeed seized by the current white owners from blacks in the first place, as just another contestable claim and to establish as fact that war veterans were farm invaders and whites, owners of the farms.

Villains and victims, beneficiaries and benefactors of FTLRP

It is important to note here, that if government resettlement policy on the ground reinforced rather than challenged colonial white supremacist discourses categorising farmers as commercial or subsistence farmers solely on the basis of skin colour in the early days of independence, then mainstream media would scarcely be expected to debunk those myths.

Crucially, the responsible ministries did not challenge the beliefs and practices which had informed Rhodesian 'technical development', the set of

152 *The Daily News and 'telling the land story'*

> modernising policies which had long shaped interventions in African farming, and which reached their height in the Native Land Husbandry Act (NLHA) of 1951. The colonial myth of African farmers as traditional, subsistence-oriented and inefficient, in contrast to the 'commercial white farmers, was left largely intact in the early 1980s ... Land redistribution was rapidly construed as a technical exercise, and one in which the goal of productivity came to hold a central place. (Alexander et al., 2003: 84)

Thus by 2000 when government intensifies its resettlement drive still based on the same logic as in the 1980s, the news stories on the agrarian reform then would expectedly borrow from and elaborate or seek to debunk age-old colonial myths about the whites' ability to farm and African laziness as justification for continuation with a land ownership pattern established under colonial rule. *The Daily News* took it as its mission to articulate white opinion, defend white farmer entitlement over the commercial farmland. One thing that is evident in many of the news stories on the FTLRP developments on the farms is that white farmers were represented as the legitimate owners of the land from which they were being unjustly driven away, and that they were commercial farmers, while Africans taking over those farms were represented as marauding mobs, farm invaders, squatters, new farmers or some such appellation connoting denial of the African as a farmer.

> The success of resettlement would lie in its ability to produce marketed surpluses. To achieve this, officials stressed the need for bureaucratic control over settler selection and careful land-use planning. In this vision, there was little room for popular participation or the historically informed claims to restitution that had animated the liberation war. By far the most dominant resettlement model followed the pattern of the NLHA. (Alexander et al., 2003: 65)

But even this model had not been applied in the strict sense in the early models of resettlement based on the willing-buyer willing-seller nor was it used as the basis for resettlement under the FTLRP. A serious flaw that characterised all resettlement programmes implemented by government since independence is that they largely skirted addressing restitution of rights to lost ancestral lands for most Africans who were forcibly removed by white settler governments of Rhodesia. Although grievance over lost land was the rallying point around which guerrillas mobilised popular support for the war of liberation, the independence government never committed itself to tackling the land imbalances as a justice issue. It had been hoped that an African nationalist government would commit itself to a speedy redress of the racially skewed entitlements to land between blacks and whites on attainment of independence as a matter of priority (Palmer, 1977). But, as Marongwe (2003: 156) rightly points out, 'that did not happen' particularly in the early phases of resettlement programmes of the 1980s based on a willing-buyer willing-seller principle enshrined

The Daily News and 'telling the land story'   153

in the Lancaster House agreement of 1979. That land reform process was not only blind to claims for land restitution by Africans but it also did not pay due attention to the structural violence that Africans had continued to suffer in the 'Tribal Trust Lands' to which they had been banished by the colonial regime.

The TTL as a system continued to generate what it had always been intended to; a steady stream of cheap black labour flowing into the modern economic sector escaping from poverty, malnutrition and starvation among blacks after independence as much as they had done before, under colonial rule. Around 2000 the problem of population density and congestion in some rural areas such as Mhandamabwe, Chiundura, Chachacha to name just a few had reached crisis proportions. The resulting land degradation from population pressure was becoming all too evident, but media discourses on the FTLRP, across the media divide, did not construct that programme as in any way related to the actual existing problem of seeking to decongest these rural areas. What we are not told in the FTLRP story is how the new resettlement programme could possibly relate to the liberation movement's aspirations for the dismantling of a pillar of the colonial economy and the fount of black man's sense of inferiority to the white man – the native reserve. The economic value of the native reserve, now communal area, to the colonial system was in so far as it contributed to breaking the black man's spirit, his pride and self-confidence in his humanity. Confinement to native reserves was an instrument through which white settlers subjugated and pacified the subject races in many parts of colonial Africa.

The success of the colonial project hinged on the realisation that 'the corollary of deliberately fostered African inferiority is the perpetuation of white superiority' (Austin, 1975: 35). It was the principal instrument in the process of what Fanon (1970: 4) calls 'the epidermalisation of this inferiority' complex. There is something uncanny about how discourse makes the whole difference between what can be accepted, legitimated and that which can be considered with revulsion and there is a history to it. Torture and extermination camps implemented in German South West Africa from the close of the nineteenth to the beginning of the twentieth century against the native population of that country were labelled concentration camps and were on that basis condemned as more inhumane than similar structures used for similar purposes against British South Africa's own indigenous population much earlier probably because the latter went under the appellation of 'refugee camps' not 'death camps' which they were. The native reserve was only slightly more humane, in at least its claimed paternalist purposes, than the concentration camps in Germany-owned South West Africa (now Namibia) of the early 1900s or the Nazi gas chambers at Auschwitz (Erichsen and Olusoga, 2010). The native reserve was an inexhaustible and inexpensive source of cheap labour, without which the often celebrated rise of Rhodesia's commercial farming sector to the status of being regarded as 'the bread basket' of Southern Africa would not have been possible. As Austin (1975: 35) points out:

> The African majority has been placed in an economically weak position from which it is virtually impossible to recover unless fundamental changes are

> made. It has been cut off from the economic power which goes with land ownership. The minority pursues this policy … because of a direct desire to ensure a mass of semi-skilled labour.

It never seemed to occur to the news reporters of the FTLRP that the white-owned commercial farm, the target of the war veterans' invasion had a very close affinity with the native reserve (now communal area) to a point of one being the corollary of the other. It was so, at least, to the architects of colonialism who realised early enough that you would not have the one without the other. There was no better way to smoke Africans out of their complacency into willingly joining queues of job hunters in the European sector than confining them to native reservations. It did not occur to the news workers that in its discursive architecture the FTLRP needed to appear as structurally designed as a means to undo the racial dehumanisation visited on indigenous people by being confined in the native reserves renamed communal areas at independence. Lost to them was the fact that the black farm worker now being evicted from the commercial farms was the same rural tribesman turned migrant labourer from the TTL because of the same problem of landlessness which the FTLRP was ostensibly meant to address. But due to the manner in which FTLRP was implemented and reported in the press, many thousands of former farm workers wound up having been offloaded back to the TTLs, worsening an already bad situation of population pressure on the limited land available in the rural areas.

Journalistic blindness to the structural link between rural areas as the foundry of the country's largely semi-skilled black labour in factories, mines and commercial farms and estates probably explains the almost ideologically innocent and unproblematic way *The Herald* (21 August 2002: 1) could use a photograph with its headline story – 'Farmers' defiance' – on evicted white farmers, showing a farm worker, wife and children seemingly happy after having received gratuity from the white employer who has been evicted from his farm. The caption explained the picture in the following words:

> Farm worker for 24 years, Mr Misheck Karuru, says he has received his gratuity and is ready to leave Turner Farm, just outside Harare along Mazowe Road, for his rural home in Mount Darwin. Some farm workers claim that they will have nowhere to go when their employers, the white commercial farmers whose properties have been designated for resettlement, leave.

The expression 'ready to leave … for his rural home' implies someone who has gladly embraced his fate as if he has always looked forward to such a happy moment when he would be relieved of the harsh and oppressive work at the farm and leave for what he and many black Zimbabweans now call 'home'. The intended rhetorical effect was probably to orchestrate the white farmers' defiance by contrasting it with the compliance and readiness to cooperate demonstrated by the farm worker. If he has been away from his rural 'home' for 24 years, working at a commercial farm, the reader can only speculate at what sorts of comforts awaited to attend his homecoming.

Colonial culture had firmly impressed it upon the African mind that his home was in the reserves not in towns or farms where he worked, and it seems The Herald, instead of challenging this reinforces it as the natural order of things. The picture and caption in fact raise more serious questions than they help to answer. They conceal more information than they reveal. Why do Mr Karuru and fellow workers on the farm not resist this uninvited displacement? Are they happy and glad that their employment has had to end this way? In fact, what different purposes does this rural home serve now in postcolonial Zimbabwe than those it served from when it was designated as such under colonial rule – a place to return to for those whom the white economy no longer needed – a place for the 'discarded' people as Desmond (1971) would call them? The reporter at The Herald fails to apprehend the paradox in representing a farm worker happily looking forward to going 'home' from where some villagers are so desperate to escape that they found it necessary to accompany war veterans on the march to invade white-owned farms. Thus in this particular story the "Famers' defiance" to leave the farms is being contrasted with Mr Karuru the black farm worker's readiness to comply with the outcome of a government eviction notice served on his employer.

The intended effect was probably to legitimise government policy in dealing with recalcitrant white farmers. The picture above would have conveyed a completely different sense had it been captioned alternatively as follows: "...Mr Karuru and family face a bleak future as they prepare to leave the Farm for 'home' in the former 'native reserve' of Mount Darwin where he had come from 24 years ago...."? A caption like that would obviously rehash the black government's betrayal of the liberation promise to end the dehumanising effects of life in the former native reserves, a life that had pushed many blacks like Mr. Karuru into accepting servitude to their white masters on commercial farms in the first place.

Note

1 Gile na Gile 19 June 2008, 'No sign of an end to the horror. Zimbabwe's travesty of a presidential election'. *The Economist.* https://www.economist.com/node/11603612/comments?page=1.

References

Alexander, J., Hammer, A., Raftopoulos, B., Jensen, S., 2003. *Zimbabwe's unfinished Business: Rethinking land, state and nation in the context of a crisis.* Weaver Press.

Apter, A., 2007. *Beyond words: Discourse and critical agency in Africa.* University of Chicago Press.

Ashcroft, B., 2001. *On post-colonial futures: Transformations of a colonial culture.* A&C Black.

Austin, R., 1975. *Racism and apartheid in southern Africa: Rhodesia: a book of data.* Unesco Press.

Bednarek, M., Caple, H., 2014. Why do news values matter? Towards a new methodological framework for analysing news discourse in critical discourse analysis and beyond. *Discourse Soc* . 25, 135–158.

Bird, S.E., 2010. *The anthropology of news & journalism: Global perspectives.* Indiana University Press.

Cesaire, A., 1972. *Discourse on Colonialism* (J. Pinkham, Trans.).Monthly Review Press.

156 The Daily News and 'telling the land story'

Dombo, S., 2014. Daily struggles: Private print media, the state, and democratic governance in Zimbabwe in the case of the *Africa Daily News* (1956–1964) and *The Daily News* (1999–2003). (PhD Thesis). Accessed 11 May 2019 from: http://ukzn-dspace.ukzn.ac.za/bit stream/handle/10413/11104/Dombo_Sylvester_2014.pdf?sequence=1&isAllowed=y.

Erichsen, C., Olusoga, D., 2010. *The Kaiser's holocaust: Germany's forgotten genocide and the colonial roots of Nazism.* Faber & Faber.

Fairclough, N., 2013. *Critical discourse analysis: The critical study of language.* Routledge.

Fanon, F., 1970. *Black skin, white masks.* Paladin.

Hanlon, J., Manjengwa, J., Smart, T., 2012. *Zimbabwe takes back its land.* Kumarian Press.

Hasty, J., 2005. *The press and political culture in Ghana.* Indiana University Press.

Heise, N., 2018. Malcolm X and Black Lives Matter: How media bias, globalization, and exigence affect the messages of rhetorical movements. Honours Thesis AY 17/18. 74. Accessed 11 May 2019 from: https://repository.uwyo.edu/cgi/viewcontent.cgi?article=1075&context=honors_theses_17-18.

Kagoro, B., 2003. The opposition and civil society, in: B. Kagoro, J. Makumbe and J. Robertson (eds), *Zimbabwe's turmoil problems and prospects*, pp. 4–15. Accessed 21 June 2019 from: http s://www.africaportal.org/publications/zimbabwes-turmoil-problems-and-prospects/.

Laakso, L., 2003. Opposition politics in independent Zimbabwe. *Afr. Stud. Q.* 7, 119–137.

Loomba, A., 2007. *Colonialism/postcolonialism.* Routledge.

Marongwe, N., 2003. Farm occupations and occupiers in the new politics of land, in: A. Hammar, B. Raftopoulos and S. Jensen (eds), *Zimbabwe's unfinished business: Rethinking land, state and nation in the context of crisis.* Weaver Press, pp. 155–190.

Matusitz, J., Breen, G.-M., 2007. Unethical consequences of pack journalism. *Glob. Media J.* 6, 54–67.

Mbembe, A., 2001. *On the postcolony.* University of California Press.

Moretti, V., 2017. Robert Mugabe in Zimbabwe: The endgame?. Notes de l'Ifri, Ifri. Accessed 21 June 2019 from: https://www.ifri.org/sites/default/files/atoms/files/m oretti_zimbabwe_en_2017.pdf.

Moyo, S., Chambati, W., 2013. *Land and agrarian reform in Zimbabwe.* African Books Collective.

Mudimbe, V.Y., 1988. *The invention of Africa.* Indiana University Press.

Mugari, Z., 2015. Colonial designs, landscapes and the mediation of forced removals in post-independence Zimbabwe, in: Z. Makwavarara, R. Magosvongwe and O.B. Mlambo (eds), *Dialoguing land and indigenisation in Zimbabwe and other developing countries: Emerging perspectives.* University of Zimbabwe Publications, pp. 64–90.

Mungoshi, C., 1975. *Waiting for the Rain.* Heinemann Educational.

Palmer, R.H., 1977. *Land and racial domination in Rhodesia.* Heinemann Educational.

Parker, J., 1972. *Rhodesia: Little white island.* Pitman.

Raftopoulos, B., 2009. The crisis in Zimbabwe, 1998–2008, in: B. Raftopoulos and A.S. Mlambo (eds), *Becoming Zimbabwe: A history from the pre-colonial period to 2008.* Weaver Press, pp. 201–232.

Ranger, T.O., 1970. *The African voice in Southern Rhodesia, 1898–1930.* Northwestern University Press.

Riddell, R.C., 1978. *The land problem in Rhodesia: Alternatives for the future.* Mambo Press.

Saunders, R., 1999. Dancing out of tune. R. Saunders.

Scarnecchia, T., 2006. The 'fascist cycle' in Zimbabwe, 2000–2005. *J. South. Afr. Stud.* 32, 221–237.

Selby, A., 2006. Commercial farmers and the state: Interest group politics and land reform in Zimbabwe. (Doctoral dissertation, University of Oxford). Accessed 11 May 2019 from: http://mokoro.co.uk/land-rights-article/commercial-farmers-and-the-state-inter est-group-politics-and-land-reform-in-zimbabwe/.

Van Onselen, C., 1976. Chibaro: African Mine Labour in Southern Rhodesia. Ravan.

Willems, W., 2004. Peasant demonstrators, violent invaders: Representations of land in the Zimbabwean press. *World Dev.* 32, 1767–1783.

Worby, E., 2001. A redivided land? New agrarian conflicts and questions in Zimbabwe. *J. Agrar. Change* 1, 475–509.

6 *The Herald* and patriotic news on the land issue

Introduction

The front cover illustration of Richard Saunders' book *Dancing out of tune* (Saunders, 1999), in which he traces the onset of a stricter media surveillance and control regime by the state in Zimbabwe at the turn of the twenty-first century shows a figure bestride the keyboard of a journalist's typewriter performing what appear to be arrhythmic dance moves. The cause, hardly visible puppet strings that pull the figure in different directions. That figure vividly captures the coloniality of news media in Zimbabwe and lack of editorial independence. When journalists report they do not do so freely in response to the dictates of the tunes and rhythm of the events themselves. Rather they do so, constrained by invisible puppet strings from within and from without that pull at journalism practice in different directions. Just like Karl Marx once commented of history, journalists in postcolonial settings may write their own news but they do not write it just as they please under conditions chosen by themselves but under discursive circumstances and practices shaped and constrained by the colonial archive they draw upon (Manning, 2001).

The newspaper's morgue thus stands as an epistemic monument in honour of the ossified news versions of Zimbabwe's colonial past, and presents to historians and researchers the 'first draft' of postcolonial Zimbabwe's history, only that version of it colonially choreographed for posterity to have access to. That version, it must be remembered, had very little to say about the colonial violence, mass dispossession and displacement suffered by the black people of this country. With more than a century of publishing in a market with little competition, *The Herald* easily enjoyed a hegemonic status as the newspaper of record throughout the greater part of its life as a newspaper in Zimbabwe. Competition coming from rival weekly newspapers and monthly magazines only offered a very feeble challenge to *The Herald's* status as the primary definer of the socio-political realities in Zimbabwe. In fact, *The Herald* did not only provide the lead in news publication throughout the country's recorded history but in the early years of independence it also provided the much needed training for freshmen usually joining the newsroom with no background training whatsoever in news writing through its on-the-job-training cadetship programme. The newspaper had continued in this role of offering apprenticeship, even beyond the time when the first journalism training programme was established at the Harare Mass Communication Institute and later at other private colleges and universities. So critical was *The Herald*'s internal on-the-job-training programme that the late William Saidi, one of the veteran journalists in Zimbabwe at the time of this study once quipped that: 'there was a commonly held view among seasoned journalists in the country that if a journalist hasn't been through *The Herald* then they ain't going anywhere at all'.[1] *The Herald* tradition of news gathering and reporting has been so pervasive in Zimbabwe that there is no escaping its influence.

By the turn of the century, a culture of journalism dependence on government officials had been fully internalised and institutionalised at *The Herald*. Years of Rhodesia censorship had taught that only government were the sole custodians of the truth and could be relied upon to judge what was in the public interest to report. Mr Ian Smith is often not given due credit for laying the foundation for patriotic journalism in Zimbabwe when during the crisis years following his unilateral declaration of independence (UDI) from Britain, he admonished the press that in making editorial choices to publish or not to publish a story: 'one has to get back to the primitive thing "my country right or wrong"' (Wengraf, 1964: 47). It is against this background that when Ranger (2005) points to the emergence of what he called patriotic journalism in Zimbabwe after 2000, it should not be viewed as a new phenomenon unique to Mugabe's Zimbabwe. It was, in actual fact, a resurgence. While Ranger does acknowledge this fact, in his analysis somehow, he only draws parallels with similar practices in war time propaganda broadsheets of the ZANU nationalist movement during the internecine power struggles within the struggle (Sithole, 1999). The white colonial regime's own version of patriotic journalism somehow escapes his analytic censure. Thus, when Bornwell Chakaodza, the then editor of *The Herald* just before the start of farm invasions by ex-freedom fighters in 2000, stated that: 'In any given situation, crisis or conflict, the idea is not to tell the truth, but ... to reflect the issue in such a way that the majority interests are guaranteed', (Saunders, 1999: 50) he was merely restating a time-honoured principle at *The Herald*. The reality in Zimbabwe irrespective of who may be affected was to be represented in line with the editors' understanding of 'the national interest as articulated by the elected government of the day'.[2] Editorial autonomy at almost all newspapers under the Zimpapers stable was increasingly getting eroded and undermined by government interference. This was increasingly becoming evident through the mechanism of editorial appointments, rewards, promotions and sanctions to whip editors into toeing the government line on issues. Geoffrey Nyarota and his deputy at *The Chronicle* had been silenced by being promoted into positions in which their critical reporting was silenced. In 2000, the then editor of *The Herald* was relieved of his duties on 31 August 2000 for criticising land invasions in an editorial comment. The editor who came after him, Ray Mungoshi, could only serve as editor for *The Herald* for seven months before being fired together with Funny Mushava, editor of *The Sunday Mail* coming as it did hot on the heels of the dismissal of Tommy Sithole,

160 *The Herald and news on the land issue*

managing director of Zimpapers by the newly appointed Minister of Information and Publicity: their crime, defying the minister's directives on editorial decisions at their papers. In an exclusive interview with the US Embassy's Chargé D'Affairs, Mungoshi made the revelation that the minister was literally running the paper, through directives on what stories to carry on the front page and how to write them. The situation had degenerated to a point where the minister would bypass and under-cut *The Herald*'s editorial oversight by directly planting stories in the paper outside the editor's knowledge as revealed in an American Embassy Cable published on WikiLeaks:

> Information minister Jonathan Moyo called Mungoshi on an almost daily basis, usually at about 0600 in the morning. Mungoshi said that these calls often lasted 30 to 45 minutes, and were often angry diatribes about "*The Herald*'s" lack of support for the government. Moyo also used these phone calls to tell Mungoshi what the next day's editorial should be, or what story he wanted to see on the first page. Mungoshi also told us that Minister Moyo would send ready-to-print stories to the paper and expect to see them published without question or alterations ... Mungoshi says that he became accustomed to finding stories in the newspaper that he had never before seen or approved. Minister Moyo went directly to Sub-Editors and production staff to have stories placed in the paper after Mungoshi had approved an edition and "put it to bed". (American Embassy, Harare, 30 March 2001)

The cumulative impact of developments like these involving editorial interference and harassment and intimidation and the sacking of senior staff at Zimpapers was to break the spine of editors and send an unmistakable sign that editorial sovereignty was henceforth not tolerated at *The Herald*, and that editors only served at the minister's pleasure. That the Minister of Information had usurped the powers of the editors at Zimpapers and had installed himself as the de-facto editor of *The Herald* was corroborated by many reporters interviewed for this research at *The Herald* who pointed out many occasions when some members of the editorial team would wake up the following morning to find their paper carrying stories they would never have discussed in the previous diary meeting.

> Some stories, especially the politically controversial ones, just find their way straight onto the pages of the paper without ever having been discussed at diary meetings. Sometimes you are just called by the Editor and assigned to work on a story, you are specifically told who to interview for the story and when you phone such commentators you often got the impression that the answers will have been well rehearsed beforehand. It will be so well choreographed because all the sources will speak as if they had sat in a meeting before and agreed on what to say.[3]

The Herald and news on the land issue   161

That lack of editorial independence from government influence had become so naturalised as can also be inferred from the President's remarks in a speech at the burial of Nathan Shamhuyarira, Independent Zimbabwe's first Minister of Information. In that speech the President castigated Minister Jonathan Moyo for abusing 'our papers' by using them to fuel factional fighting in the ruling party ZANU-PF arguing that: 'all the men that we had, who were leading the newspapers, were fired and replaced by those from the MDC' (New Zimbabwe.com 6 June 2014). Thus, in analysing *The Herald* story of the FTLRP below, there is a limit on how much of that story can be attributed to journalistic agency, given the extent of the minister's direct influence on content through directives and through his power to appoint high-level decision makers and gatekeepers at the newspaper. Thus, in analysing the stories one should be under no illusion that the story could possibly have been a window to the reality it reported on, rather the story actively constructed that reality. The intention therefore, is not to hold *The Herald* story to some truth test because such a truth would be so slippery, elusive and inaccessible by journalistic means, let alone of a patriotic mould introduced at state-controlled media by the Minister of Information Jonathan Moyo at the turn of the twenty-first century (Ranger, 2005).

In as far as the press was concerned, Zimbabwe Newspapers Company (Zimpapers 1980 Ltd) had retained its dominant position in the newspaper publishing industry since independence. This was particularly the case in the dailies market where *The Herald* and *The Chronicle* enjoyed a duopoly until 31 July 1999 when *The Daily News* was then launched as a private daily newspaper. *The Herald* (formerly *The Rhodesia Herald*), Zimpapers' flagship publication, has the longest uninterrupted tradition as a daily newspaper. It straddles the colonial and postcolonial mediascape like a colossus. The change in the ownership structure of Zimbabwe's leading newspaper publishing company that happened when the government of Zimbabwe acquired a controlling stake in the former Rhodesian Printing and Publishing Company a subsidiary of the South African Argus Company in 1981, did not mark a rapture with its colonial past, nor did it introduce a significant shift from the structural relationship that subordinated the news production process to influence by the dominant political and economic class in the country.

The ZMMT experiment, though, had somehow tempered government's exercise of direct editorial oversight at *The Herald* over the years of its existence albeit under very difficult and constraining circumstances. As the news headlines that broke the story of the war vets-led campaign to invade white-owned farms indicate, editors of *The Herald* did enjoy a semblance of editorial independence before Minister Jonathan Moyo's first advent at the Ministry of Information. During the early phase of farm invasions, in 2000, it was not uncommon to encounter story headlines clearly critical of some of the excesses of the campaign by war veterans to occupy white commercial farms. *The Herald* could carry such headlines as listed in the table below:

162 *The Herald and news on the land issue*

Table 6.1 News story headlines 'critical' of the land reform programme

Story headline	*Publication date*
Zimbabwe makes UK liable for *farm seizures*	7 April 2000
Conditions set for end to *invasions*	4 May 2000
Over 240 000 farm workers stand to lose jobs	20 August 2000
Farmers sue government over land acquisition	19 September 2000
Legality of land reform challenged	7 November 2000
Court gives State until July to stop land acquisitions	22 December 2000

The Herald clearly prevaricated on the desirability and legitimacy of the land reform programme in the form that it took in early 2000. Just as there appeared to be no coherent policy in government over the land issue at this early stage of the fast track land reform that policy inconsistency also tended to be reflected in *The Herald*. This is quite evident in the paper's use of such phrases as: 'farm seizures' and 'land invasions' terms which the paper clearly stopped using as the land acquisition programme continued to unfold in a manner that increasingly indicated its irrevocability. At first, *The Herald*, far from presenting a coherent and consistently pro-government 'patriotic' reporting on the FTLRP, most of its news representations of the FTLRP events tended to betray a largely ambivalent and sceptical view of the political development. It mostly took a middle-of-the-road approach which produced stories rather ambivalent and inconclusive on the whole subject of the fast track land reform. In fact, a comparison of its headlines on the unfolding land saga, differed little from those of its rival, *The Daily News*, in the early phase of the war veterans campaign to occupy white-owned farms. The diction was not different. For example, war veterans' actions were described as 'raids', 'land invasions', 'farm seizures' land grabs etc., terms that by their use denoted the illegality of the land acquisition programme – the following front page headlines of the two newspapers illustrate this point.

In those early stages of the FTLRP, *The Herald*'s editorial was clearly more sympathetic towards white farmers' cause and represented war veterans' actions as disruptive, chaotic and invasive on an otherwise key sector in Zimbabwe's economy. This was in spite of the President on several occasions having signalled tacit endorsement of what the war veterans were doing on commercial farms.

At this time the newspaper strove to give a balanced account of political events in the country, affording a fair opportunity to competing shades of elite opinion on the subject of land takeovers. War veterans' views were juxtaposed and counter-balanced with those of the Commercial Farmers Union (CFU) the representative body of mainly white commercial farmers. President Robert Mugabe's views of condoning war veterans' actions were contrasted with those of some of his cabinet ministers in government and members of his party who seemed to contradict his. On 3 March 2000, the paper led with the story headlined: 'War vets ordered to move off farms' attributed to the Minister of Home Affairs,

Figure 6.1a and b. Comparable headlines in the two newspapers. Reproduced with permission from *The Daily News* and *The Herald*.

Figure 6.1b Continued

Dumiso Dabengwa. As if to play out the contradictory attitudes and policy inconsistencies within ZANU-PF and in government, that story was laid out on the same page with an insert story written in bold typeface and attributed to the President introducing a competing interpretation of war veterans' actions on commercial farms, decriminalising them as a mere protest demo. The story's headline announced: 'Invasions protest against "no" vote: President'. The vacillation between approval and disapproval of farm occupations by war veterans and land-hungry villagers continued to play itself out on the pages of *The Herald* throughout the first and second months of the FTLRP programme. The paper, just like its rival *The Daily News*, seemed to orchestrate the divergence of opinion within the ruling ZANU-PF on the form and content of the new government driven land acquisition policy. The fault-line of disagreement took an intra-party conflict inflexion with the former ZAPU elements (Dumiso Dabengwa, Joseph Msika and John Nkomo) in the recently reconfigured ZANU-PF, calling for the halting of the seizures of white-owned commercial farms and the reining in of errant war veterans by issuing pronouncements and proclamations ordering war vets to leave occupied farms. The ZANU element led by President Mugabe and leader of the war veterans association Dr Chenjerai Hunzvi threw their weight behind the ongoing land occupations.

This ambivalence and policy ambiguity within ZANU-PF manifested themselves through *The Herald*'s headline stories on the FTLRPP for the greater part of its early phase in 2000 and 2001. Pairs of stories like 'War vets ordered to move off farms' with an insert story, 'Invasions protest against "no" vote: President' (*The Herald*, 3 March 2000: 1) and 'Government orders war veterans to leave farms' (*The Herald*, 14 April 2000: 1), 'President won't order war vets off farms' (17 April 2000) highlight lack of policy coherence and the paradoxes and contradictions in government's approach to implementing FTLRP programme in the early stages.

HEADLINE: War vets ordered to move off farms
BYLINE: Herald reporters
LEAD: War veterans have been ordered to move out of white-owned commercial farms by today or face unspecified police action, but the war veterans said the invasions were likely to continue.
BODY: The Minister of Home Affairs, Cde Dumiso Dabengwa, told reporters yesterday that the war veterans could be whipped into line unless they immediately withdrew from the farms.

War veterans' association chairman Dr Chenjerai Hunzvi, however told a separate Press conference held simultaneously with Cde Dabengwa's in a different part of town that the "spontaneous" farm invasions, which had attracted hundreds of landless villagers and farm labourers, were likely to continue.

The passivisation construct in both the main headline of the story and the lead conceals or at least downplays the importance of the agent in ordering the evacuation of war veterans from farms. This has the effect of placing the authority of

166 *The Herald and news on the land issue*

the ordering agent and the inevitability of its action beyond questioning. This threat of ejection from occupied farms is juxtaposed with war veterans' expressed commitment to continue with the farm invasions. The fact that the paper uses the word invasions not in quotation marks here, and in many of its early descriptions of war veterans' actions on white-owned farms and also given that the story is not attributed to any specific reporter but to 'Herald Reporters' clearly demonstrates that the paper's editorial leadership was unambiguous about the illegality of 'spontaneous' farm occupations by war veterans. The story counterpoises Home Affairs Minister Dumiso Dabengwa's statement with that of war veterans' leader Chenjerai Hunzvi.

The Herald story at this stage is very clear about the owners and who invaders are between whites and ex-freedom fighters on the commercial farms. That the paper was very sceptical about the spontaneity of the farm invasions and that its editors felt that the invasions were anything but orderly and successful is made evident by their placing such descriptors as 'spontaneous', 'the orderly farm invasions', and 'successful', in quotation marks. In this story, typical of *The Herald*'s elite-centric reporting, the reporters are satisfied to balance off the views of government officials against those of organised interests of war veterans and white commercial farmers represented by Home Affairs Minister Dumiso Dabengwa, war veterans' leader Dr Chenjerai Hunzvi and CFU president, Tim Henwood respectively. The paper bases its construction and interpretation of the complex 'reality' of the FTLRP on what they consider to be the most credible representatives of three key protagonists (sources) in the unfolding conflict situation on farms.

Through this process of selective affordances of voice the evolving land redistribution exercise can only be imagined along the normative prism of a liberal world order where government's remit is to enforce law and order, protect human rights including right to private property and to be a neutral arbiter between the competing interests of war veterans bent on forcibly extracting a fair share of Zimbabwe's most fertile land against white commercial farmers' ownership claims.

INSERT STORY HEADLINE: Invasions protest against 'no'vote: President
BYLINE: Herald reporter
INTRO: The government will not stop war veterans from invading white-owned commercial farms because they are demonstrating peacefully for equitable redistribution of land, President Mugabe said in Harare yesterday.
BODY: He said the invasions were a peaceful demonstration against the rejection of the draft constitution, which would have given the government the right to acquire land for resettlement without paying compensation.

"They are just demonstrating the greatest disappointment that there was this 'no' vote which negated the clause in the (draft) constitution that was going to give government power to acquire land without hindrance, he told journalists at state house yesterday. He said the invasions were a demonstration of the "greatest desire and demand on the part of the people for more land".

"The ex-combatants feel it much more because they sacrificed their lives for us to get back our land ... and sovereign dignity."

Through the layout technique of embedding a separate story as an insert in the general outline of another story, the editors cue their readers to consider the second story as presenting or reporting on an issue closely related to the main story and that the two ought to be read together. The insert will be capturing a sub-plot to either amplify, clarify the themes dealt with in the main story, or to challenge, contrast or question the main story's propositions. In this particular case, the insert story headline presents the President's contrary view of the issue reported in the main story. In the first paragraph the story appears to contradict and subvert the claim made in the headline of the main story. Instead of affirming a position stated at a press conference by his minister, President Mugabe in this insert asserts a contrary position that government would not stop war veterans from invading white-owned commercial farms.

Unlike the view expressed by the commercial farmers and shared with the Minister of Home Affairs which condemned the war veterans led farm invasions as a breach of law, President Mugabe's sentiments seem to condone and even abate that action as legitimate and in that way signals to the police to back off and not to interfere with war veterans who were exercising their democratic right to protest as long as they did so peacefully. Implied in the sub-plot was that the war veterans' protest action would be allowed to go on for as long as they met the government's criterion for a 'peaceful demonstration'. That the reporter in this story is satisfied to present the President's views on the issue without asking any questions illustrates the ideological operation by which elite views are presented as the only valid accounts of reality. For example, the President's tolerance of ex-combatants' democratic right to peacefully organise and protest against the 'no' vote, which itself was an outcome of a democratic process seems to be a contradiction in terms, but the reporter is content to just report what the President said.

It is important to note that at this stage the campaign to occupy white-owned commercial farms is represented as only a 'peaceful demonstration' meant to protest against whites for instigating the rejection of the draft constitution in the referendum. The impression created was that farm invasions were token and ephemeral and would end as soon as government had taken sufficient steps to correct what the 'no' vote had wronged. In the two stories above, as in many headline stories that followed during the first two months since the outbreak of farm invasions, *The Herald* was consistent in presenting to its readers, versions of the material reality on the farms as seen through the eyes of commercial farmers, war veterans or government ministers. Perspectives that were conspicuous by their absence at this early stage of *The Herald's* coverage of the FTLRP programme were those of affected farm workers and of the ordinary land-hungry rural Zimbabweans in whose name the farm invasions were purportedly being effected. Their voice on the land reform was irretrievably lost as an artefact of news writing processes and news sourcing practices which favoured elite views at the expense of those of the subaltern groups.

In fact, when the farm invasions erupted and as the journalists attempted to cover the story, there were no premeditated obvious consensus positions from which the different reporters at *The Herald* covered the developing story in the first

168   *The Herald and news on the land issue*

month of its occurrence. But that farm invasions would pan out for the long haul as they eventually did was generally not anticipated in *The Herald* newsroom, nor among war veterans themselves, nor in some government quarters with the exception probably of President Mugabe himself and top leadership of the war veterans. The headline story cited below demonstrates this policy uncertainty:

HEADLINE: War veterans vow not to leave farms
BYLINE: Ray Mungoshi
LEAD: War veterans yesterday set themselves on a collision course with the police
    when they vowed not to leave white-owned commercial farms they occupied
    last month.
BODY: Zimbabwe Liberation War Veterans Association Secretary General, Cde
    Cosmos Gonese, said the former freedom fighters would not bow to the
    Government's demand despite its threat to kick them out of the farms.
        "We are not moving out of the farms but rather we will sit out the 30 days
    it will take the Government to gazette the amendment on land, said Cde
    Gonese in an interview.
        Our intention is not to chase out white farmers but to make a statement
    that our patience has run out. We are not going anywhere until we get the
    land for the people ...
        The war veterans' stance flies in the face of the Minister of Home Affairs
    Cde Dumiso Dabengwa who on Thursday gave them an ultimatum to
    retreat from the farms by yesterday or face unspecified consequences ...
        The minister who admitted in an interview that the authorities did not
    move fast enough to stop the invasions, said he would now move cautiously.
    "I think we will sit down with their leaders first because they too now realise
    that these (the invasions) have become disorderly. We cannot allow this to
    continue spreading."

What comes out very clearly from this and other subsequent newspaper reports on the farm invasions by war veterans is that war veterans were on white-owned commercial farms for purposes other than repossession of land from white farmers. Their ultimate goal as Gonese intimates in this story was to 'get the land for the people'. Implied by 'the people' is probably all landless blacks the majority of whom had been pushed into reserves during colonial rule. It is in the interests of the generality of black Zimbabweans that Gonese and his fellow comrades were ostensibly invading white-owned farms. The fact that the reporter does not take Gonese to task to explain and specify exactly who he was referring to by 'the people' shows how taken for granted and common-sensical it often is for journalists to base their own assumptions of reality on what the elites say and then proceed to reproduce that as the only valid knowledge about reality. The context in which Gonese can make the claim that the actions of his organisation enjoyed a popular mandate becomes all the more questionable when considered in the light of the fact that the invasions were triggered by the democratic rejection of the draft constitution in which a clause seeking to expedite the equitable redistribution of land had been enshrined. The so-called people for whom war veterans are invading white farms are never given an opportunity in this story to speak. The exclusion of 'the people's' voice, or the 'silent majority' in a news story is perfectly understandable here. the silent landless black poor lack organisational capacity. Unlike the commercial white farmers who can speak through their representative organisations like the CFU, the landless villagers have no representative organisation to articulate their view point on matters that affected them individually.

In March 2000, of the 26 stories dealing directly with the subject of farm invasions 17 of them tended to cast the farm invasions and their perpetrators in negative light either expressing the writer's general sense of apprehension at the spontaneous and therefore anarchic nature of the phenomenon. Only nine stories were clearly in support of the farm occupations by war veterans. The cartoon strip by Innocent Mpofu of 6 March 2000 palpably reveals the scepticism with which the editorial staff at *The Herald* regarded the farm invasions led by war veterans. The cartoon depicts a police officer ordering a group of war veterans, one of whom was brandishing a hoe, to 'invade the constitution and amend it instead!' By publishing a cartoon whose message was so unambiguously critical of the continuing farm invasions by war veterans, it is clear that *The Herald* enjoyed a modicum of editorial independence from government during this early stage of the crisis on the farms or simply that *The Herald*'s editorial leadership was itself very sceptical of the merits of the war veterans led farm invasions.

The editorial sovereignty at *The Herald* becomes even more evident when one takes into account that this cartoon was published three days after President Mugabe's utterances published in the same paper on 3 March expressing tacit support for the farm invasions and clearly reversing Home Affairs Minister Dumiso Dabengwa's order to the war veterans to vacate white-owned farms. By publishing the cartoon, the editorial staff at *The Herald* showed that they were sympathetic with the view that war veterans' actions were illegal and in violation of the country's constitution and that until such a time when the constitution had been amended to allow it, they should end their invasions of white-owned commercial farms.

Given the fact that government pronouncements and directives ever to be given to war veterans to end their siege of white-owned commercial farms came from the Home Affairs Minister Dumiso Dabengwa and Acting President (Vice President) Joseph Msika was not lost to the observing public who might have interpreted this as a sign of a policy rift between former ZAPU members and the rest of the now reconstituted ZANU-PF. This probably partly explains why it became necessary for the former Zipra cadres to explain their stance and give assurances of where they stood on the land issue in a story published by *The Herald* (25 April 2000: 6) under the headline: 'We support Zanu (PF) on land issue – former Zipra members'. There were in those early phases of the FTLRP, clear 'divisions within Zanu-PF as to the way forward on land reform, between those favouring an orderly legal process, and those urging a 'revolutionary' political solution to the problem' (Human Rights Watch, 2002).

Figure 6.2 *The Herald* leader page 6 March 2000, cartoon caricature of farm invasions. Republished with permission from *The Herald*.

Table 6.2 Headline stories on farm invasions in *The Herald,* March 2000.

Negative portrayal	Positive portrayal
FTLRP programme as ill-timed, violent and chaotic invasions of white-owned farms by government sponsored war veterans.	FTLRP programme as spontaneous ex-combatants led peaceful and popular demonstrations to protest delays in the resettlement of land-hungry blacks.
War vets raid 27 farms countrywide, 2 March 2000	War vets ordered to move off farms, 3 March 2000
War veterans vow not to leave farms, 4 March 2000	Invasions protest against 'no' vote: President, 3 March 2000
Tobacco worth $75 million lost, 8 March 2000	President castigates opponents of land redistribution exercise, 4 March 2000
Calls for war vets to end farm invasions grow louder, 9 March 2000	War veterans can remain on farms, says President, 11 March 2000
Mixed feelings over continuing farm invasions by ex-combatants, 13 March 2000	CFU's record on land reform speaks for itself: Henwood, 8 March 2000
War vets defy court order to leave commercial farms, 20 March 2000	Not much crop disrupted by farm occupations, 14 March 2000
Arms seized as Hunzvi leads Nkayi farm invasion, 31 March 2000	Zanu (PF) will adhere to court ruling, 20 March 2000
'Farm invasions impact negatively on economy', 21 March 2000	Villagers support farm invasions, 17 March 2000
Farm invasions threatening plantation workers' jobs, 22 March 2000	CFU seeks court order declaring farm occupations illegal, 14 March 2000
ZRP seeks court order on farms, 24 March 2000	Land reform is crucial to Zimbabwe's future, 31 March 2000
War vets continue to invade farms, 24 March 2000	Britain to help private sector implement resettlement projects, 17 March 2000
Farm invasions worry church organisations, 28 March 2000	

Farm invasions or peaceful demonstrations

The first month of farm invasions comes to an end with no solution to the impasse between war veterans and white commercial farmers. Farmers' appeals for protection seem to go unanswered. The police are either complicit or have proved virtually powerless to evict war veterans from farms and restore law and order. Attempts by white commercial farmers, organisation (the Commercial Farmers Union) to mount a campaign to link decline in productivity on the farms to the disruptions caused by farm invasions fail to elicit any significant sympathy from government. Opinions of Harare city residents appeared to favour an end in farm invasions as illustrated in *The Herald*'s (8, 9, 13 March, 2000: 1) front page stories: 'As war veterans continue to invade farms ... Tobacco worth $75 million lost'; 'Calls for war vets to end farm invasions grow louder' and 'Mixed feelings over continuing farm invasions by ex-combatants'. The fact that most urban

172 *The Herald and news on the land issue*

residents had long become disillusioned with ZANU-PF policies and had jumped ship and begun to put faith in the opposition MDC was not so evident at that early stage of the formation of a credible movement for opposition politics. This only dawned on *The Herald* reporters much later and the paper avoided the practice of basing their stories on street vox-pops altogether as a senior reporter at *The Herald* pointed out in an interview (Herald House, Harare 21 December 13).

> Normally they say it's those big people who make news not ordinary people. Rarely do we go onto the streets to hear what the ordinary people say, but opinion leaders like the Jonathan Moyos, Makumbes, Eldred Masunungures or some university lecturer. The challenge is that if you decide to do a vox-pop and you're writing for *The Herald*, if you go on the streets and ask people 'what do you say about the constitution or this other development?', the views you are likely to get especially from Harare are anti-policy, I mean editorial policy. So you rarely get anything which you can come here and write. Harare being Harare, it's an MDC dominated thing, so you may collect it but you won't use it.

On the other hand, the President and those in rural areas appeared more sympathetic to the war veterans' cause as evidenced by *The Herald*'s (11, 13, 14, 17 March 2000) stories: 'War veterans can remain on farms, says President'; 'War veterans, villagers occupy 8 farms in Gwanda, Mash East'; 'Not much crop disrupted by farm occupations'; and 'Villagers support farm invasions'. Such story headlines, clearly demonstrate how polarising and divisive the farm invasions issue was increasingly becoming in Zimbabwe. Tensions continued to escalate between commercial farmers and the war veterans as Zimbabwe entered the second month with no respite in farm invasions. All along war veterans' actions were construed in *The Herald*'s reportage, as altruistic and solely driven by a selfless desire to capture some excess land from whites for redistribution to land-hungry Zimbabweans. It had also been explained as the inevitable though unfortunate blow-back in response to the rejection of the government sponsored draft constitution blamed on white commercial farmers and their black farm workers. No attempts had been made to explore the relationship between war veterans' organisation and the ruling ZANU-PF party or the possibility of farm invasions serving as a Trojan horse in ZANU-PF's political campaign to win the impending parliamentary elections. The only substantial clue *The Herald* gives of farm invasions' role and connection with ZANU-PF party politics and campaign strategy for the forthcoming parliamentary elections was in a front page story, 'War vets threaten war if Zanu (PF) loses election' (16 March 2000):

HEADLINE: War vets threaten war if Zanu (PF) loses election
BYLINE: Herald Reporter
LEAD: War veterans will "go back to the bush" if the opposition wins next month's parliamentary elections and tries to obstruct their efforts to repossess land, a leader of the Zimbabwe National Liberation War Veterans Association said yesterday.

BODY: ZNLWVA national secretary for projects Andrew Ndlovu told reporters in Harare that people who obstruct the former combatants from 'repossessing' land, so as to win the economic struggle, are declaring war and inviting a civil war in the country.

This therefore means that all those who try to obstruct us from winning our economic struggle would simply be declaring another war with us ...

Should the party fail us we would rather go for military government for a period of five years to set things straight," Cde Ndlovu said in a statement.

Zanu (PF) is a liberation party name, meaning we are still a patriotic front ... and those of our enemies whom we gave amnesty are the ones insulting us and causing instability within the country. Their ignorance of war is no defence because when the war starts (MDC president Mr Tsvangison) Tsvangirai is bound to suffer ...

Cde Ndlovu said the war veterans were not invading farms but "repossessing them". Moving onto farms, as we are doing now, is not a mistake, because, initially, when we went to join the struggle, our intention was to liberate Zimbabwean land through conventional warfare.

This story sheds some light on a very significant aspect of the farm invasions by situating them in the prevailing political conundrum between the ruling ZANU-PF and the opposition party, MDC. One important fact that this story establishes is the close link between the Zimbabwe National War Veterans Association and ZANU-PF. In fact, the main source, Cde Andrew Ndlovu, speaking on behalf of his organisation, falls short of admitting that his organisation was an organ of the ruling party ZANU-PF and that in invading the white-owned farms they would be doing their party's biding, and thus acting in the interests of the party. Ndlovu also drops another very important hint on the true nature and essence of the war veterans led campaign on white-owned commercial farms by stating that they 'were not invading farms but "repossessing them"'. This represents a clear departure from earlier media constructions of the farm invasions as a mere peaceful demonstration which was bound to be called off as soon as the twin objectives of protesting the 'no' vote as well as the urgent need for government to put in place constitutional measures for a speedy land redistribution exercise had been sufficiently communicated. All along an impression had been created that the presence of war veterans on commercial farms would be temporary. But Ndlovu intimates a much more radically different understanding of the nature and purpose of war veterans' presence at white-owned commercial farms – repossession. The contradictions and the struggle over land were clearly manifest on front pages of newspapers as the figure below shows. Editors must have had serious challenges in making decisions about which story to give greater prominence between the President's commentary on the situation on the farms or the killing of the Macheke white farmer. To resolve that difficult choice, the newspaper decided to use both stories on front page. Simply ignoring the story altogether would mean losing the initiative to the newspaper's competitor *The Daily News,* on the one hand. On the other, running the story on the fatal shooting of the white farmer in Macheke would run counter to the narrative of war veterans engaged in peaceful demonstrations on white-owned farms. Here was evidence to the contrary. The challenge had to be resolved discursively through passivisation in the headline that elided the agent of the shooting.

The thin mask of peaceful demonstration quickly peeled off and was irreparably damaged when the shots were fired which killed the first white farmer to die in clashes with the farm invaders on 3 April 2000 at his farm in Macheke, followed a few days later by another white farmer also killed at his farm in Nyamandlovu. Those killings got such publicity that the Human Rights Watch reported that 'overt attacks on white farmers attracted greater international and national publicity than those on black Zimbabweans'.

The framing of the shooting of the white man in the headline: 'White Macheke commercial farmer shot dead' emphasises the Macheke based white man's identity as a farmer and downplays his other identities, for example, as an MDC political activist. In this way the story, through implicature, conveys the view that it was solely because of his identity as a white farmer that he was targeted for killing. This made it the single most important story to have drawn and focused the world's attention on the farm invasions story in Zimbabwe. It is important to contemplate the different responses that headlining the story something along the lines of: 'White Macheke MDC supporter shot dead' would have elicited. The incident would have been interpreted as resulting from politically motivated violence between ZANU-PF and MDC, in which case his unfortunate killing would not have been unique since there had already been similar killings of opposition politicians before. The accusatory finger would have been directed to ZANU-PF as a violent political party and not to farm invadors as happened in this case.

It is important to note that the farm invasions story remained the single most important story in the media for a very long time. From when it started in February 2000 it continued to occupy front page status in the main news outlets in Zimbabwe. Other newsworthy events would erupt from time to time such as election campaigns but they only grabbed media attention for very limited stretches of time and then faded into oblivion, but the FTLRP story differently imagined by different news organisations in Zimbabwe remained the alma mater for much of Zimbabwean media coverage of events that happened concurrently and subsequent to it such as political contestations between the ruling party and the main opposition party, the famines, economic crisis etc. Election campaigns were lost and won on the basis of how they related to the land issue. Political party manifestoes were structured around the land issue. Famine, economic decline and any social and political condition in Zimbabwe had to be re-imagined through the lenses of the fast track land reform. Economic sanctions and travel restrictions imposed on the country were explained away as punishment being visited on Zimbabweans for having dared to tackle historical imbalances in land-ownership between blacks and whites through the FTLRP.

Figure 6.3a and b. Front pages of *The Herald* reporting the killing of white farmers in clashes with war veterans on 17 and 19 April 2000. Reprinted with permission from *The Herald*.

Figure 6.3a and b Continued

The number of people who were victims of it, who were evicted and displaced because of land occupations cannot fully account for the media attention it attracted. The largest group statistically, to suffer displacement as a result of farm occupations by war veterans was that of black farm workers whose own fates were largely intertwined with those of their employers. That story was late in coming and when it did, it never commanded the same media attention that the plight of white farm-owners mustered. In fact, an analysis of the story headlines goes on to illustrate how the farm workers as a group became even more marginalised by being written about. In either case they were just being used as fodder in the bruising fight over ownership of land between white farmers and war veterans. These self-appointed spokespersons only highlighted the farm workers' plight in a way that furthered their own interests. The story when written from the war vets' standpoint, it often highlighted how farm workers were being abused by their employers in order to legitimise their own invasion of white-owned farms. Stories like 'Farmers accused of abusing workers' (*The Herald* April 2000: 1) and 'Abused! Farm workers are threatened: Vote Zanu (PF) and you are out of here' (*The Herald*, 25 April 2000: 9) through sourcing practices of the reporters privileged war veterans' perspectives on the impact of farm occupations on farm workers.

When the story was written from the farm-owners point of view its point of emphasis was on how farm invasions by war veterans were disrupting productivity on the farm and resulting in loss of farm workers' jobs. *The Herald* (March 2000) story "Farm invasions threatening plantation workers' jobs" is typical of such constructions. In those instances when farm workers' organisational spokespersons' views were sought they were invariably framed in support of either the white farmers or the war veterans' position on the issue under discussion and never on their own terms. The other group to be seriously marginalised by the media narratives on the FTLRP were those whom the former Prime Minister of Rhodesia had euphemistically called 'the silent majority' (Frederikse, 1982), the rural folk. The FTLRP was reported in both the privately owned press and the state-controlled press with no reference to systematically decongesting rural areas to restore their productivity. Although war veterans and government officials were wont to represent the FTLRP as a third Chimurenga being waged in the name of and for the ultimate benefit of those who had been dispossessed as a result of the oppressive colonial land policies, ordinary rural folk's comment on the programme and how it affected them was never actively sought nor given expression through the newspaper reports serve for one story headlined: 'Villagers support farm invasions', published by *The Herald* (Chris Chivinge, 17 March 2000: 1). The story took the format of a vox-pop. The story is based on the views of seven named villagers who were interviewed by the reporter in different parts of Mudzi district. The extent to which the views of these seven villagers could be generalisable to all villagers in Zimbabwe is often brought to question and challenged. But if views are expressed by some expert in the field, or if they have an official stamp of authority according to journalistic logic, they become valid knowledge. An even more important point that this story makes clear is the fact that the FTLRP was politically engineered from above and that it largely

178 *The Herald and news on the land issue*

excluded the grassroots villagers. In doing the FTLRP story the reporters for some unknown reason suffered a serious amnesia. It did not occur to them to link this story to earlier attempts of 'spontaneous action by villagers of the Svosve people. The FTLRP was being reported as though it was unrelated to similar grassroots struggles in the past.

In the story the reporter states that:

> Most villagers threw their weight behind the ongoing farm invasions by war veterans, and said they would join in the land self-redistribution programmes if they had more details on its modalities. 'We have nothing against the war veterans. Given the frustration we have over inadequate land we might have done the same,' said a man at Gosha village in Murewa. (*The Herald*, March 17, 2000)

It is clear from the villagers' statement above that villagers perceived the land invasions as invasions by war veterans, and that they had been excluded by the modalities of how the programme was being implemented. According to this story, villagers were certainly not part of the programme as actors much least as beneficiaries and yet it was them who were most historically justified to lay a claim on white-owned farmland in Zimbabwe. It is against this background that Sithole et al. (2003: 84) rightly contend that:

> in the later invasions, we see a gradual replacement of genuine peasants by 'manufactured' peasants comprising state and party-financed militias (unemployed youths, war veterans, displaced farm workers and party supporters) in order to promote systematic invasions throughout the country. The peaceful and spontaneous peasant invasions were transformed into violent and systematic "drive in and set up camp" invasions. Thus media and other reports labelled these later invasions as "the war veterans' invasions" rather than as peasant invasions.

Thus from the argument above it could be concluded that the FTLRP was in its design and implementation, a land reform programme instituted ostensibly for the benefit of landless villagers but without them. And, *The Herald*'s reportage largely sought to represent the programme as enjoying a broad based legitimacy as a people's programme for self-empowerment.

'Readers' write back on land

The letters to the editor section of *The Herald* carried a very robust and nuanced debate on the land issue in the early days of the war veterans-led land occupations. The letters succeeded to place the land issue in its proper historical context. For example, *The Herald* of 6 March 2000 published two letters on its letters page which took diametrically opposite views of the farm invasions issue. One letter ran under the headline: 'War veterans are digging the ground they are standing on'. It registered strong disapproval of the reasons given to justify the farm invasions by war veterans whom the writer characterises as selfish and self-centred, 'the war veterans" reason for invading white owned farms is to retaliate for the "no" vote'. Clearly to cite the 'no' vote as the reason for land invasions was not only a weak justification but a subversion of the democratic process which the government professed to uphold by subjecting the draft constitution to a referendum in the first place. Similar sentiments were voiced in another letter to the editor published on 8 March 2000.

LETTER HEADLINE: Isn't Hunzvi going against bail conditions?
BODY: Editor – I must admit to being confused. I understood that the 'freedom fighters' went to war to fight for democracy and one man one vote, among other things. Now they say the latest farm invasions are being undertaken in response to the 'NO' vote in the recent referendum, held under a one man one vote system and lauded as being free and fair democratic process. I now read that they are promising to go to war if Zanu (PF) loses the election ...
SIGNED: Confused. Avondale, Harare

The second letter published on the same page and side by side with the earlier mentioned letter was headlined: 'Invasion of farms a challenge to put property rights into perspective'. Thus it appears as if the paper's more open and generous accommodation for diverse views and opinions on the land question in the letters to the editor section made up for any limitations in the news sections of the paper. It was mainly in the letters section that questions about the legal basis of the current owners of land in Zimbabwe were raised, a connection made between the current crisis with the colonial historical processes by which Africans ended up being dispossessed and impoverished. As the writer of this letter points out, by crying foul about the behaviour of war veterans, white farmers were actually 'hiding the fact that those farms are stolen property which should be returned to its rightful owners ... all farms owned by white farmers were not justly acquired' The Herald 6 March 2000). In another letter to the editor published in the 8 March edition of The Herald a similar connection is made between the current structure of land-ownership and the landlessness among Africans.

HEADLINE OF LETTER: Farm invasions are about delayed justice
BODY: Editor – What is called farm invasions in Zimbabwe today is basically delayed justice. When black Africans of the 1890s were dispossessed of their land nobody cried injustice, no invasions were claimed. The real invaders then used fire-power and pieces of British legal papers to justify the occupation of the black man's land. We went to Chimurenga war to fight, not for street names and poverty but to recover land stolen from our forefathers ...
SIGNED: Chitumba Jiti. Harare.

180 *The Herald and news on the land issue*

Both Chitumba Jiti and T. Thomas above raise issues about the land invasions by war veterans which are somehow not raised in the main sections of the paper – that land reform should be about restorative justice. It is clear that the editorial somehow let the 'public', through the letters pages, raise and debate those uncomfortable questions they found it difficult to ask their sources themselves.

But this lively debate on the land reform issue does not last long at *The Herald* as the Minister of Information and Publicity Professor Jonathan Moyo consolidates his grip on all state-controlled media through policies and direct editorial interventions at *The Herald*. Thus as the farm invasions enter the second month and tensions continue to rise between war veterans and white farmers *The Herald's* coverage increasingly becomes one-sided, in support of the farm occupations by war veterans and doing damage control as *The Daily News* took the offensive in voicing concern and giving space to white farmers and civil society voices critical of the government's softly, softly approach in dealing with farm invaders.

Evictions and displacements

In any conflict situation news coverage of events and the developments of the conflict tends to accentuate how news as language use is always ideologically implicated in hegemonic struggles between competing elite centres of power. The analysis in the preceding section showed how difficult it was to pin down with some objective exactitude the true essence of the presence of war veterans at white-owned farms. The truth kept shifting as reported within the same newspaper over time. The non-discursive aspects and materialisations on the farms verbalised and non-verbalised in news reports form an important continuum and contribute to the totality of meaning of news texts. 'The manifest discourse therefore, is really no more than the repressive presence of what it does not speak about: and this "not-said" is a hollow that undermines from within all that is said' (Foucault, 1972: 25). Thus in the study of news reports that which constitutes the news' absences and how those absences get produced is just as much part of the productive process of the overall discourse as the manifest text. In a project that is committed to the discovery of how news silences construct and are in turn constituted by elements of social power relations, there is need to go beyond a concern with linguistic engagement with published reports of the news. Of greater importance is the unsaid of the news which cannot be analysed and understood by lexical and semantic means. In this section the reader is invited to turn their analytic gaze on the newspapers' reporting of the evictions of white farmers and their black employees. These events were subsequent to the compulsory acquisition and redistribution of white farms most of which had already been occupied by ex-liberation fighters and landless villagers.

Critical to understanding the nature of the farm eviction story is the question of whom the newspapers were possibly writing for when they set out to cover the story. To what extent was the content of newspapers under study geared to 'prioritising sensibilities and interests of the majority black poor, the so called masses', (Willems, 2010: 320) as their primary audiences is the question. The

The Herald and news on the land issue 181

unfortunate pattern of economic demographics which characterise Western societies as described by Richardson also tended to pattern Zimbabwe's demographics in the early 2000s. Blacks were 'significantly overrepresented in the impoverished and ill-educated social strata' (Richardson, 2006: 80), a strata which it would not be economically prudent for any newspaper that is run as a business entity to invest in trying to attract. The racially determined economic relations in Zimbabwe represented that 'complex amalgam of economic and racial factors' operating to anchor Zimbabwe of 2002, firmly to its colonial past (Loomba, 2007: 129). Spatial land distribution planning in post-independence Zimbabwe during the first two decades of independence had skirted the issue of redistributing economic resources including land to those who needed it most, the rural black population. 'The primary focus of resettlement', according to Alexander et al. (2003: 89) 'shifted to the deeply unpopular policy of communal area reorganisation, i.e. land-use planning within the former reserves'. This means that land-hungry peasants in rural areas as a category of people were largely missed by the first resettlement phase. They were also largely missed by the fast track land resettlement exercise in the post-2000 period as media reports seemed to indicate. Villagers simply did not know when where and how the 'farm invasions' were being effected much less how they could participate (*The Herald* 17 March 2000).

The unchanging landscapes and land-ownership patterns appeared to be reinforced and reflected at the level of discourse. Colonial myths about Africans as primitive and ineffective peasant farmers in contrast to images of successful white commercial farmers, of blacks who sought to reclaim their lost lands as squatters, discursively supported the status quo in land-ownership structures. If government policy had over the 1980s and 1990s, consistently discouraged as impractical a bottom-up land resettlement exercise driven by popular demands for restitution of the lost lands based on colonial evictions (Alexander et al., 2003), then after 2000 it can be argued that the discourse of land restitution was dead and buried and in its place a new discourse of land redistribution emerged using participation in the war of liberation and political affiliation to the ruling ZANU-PF party as its new criteria of legitimation.

The idealistic view that newspapers ought to be democratic and representative of all fractions of the nation's population often misses the simple fact that as business entities, newspaper organisations ultimately make decisions and choices about their product based on hard-nosed economic considerations with an eye on the bottom line. Throughout the colonial period Zimbabwe's indigenous population, particularly those confined to the former native reserves, largely existed outside the media and communication loop. Mainstream colonial press establishment with the exception of few missionary newspapers like Umbowo and Moto, did not ordinarily address its content to them as audiences. That one or so of such newspapers wound up in the hands of few literate Africans would not make the difference in terms of the nature of content and its intended addressees. In the few instances that newspapers were set-up directed to an African readership, these simply spoke down to them. They carried not their thoughts but the views and opinions of those in power, their commandments and announcements ordering

182 *The Herald and news on the land issue*

them on what to think how to think and act in a manner prescribed for them. Thus, before attainment of independence in 1980, the primary addressees of *The Herald*'s news content who also turned out to be the primary definers of its news were largely white middle class. The decolonial impulse of deracialisation ensured that by 2000 the exclusive class of rich white middle-class men had been forced to accommodate in its ranks a reasonable number of the new black bourgeoisie class largely fashioned in its own image in terms of sensibilities and cultural orientation. So although, as Hanlon et al. rightly point out: 'racial discrimination in land ownership ended just before independence, the new government did not move to change the inherited system of a few very large commercial farms and most farmers densely packed in what were simply renamed from 'Tribal Trust Lands' to 'communal areas' (Hanlon et al., 2012: 27).

In terms of the new constitution white privilege had ended and henceforward it was going to be equal opportunity for all but nothing in the new constitution suggested that ill-gotten wealth already in white hands would be equitably redistributed between the races. If anything ratification of the Universal Declaration of Human Rights in 1980 enjoined the new independent state of Zimbabwe to non-discriminatory respect of human rights which further entrenched the economic status quo which favoured whites as owners of property. Thus, when war veterans with tacit or implicit government support invaded white land in 2000 under government's Fast Track Land Reform Programme (FTLRP), critics working with some sections of the private press were on the look-out for evidence of government complicity in what according to them, amounted to a violation of white farmers' property rights. On the other hand, government-owned and controlled press was out to present evidence to the contrary. Thus, in covering FTLRP, the press engaged in a divisive and polarising propaganda war. In the early phase of the FTLRP *The Herald*'s story, on the other hand, was at pains to portray war veterans as law abiding citizens engaged in organised peaceful nationwide demonstrations and any violence on their part as reasonable response to extreme provocation by the white farmers. After the passing of the Land Acquisition Amendment Act and other legislative measures that retroactively legitimated the farm occupations by war veterans and other landless Zimbabweans the government could 'legally' compulsorily acquire land and evict white farmers from their farms. By this time, the New Minister of information had introduced wide-ranging editorial policy and personnel changes at *The Herald* to enlarge direct ministerial control of the medium. This section focuses on how those changes were reflected in *The Herald*'s representation of the different groups affected by the FTLRP. How did the newspaper report the story of the government's monumental failure to use the opportunity presented by FTLRP to tackle the single most enduring feature of racial land segregation? Many independent assessments of the FTLRP pointed out that the programme's impact on rural decongestion were very negligible, (Zimbabwe. Presidential Land Review Committee, 2003).

Journalistic blindness to the structural link between rural areas as the foundry of the country's largely semi-skilled black labour in factories, mines and commercial farms and estates probably explains the almost ideologically innocent and unproblematic way *The Herald* (21 August 2002: 1) could use a photograph with its headline story – 'Farmers' defiance' – on evicted white farmers, showing a farm worker, wife and children seemingly happy after having received gratuity from the white employer who has been served with eviction orders from his farm. The caption explained the picture in the following way:

> Farm worker for 24 years, Mr Misheck Karuru, says he has received his gratuity and is ready to leave Turner Farm, just outside Harare along Mazowe Road, for his *rural home* in Mount Darwin. Some farm workers claim that they will have nowhere to go when their employers, the white commercial farmers whose properties have been designated for resettlement, leave.

The expression 'ready to leave ... for his rural home' implies someone who has gladly embraced his fate as if he has always looked forward to such a happy moment when he would be relieved from the harsh and oppressive work at the farm and leave for what he and many black Zimbabweans learned to call 'home', the reservations to which their forebears were forcibly driven under colonial rule. The intended rhetorical effect was probably to orchestrate the white farmers' defiance by contrasting it with the compliance and readiness to cooperate demonstrated by the farm worker. If he has been away from his rural 'home' for 24 years, working at a commercial farm, the reader can only speculate at what sorts of comforts await to attend his homecoming. The need for redress of the colonial displacement of Africans into 'native reserves' which colonial authorities preferred to call resettlement of Africans throughout the many decades of post-Land Apportionment Act racial redrawing of the demographic map of the then Rhodesia was buried under the rubble of the FTLRP story. Instead of the story of the epic return of Africans formerly displaced under colonialism to their ancestral lands, the chroniclers of power at *The Herald* give us the story of former farm workers actually returning 'home' to the same rural areas where colonialism had always wanted them to be in the first place. The government's fraudulent elite highjacking of what had started off as a spontaneous ordinary landless people's revolution to reclaim their land from which they had been driven away by white settlers (Moyo and Yeros, 2005) ended up banishing Africans to their rural homes more permanently than ever before. The incarceration of Africans to colonially demarcated labour reserves and the complicity of the black government in keeping them there, coupled by media silence about it is not dissimilar to the treatment of the Ilois people, former native inhabitants of the Indian ocean island of Diego Garcia who now permanently live in Mauritius after the British colonial authorities evacuated them from the island in 1965 and went on to represent the island as never having had inhabitants. This was only possible because according to Pilger (2010: 21) 'there was silence on the British atrocity in Diego Garcia' and there was no hope of redress for 'the suffering of the forgotten Ilois people whose story has been consigned to oblivion, routinely, by the reporters and historians of power'.

Figure 6.4 An example of how the plight of the farm workers caught up in the milieu of land occupations was seldom narrated in newspapers. Reprinted with permission from *The Herald*.

The demands for restorative resettlement by victims of colonial displacement rarely made it into the news for the same reason that their initial forced eviction was a non-issue and was largely ignored by the press. Stories that tried to put the land restitution on the agenda were rare, as Pekeshe points out in an article published in *The Patriot* (26 February 2015) 'Opportunity for restorative justice came with the Land Reform Programme. Unfortunately the resultant resettlement programme was more concerned with distributing land to land-hungry Zimbabweans than with restorative justice with regards cultural rights and return of ancestral lands.' With the exception of Chief Jahana and his people, who successfully petitioned government for permission to return and resettle in the land from whence they had been forcibly removed and relocated to Gokwe in 1965 (Kufakurinani and Bamu, 2015), the FTLRP story gave a wide berth to restorative justice issues in land reform. The land conflicts between the returning Jahana people and early beneficiaries of the FTLRP which made news headlines brought into sharp focus the contradictions about the extent to which the FTLRP was about land repossession by its rightful owners or about opening up opportunities for the replacement of the white occupiers with a new class of black occupiers. The anti-climax to the Jahana's epic return story was poignantly captured by *The Patriot* newspaper's report on Chief Jahana's untimely death before the land dispute between the Jahanas and the early settlers had been resolved. The Chief's dead body could not find a final resting place in Insiza, the land of his ancestors, but as the newspaper commented: 'sadly and not surprisingly his body was taken back to Gokwe for burial' (ibid.). The use of 'not surprisingly' suggests that the repatriation of Jahana's body to Gokwe enjoyed the blessings of the authorities. The reasoning being that the triumph of the Jahana case might set 'such a successful example as to be contagious – "the fear of a good example"' (Pilger, 2010: 28). This had the symbolic significance of a reversal to his triumphal return to the land of his forefathers. Had his remains been interred in Insiza, this would have set an 'unfavourable' precedent of a consummate example of the superiority of the claim to land based on historical dispossession.

Colonial culture had firmly impressed it upon the African mind that his home was in the reserves not in towns or farms where he lived and worked as a migrant. It seems *The Herald*, instead of challenging the colonial myth that the African's home is in the reserve, reinforced it as the natural order of things. The picture and caption in fact raise more serious questions than they help to answer. They conceal more information than they reveal. Why do Mr Karuru and fellow workers on the farm not resist this uninvited displacement? Are they happy and glad that their employment has had to end this way? In fact, what different purposes does this rural home serve now in postcolonial Zimbabwe than those it served from when it was designated as such under colonial rule – a place to return to for those whom the white economy no longer needed – a place for the 'discarded' people as Desmond (1970) would call them? The reporter at *The Herald* fails to apprehend the paradox in representing a farm worker happily looking forward to going 'home' from where some villagers are so desperate to escape that they found it necessary to accompany war veterans on the march to

186   *The Herald and news on the land issue*

invade white-owned farms. Thus in this particular story the 'Famers' defiance' to leave the farms is being contrasted with Mr Karuru the black farm worker's readiness to comply with the outcome of a government eviction notice served on his employer. The calculated effect probably was to justify government's high-handed approach in dealing with non-complying white farmers. But what would have been the difference if the caption had read: '... Mr Karuru reluctantly prepares to go back to his rural "home" in the semi-arid former "native reserve" in Mount Darwin where he had come from 24 years ago ...'? A caption like that would obviously rehash the present government's betrayal of the liberation promise to end the dehumanising effects of life in the former native reserves, a life that had pushed many blacks like Mr Karuru into accepting servitude to their white masters on commercial farms.

Ignoring the fate of many thousands of black farm labourers and the interests of many more thousands of Africans whom colonialism had dispossessed and banished to the Rhodesian gulags did little to place the FTLRP on a firm moral ground. If FTLRP was meant to reverse colonial imbalances in land-ownership patterns, then the 'native reserve', that stark reminder and symbol of colonial dispossession and humiliation of Africa's indigenous population would surely need to be addressed by such a programme. But such a discourse fell outside professional journalism's remit. Journalists were content to report events as discreet occurrences unrelated to other events dispersed across space and time.

This weakness which characterised *The Herald*'s reporting on the FTLRP probably accounts for what passed as *The Herald* 's very feeble apology for what the paper itself saw as a senseless, unjustified chaotic land grabbing exercise by war veterans. The paper failed to place the events in their proper historical context where the process of land dispossession and impoverishment of Africans was the cornerstone of the racial division of labour that had inscribed as a fact of life the roles of employer to whites and employee to blacks as the basis for their insertion into a capitalist modernity. The discursive and non-discursive materialisations that had reified white supremacy as 'the symbol of capital' and black inferiority as 'that of labour' had remained unchallenged (Fanon, 1970: 101). Affluence took the colour of whiteness while poverty and the condition of employment/unemployment almost always adorned itself in the colour black.

This is perfectly captured in one of Zex Manatsa's songs: '*Hona vakaita musangano mapostori ekwaMarange pamusana pokuda kuziva akatipenda nependi nhema yaive-e mugaba mugaba rourombo*' (Look, they called a meeting the members of the Marange Apostolic sect to find out who had painted us with the black paint from the tin of poverty). The permanence of this colonial symbolism becomes all too evident in the discursive constructions of the FTLRP by both *The Herald* and *The Daily News* newspapers. One continues to witness the use of labels 'white commercial farmers' or simply 'farmers' with reference to whites whether on the land or off the land as opposed to 'farm workers', 'farm invaders', 'land grabbers', 'squatters' 'new farmers' or 'peasant farmers' in the two papers, signifiers which depend for their sense making on an archive of discursive constructions of the colonial difference between white masters and black servants. No reader of *The Herald* or *The*

Daily News would ever misconstrue the label 'farm worker' or 'new farmer' as also including white employees at a farm or white farmers recently embarked on farming. The signifier 'farmer' when unalloyed with a qualifier almost always referred to a white person and connoted success at farming. *The Herald*, however, should be given the credit for reporting in a more sustained manner on the plight of the largely black farm workers in the FTLRP saga. Stories such as:

> "White farmers' hypocrisy: Workers some of the poorly paid, neglected" (16 August 2002: Opinion page)
> "New rule on farm workers' benefits" (20 August 2002: 1 Headline story)
> "Farmers' defiance" (21 August 2002: 1 Headline story)
> "Farm workers benefit from resettlement programme" (28 August 2002, Opinion page)

were some of the stories that kept the plight of the farm worker in the spot light.

Those stories that reported on the white farmer generally cast him as an unrepentant racist and violator of the rule of the same law from which he expected to gain protection. John Nkomo, Joseph Msika and President Mugabe all at different stages issue stern warnings on defiant farmers for resisting a lawfully issued government order to vacate their farms. Another departure in *The Herald*'s reporting on the farm occupation story is evidenced by the paper's increased focus on the newly resettled farmer. Where in the past the paper had almost exclusively relied on white farmers' organisations, the ZCFU, and ZTFA for expert comment on farming, now there is a marked shift to rely instead on leaders of the black farmers' organisation the Zimbabwe Farmers Union (ZFU), for comment on farming issues.

By August 2002 *The Herald* had completely changed both in tone and outlook. At this stage *The Herald* also begins to draw on a counter-hegemonic archive of discourses of black resistance against settler colonial domination, when it coins the term third Chimurenga as a code name for the radical land repossessions led by veterans of the guerrilla war that brought independence to Zimbabwe. The term Chimurenga which means revolutionary struggle was first used to denote the first widespread resistance and uprisings (1896–7) staged by Africans against colonial occupation by the British South Africa Company (BSAC). The letters pages began to carry increasingly one-sided opinion articles seldom in open disagreement with the government's official position on the land reform question. The robust public sphere that its letters page used to offer had seriously been whittled and toned down. Instead of serving as the ideal space allowing different shades of opinion to freely clash, it became re-feudalised by fewer voices of selected pro-establishment columnists whose role was to manufacture and publicise politically correct opinion particularly on the land issue. Space which used to be dedicated to letters from readers was drastically reduced to accommodate a standard four letters per day reserving the rest of the page instead to carrying long opinion and analysis articles from selected establishment columnists and intelligentsia. In no other section of the paper than the letters page did the gatekeeper's hand and

188   *The Herald and news on the land issue*

manufactured nature of public opinion become more apparent at *The Herald*. Some of the letters exhibited clear signs of having been authored in the newsroom itself by junior reporters as admitted by one informant in an interview:

> It is not an uncommon practice for interns to be ordered to write letters to the editor as part of their normal assignments before they knock off, when no such letters have been received from readers. At other times the sub-editor assigned to layout the letters page finds themselves with the unenviable task of having to author one or rewrite a short letter if they find not enough letters in the letters basket to fill up the page.[4]

This strategy of dedicating the opinion pages to selected regular commentators as well as restricting the chances for authentic unmanaged expressions of opinion by members of the public external to the newsroom, through the editorialised letters page, further entrenched the manufacture of reality in the hands of the newspapers' editors with the result of putting the task of production of versions of reality that much more firmly under control. These strategies complemented by carefully guided selective sourcing practices had the effect of subordinating if not altogether silencing alternative regimes of truth and sense making of subordinated groups (Manning, 2001). Careful selection, rewriting and republication of opinion pieces originally published in the foreign press became common practice at *The Herald* sometimes without even acknowledging the paper's own changes to the original document. The propaganda purposes of this practice was almost always to give the impression that the land resettlement programme enjoyed wider acceptance even beyond the borders of Zimbabwe. George Monbiot's article originally published in *The Guardian* under the heading: 'Our Racist Demonology' and republished in *The Herald*'s opinion page, presents a typical case as shown below:

HEADLINE: Land reform not brutal
BYLINE: George Monbiot
LEAD: The most evil man on earth after Saddam Hussein and Osama bin Laden, is Robert Mugabe, the President of Zimbabwe. That at least is the view of most of the Western world's press.
BODY: His assault on white-owned farms has been cited by the Daily Telegraph as the principal cause of the current famine. Now the paper maintains, he is using "food aid as a political weapon". To suggest that the land seizures are largely responsible for the nation's hunger is sheer mischief. Though the 4500 white farmers out there, own two-thirds of the best arable land, many of them grow tobacco not food.

Seventy percent of the nation's maize – its primary staple crop – is grown by black peasant farmers eking a living from the marginal lands they were relegated to by the whites. The seizure of the white farms is being portrayed as both brutal and illegal. But it is only one small scene in the tragedy now playing all over the world.

Every year, some tens of millions of peasant farmers are forced to leave their land, with devastating consequences for food security. For them there are no tear stained descriptions of a last visit to the graves of their children. If they are mentioned at all, they are dismissed by most of the Press as the unavoidable casualties of development ... These are dark-skinned people being expelled by whites, rather than whites being expelled by black people. They are as such assuming their rightful place as invisible obstacles to the rich world's projects. Mugabe is a monster because he has usurped the natural order. Throughout the coverage of Zimbabwe there is an undercurrent of racism and of regret that Britain ever let Rhodesia go.

The Herald's story, though wholly attributed to George Monbiot is a modification of the original version published in *The Guardian* on 13 August 2002. Monbiot's original article gave a far more balanced and nuanced analysis of Zimbabwe's farm evictions and of Mugabe's policies in general. His criticism of Mugabe, though it pales into insignificance when considered against his upbraiding of the big powers and their media, was just as scathing. In the second paragraph of the original story – which *The Herald* edited out of its own rendering – Monbiot had written as follows:

Yesterday Mugabe insisted that 2,900 white farmers will have to leave their land. He claims to be redistributing their property to landless peasants, but many of the farms he has seized have been handed instead to army officers and party loyalists. Twelve white farmers have been killed and many others beaten. He stole the elections in March through ballot rigging and the intimidation of his political rivals ... As a candidate for the post of World's Third Most Evil Man, he appears to possess all the right credentials ... There is no doubt that Mugabe is a ruthless man, or that his policies are contributing to the further impoverishment of the Zimbabweans ... The seizure of the white farms is both brutal and illegal ... (Monbiot, *Guardian*, 13 August 2002)

But these sections critical of Mugabe were conveniently edited out to ensure a clear white-washed, sanitised and one-sided positive commentary on Mugabe's policies on land redistribution as anything but bad. The recasting of the headline from 'Our Racist Demonology' to *The Herald*'s 'Land reform not brutal', is even much more misleading. When this is added to the unacknowledged surgery in some parts of the original it gives the impression that George Monbiot condones Mugabe's land reform programme, and that he absolves him of any wrong doing that the author is totally on Mugabe's side on this issue eviction of white farmers from their land. Monbiot's is made to appear and sound like a member of Mugabe's party apparatchik. The paper appears to be saying lo-and-behold here is one British citizen who endorses Mugabe's land policies. If *The Herald* editors had acknowledged their own input into the story by indicating in the credit line or byline then at least it would not have been that misleading to the reader who

190 *The Herald and news on the land issue*

may not have had access to the original article. *The Herald's* action here represents a different kind of role relationship between the local and the global media. While some local newspapers – and *The Daily News* provides a good example – would readily surrender their initiative to set the news agenda and to define the news situation to the global media giants from the West, *The Herald* through this story presents a break with tradition. Notwithstanding the ethical issues, through 'voicing over' Monbiot's story *The Herald* asserted its own epistemic imprint by adopting, reinterpreting and adapting the *Guardian* story to give it an inflection in accordance with its own purposes.

Overall, for the paper to write on white farmers' evictions from farms, the way it did at this stage, should be understood in a context where the paper availed the only space the nationalist leadership in government had, to offer a rebuttal to a growing shrill condemnation of Mugabe's land reform policies by the international media and in some sections of the local private press. It represents a sort of decolonial usurpation of a form of knowledge production and turning it against imperial power, a form of doing journalism against the Holy Grail.

A sea change had happened in *The Herald's* general thrust in reporting the land reform issue. Expressions like 'land seizures', 'farm invasions', 'raids of white-owned commercial farms' disappeared. In their place we now had 'land acquisitions' 'newly resettled farmers', or 'farm occupations'. The tables have completely turned against the commercial farmers with court orders of eviction being issued against white commercial farmers instead of against farm invaders and squatters of yesteryear. It is the white farmer who gets represented as in breach of the law not war veterans. The change in *The Herald's* reportorial stance on the land issue does not only extend the debate on the interface between structural constraints and journalistic agency but also complicates it with the role of the discursive unconscious in shaping the news agenda. *The Herald's* main weakness in its reporting of the farm occupations story stemmed from the same original sin where it is not journalistically possible to represent the 'silent majority's' views on the land issue. The press was and has largely remained an institution of power. From when it started during colonial times its practices and its language de-authorised African epistemes. Through such practices the African was constructed as un-representable by journalistic means. Africans were not entitled to hold views of their own. They only existed as types not as individuals. Thus when Cecil John Rhodes wanted to dig for gold in the land across the Limpopo it was sufficient for him to secure an agreement with one man, the chief among Africans whose views were taken as representative of those of the people. It was sufficient for the world to know what the European had to say or write about what was happening in the making of the then Rhodesia. It was standard practice to imagine the white man as writer and the black man as the written, the white man as the knower and the African the known, the white man's language as the language of news. To borrow Chakrabarty's (2008) turn of phrase it could be argued that at *The Herald* the coloniality of news coverage of events on white-owned commercial farms produced their work in relative ignorance of black farm workers and landless blacks' ways of knowing and this did not seem to affect the quality of the news. 'This is a gesture, however that we cannot return. We cannot even afford an equality or symmetry of ignorance' (Mignolo, 2000: 204). This fact partly explains how and why even while supporting the black government's policy on land as *The Herald* did, it could not afford to do the news in total ignorance of what was happening to the white farmer. It was ignorance no newspaper could afford. This fact alone accounts for the comparatively large volume of the stories on farm occupations and eviction of white farmers in the press. A whole new lexicon emerged around ways of naming what was going on in the farms depending on the discursive orientation of the newspaper. Farmers were no longer just farmers. They were either white commercial farmers or simply commercial farmers if they were white, new farmers or newly resettled farmers, if they were black. The process itself of transferring land from former white farm-owners was land acquisition, FTLRP or farm occupations in *The Herald*'s reporting. In *The Daily News* the new owners were land invaders or land grabbers and the process itself was referred to as farm invasions, land seizures etc. During the UDI chiefs' views were taken as proxies of the silent majority. After independence a new breed of chiefs had installed itself as the spokespersons of the silent majority and the media does not in any way act differently towards them under the independence rule. The headline story 'New farmers upbeat' (*The Herald*, 26 August 2002: 1) is representative of the same news logic which operated to produce the white settler colonial government propaganda based on official perspectives of Africans' acceptance of the government's policies. In the present case the land reform programme is officially constructed as enjoying popular support from all landless blacks who stood to benefit most from the government's resettlement programme. Government officials' views and comments are foregrounded:

HEADLINE: New farmers upbeat
KICKER: Most A2 beneficiaries start tilling land, buying inputs
BYLINE: Herald Reporters
LEAD: Hundreds of newly resettled commercial farmers have started tilling their land and buying inputs in preparation for this year's farming season.
BODY: Most Model A2 farmers who got land in commercial farming areas are busy tilling their land just before the onset of the rains in October. Ministry of lands, Agriculture and Rural Resettlement officials in various provinces throughout the country confirmed that thousands of model A2 beneficiaries had accepted Government's offer for land and were now preparing for the coming season.
"We are working hard to prepare the land", said Mr Alois Chidzimi. A tractor driver at a farm in Mazowe. "I used to doubt that we blacks can do it. It's amazing that a number of black commercial farmers are keen to farm on a large scale."

If decolonisation was about fighting the system and not just against personalities and the colour of their skin, then the land resettlement model represented in the story above where former commercial land holders are replaced by black commercial land

Figure 6.5 *The Herald* early reporting on farm occupations used delegitimising language, e.g. 'farm invasions' 'invading ... farm', including accompanying photographs of axe-wielding mobs on the march to invade the next farm. Reprinted with permission from *The Herald*.

holders represents no huge departure from the colonial model. Such a system would continue to leave majority blacks excluded from playing a meaningful part in the mainstream economic production of the country. Its viability as a model of organising agricultural production would continue to rest on the guaranteed existence of a reservoir of cheap black labour – former tribal trust lands now communal areas. The success of black commercial farmers 'keen to farm on a large scale' would pivot on a steady supply of cheap black labour just like their white predecessors. In this news report, a commercial farm worker, Mr Alois Chimidzi who is a tractor driver, is represented as embracing and accepting his new black employers. He used 'to doubt that we blacks can do it'. The use of 'we' here rhetorically indicates the speaker's acceptance and endorsement of the land reform programme of which he feels a part by racial affinity to the new owners of the farms for whom he now works. Nothing is said in the story about any material change that the programme would bring to Chimidzi and other farm workers' conditions of work.

Manufactured silences

The press by representing the FTLRP as a conflict between mostly white commercial farmers and veterans of the liberation struggle over ownership of land in Zimbabwe succeeded in muffling other stories about economic hardships that continued to be the unhappy lot of most rural-based black population in independent Zimbabwe. It steered attention away from issues of land restitution for those communities who had directly suffered loss of their land through racial land policies in colonial Zimbabwe. The story was told at the cost of killing the story of unrequited pleas for justice by those who continued to suffer in the iron cages of rural poverty. The whole issue of land segregation got also de-historisised in the telling of the story of farm invasions by war veterans. There is no doubt that some ordinary blacks did benefit from the land resettlement under FTLRP but it has to be underlined that the basis and criteria of selecting beneficiaries were completely different from those which had been promised during the liberation struggle as a solution to the land question in Zimbabwe. By just focusing on the takeover of land from the whites without relating it to the story of land dispossession in the first place in the initial land grab by whites tends to legitimate and naturalise the Tribal Trust Land as the home of the African. Tribal Trust Lands, formerly referred to as native reserves and more recently renamed communal areas, were an important component in the colonial system for drawing Africans into the colonial economy as a source of cheap labour.

Cheap labour was as much a necessary component of the Rhodesia colonial economy as it was for King Leopold II's Congo. The difference lay only in how that cheap labour was secured and obtained from the Africans in the respective colonies. Where the white overlords used the 'chicotte' in the Congo and the taking of African women and children hostage to force African men into accepting porterage and into the equatorial rain forest to harvest rubber (Hochschild, 1998), Africans were forcibly driven and containerised into the 'native reserve' as a way of forcing their men to 'volunteer' their labour on the

194   *The Herald and news on the land issue*

European mines and estates at slave wages in colonial Rhodesia. Thus any land reforms that left the native reserve system intact in Zimbabwe would not be any different from reforms that sought to humanise and mitigate the brutality of the internal slave system in colonial Congo without abolishing the use of chicotte. The chicotte was an instrument of colonial violence used to civilise the savage race as well as extract free labour from the lazy African in Leopold's Congo of the late nineteenth century. But thanks to the campaign of the Congo Reform Association against the system, the chicotte was removed though without restoring the stolen land back to the indigenous people of the Congo. In the Zimbabwean case the land was repossessed without undoing the native reserve – that factory for the production of an endless supply of cheap black labour. The news reportage simply made no connection between the need for repossession of land from commercial white farmers with the need to reform or reverse the native reserve system as an instrument of colonial domination. The independence government still has to confront the embarrassing reality that it has continued with the same system of mass-producing Africans as half-humans and half-beasts of burden without thinking through the question of on whose behalf do they want to continue producing these quant but profitable creatures. Fanon's prophetic characterisation of the national bourgeoisie that takes over government at independence is vindicated in the Zimbabwean case where, 'far from embodying in concrete form the needs of the people in what touches bread, land and the restoration of the country to the sacred hands of the people' the nationalist leadership proves too eager and content to put into its own hands the same unfair privileges 'which are a legacy of the colonial period' (Fanon et al., 1963: 122, 133).

The stories generally failed to make the connection between the competing rights of white farmers over their land and the current status of blacks as landless and poor. The inbuilt structural racism in land-ownership patterns was an 'absence' in the media discourses and debates about land reform. By inscribing the white commercial farmer as the victim of Mugabe's brutal and violent seizure of land, and by representing the whole process of land acquisition as lawless and chaotic the news coverage further legitimised the old order without questioning the equally brutal process of colonial conquest by which it had come about in the first place. Eventilisation in news stories on the FTLRP resulted in the exclusion of the broad historical context without which it is not possible for a reader unfamiliar with the Zimbabwean colonial history to fully understand the nature and cause of the conflict. The hard news story style of presentation which concentrates on reporting what happened or did not happen, who was involved and probably the effects of the event on the protagonists in the conflict and all of this narrated, cross-checked and validated from the standpoint of power is bound to produce silences of its own. The newspaper is no museum or monument for commemorating and celebrating the vanquished. One cannot look up to recorded news in search for statuary and other reminders of the unjust treatment of those on whose sweat and blood postcolonial civilisation was founded. This is notwithstanding the fact that 'the world we live in' as Hochschild (1998: 294) aptly reminds us, 'is shaped far less by what we celebrate and mythologise than by the painful events we try to forget'. The true victims of the FTLRP (Africans dispossessed and displaced in the colonial land theft by white colonists and their descendants) still remain invisible in both *The Daily News*'s and *The Herald*'s narratives of the fast track land reform.

The two newspapers' approaches to covering the FTLRP differed in the propaganda purposes they served. While it is Waldahlr's (2004) contention that pro-government press like *The Herald* unlike their pro-opposition counterparts, represented the FTLRP as a struggle meant to benefit landless black people in rural areas, I contend that both papers largely missed on making this connection as they rather engaged in a war of words over whether the FTLRP was a violation of human rights or not. In both papers landless peasants' voice is conspicuous by its absence. Both papers suffer from what Schudson (2011) considers to be professional journalism's original sin that of reliance on official sources and professionalism which tends to produce its own biases against the marginalised groups in society and tends to privilege a statist version of reality. *The Daily News* orchestrated the white farmer's stoicism in the face of a resurgent savagery perpetrated by unruly war veterans condoned and egged on by a demented African president turned dictator by over-dramatising the moral, legal and ethical repugnancy of the programme, while *The Herald*'s representation of the programme on the other hand, consisted mainly in marshalling facts and evidence to the contrary and mounting a refutation of all criticism and charges of wrong doing on the part of government. The story which neither of these papers ventured to run in a sustained manner was one which made a connection between what was going on with the legitimate quest for social justice and redress of past colonial racial injustices. The story that was not told is that the FTLRP in its current trajectory was at risk of replacing one set of land robbers with another except that the latter's skin colour was of a darker hue, that it was in danger of missing a great opportunity for requiting the majority of rural Zimbabweans made poor and subservient to the white colonists by theft of their land. The only images that loom large in the FTLRP story in both papers are those of the individual white commercial farmers as victims, Mugabe, 'Hitler' Hunzvi and his 'marauding hordes' of war veterans as perpetrators.

Journalistic silencing

Journalistic silencing occurs where information outage is sustained on an event or issue usually affecting or of interest to the poor or subaltern. It happens as an artefact of established professional practice and routines of news production itself. This form of silence is far more difficult to expunge due to the fact that it results not from journalism gone wrong but rather when there is strict but uncritical adherence to the creed of the journalistic profession, where editorial choices about what to report or not are informed by a universalistic set of ethnocentric news values. Events that affect elite people (of which white rich middle-class owners of large commercial farms and estates in Zimbabwe form a core), what elite people do and their views and opinions on issues would more easily pass the news credibility test than events that affect ordinary people, what they do and say.

196 *The Herald and news on the land issue*

The news, like other 'conventional, published sources' as texts of power, is not the most suitable place to look for stories about powerless people (Hochschild, 1998: 104). Thus as Hall argues, content analysis alone fails where the main mode of racial prejudice takes the form of silence, where no content is produced in the first place about the subject race's realities. If the preferred and most effective mode of aiding forgetfulness and silencing is not documenting in the first place, then a methodology would need to be developed that not only focuses on the manifest content of the media but one that also attends to:

> what people could not say about race. It was the silences that told us something; it was what wasn't there. It was what was invisible, what couldn't be put into frame, what was apparently unsayable that we needed to attend to … You can count lexical items if they're there; but you need a different approach if you really want, as it were, to read a society and its culture symptomatically. (Hall, 1992: 15)

The implications of Hall's argument above would entail going beyond considerations of the actual stories published on the FTLRP by the two newspapers and looking at the larger context within which certain stories are possible and not others. The peculiarities of the FTLRP stories can begin to make more sense when looked at against and in contradistinction to how similar land grabs were reported in an earlier epoch that of colonialism as presented in the previous chapter. The fact that white theft of land from blacks as an inevitable process of colonial occupation of Zimbabwe by whites did not attract as much media attention as land repossession by blacks from whites discursively reproduces racial difference probably in a more subtle way. Some versions of reality systemically get drowned in the din of other competing news versions. In this regard news is comparable to any other commodities sold on the open market where through repetition some news out-compete other news and soon establishes itself as the only news in town. This form of silencing happens where some news stories or versions of them due to infrequent publicity simply fade away from conscious memory as was the case with the displacement and forced evictions of Africans from their ancestral lands discussed in the preceding section.

Context of news production

The news pieces discussed here would make little sense if considered outside their historical contexts of production. The decade starting from the year 2000 is marked by very intense political contestations for hegemonic control of the country between ZANU-PF and newly established opposition party, the Movement for Democratic Change (MDC). During the first two decades of independence ZANU-PF had enjoyed an almost unassailed dominance in the political arena of Zimbabwe. But the MDC's formation towards the end of 1999 posed the first real threat to ZANU-PF's monopoly hold on political power in Zimbabwe. Competition for political office by both parties was largely fought around the long-standing and unresolved land question dating back to the racially skewed land-ownership structures that remained largely unchanged many years after the end of white colonial rule in Zimbabwe (Scoones et al., 2010). It can reasonably be argued that the discourse on repossession of land by landless black Zimbabweans remained top of ZANU-PF political campaign agenda for the parliamentary elections of 2000, presidential elections of 2002 and subsequent harmonised elections of 2005, 2008 and 2013. The MDC on the other hand foregrounded a discourse on the human rights, rule of law and good governance deficit as the most urgent issues. During this period civil society including the media became riven and polarised along these political contestations between the two dominant political formations.

All media organisations in which the government held a controlling stake became patently partisan in favour of ZANU-PF and they shed any pretence at being just pro-government in reporting political developments of the time and *The Herald* was most typical in this regard, guaranteeing ZANU-PF a ready conduit for wider national dissemination of its perspective and interpretation of the political situation in the country including on the unfolding developments on the FTLRP. It ensured that 'ZANU-PF's policies were not only widely discussed, they were also praised. Political events were constantly presented from a ZANU-PF point of view' (Waldahl, 2004: 129).

Most privately owned media organisations or the so-called independent press on the other hand, reported in a manner largely sympathetic to the political cause of the opposition MDC party and *The Daily News* became increasingly viewed as the chief critic of ZANU-PF's political programmes and policies as enunciated through the pages of *The Herald* while providing space for the MDC political formation (Waldahl, 2004). The upshot of the media polarisation was the mystification of the FTLRP. It became difficult to ascertain the reality on the ground from media reports on the issue. It was such scepticism about media representations of the FTLRP that inspired ethnographic studies particularly by Scoones et al. (2010) and Hanlon et al. (2012) which were intent on going beyond the media myths and stereotypes by exposing themselves to empirical evidence on the ground in selected specific case studies. Scoones et al. (2010: 1) clearly specify the object of their work as one in which they sought to look 'at the realities behind the headlines, and ... try to tackle some of the oft-repeated myths about Zimbabwe's land reform with a hard look at empirical data'. While their work gives valuable alternative insights and understandings of the FTLRP to those that could be gleaned from media reports, it does not address the question of how those media myths were created, legitimated and made possible in the first place. This is the gap that the present work seeks to address by focusing on how a process of inter-media agenda setting between international and local news outlets and a blind application of an ethnocentric news value system (Conboy et al., 2014) works to project African realities in line with pre-existing tropes of Africa as the place of darkness always being prevented from descending into barbarism and anarchy by a remnant of white colonialists' descendants still on the continent.

News and the truth claim

The reason why society places such importance on the news is because of its truth claims. News is often regarded as an accurate reflection of what actually is happening out there. One reason why this is the case is because of the claims news makes about itself. It disavows its own discursive signature on that reality by purporting as Bird (2010: 5) argues 'to be (and is often received as) an accurate reflection of reality'. History is replete with cases where publicity in the press or lack thereof had direct ramifications on public policy locally and internationally. For example, publicity of the Soweto uprising and the brutal murder of Steve Biko by the press precipitated the imposition of sanctions on apartheid South Africa by the international community in the 1970s (Brown, 1980).

Hochschild's book *King Leopold II's ghost* is a detailed account of how E.D. Morel's media publicity crusade against atrocities in King Leopold II's Congo drew the world's attention to the inhuman treatment of natives in the Congo under Leopold's imperial rule in a manner that lead to a reform of the system. What is worth noting and instructive as Hochschild (1998) points out is that similar if not worse treatment of natives was common practice and quite widespread in colonial Africa of the period. That no international outrage was ever voiced against the British's treatment of her colonial subjects in her imperial rule in Africa and elsewhere in the world is testimony to the benignity of her system. Germany's acts of genocide against the Herero and the Nama people of Namibia did not elicit any response from the civilised world at the point of their commission because the world's news media took no notice of them. Closer to home in 2014, serious political consequences followed a sustained and unrelenting media battering of the political image of Zimbabwe's former Vice President Joyce Mujuru and all those viewed as aligned to her within ZANU-PF.

The Daily News's exposé of human rights violations on white-owned farms, as government sponsored invited a raft of restrictive media laws and policies from the ZANU-PF government in response, which contributed to a large extent to the closure of that newspaper and other publications seen as 'too' critical of ZANU-PF government policy. The same media glare on the FTLRP in Zimbabwe is not unrelated to the international community's foreign policy towards Zimbabwe in the form of declared and undeclared sanctions imposed on the country by Western nations post-2000. Given that 'media, especially news media, do have enormous power to shape the reality experienced by readers and viewers', it is of material importance to want to know 'what stories that people in any given society are being offered as tools to make meaning?' (Bird, 2010: 7–8).

That the pattern that news media produced on the African continent should elicit policy responses from Europe is no new phenomenon. It has a history that dates back to the era of David Livingstone and Henry Morton Stanley's travelogues of the mid to late nineteenth century. Their news stories about the parts of Africa they travelled contributed significantly in shaping Europe's knowledge and attitudes towards Africa and its aboriginal peoples. The nature of Stanley's journalistic assignment to Africa in many ways acts as a template for doing journalism

The Herald and news on the land issue   199

in Africa. The story he was sent to get which his newspaper would be interested to read back home was not a story about the dramas and vicissitudes of so many savages who peopled the uncharted jungles of Africa's interior. It was a story about the whereabouts and health of the Scottish doctor and explorer gone missing. It was a story about the white man in Africa addressed to an European audience. This raises the question: whom do journalists in postcolonial Africa write for and about? Who were *The Daily News* and *The Herald* reporters writing for when they covered the FTLRP the way they did? Could it be that they targeted their local readership or a foreign audience with sufficient power to react and change the reality as reported consistent with Fanon's (1970: 8) dictum that 'what matters is not to know the world but to change it'. The wish to grab and retain a Western European readership's attention has ever been a prized goal for many newspapers in Africa before and after attainment of independence because of the perceived capacity of the West to translate their media-based knowledge to action vis-à-vis Africa's realty. This reduces African journalism to the role of placard waving. Just like placards, African newspapers by design do not address a local readership. Their primary addressee is always the distant Western other. An other who wields sufficient political and economic power to not only read and know the realty conveyed on the placards but also act to change it. Thus for different and often competing purposes *The Daily News* and *The Herald* hoisted aloft placards often with contradicting messages about the prevailing situation on white commercial farms during the FTLRP. Cognisant that imperial centres in Europe had the power to change reality in their African colonies, successive white settler governments in colonial Rhodesia had taken a direct interest in nurturing a captive press that would put out 'safe' news.

Since life-changing policies have been known to emanate from elsewhere both before and after independence, journalism in Africa then as now has always been an exercise in placard waving never truly meant for local awareness building, informing and educating the citizens but oriented to external others addressing them as its primary audience the powers in the world who have the capacity to alter the fates of the local for ill or for good. This probably partly explains Zimbabwean news media's continued obsession with the use of English as the vehicle of news – a colossal relic of a systematic devaluation of the black subject's language and humanity under British colonial rule. (Wa Thiong'o, 1992)

Given this close correlation between news media and policy and given that news is not a natural occurrence but a 'cultural construction that draws on narrative conventions and routine practices' (Bird, 2010: 5), the present work seeks to establish by analysing selected specimens of news stories from the two newspapers just how democratically representative were journalists' selection of the voices that spoke in those stories.

Thus, when the land occupations or Jambanja broke out in 2000, the media covered that process in a manner that further fractured society than in ways that sought to mend bridges. The media became polarised as well as polarising in the manner in which they reported that high-profile land conflict in Zimbabwe. The conflict which pitted commercial white farmers on one side and war veterans on

200 *The Herald and news on the land issue*

the other with farm workers and landless rural peasants suffering collateral damage. Farm workers and some landless rural peasants were the most powerless in the conflict. They were the subaltern whose interests counted for little in the ensuing struggle to claim legitimate space on the newly redrawn geographical landscapes as much as the story of their systemic exclusion was not fully articulated in Zimbabwe's mediascapes to command any meaningful policy attention. In terms of existing news values farm occupations or seizures met the criteria for selection and inclusion as news to the extent that those occurrences affected either white farmers or the war veterans and not as they affected farm workers and even much less so as they affected rural peasants. Media silence on legitimate claims for land restitution clearly appeared to work in the interests of both the government and the white farmers facing eviction. Stephen Ndlovu makes this important observation in a feature story published by *The Sunday Mail* (12 March 2000) that: 'History had shown that throughout the world, all natives that had lost their land to colonialists had either been "compensated" or given back. This had not happened in Zimbabwe'. And the news is more about what happened than what did not. Land redistribution therefore was not being pursued as a justice issue. And the story that the media had not been telling or was rather actively suppressing was how the fast track land reform would include/exclude the peasants who were the victims of land seizures by whites under colonial rule. Their losses were to remain unrequited even under the new FTLRP.

Reporting land reform as if colonialism did not happen

If volume and prominence of media content alone were an accurate measure of salience then no other event or issue could equal the Fast Track Land Reform Programme in remaining on top of news agendas of the two newspapers considered in this investigation for the three years running from February 2000 to August 2002. The reason for this could not be fully explained in terms of Galtung and Rudge's list of news values. Farmers as a class of people would not normally count as prominent people. The Zimbabwe National Liberation War Veterans Association, which spearheaded the farm invasions cannot be regarded as such an elite organisation to warrant the news attention its activities attracted. The reason cannot be fully supplied by the fact that the issue had the ingredients of a racial conflict, pitting blacks (war veterans and villagers) against whites (white commercial farmers). As shown in the previous chapter, an equivalent racial dispute over land-ownership between blacks and whites in colonial Rhodesia failed to generate any significant and sustained media interest as the FTLRP did. If scope and potential impact in terms of numbers of people affected is considered then land grabs by white settlers in the then Rhodesia were themselves not insignificant by comparison to the FTLRP.

The only plausible account for the apparent disparity in the media's coverage of these similar events can be inferred from the genealogical link between post-colonial media and their colonial progenitors. Basing on a cursory look through the pages of *The Rhodesia Herald* before the 1970s, one could be justified to define the news according to *The Rhodesia Herald* as, the white man's story in Africa, about and by him. My analysis of the news coverage of the FTLRP in this section demonstrates our media's definition of news more than 30 years after attainment of independence has changed but little. What makes the FTLRP story perhaps such a big story for both papers may be partly because it concerns the white farmer and his interests. The only difference is that, that story is no longer being physically written by white journalists as in the past, but in any event, the perspective remains the white man's, at least in some of *The Herald*'s stories and most of *The Daily News*'s. This pattern of under reporting situations and cases where blacks are the victims and excessively over-dramatising the story when the victim tends to be white has a very long history to it. It was not through the efforts of journalists that atrocities of genocidal proportions against the indigenous black populations of King Leopold II's Congo Free State were brought to light. If anything the celebrated travelogues by journalist Henry Morton Stanley helped in covering up those crimes against humanity in the Congo (Hochschild, 1998). The press in colonial Africa was an appendage of and too cosily embedded with imperial white power to concern itself with the plight of colonised Africans. Derrick Nault's article: 'What signify these dark races to Us?: Progress, dehumanisation, and black concentration camps in early twentieth century southern Africa' brings out most forcefully the differential silences on any negative impacts of colonial policies as they affected particularly blacks. He states that in an effort to shine light on how the first concentration camps ever to be devised as part of a military strategy and used by the British against the Boers in the South African Anglo-Boer war (1899–1902):

> Emily Hobhouse, the humanitarian campaigner who almost singlehandedly shamed the British government into tackling the appalling conditions found in the Boer concentration camps, learned from clergymen and others of "sad tales of the sickness and mortality" in the black "refugee" camps, but no one – including her – took up the cause of African prisoners. Photographs of emaciated white children and shocking reports outraged the international community and resulted in improvements in camp conditions for Boer prisoners by late 1901, but the humanitarian crisis in the black concentration camps raged on, hidden from public view. (Nault, 2013: 9)

News media have, in colonial and postcolonial contexts, most certainly in the case of Zimbabwe's FTLRP, been accessory in keeping negative effects on blacks 'hidden from public view'. It was not through a feat of journalistic accomplishment that the world came to know about how the Herero and the Nama of Namibia were nearly exterminated in concentration camps in Germany ruled South West Africa in the early 1900s. That crime would have remained under wraps had it not been for the investigative zeal and sense of justice that compelled O'Rielly, a lawyer by profession, to dig up and expose every detail of Kaiser Germany's secret plan to annihilate the lower races in its South West African colony (Erichsen and Olusoga, 2010). It was not by reading the newspapers that

202 *The Herald and news on the land issue*

Pilger (2011: 197) learnt about what he called apartheid South Africa's 'rural concentration camp' into which 'some 3.5 million black South Africans were forced', but thanks to the fearless efforts of a Catholic Priest Cosmas Desmond whose book The Discarded People helped expose apartheid South Africa's most heinous crime against its black population.

Censorship by professional journalism

Journalists are often the first to protest and cry foul when other centres of power particularly government impose any form of restrictions on their right to free expression and right to knowledge and information however justified that might be (Hasty, 2010). But this form of censorship is less virulent and dangerous than that brand of censorship that is wired into journalism's own DNA. Those barricades and inhibitors to information that journalism's mode of work imposes has the same effect as that of burning books. The only difference is that journalism's way is far more complete in its destruction and concealment of truth.

Certainly the journalistic imperative to cooperate with elites contributes to an overall tendency of newspapers to represent the perspectives and interests of authority, particularly economic and political authority sometimes to a point of making 'reality' stranger than fiction (Hasty, 2010: 138). What was the independence government going to do with the 'reserves of cheap labour' that the British colonial administration had so painstakingly established over many decades in Rhodesia? In spite of all the nationalist rhetoric of the ZANU-PF government, policy on the ground skirted the issue of dismantling the labour reserves from which the modern postcolonial capitalist economy continued to draw. The news media from the left or from the right also shied away from relating the native reserves question to the ongoing land reform process. Although in principle racial discrimination was abolished in 1980 with the attainment of independence, the structures that supported continuation with racial inequality remained geographically inscribed in Zimbabwe. Africans remained far removed from the levers of power. They continued to be treated condescendingly as a 'subject race' to be spoken for in news spaces or altogether excluded (Van Schoor, 1986: 14). Journalists in postcolonial settings scarcely think of their profession as inherently designed to favour one race over another in news reporting. The taken for granted assumptions about what makes the news are as Stuart Hall warned:

> One of the most opaque structures of meaning in modern society journalists speak of "the news" as if events select themselves. Further, they speak as if which is the "most significant" news story, and which "news angles" are most salient are divinely inspired. We appear to be dealing, then, with a "deep structure" whose function as a selective device is un-transparent even to those who professionally most know how to operate it. (Hall et al., 1978: 181)

This argument reinforces Foucault's view that people including journalists do not produce discourse, rather what is more the case is that discourse produces speaking positions for journalists so that by extension it can reasonably be argued that the farm invasions news/discourse shaped the journalists' way of thinking and writing about it.

Diversity of news interpretive frameworks

There was very limited diversity in interpretive frameworks availed to the reader by the two newspapers on account mainly of the news gathering and sourcing practices at the two media organisations. Adherence to the same set of news values, news sourcing practices that position official representatives of elites and elite organisations at the top of a hierarchy of credibility lead to very limited range of interpretive frames being made available in the news. (Manning, 2001). 'Are journalists elites or subaltern?' Jennifer Hasty once posed this rhetorical question in the light of her ethnographic studies of Ghanaian newsrooms in 1995. This question is very material in the light of the importance of one's locus of articulation in the epistemic view of material realities journalists report on. Her answer to that question was:

> As highly literate discursive producers with privileged access to the political field, they may seem to be elites. However, most journalists are poorly paid and lack the social and intellectual capital of local elites, which tends to subordinate them in everyday interactions with representatives of power. (Hasty, 2010: 143)

In reporting FTLRP journalists from *The Daily News* differed from those at *The Herald* only in terms of which elite segment of Zimbabwean society they chose to align themselves with and which one they chose to vilify and demonise. The reporting oversimplified an otherwise complex and variegated problem reducing it to an either black or white binary issue. In the period soon after Jonathan Moyo's appointment to head the Ministry of Information and Publicity the media became deeply divided and polarised into patriotic press and a sell-out press. Their reporting demonstrated their lack of capacity to challenge the elite perspectives that were dumped down on them by their favoured elite segments. The reporting became so committed to a point of becoming some brand of activist journalism or what Terrence Ranger termed patriotic or hate journalism with no capacity for self-introspection. 'It prevents any self-reflection' (Ranger, 2005: 15).

Decolonial liminality

Land reform without addressing the modernity/coloniality binary introduces a new and more dangerous form of colonialism in search of its own undoing or antithesis. It is colonial envy seeking to access the benefits of decoloniality without subjecting itself to the means thereof (Mignolo, 2000). News reporting on the land reform project that is essentially indifferent to whether colonial land occupation ever happened is itself part of the colonial continuity. The situation in Zimbabwe at the height of the FTLRP exemplifies what happens when new signifiers name the same old concepts and referents. This can only have the effect of masking and mystifying unchanging patterns of domination and unequal relations of power on

204 *The Herald and news on the land issue*

the ground. In postcolonial environments, a blind and unconscious application of ethnocentric news values tends to produce news content that reinforces the same division of labour between whites and blacks, along the lines of a master race and a servant race as it has always done between coloniser and colonised in the past. This unfortunately often happens as it often does against the best intentions of well-meaning African journalists and editors. On reading through the many news reports on the FTLRP published in both newspapers, one soon learns of many white farmers by name as they are referred to for comment sometimes in their individual capacity, but not so about the war veterans and the nameless, faceless hordes of landless villagers.

Conclusion

The analysis of the evolving manner in which *The Herald* covered the FTLRP presented here was not premised on the assumption that some of its stories were less true than the others. The aim was to demonstrate the constructedness of mediated reality no matter who is doing the construction. This does not, however, signal denial of the existence of material realty but simply to suggest that such a reality will always remain slippery, contestable and difficult to access if 'our only access to it is through the constructionist prism of discourse' (Macdonald, 2003: 17). The eventalisation of the farm invasions largely masked the colonial rooted-ness of Zimbabwe's land problem. The story was reported by both newspapers as if colonialism never happened in Zimbabwe and because of this tendency in journalism, colonialism's silent majority also remained silent in this story in spite of the claim on both sides of the conflicting parties to act in their name. *The Herald* morphed from incredulity to a clear, unambiguous and unequivocal pro-government line on farm occupations. After consideration of the newsification of the FTLRP in *The Herald* discussed above, one cannot but come to the same pessimistic conclusion that Mignolo (2011: 161) arrives at, that 'the epistemic colonial and imperial differences did not end with decolonisation in Asia and Africa'. The next chapter explores how forced evictions of the poor urban slum dwellers, some of who were former farm workers, were reported in the state press and in privately owned press.

Notes

1 Interview with Mr Bill Saidi at Herald House, 13 December 2013.
2 Interview with Caesar Zvai at Herald House, 19 December 2013.
3 Interview with a senior reporter at Herald House, 6 January 2014.
4 Interview with a sub-editor at Herald House, 23 December 2013.

References

Alexander, J., Hammer, A., Raftopoulos, B., Jensen, S., 2003. *Zimbabwe's unfinished business.* Weaver Press.
Bird, S.E., 2010. *The anthropology of news & journalism: Global perspectives.* Indiana University Press.

Brown, T., 1980. Did anybody know his name? Coverage of Steven Biko and the Black Consciousness Movement in South Africa by the *New York Times* and the *Washington Post* 1969–1977. *Ecquid Novi*. 1, 29–49.

Chakrabarty, D., 2008. *Provincializing Europe: Postcolonial thought and historical difference*. Princeton University Press.

Conboy, M., Lugo-Ocando, J., Eldridge, S., 2014. Livingstone and the legacy of empire in the journalistic imagination. *Ecquid Novi*. 35, 3–8.

Desmond, C., 1970. *The discarded people: An account of African resettlement*. Christian Institute of South Africa.

Erichsen, C., Olusoga, D., 2010. *The Kaiser's holocaust: Germany's forgotten genocide and the colonial roots of Nazism*. Faber & Faber.

Fanon, F., 1970. *Black skin, white masks*. Paladin.

Fanon, F., Sartre, J.P., Farrington, C., 1963. *The wretched of the earth*. Grove Press

Foucault, M., 1972. *The archaeology of knowledge* (A.M.S. Smith, Trans.). Tavistock.

Frederikse, J., 1982. *None but ourselves: Masses vs. media in the making of Zimbabwe*. Heinemann.

Hall, S., 1992. Race, culture, and communications: Looking backward and forward at cultural studies. *Rethink. Marx*. 5, 10–18.

Hall, S., 1978. The social production of news, in: S. Hall, C. Critcher, T. Jefferson, J. Clarke, and B. Roberts (eds), *Policing the crisis: Mugging, the state, and law and order*. Macmillan, pp. 53–75.

Hanlon, J., Manjengwa, J., Smart, T., 2012. *Zimbabwe takes back its land*. Kumarian Press.

Hasty, J., 2010. Journalism as fieldwork: Propaganda, complicity, and the ethics of anthropology, in: E. Bird (ed.), *The anthropology of news & journalism: Global perspectives*. Indiana University Press, pp. 132–148.

Hochschild, A., 1998. *King Leopold's ghost: A story of greed, terror and heroism in colonial Africa*. Houghton Mifflin.

Kufakurinani, U., Bamu, W., 2015. Resettled yet unsettled?: Land conflicts and food (in)security in Insiza North, Zimbabwe 2005–2013, in: E. Bird (ed.), *The anthropology of news & journalism: Global perspectives*. Indiana University Press, pp.132–148.

Loomba, A., 2007. *Colonialism/postcolonialism*. Routledge.

Macdonald, M., 2003. *Exploring media discourse*. Oxford University Press.

Manning, P., 2001. *News and news sources: A critical introduction*. Sage.

Mignolo, W., 2000. *Local histories/global designs: Coloniality, subaltern knowledges, and border thinking*. Princeton University Press.

Mignolo, W., 2011. *The darker side of western modernity: Global futures, decolonial options*. Duke University Press.

Moyo, S., Yeros, P., 2005. *Reclaiming the land: The resurgence of rural movements in Africa, Asia and Latin America*. Zed Books.

Nault, D.M., 2013. What Signify these Dark Races to us?': Progress, Dehumanisation, and Black Concentration Camps in Early Twentieth Century Southern Africa. Presented at the 'On the Move: People, Protests and Progress' the 8th international Conference of the Asia Association for Global Studies (AAGS), First Hotel, Bangkok, Thailand, pp. 3–5. Accessed 12 June 2019 from: https://www.academia.edu/2189531/_What_signify_these_dark_races_to_us_Progress_Dehumanization_and_Black_Concentration_Camps_in_Early_Twentieth_Century_Southern_Africa.

Pilger, J., 2011. *Freedom next time*. Random House.

Pilger, J., 2010. *Hidden agendas*. Random House.

Ranger, T.O., 2005. The rise of patriotic journalism in Zimbabwe and its possible implications. Westminster Papers in communication and culture, 2. Accessed 11 May 2019 from: https://www.westminsterpapers.org/articles/abstract/10.16997/wpcc.38/.

Richardson, J., 2006. *Analysing newspapers: An approach from critical discourse analysis.* Palgrave.

Saunders, R., 1999. *Dancing out of tune.* R. Saunders.

Schudson, M., 2011. *The sociology of news* (2nd edn.). W.W. Norton & Company.

Scoones, I., Marongwe, N., Mavedzenge, B., Mahenehene, J., Murimbarimba, F., Sukume, C., 2010. *Zimbabwe's land reform: Myths & realities.* James Currey.

Sithole, B., Campbell, B., Doré, D., Kozanayi, W., 2003. Narratives on land: State-peasant relations over fast track land reform in Zimbabwe. *Afr. Stud. Q.* 7, 81–95.

Sithole, M., 1999. *Zimbabwe: Struggles within the struggle, 1957–1980.* Rujeko Publishing.

Van Schoor, W.P., 1986. *The origin and development of segregation in South Africa.* Apdusa.

Wa Thiong'o, N., 1992. *Decolonising the mind: The politics of language in African literature.* East African Publishers.

Waldahl, R., 2004. *Politics and persuasion: Media coverage of Zimbabwe's 2000 election.* Weaver Press.

Wengraf, T., 1964. Zimbabwe. *New Left Rev.* 39.

Willems, W., 2010. At the crossroads of the formal and popular: Convergence culture and new publics in Zimbabwe, in: *Popular Media, Democracy and Development in Africa.* Routledge, pp. 62–78.

Zimbabwe Presidential Land Review Committee. 2003. *Report of the Presidential Land Review Committee.* Presidential Land Review Committee.

7 Operation Restore (colonial) Order

Introduction

The last two chapters have dealt with cases of forced removals of farming communities as they were reported in the newspapers. Evidence presented and discussed showed how the methods of professional mainstream journalism impose limitations on what events, and what people make it into the news domain in the writing. It also became clear that dominant ideological frameworks such as white supremacy, and patriarchy operated on and intersected with journalism's conventionally accepted rules about what is newsworthy to discursively produce a very predictable run of the news where African men and women and their views were largely absent. Chapters 5 and 6 in particular extended the same critical discourse analytic framework on the newsification of forced removals occurring in a postcolonial context, two decades after Zimbabwe gained independence. The racial dynamics and role relationships of perpetrator/victim between whites and blacks had switched, in the Fast Track Land Reform Programme (FTLRP), ostensibly meant to right the colonial wrongs in favour of the majority landless black Zimbabweans. In spite of the changed political context, it was clear that the news somehow retained its white-centrism. Whites remained just as newsworthy regardless of changed circumstances. The evidence seemed to suggest that contemporary news work practices were genealogically rooted in Zimbabwe's colonial news archive. The news on the FTLRP continued to produce echoing silences on the plight of the marginalised sections of the black population specifically the land hungry rural black peasants and black farm workers affected by the FTLRP. Their voices were simply left out, marginalised as before independence. On the other hand, a similar erasure was a favour black journalists working in black owned and run newspaper organisations were somehow unable to return on the white former farmers, now victims of forced eviction.

The chapter came to the conclusion that the largely unchanged racial geography of Zimbabwe was largely responsible for reproducing racial and gendered inequalities in the news. Rurality socially engineered over a century-long period of white settler rule was weaponised as an instrument of racial domination of blacks by whites and was used to manufacture Africans suited for exploitation in the mainstream European economy. Some former black farm workers now

208   *Operation Restore (colonial) Order*

evictees as a result of the FTLRP managed to find their way back to their rural 'homes' to re-establish their livelihoods as peasant farmers. Some analysts put the estimate of farm workers who were displaced as a result of what they describe as the chaotic ad-hoc and unplanned FTLRP, at about 200,000 (Mazingi and Kamidza, 2011). Part of this population of former farm workers, particularly those of foreign descent were left with no option but to join the ranks of the urban unemployed and hordes of informal traders and in the process over-stretching the city's population carrying capacity to breaking point. A majority of them simply did not have the wherewithal to acquire proper urban housing or to access proper rented accommodation. The inevitable increase in demand for urban housing coupled with a deepening economic decline led to a marked rise in the phenomenon of urban slums and informalisation of the economy. Given the non-existence of a news archive on how forced removals under the FTLRP affected thousands of former farm workers, it can be reasonable to anticipate further silence on subsequent displacements of victims of earlier displacements.

On 19 May 2005 the government of Zimbabwe made an announcement that it wanted to rid the city of all illegal structures as these had become havens of thieves and criminals. It was also going to launch a police blitz to drive out all those engaged in informal and illegal trade, off the streets of main city centres such as Harare. That police blitz was initially codenamed Operation Murambatsvina (drive out trash) (OM) or Operation Restore Order. After an outcry by the international community over what were perceived as human rights violation aspects of that operation, the demolitions then graduated into the phase of re-construction of cheap but decent housing provision for those who had been affected by the earlier operation. To mark it out as different from OM, the new phase was then codenamed Operation Garikai of Hlalani Kuhle (live in prosperity). Many theories have been advanced by different scholars to explain the main motive behind the timing and ferocity with which government went about implementing OM. One argument pointed to the possibility that Robert Mugabe's regime was probably afflicted by a malignant symptom of colonial nostalgia and was impatient to restore the city of Harare to its former sunshine city status. Another school of thought advanced the thesis that it was mainly political retribution; the just-ended national elections had sent the clear message that Mugabe's party had lost ground to the opposition party in urban areas. This chapter begins by giving a historical outline of the cityscape in colonial Rhodesia as a backcloth and context against which to understand the developments that led to government implementing the operation restore order in the winter months of May to July 2005 and news media coverage of the operation.

Contextualising Operation Murambatsvina

Conceptions of the city as a place only fit for (amadoda sibili) Ndebele for 'real men' comes from and builds on a century-long tradition of black male migrant labourers being tolerated to come into contact with white people in urban areas (where this was unavoidable) to work for them, leaving their wives and children

Operation Restore (colonial) Order   209

behind in the reserves. Even the black male migrant labourers were not allowed to permanently establish themselves in the city as home. The early city and colonial urban planning had ensured that locations or African townships which consisted of male-only hostels were established usually on the western outskirts of the city to provide temporary accommodation for the male black migrant labourers. The central business district was a no-go area for Africans. It was one of those highly racially regulated spaces. For example blacks were forbidden to walk on pavements lest they came into physical contact with the white master. The city centre was therefore almost permanently white and very uncongested as early pictures of Harare city centre would show. Its whiteness became a synonym for cleanliness thus earning for itself the epithet of 'the sunshine city'. That status had completely changed by 2005 and understandably so more than two decades after the heinous and racist policies that had literally excluded blacks from making Harare their home had been removed with the coming of the independence government in 1980. Harare had morphed from a white city to a black city. The city centre had become heavily congested with an influx of unemployed people hustling to earn a living.

It is important to note here that the phenomenon of illegal housing structures in the shape of shacks built of bits of wood, discarded cardboard boxes, plastic, tarpaulin, or sacks was not an altogether new development on the outskirts of Zimbabwean cities. Shack building and shack dwelling is deeply rooted in a culture of black urban resistance which was itself a part of the broader struggle for liberation. Because the shacks always gave one the impression of structures put up in a hurry, temporary and contingent upon immediate pressing need for accommodation with no view of permanence, urban slums in Zimbabwe came to be ordinarily referred to as *Zvitangwena*, black people's way of acknowledging the Tangwena people, as the first to originate the architectural design of housing units fabricated in a hurry in defiance of oppressive legalistic injunctions against their right to occupy what they had considered to be their land by right of birth. Thus although the context was now different, the sprawling urban housing structures and slums always bore the mark and characteristic traces of a people in resistance against marginality. For such poor people the very act of being present in the city was in and of itself criminal and a statement of defiance against authority. It is when this fact is looked at in a context of ZANU-PF' waning popularity especially in towns and cities, which national elections of 2000, 2002 and more recently the 2005 harmonised elections had consistently confirmed. The voting patterns had shown that the ruling party had lost political ground to the opposition party in urban centres.

So, whether government's motive was to punish the poor sections of the urban population for voting 'wrongly' or to arrest the growing threat to urban stability which uncontrolled growth of urban population remains a moot point. Government, on 19 May 2005, launched a massive campaign to drain the urban swamps and restore some sort of order in the cities except that the new order had many colonial reminiscences. The vision of towns and cities as nodes of power and exclusive spaces of elite domination had to be reinscribed by force (Potts, 2011).

210 *Operation Restore (colonial) Order*

'Operation Murambatsvina' (drive out trash) was embarked upon to physically demolish the slums and drive their occupants out of the city. Initially city authorities issued out an order for those who owned and lived in what were described as illegal structures to pull them down themselves and salvage whatever they could by a given date, failure of which government bulldozers would roll in to demolish those structures. The focus of this chapter is on how, while the physical demolition of illegal structures was taking place, the press was effecting symbolic erasure and demolition, of the voices of those affected, from its news pages as is made apparent in the newspaper stories about Operation Murambatsvina in the period May to July 2005, which are discussed below.

The idea of maintaining a dual society with people belonging in the two sections of the country kept apart and following separate paths of development was not an original one to the nationalist leaders in ZANU-PF of the early 2000s. In fact, it had been the hallmark of the Rhodesian society imposed by colonial fiat and upheld and maintained by a regime of legislative measures since colonial conquest and occupation by white colonial settlers by the end of the nineteenth century. During that time it had been envisaged that such a policy based on racial difference between whites and blacks was to be physically enforced and supported by the force of law. The government of Rhodesia, under Prime Minister Sir Godfrey Huggins (1933–1956), had sought to put in place policies that ensured that as far as possible Africans would be kept away from European areas. Protection of white economic interests from competition by a bourgeoning black population in European areas, particularly in urban areas, was given as the main reason for pursuing the policy of racial partnership, which in reality was only different from racial apartheid in name. Then, the unchecked growth of a 'detribalised urban black population' was generally viewed as a contaminant that threatened white interests and white purity. Huggins as Prime Minister of Southern Rhodesia in 1938 is cited in Rifkind as having summed up the rationale for a policy of separate development in Rhodesia in the following terms:

> The European in this country can be likened to an island of white in a sea of black, with the artisan and the tradesman forming the shores and the professional classes the highlands in the centre. Is the native to be allowed to erode away the shores and gradually attack the highlands? To permit this would mean that the leaven of civilisation would be removed from the country, and the black man would inevitably revert to a barbarism worse than ever before. (Rifkind, 1968: 58)

Moffat before him and many white colonial administrators of that time were generally agreed on this policy of territorial segregation between the races in colonial Rhodesia. An influx of Africans in towns and cities was a general cause of apprehension and had to be kept in check through a cocktail of legal measures the Land Apportionment Act (1930); the Natives Registration Act (1936); the Native Land Husbandry Act (1951) etc. as well as force to control, regulate and limit the flow of Africans into urban areas.

Operation Restore (colonial) Order 211

Given this historical background it was thus paradoxical that a government led by a decorated liberation fighter of Mugabe's standing could have possibly conceived and implemented a policy so reminiscent of that dark colonial past against his people. It has remained enigmatic to date, for analysts to find so much resonance between what the type of city the Zimbabwean government sought to achieve by implementing Operation Muramabatsvina and the city in the colonial government's imaginary. The UN Special Envoy on Human Settlements Issues in Zimbabwe's report points out this contradictoriness and irony in the nationalist government retaining most of the colonial legal framework which had been used against blacks in the past:

> The institutional framework of governance in post-colonial Zimbabwe retained structures, laws and an 'elite' attitude and culture used during colonial times despite the liberation from minority rule in 1980. The nationalist elite seemed to have perpetuated the colonial mentality of high standards for a few at the expense of the majority. In the end, while the liberation struggle was against the 'white settlers' and the economic and political power they monopolised, the Government was not able to reverse the unequal and exploitative nature of colonial capitalism itself. (Tibaijuka, 2005: 16)

Many reports based on independent investigations carried out on Murambatsvina concur that the ruthlessness with which the programme to rid towns of people whose presence in towns and cities had been declared illegal under Operation Murambatsvina/Restore Order would make any racist colonialist of the past century turn green with envy (International Crisis Group 2005; Solidarity Peace Trust 2005, 2010). Driving people, mainly poor African urban residents out of town, as an idea, was premised on pernicious colonial assumption that the African's home is in the former 'native' reserves, and that his sojourn in town was therefore temporary. In colonial practice, the African man, as a migrant labourer, was supposed to be always mindful of the fact that one day he would return to reunite with his wife and children in his rural 'home'. The rural area was the source of his identity as an African. Only white people could call town, home. On attainment of independence the former colonised and marginalised black majority had been led to believe that the new government would pursue social justice policies to undo the marginalisation and dehumanisation they had suffered under racial segregation. So, most of those affected by OM must have had a rude awakening when they found themselves targeted for eviction and their shelter, which they had built at times with the tacit encouragement by the same politicians, demolished as illegal settlements or structures. They were disillusioned to find that in 2005, more than two decades after independence that white racist attitudes towards Africans were now embraced by black elites in government and being used against the urban poor. The black government:

> found it convenient to assert that rural-urban linkages were universal for 'proper' Zimbabweans and thus those displaced by Operation Murambatsvina

212 *Operation Restore (colonial) Order*

> could all return 'home' to rural areas, if they had to. Again there were con-
> tinuities with the colonial past and the various policies which had forced urban
> Africans to maintain their rural link in order to neutralise both their political
> and economic claims on white space and the cities. (Potts, 2011: 33)

Operation Murambatsvina was one clear instance of the colonial past catching up
with and surviving in the postcolonial present. Instead of rethinking the city as a
more inclusive space, the political class that took over government demonstrated
a lack of imagination beyond the straight colonial jacket they had inherited and
actively sought to repair and maintain. They were just content with replacing the
white masters as the managers of the old oppressive order which they were now
as committed to defend just as vigorously as they had fought against and criticised
it in the struggle for liberation. Due to the event-based reporting nature of professional newsroom practice in Zimbabwe as anywhere else in the world, few
stories on Operation Murambatsvina ever attempted to explore the underlying
structural inequalities behind urban poverty. The genealogical link between the
ongoing government blitz to drive poor black people out of the urban space to
colonial precedent of white racist exclusion of blacks from European areas was
occluded by the narrow (5Ws and an H) news algorithm on OM. Only Ray
Matikinye's story published in the *Zimbabwe Independent* newspaper attempted to
relate what was happening to similar events in Zimbabwe's colonial past in a
story titled: 'Chief Tangwena turning in his grave'. In his analysis the reporter
drew parallels between the current forced evictions of urban slum dwellers to
those of the Tangwena people in the late 1960s when he states that:

> Trudging along the main highway in search of alternative homes, they por-
> trayed scenes reminiscent of villagers evicted by the colonial regime from
> Gayeresi Ranch under the Land Tenure Act of 1969. But this time there was
> no famed traditional chief like Rekayi Tangwena to lead them in resisting
> state sponsored removals. (*Zimbabwe Independent*, May 2005).

What made Operation Murambatsvina uniquely different and extreme in its
violence is the fact that those displaced by this state sponsored displacement were
not relocated by the same government. There was no planned programme or
specified and designated geographical spaces the government offered as alternatives for resettlement. After the demolition of their homes, displaced people
were just expected to go away, to vanish or risk arrest and incarceration charged
with loitering. In fact preceding the operation, it had become common cause that
any woman found on the streets would be rounded up by police in evening raids
(Tibaijuka, 2005). Comparatively, the colonial regime's forced evictions of rural
communities discussed elsewhere in this book were far much more benign in that
the evicted were always displaced in a way that preserved their community ties
undisrupted, and they were always relocated to a specified geographical space
albeit of a more inhospitable type that Chabal (2013: 153) describes as: 'the forcible displacement of people to regions of a country that are unsuited to

Operation Restore (colonial) Order   213

agriculture, where they sink into poverty, despair and hunger'. But, this would happen as a slow and drawn-out process. Under Operation Murambatsvina, on the other hand, the social shock and awe was immediate, drastic and unmitigated. Operation Murambatsvina was not a resettlement programme, as was made clear on a number of occasions in official statements by police officers in charge of conducting the operation. Police Officer Commanding Harare Province Senior Assistant Commissioner Edmore Veterai was quoted as saying: 'The purpose of the clean-up was not to resettle people but to wipe out vice on the streets' (*The Herald*, 25 May 2005: 1). So generally those affected by the operation had to be classified under the general category of law breakers and common criminals to justify their treatment as such by the law enforcement agents. First they had to be constructed as other than human at the discursive level before inhuman treatment was meted out on them.

Criminalisation of urban poverty

The very naming of the police blitz to drive poor people out of town, Operation Murambatsvina or alternatively Operation Restore Order, was couched in a manner that made it sound as if the government meant well for its citizens, that it was a pro-people intervention and therefore to be accepted. *The Herald* newspaper played no small role in sanitising and smoothening the rougher sides of the operation so that in the reader's mind the police eviction of poor people from towns and cities appeared as justifiable war on crime. Some of the paper's early headlines on the subject clearly demonstrate the paper's ideological orientation as one of setting the broader parameters and interpretive frameworks within which its readers were expected to make sense of the ongoing campaign in terms of regular policing. For example, the following headlines illustrate this point:

> "Blitz targets tuck shops, shacks" with bullet points that announced police victory over urban crime. "Owners given 3-month ultimatum; More criminals, dealers arrested" (*The Herald*, 24 May 2005)
> "Police demolish tuck shops, flea market stalls in Harare" (*The Herald*, 25 May 2005)
> 'Rise in criminal activities necessitated the clampdown' (*The Herald*, 27 May 2005)
> 'Criminal activities decline in Harare' (*The Herald*, 27 May 2005)

The Herald's front page story of 24 May 2005, set out below, was key in setting the tone for the paper's reportage on subsequent events associated with the government-sponsored operation to clean-up the cityscapes:

HEADLINE: Blitz targets tuck shops, shacks
KICKER: Owners given 3-month ultimatum; More criminals, dealers arrested
PICTURE CAPTION: Property owners in Harare have been given three months' notice to destroy illegal structures such as shacks and tuck shops. Here are

CITY OF HARARE

SPEECH BY THE CHAIRPERSON OF THE HARARE COMMISSION CDE. SEKESAI MAKWAVARARA ON THE OCCASION OF THE OFFICIAL LAUNCH OF *"OPERATION MURAMBATSVINA"* AT THE TOWN HOUSE ON 19TH MAY, 2005 AT 12 NOON

The City of Harare wishes to advise the public that in its efforts to improve service delivery within the City, it will embark on **Operation Murambatsvina**, in conjunction with Zimbabwe Republic Police (ZRP). This is a programme to enforce by-laws to stop all forms of illegal activities.

These violations of the by-laws are in areas of vending, traffic control, illegal structures, touting/abuse of commuters by rank marshals, street-life/prostitution, vandalism of property infrastructure, stock theft, illegal cultivation, among others have led to the deterioration of standards thus negatively affecting the image of the City. The attitude of the members of the public as well as some City officials has led to a point whereby Harare has lost its glow. We are determined to bring it back.

Harare was renowned for its cleanliness, decency, peace, tranquil environment for business and leisure; therefore we would like to assure all residents that all these illegal activities will be a thing of the past.

Figure 7.1 Notice of official Launch of Operation Murambatsvina. Reprinted with permission from *The Herald*.

some of the structures in Mbare which are to be demolished. (Aerial picture of Mbare before the demolitions)

BYLINE: Herald reporters

LEAD: The clean-up campaign in Harare has moved into residential areas where property owners with shacks and illegal extensions as well as tuck shop operators have been given a three-month ultimatum to demolish or legalise structures on their properties.

BODY: The move came as police arrested 72 more people in Harare, 654 in Mashonaland West, 518 in Masvingo and 10 in Mashonaland East provinces under the operation to rid urban centres of crime and other illegal activities.

In Harare, they confiscated 1200 litres of diesel, 1070 litres of petrol and various quantities of several basic commodities worth billions of dollars, as they intensified their clampdown on criminals, illegal dealers, touts, flea market operators and general lawlessness in the capital city on Sunday.

The 72 arrested in Harare brought the number of those rounded up in the capital to 9725 under a swoop code-named "Operation Restore Order" which was recently launched to clean up the city. Several street people were also rounded up and some of them were yesterday taken to a farm on the outskirts of Mabvuku.

The headline accurately describes the police operation as 'a blitz' to capture the scope and scale of its devastation and the seriousness of its effects on those targeted. It is indeed a blitzkrieg. The target of the police offensive is tuck shops and shacks, the headline announces. So, people, their owners, are somehow not the direct target of the police operation. They are only indirectly affected. They suffer collateral damage. To minimise and understate the social consequences of the blitzkrieg and its discriminatory dimensions against the urban poor, these social dimensions are only introduced by way of a kicker with two bullet points; 'Owners given 3-month ultimatum; More criminals, dealers arrested'. The concept 'criminals' is introduced as so obvious a characteristic of those arrested that the paper need not wait for their trial and conviction as such in a caught of law. Since news as a genre of discourse conceals its constructedness under the cloak of truth and facticity (Bird, 2010), what it states is often accepted as a record of fact with the result that the police operation in this case, is understood as ultimately beneficial to law abiding members of society, since those who suffer under it are 'criminals' after all. The list of offenders and their offences, which included, among other things, touting, engaging in informal trading/dealing, operating flea markets, panning for gold, vending and just being unemployed and loitering on the streets, clearly show that poverty was the underlying factor in all the livelihoods strategies now being delegitimised as crimes. Such an inordinately large number of those arrested in Harare alone (9,725) is stated mater-of-factly by the reporters who do not find it warranting their wonderment. That fact did not raise any suspicion among the journalists covering the story to seek out the comment of those accused. Their construction as criminals is one in which they are not invited to participate or mitigate.

216 *Operation Restore (colonial) Order*

But this story is probably one example that fits a lazy journalist's story which could have been written without the reporter ever leaving the newsroom. All the reporter needed to do was telephone various police provincial headquarters and ask the presiding officer at the rank of Police Commissioner (for attribution purposes) and get statistical information about those they had rounded up and the nature of charges preferred against them and present this as the news. Such an assumption is strongly supported by the way the story is sourced. The officialdom in this story is striking, though not exceptional. The table below shows the story's sources who spoke in their official capacities:

Table 7.1 Officialdom in news sourcing at *The Herald*

Source	Position and institution represented
Oliver Mandipaka	Superintendent police spokesperson
Nomutsa Chideya	Town Clerk, Harare
Paul Nyathi	Police Assistant Inspector Mashonaland West, provincial police spokesperson
Darlington Mathuthu	Police Inspector Mashonaland East, provincial police spokesperson
Patson Nyabadza	Police Inspector Masvingo, police spokesperson

The blitzkrieg on urban slum dwellers was only matched with its equivalent in the avalanche of news disinformation that *The Herald* spearheaded. With *The Herald* as the only national daily paper in circulation after the closure of *The Daily News* in 2003, a campaign of disinformation and misinformation was mounted on the brutal violations of poor people's rights under Operation Murambatsvina. As evidenced in the way the above story and many others after it were sourced the demolitions of poor people's shelter as illegal was itself symbolic of the even more ruthless and brutal annihilation and silencing of the same poor people's voices and opinions in *The Herald*'s stories about their circumstances. Through news sourcing practices *The Herald* symbolically produced subaltern silence on Operation Murambatsvina.

Nationalists and colonial nostalgia

In a headline story published on 28 May 2005 under the headline: 'President backs cleanup', *The Herald* as had become its standard practice drew out President Mugabe's view on the controversial and highly sensitive issue and his comments were marshalled in a story whose aim was to communicate that the clean-up campaign enjoyed support and legitimacy at the highest level of government. Mugabe's endorsement of OM betrays a neurotic desire to escape and break free from the prison of his black skin into whiteness, a nostalgic yearning for a return to the lost colonial paradise of ordered and neat white cities. It is revealing of a debilitating nervous condition afflicting the national bourgeois class so well theorised by Fanon (1970) in 'Black Skin White Masks'. The national bourgeois is afflicted with a sudden realisation that their interests as a class were all along co-terminus with those of the white settler colonialist master class whom they had now replaced in power, and that they would be better served by the same discriminatory institutional framework on the basis of whose criticism they had mobilised grassroots support to dislodge colonial rule.

They were now committed to reviving it and where it had been dismantled, to see to it that it was repaired and restored. It has arrived at that stage when the new ruling caste realises, as Fanon et al. (1963: 142) aptly points out, that decolonisation should never have meant anything 'more than the takeover unchanged the legacy of the economy, the thought and the institutions left by the colonialists'. *The Herald*'s news work on this and other issues in which the dominated classes were caught up represents the most apt exemplification of how the legacy of colonialism was fraudulently continued with in service of the new black political class, beyond attainment of political independence.

For their part, as the inheriting class, they would spare no effort in arresting the momentum towards national transformation they had promised during the struggle for liberation. It redefines its national vocation as one of simply ensuring that 'the unfair advantages which are a legacy of the colonial period' (Fanon et al., 1963: 122) are securely transferred into their (native) hands. So now that they have replaced or rather joined the whites in the leafy suburbs of Harare, Bulawayo, Gweru or Mutare, they become victims of the same siege mentality uneasy at the prospect that if left unchecked the rural/urban drift of the poor 'unwashed' masses, posed an unusual threat to their newly acquired comforts. The seductive cleanliness which settler governments had maintained by edict and coercion, the independence government now sought to restore by brute force. In *The Herald* story of 28 May 2005 below, President Mugabe gives his nod to the coercive means being employed by government's uniformed forces to drive mostly poor people from urban areas without providing them with alternative shelter in the midst of the cold season. Below are excerpts from *The Herald* story.

HEADLINE: President backs clean-up

BYLINE: Herald reporters

LEAD: President Mugabe yesterday threw his weight behind the ongoing clean-up campaign as police razed to the ground Harare's biggest illegal settlement – Tongogara Park at White Cliff Farm along the Harare-Bulawayo road.

BODY: Cde Mugabe who was addressing the 162 ZANU-PF Central Committee extraordinary session in Harare, said Government was fully behind the clean-up campaigns by the police aimed at restoring the status of the cities and towns. President Mugabe said the Government had to act in cleaning up the mess in towns and cities in order to restore their old fame of cleanliness and safety.

'Our cities and towns had deteriorated to levels that were a real cause for concern. Apart from the failing reticulation systems and broken roads and streets, our cities and towns, including Harare, the capital, had become havens for illicit and criminal practices and activities which just could not be allowed to go on,' he said.

'Those who have wrongly suffered damage (of their properties) action will be taken to remedy what will have been damaged. From the mess should emerge new businesses, new traders, new practices and a whole new and salubrious urban environment.

That is our wish and vision. Our tourists and visitors first look at our capitals and towns. Capitals, cities and towns are what shape the impressions of a country,' he said.

Police in Harare have embarked on a campaign to clean up the city by destroying such illegal structures as homes, tuck shops and flea markets. The illegal settlement near Snake Park was demolished amid minor resistance from disgruntled settlers. When *The Herald* visited White Cliff Farm yesterday morning, some unruly youths had gathered and attempted to resist the move but riot police reacted swiftly and calmed the situation.

This story served to clear any lingering doubts on whether the operation was just an act arising from police overzealousness or whether it was fully sanctioned by the state. The story's emphasis is on the desirability of the move to clear the mess in towns and cities without explaining what and how the mess had come about in the first place. The President has thrown his weight behind the clean-up campaign, we are told. The newsworthiness lies in the timeliness of the President pronouncing himself on the matter. His remarks come at a time it would have been least expected, coming as it did at a time when Harare's biggest 'illegal' settlement was being razed to the ground by the police. It could not have been more ironic that President Mugabe could give a nod to the demolition of a settlement as illegal, whose very name 'Tongogara Park' invoked and celebrated one of the most revered fallen heroes of the second Chimurenga and decorated icon of the revolutionary struggle, a fact which would have suggested that the settlement enjoyed the President's and the ruling ZANU-PF party blessings as a shining example of black empowerment projects. Structurally this story foregrounds what the President said and not the police demolition of so-called illegal settlements, the sheer numbers of those affected by such action or how owners of such demolished properties were affected as the basis of the story's newsworthiness. In the rest of the story the reporter sustains the play of irony and ambiguity through exposing and juxtaposing statements with contradicting evidence. Here is a president whose government's inaction against 'illegal' farm occupations only a few years back in 2000 now unleashes the full force of his state machinery to evict those urban dwellers whose action was in many ways similar to and in part inspired by that of newly resettled farmers who had invaded and also illegally settled on white commercial farms. The only difference, the urban squatters had chosen to settle in the wrong places – towns.

The President's remark that 'the Government had to act in cleaning up the mess in towns and cities in order to restore their old fame of cleanliness and safety' is equally liable to interpretation as betraying nostalgia for the restoration of the lost lustre of cities and towns in colonial Rhodesia. Difficult questions could have been asked of the President to clarify which 'old fame of cleanliness' he had in mind, which he wanted restored. But with the journalist type at *The Herald*, when the President speaks then theirs is to write with no questions asked. It would also be difficult to imagine how restoration of cleanliness and order would be accomplished without resorting to the same control mechanisms and institutional arrangements by which that cleanliness had been instituted and maintained by white settler governments in the first place. Under racial segregationist management and spatial arrangement of urban centres, cleanliness and orderliness of the city was synonymous with strict restriction of Africans as far as possible in rural confinement where they belonged. Under such arrangements black's stay in town was only temporary and closely monitored and regulated. The logic of Operation Murambatsvina was different only in that instead of using racial difference as the basis for segregation it used class. The black poor had no place in towns and cities. Only the professional class in formal employment had the right of citizenship in towns and cities.

The operation to rid cities of poor people 'was based on the assumption that those pushed out of the urban areas could "return" to homes in the rural areas' (Raftopoulos, 2009: 221). The idea that the evicted town dwellers would return to their rural homes represents a return to the colonial order which had defined urban areas as exclusively white areas and tribal trust lands (TTLs) as spaces fit for blacks to call home. The restoration sought, under this programme, was the restoration of the old order and the benefits it would guarantee for the new black ruling elite. It must be remembered that 'the permanence of its black urban population' was a blemish, an egregious fact white 'Rhodesia had come to terms with' only by-and-by (Chennells, 2015: 5).

By representing the urban poor who lived in backyard shacks, who owned and operated the tuck shops as well as engaged in informal trade as the 'mess' that needed to be gotten rid of, the story rhetorically justifies the dehumanising treatment victims of Operation Murambatsvina suffered. Portrayal of people as other than human, as refuse or garbage rationalises their treatment as such. Even this clearly exclusionary eviction of poor people from towns is spoken of as in the general interest of the nation as a whole through the repetitive use of the inclusive possessive 'our' in 'That is *our* wish and vision. *Our* tourists and visitors first look at *our* capitals and towns' (emphasis is mine). The journalist and his implied reader are lexically constructed as sharers in the same wish and vision as the President on the issues under discussion in the story. They supposedly share the same concerns with the President about taking the necessary steps to ensure that the country makes the right impression on 'our tourists' even if such action may mean police razing to the ground some people's shelter and forcibly driving a section of the urban population out of 'our towns and cities'. Ironically in seeking to restore order in towns the political elite is conveniently silent about the type of order they seek to restore – a colonial capitalist order. '*Our tourists*', the imaginary final consumer of the city's restored cleanliness, is a signifier of how the local national bourgeois class is extroverted and articulated with the international capitalist class at the expense of its exploited poor classes.

As a paper committed to serving the government of the day, *The Herald* typically privileges government official line on national issues such as Operation Murambatsvina. The above story is an illustrative case of how *The Herald*'s presentation of news structures it according to a hierarchical pyramid of credibility of attribution, beginning with comments made by the President as the most significant and therefore credible source, followed by those of his cabinet ministers most directly connected with the issue being reported in a descending order of importance to the most junior police officer, with comments by eye witnesses and ordinary victims coming right towards the tail-end of the story just to give confirmatory evidence as shown in the table below. *The Herald*'s arrangedd its sources in the order of credibility in story above beginning with President Mugabe who is extensively quoted at the beginning of the story. Minister of Local Government Ignatius Chombo is indirectly reported handing over newly built Siyaso Industrial Complex for use by informal traders. Minister of Small and Medium Enterprises Development, Sithembiso Nyoni is quoted directly reassuring the affected informal traders. Harare Metropolitan Governor David Karimanzira is indirectly reported as encouraging informal traders to access government loans for their businesses. Chairperson of Harare Commission, Sekesai Makwavarara and Minister of Mines Amos Midzi are just mentioned as witnessing the occasion way down the story. Police spokesperson, Superintendent Oliver Mandipaka is last to be quoted directly warning as well as urging compliance with police orders. One of the affected residents at Tongogara Park is quoted but largely described as complying with police the order to participate in demolishing his own 'illegal structure'.

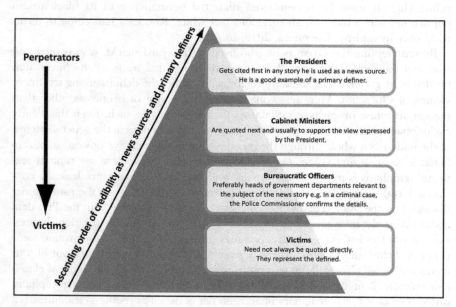

Figure 7.2 The hierarchy of primary definition on the Operation Murambatsvina story at *The Herald*.

Operation Restore (colonial) Order   221

The President's tacit endorsement of the clean-up campaign seemed to have the effect of emboldening *The Herald* reporters in their near-celebratory coverage of police triumphal march to rid cities and towns of 'criminal elements'. Two days later the paper publishes three different stories on the subject. One of the three stories published on front page is cited below for closer analysis (*The Herald*, 30 May 2005):

HEADLINE: Police storm Mbare
BULLETS: *Illegal structures* ripped down; Demolition continues today
BYLINE: Nelson Chenga
LEAD: A dark cloud of doom and gloom hung over Harare's oldest suburb, Mbare, yesterday as police demolished some *illegal structures* in their clean-up swoop dubbed Operation Murambatsvina (No Tolerance to *Filth*).
BODY: It was a hive of activity as shack dwellers – mainly in Mbare's Jo'burg Lines section – ripped down structures, jam-packed their bags and headed for various destinations. Police said the operation in Mbare would be intensified today.

Mbare – the country's most densely populated urban settlement – has been a notorious *criminal hideout* for decades. Police last week recovered 30 tonnes of sugar worth $300 million, 8000 liters of diesel and 13500 litres of petrol at an *illegal warehouse*.

This comes at a time when the former *illegal settlements* of Tongogara Park in White Cliff Farm, Hatcliffe Extension, Nyadzonya, Chimoio and New Park near Mt Hampden in Good Hope now resemble the aftermath of a devastating earthquake.

Officer Commanding Harare Police Senior Assistant Commissioner Edmore Veterai yesterday vowed to clean up all the *illegal settlements* around Harare and its satellite towns of Chitungwiza, Ruwa, Epworth and Norton. He urged residents to pull down any *prohibited structures* on their properties, adding the clean-up campaign was at full throttle in Mbare and other suburbs.

Hundreds of distraught people still adjusting to the situation were busy going through the debris picking up their belongings and organising transport yesterday. Still in shock and grim-faced, others were milling around their former homes that were now just heaps of rubble.

"I have no idea where to go and I have been told that they (police) don't want to see me here again," said one settler at Tongogara Park, moving about a thriving garden of cabbages and carrots.

Yesterday, police patrolled all the settlements around Harare which were razed to the ground last week to ensure *the illegal former occupants* moved out as required. (emphasis mine) ...

This story was also accompanied by a large landscape close-up photograph showing the evicted shack dwellers loading their household furniture and goods on to a lorry to an unknown destination according to the caption. They stand

222　*Operation Restore (colonial) Order*

with their backs to their former illegal shelters in the background now reduced to heaps of rubble. The style of reporting in the above story is reminiscent of *The Rhodesia Herald*'s reporting of the aftermath of the demolition of the Tangwena villages and the forcible eviction of the Tangwena people in 1969. The reportorial intention cannot be easily pinned down as one serving the propaganda purposes in favour of government's position on the issue of Operation Murambatsvina. Careful selection of lexical items in the headline and the lead paragraph emphasise the imagery of doom, gloom the devastation and destruction caused by police action bring into poor people's lives. This comes out very evidently in the reporter's diction of 'storm' ripped down, demolition 'swoop, words that have strong associations of violence and aggression. Although the story draws on and unproblematically uses such labels as 'illegal former occupants' to refer to those being evicted by police and such negative epithets as 'illegal structures' to refer to the buildings being demolished by police, the reporter's ambivalence on whether he believes this to be right becomes evident in his description of the victims as 'distraught people still adjusting to the situation were busy going through the debris picking up their belongings and organising transport yesterday. Still in shock and grim-faced, others were milling around their former homes that were now just heaps of rubble' and the demolished 'illegal settlements' … now resembling the aftermath of a devastating earthquake'. Such language may have been meant to elicit sympathy for the victims of police demolitions or alternatively to portray the police as invincible.

In this and other stories on the clean-up campaign *The Herald* introduced and consistently used negative labelling as a strategy to invite the reader to participate in its condemnation of urban poor people, their informal businesses and their shelter as illegal and therefore deserving of any negative consequences arising from the government operation to restore order in the cities. The discursive operation of *The Herald* story on Operation Murambatsvina epistemically produces those being evicted as having invited the wrath of the police upon themselves and deservedly so, because their presence in the city is illegal, their dwelling structures were built in breach of the law and are therefore illegal and their businesses, that of informal trading, touting and vending are also illegal. The suburbs they live in have become havens of crime. They represent the filth, hence the need for the clean-up campaign. Such language delegitimates and criminalises the poverty of the poor and justifies our (police's) 'inhuman' actions carried out on them, in the form of arbitrary arrest and rounding-up for police interrogation, and demolition of their houses. The slum dwellers do not even deserve the presumption of innocence until proven guilty. Suspicion is enough grounds for treating them as guilty of crimes until they can prove themselves otherwise. Those found to be out of formal employment are either guilty of engaging in illegal dealing, and trade, or if they are women, guilty of loitering for purposes of prostitution.

Maggotisation of the urban poor

As a way of justifying their brutal treatment of the urban poor people, dominant elites often begin by discursively constructing their target victim as somehow deserving of such treatment by use of language that demeans them and objectifies them as other than human. *The Herald* story below is one such example of delegitimation of the poor's presence in cities and towns (*The Herald*, 16 June 2005):

HEADLINE: 'Government not punishing people'
BYLINE: Herald reporter
LEAD: The Government is not punishing people under the ongoing Operation Murambatsvina/Restore Order but is merely restoring sanity in the country, Police Commissioner Cde Augustine Chihuri said yesterday.
BODY: Cde Chihuri said the exercise was restoring sanity in major cities and that the joint operation with other Government departments and local authorities would be sustained.

This would clean the country of the "crawling mass of maggots bent on destroying the economy and also to spruce up the images of our cities"

"Under Operation Murambatsvina, the Government is re-inventing things properly and it is not true that it is punishing the people. And I would like also to thank the people, especially those who were affected, for not going wild during the exercise, he said ...

Whenever power wants to assuage itself and others about the legitimacy of its own actions and (ab)uses of power over the subjects under its domination, it chooses to represent the targets of its violations in demeaning terms, terms that construct the dominated 'Other' as other than human. In this classic example the Police Commissioner represents the urban poor as 'crawling maggots bent on destroying the economy'. The consequences of such utterances were the brutal destruction of the poor people's shelter, leaving them exposed to the elements in the middle of the cold winter season. This behaviour has its many parallels in the history of postcolonial Africa. The genocide in Rwanda was preceded by the governing Hutus comparing Tutsis with cockroaches on their Radio Television Libres des Mille Collines (RTMC) radio station. Most recently the Zulu king's irresponsible utterances comparing foreign black immigrants in South Africa to lice and ants sparked xenophobic attacks and black violence on fellow blacks. It is important to note that the whole history of slavery and colonisation of other peoples by the west was closely connected to how enlightenment Europe produced knowledge about other peoples as Europe's inferior other (Said, 1995).

The poor are with no words

In the absence of any other daily newspaper by a different publisher from Zimpapers, the Zimbabwe newspaper reading public was left with very few sources of alternative interpretations of political realities and economic and social dimensions of the unfolding clean-up campaign. *The Standard*, a privately owned weekly newspaper under the Alpha Media Holdings stable, offered the only meaningful alternative story to that of *The Herald* on Operation Murambatsvina. There were other independent newspapers publishing this time such as

224   *Operation Restore (colonial) Order*

The Mirror, the *Zimbabwe Independent*, and the *Financial Gazette* but they together mounted to a very feeble challenge to *The Herald*'s hegemonic dominance of the Zimbabwean media market. Although *The Daily Mirror* had announced that it would follow a middle of the road editorial policy, its reportage on issues was generally viewed as more sympathetic to the ruling ZANU-PF party ideology so that its angle on any story was not significantly different from the line that *The Herald* would take. The other two weekly papers were business weeklies meant as fitting reading for business elites. That left *The Standard* to fill the void as far as news and commentary on general political subjects targeting an average reader was concerned. Its stories were therefore expected to present the only alternative views on Operation Murambatsvina to the reader. The Zimbabwean society was highly polarised along political lines throughout most of the first decade of the 21st century and the media played an instrumental role in fanning political differences through the way they reported on issues including on such contentious developments as Operation Murambatsvina. Given this background it would be rather simplistic to believe that there was any newspaper, one could turn to for the 'true' story on such an emotive and politically charged subject as the forced evictions of urban poor people. Thus, the comparative analysis of the two papers' coverage of the clean-up campaign in cities and towns is not driven by an attempt to establish which story was truer, rather the objective is to explicate the divergences and to possibly seek out the reasons for these differences and how these might throw a new light on underlying deep structures that influence how journalism continues to serve or underserve the interests of emancipation and the decolonial project.

From when the first news story on Operation Murambatsvina was broken, through to the point when the demolitions were halted after the damning report of the UN Special Envoy Report on Human Settlements, Mrs Anna Kajumulo Tbaijuka in mid-July, *The Standard*, just like *The Herald* kept the Operation Murambatsvina story on top of its news agenda. In this section, I analyse some of *The Standard*'s typical stories on the issue. *The Standard* as a weekly tabloid newspaper differed from *The Herald* in that compiling stories for a weekly paper gave its reporters ample time to conduct in-depth research and thus introduce deeper analysis than could be possible under the tight reporting schedule of a daily paper. A cursory look at *The Standard*'s headline stories on Operation Murambatsvina shows that the paper took a stand in support and defence of the victims of the operation's claims and rights against the state as can be deduced from the headlines listed below:

'Angry Residents beat up police' 23 May 2005; 'Government condemned' 29 May 2005; 'Stayaway' 5 June 2005; 'Child killed in clean-up' 12 June 2005; 'Clean-up splits Zanu PF'19 June 2005; 'Clean-up forces 300 000 pupils out of school' 26 June 2005; 'UN envoy "upset"' 3 July 2005; 'Chombo, Mohadi clash' 10 July 2005; 'Councils face huge lawsuits' 17 July 2005; 'UN orders halt to demolitions' 24 July 2005.

From when the story broke out, *The Standard* consistently led with a story on Operation Murambatsvina on its front page except only in its end of July edition. In each of these story headlines, *The Standard* was unequivocal in representing government as the aggressor and those affected by the

Operation Restore (colonial) Order 225

demolitions as innocent victims. *The Standard's* story generally read more like a story written in response to the cumulative stories *The Herald's* would have published during the week in a process that betrayed the existence of inter-media agenda setting between the papers. Thus, where *The Herald* has published stories celebrating police success and representing the police force as invincible, *The Standard* pricks a hole to deflate that confidence by publishing such stories as 'Angry residents beat up police' and 'Government condemned'. While on the surface the headlines might suggest a grassroots-up approach to stories at *The Standard*, a closer analysis of the actual stories proved to the contrary. Its style of reporting does not represent a serious departure from the dominant elite-centric paradigm that structured news reporting at *The Herald*. Below are excerpts from selected stories to illustrate this point (*The Standard* 23 May 2005).

HEADLINE: Angry residents beat up police
BYLINE: Foster Dongozi
LEAD: Frustrated residents of Chitungwiza rose up on Friday, after enduring days of brutality and intimidation and fought running battles with police officers who were demolishing tuck-shops and confiscating goods from vendors.
BODY: Police and residents, as well as children were engaged in running battles, resulting in the stoning of a ZUPCO bus and a supermarket in the area.

MDC president, Morgan Tsvangirai, lashed out at the government, saying the ongoing clampdown in urban areas to flush out alleged illegal foreign currency dealers, flea-market and tuck shop operators was a government sponsored exercise to punish urban dwellers for voting for the MDC in 31 March general elections. The police blitz was also unleashed on other MDC strong-holds of Harare, Bulawayo and Gweru.

Other areas that were also targeted include Harare's Kuwadzana Extension, Highfield and Epworth. Unconfirmed reports suggested some police details may have sustained injuries when they faced a barrage of missiles from the defiant residents of St Mary's.

Job Sikhala, the Member of Parliament for the area, confirmed the skirmishes in the volatile constituency but was quick to distance himself from the violence.

"Kwakagwiwa hondo inohlisa muSt Mary's." (There was a fierce fighting in St Mary's). Sikhala said: "It was not something that was organised. It was the people's combined eruptive anger."

Police spokesperson, Superintendent Oliver Mandipaka, was said to be "busy" according to a person who answered his cell phone when The Standard sought his comment ...

The headline of this story immediately marks the story as one dedicated to give the subaltern a voice. The headline promises a story that is a clear departure from *The Herald's* pro-government line of reporting. Instead of representing the affected residents as powerless victims of the police clean-up campaign it

226 *Operation Restore (colonial) Order*

actually gives agency to the urban poor people who are represented as capable of offering some resistance and standing up to police brutality in 'Angry residents beat-up police'. The lead of the story, however, tells of something rather different. Instead of the said member of the police force who was beaten up the reader is then told that residents rose and 'fought running battles with the police'. Such a statement does not at all suggest the residents actually beat up the police. What the headline succeeds in achieving is an over-romanticisation of the dominated groups' capability to resist their subjugation. It would have been more consistent with what the story goes on to report if the headline had announced instead that 'Angry residents stone bus, supermarket' because this is what is actually reported in the story.

The idea of subaltern seizing agency through resistance was a favoured story line with *The Standard* as it is further developed in subsequent stories on Murambatsvina. For example, in a story the paper published on 29 May 2005 headlined: 'Terror of "black boots" in Glen View', affected residents of Glenview and Budiriro suburbs are reported to have staged some acts of resistance and one of the affected residents is quoted as saying: 'We rose and we are proud. We said no to police brutality and we said no to colonial type oppression'. In this regard it can be argued that *The Standard* to a reasonable extent managed to report some dimensions of Operation Murambatsvina from the standpoint of the people affected and in that regard to bring to the fore, dimensions of the clean-up campaign which would otherwise have been lost to the newspaper reading public. What remains unsaid though is whether the slum dwellers were able to alter the course of history or extract any concessions from the authorities through their acts of resistance.

But in keeping with accepted journalistic standards, the story, after describing residents' frustration, seeks an elite figure's voice to comment, define and validate the authenticity of the event. The paper goes on to quote Morgan Tsvangirai, president of the opposition party, Movement for Democratic Change (MDC). As the story develops, an MDC Member of Parliament for the area affected, Mr Job Sikhala, is also given an opportunity to comment. As a way of balancing the one-sided comments sourced from the opposition party, the reporter then goes on to explain that efforts to get comment from the police spokesperson Superintendent Oliver Mandipaka were unsuccessful. This is important for the story as a rhetorical device to increase the credibility of the story. The reader is supposed to accept this familiar excuse for journalists' failure to write balanced stories through one-sided information sourcing. It is not enough to state that a particular source's phone went unanswered, or 'so and so could not be reached for comment'.

The way this story and many other stories published in the private press, presents issues attest to the pervasive elite nature of news. The story template of *The Standard* only differs from that of *The Herald* in the preferred elites it uses. Instead of using elites in government, it uses those in opposition to government and somehow real subaltern voices slip through the cracks and cannot be apprehended by journalism's methods of knowledge production. So, the privately owned press differed from state controlled press like *The Herald* not in principle, but only in the elites it uses as sources. They sourced their stories with a different elite group, the counter-elite. Government officials also made it difficult for privately owned newspapers to balance opposition party views with those of members of the ruling party, the majority of who controlled the state bureaucracy, by simply not being available for comment to journalists from the independent press whom they labelled as enemies of the state, agents of regime change always pandering to the imperialist interests of former colonisers. One of the most defining characteristics of powerlessness is lack of organisational strength. For example, there was no organisation that aggregated authentic views and speak for slum dwellers and act as a legitimate point of interface with institutions of power such as the media or the state bureaucracy. In spite of their numbers, they just existed as individuals and in that way they become easy prey to oppressive hegemonic forces.

In its lead story: 'Government condemned', published on 29 May 2005 *The Standard* continues to turn to opposition party leaders or to leaders of elite institutions in civil society to pronounce themselves on the government operation. Views of ordinary slum dwellers continued to suffer erasure in the private press as in the state controlled press. They tend to be spoken about or their plight simply opportunistically exhibited in support of already existing social agendas at times remotely connected to their urgent needs to bolster existing contestations of power among elites. The demolition of urban poor people's houses is important to *The Standard* and that section of elites it favours not in themselves and how they affect the evicted people, but only in so far as they can be marshalled as further evidence that the ruling elite was unfit to govern.

To underline the salience of the stories on Operation Murambatsvina, *The Standard* in its 29 May 2005 edition, dedicated the entire comment and views page to analysis and comment on the clean-up exercise. In the editorial comment, the newspaper's editors drew parallels between the ongoing government exercise to drive excess people out of towns to rural areas with colonial policies which were meant to regulate and control the flow of blacks into towns. According to the editors:

> There could not be any poignant reminder of how the colonial administration sought to protect big business, (read white interests) while emptying the townships of excess workforce, and how ironically the 'people's government' is slavishly re-enacting the same policies. (*The Standard*, May 29, 2005: 8)

The opinion piece titled: 'Freedonia's inimitable reign of terror' placed just below the editorial comment, probably as a marker of its importance was even more forthright in its satirical comparison of the current government policy of forced evictions of the urban poor with colonial policies. Below are some excerpts from the story (*The Standard* 29 May. 2005):

HEADLINE: Freedonia's inimitable reign of terror
BYLINE: Dumisani Mpofu

228 *Operation Restore (colonial) Order*

LEAD: There was fear and confusion in Freedonia. The security agencies were all over the streets and there was great gnashing of teeth and wailing. Menacing security agents, some on horseback policed the streets. It was as if there had been a military take-over and law enforcement agencies were on high alert.

Body: Freedonia's quiet old man said he had not seen such a thing since the 1950s and 1960s when the colonials were in the habit of driving indigenous people out of the city centres or raiding the locations – areas where the indigenous people were confined to in the urban areas.

Tears welling up in his eyes (we suspected it was the anger that memories of such events triggered) the old man said he saw no difference between what was happening in Freedonia and what the colonials used to. He broke the silence: "Wherever the colonials are, they must be enjoying what is happening. I tell you there were times when we were not allowed in the city, just as they are doing to the Kombis. In the locations, they raided whole areas demanding to know who had passes to stay because everyone who had no 'legitimate business, was supposed to be in the reserves (reserves of excess workforce). Most of you who are young must watch Cry Freedom".

The stinging satire in this article was far much more effective in bringing out what the issues were in the oppressive way Operation Murambatsvina was implemented by government. The continuities with the colonial order were brought home and lampooned in this satire about a country whose very name 'Freedonia' epitomised freedom. To a large extent *The Standard* and its sister papers in the independent press could be relied on to challenge the dominant discourses on Operation Murambatsvina carried in *The Herald* and other state controlled news publications such as *The Sunday Mail, The Chronicle* and *The Sunday News*. Authentic subaltern voices were almost always subordinated to other vested interests through elite sourcing of news. *The Standard's* main sources on the clean-up campaign were largely drawn from the coalition of political opposition forces within civil society and in the main opposition political party MDC, who obviously saw in the unpopular clean-up campaign an opportunity to massage popular dissent and the discourse in support of the general political programme to dislodge ZANU-PF from power.

The Standard's front page story titled: 'Stayaway' (5 June 2005) is a clear example of the manipulation of the Murambatsvina tragedy for political mileage by a coalition of opposition party leaders and those within civil society who backed them. Below are some excerpts from that story (*The Standard*, 5 June 2005):

HEADLINE: Stayaway
KICKER: MDC, civic bodies call for mass action
BYLINE: Foster Dongozi
LEAD: Opposition political parties, civic organisations and labour unions have called for a potentially crippling mass stayaway this week in protest against the government's ongoing crackdown against its citizens, The Standard can reveal.

BODY: The mass stayaway is scheduled for Thursday and Friday this week. The stayaway will see people not going to work, while protests have reportedly been plotted throughout the country, The Standard understands.

Sources close to the planned mass action told The Standard that the showdown was being organised by a coalition comprising the Movement for Democratic Change (MDC), Zimbabwe Congress of Trade Unions (ZCTU), National Constitutional Assembly (NCA), Crisis Coalition, Zimbabwe National Students' Union (Zinasu) and several other bodies opposed to the government's conduct in the clean-up campaign and crippling transport crisis.

This story in which only the leaders of the MDC, NCA and ZCTU, Morgan Tsvangirai, Lovemore Madhuku and Lovemore Matombo respectively are cited directly is a poignant example of how the most vulnerable members of society are muted by the press no matter how well-meaning and well-intentioned that press might be. Here are elite leaders rallying their constituents to engage in the only form of mass action known to themselves: stayaway. The call for mass action is directed to those in formal employment while the beneficiaries of such action are somehow expected to be those in the informal sector and the unemployed who have no work to stay away from. The call to stayaway would be misdirected if it was meant for those targeted by police brutality, because they would not have anything to stay away from. They have been already staying away anywhere, due to lack of employment. They are also least likely to be members of the organisations mobilising the mass action in their name. Part of their vulnerability consists in lack of organisational strength. They have no representative body of their own through which to articulate their peculiar interests. According to this story, their interests are somehow represented as coterminous with and coincidental to the broad goals of the political programme to remove the ZANU-PF government from power. The plight of the evicted urban poor is used only as another case to justify causes that these elite organisations had been pushing for all along. The evicted poor people's presence in a story supposedly about them is limited to appearing in the pictures showcasing them among the rubble of their demolished houses. The goal of evacuating poor people from elite geographical spaces such as urban centres is consummated and ironically mirrored in the symbolic eviction and exclusion of their voices in news stories like the one cited above. The caption describes the picture as follows: 'Peter Chisvo, his wife Susan and their baby, contemplate their predicament after their house in the background, in Harare's Mbare suburb, was demolished on Friday. The family is one of hundreds of thousands left homeless in the wake of the government's controversial crackdown on illegal settlements'. Their devastation is probably so complete that they are left *with no words* for it but to contemplate. The poor are with no words.

The pictures of Operation Murambatsvina from affected subalterns' view point would have been irretrievably lost if one had no other sources to rely on than published accounts in newspapers. The language in most of *The Herald* stories 'did not adequately narrate the story of the victims ... and neither was there adequate

230 *Operation Restore (colonial) Order*

analysis of the consequences of government's actions', (Nyamanhindi, 2008: 121). *The Herald* story as an example of the so-called first draft of history was largely a construction of that historical event from the perspectives of the victors (the police in boots) in society not because of any aberration in the way journalism was being done at the newspaper. Their story more than met the rudimentary requirements of any professionally written piece of journalistic reporting of news events. It cannot be faulted on the basis of any amateurish violations of the revered canons and codes of professional journalistic practice. Its weakness, if any, was in its adherence, too much, to a very narrowly defined professional journalism which enjoins the reporter to source his news reports from highly credible sources. The story itself had all the ingredients of newsworthiness: it was timely, and proximate if by proximity we mean closeness to elite places (towns and cities) and elite institutions (the police) it was also impactful given the sheer numbers left homeless as a result of the demolitions. Where the story may have been deficient of the news value of prominence (it affected very ordinary urban poor), the journalists wrote prominence into the story by the technique of attribution to prominent people. As long as professional journalism teaches that the more the reporters seek out highly credible sources to validate their reports the higher the credibility rating of the story, then both *The Herald* and *The Standard* news reports on Operation Murambatsvina more than passed this test. The overall outcome of the operation of such journalistic logic is, to borrow (Mignolo, 2000: 204) turn of phrase, the newspapers producing 'their work in relative ignorance of' subaltern ways of knowing 'and this did not seem to affect the quality of their journalistic work'. The upshot of all this is that the subaltern subject could not speak journalistically on Operation Murambatsvina, rendered mute in the process of news reporting.

With *The Herald* and other state controlled media unabashedly producing patently pro-government versions on the issues of the day, a quality whose genealogical roots are traceable to its colonial history, the news reading public was often pushed into accepting whatever the 'independent press' published as the valid 'truth'. Newspapers such as *The Standard* were viewed as the state media's binary opposites. If the state media were adjudged as bad, and the news they carried, as propaganda and therefore false, the 'independent' press was good and its news offerings, generally accepted as the 'truth'. This often led to the fallacy of accepting unquestioningly what the papers such as *The Standard* reported as synonymous with reality itself. This masked the fact that any news, whether by state controlled media or by so-called independent press constructed the reality they reported on. So, mainstream media whether state or privately owned was by definition just not the place to find the truth as seen by the marginalised in society. This fact tends to fly in the face of rationalisations of the image of the independent press, often enjoying purchase in scholarly literature, as the free market place of ideas giving diverse and competing ideas an equal chance of expression. The analysis in this section has given little reason for such optimism, particularly where marginalised dominated groups' interests and ways of knowing are concerned. Similar processes of deletion of subaltern interpretations and

Operation Restore (colonial) Order 231

legitimation of competing interests of different elite sections of society were at work in the news constructions of subaltern experiences of Operation Murambatsvina in the two papers.

Operation Murambatsvina stands out as a classic example of how the colonial past had continued to survive in the postcolonial present. Although now under a black government, the majority indigenous population who lived on the margins continued as before to be expunged from the mainstream platforms of self-expression and to be criminalised and thingified to justify their treatment as other than human. They were referred to as criminals, filth, dirt or crawling maggots in the press in much the same way their ancestors were referred to as primitive and a danger to civilised society in colonial times to justify their eviction and confinement away from the city to the tribal trust lands. The similarity in attitudes towards the poor between the Zimbabwe government under Mugabe's ZANU-PF and Rhodesian government under Godfrey Huggins was uncanny as Potts points out:

> After 1980, despite the removal of influx controls which dramatically altered the nature of urbanisation, periodic government sweeps of people considered 'undesirable' in the cities occurred. These included homeless people and, sometimes, women who were deemed, on the flimsiest pretexts, to be undesirable because they were alone in public spaces. The literature on these sweeps often draws the parallels between these government actions and the controls of the colonial past. The far more dramatic action against urban residents across the entire country of Operation Murambatsvina in 2005, which directly affected hundreds of thousands, attempted to force urban-rural migration too. Again, the associated literature frequently discussed the sad irony of the continuities between the campaign and the old colonial restrictions on urban residence (Potts, 2011: 23).

The similarity was also to be found in how *The Herald* became a willing ideological tool in the hands of the governing elites in postcolonial as in colonial times, to discursively construct the victims in a way that legitimised government actions against them.

Inheriting, preserving the jewel of Africa

Kwame Nkrumah's call to seek first the political kingdom met with huge political purchase among many African nationalist leaders who waged armed struggles to end colonial rule on the African continent (Ake, 2000). When ZANU-PF won the democratic mandate to govern Zimbabwe at Independence in 1980, the former colonised blacks were euphoric and ecstatic with anticipation for the realisation of socioeconomic transformation of the state to become more inclusive of their interests. But from the very beginning those who took over government, as a political class, found themselves faced with a completely different set of objectives which set them apart and on a collision course with their erstwhile comrades. Having inherited the political kingdom, the nationalist leaders saw the securing

232 *Operation Restore (colonial) Order*

and preservation of their inheritance – the unfair privileges and advantages enjoyed exclusively by white colonial settlers – as their first vocation. This tendency to negate the popular aspirations on the strength of whose promise the political class had been catapulted to power is well captured in Claude Ake's critique of the authoritarian tendencies of postcolonial governments in Africa:

> Independence changed the composition of the managers of the state but not the character of the state, which remained much as it was in the colonial era … It presented itself often as an apparatus of violence, its base in social forces remained extremely narrow and it relied for compliance unduly on coercion rather than authority. With few exceptions, the elite who came to power decided to inherit and exploit the colonial system to their own benefit rather than transforming it democratically as had been expected. This alienated them from the masses whom they now had to contain with force. (Ake, 2000: 36)

The idea of preserving colonial privilege partly accounts for the early state capture and colonisation of *The Herald* newspaper as an institution of power and now under Operation Murambatsvina exclusive occupation and monopolisation of the city by the political elite as spaces of power. That logic possibly explains the stillbirth of early independence government attempts at transformation of *The Herald* from an elite medium for use by the minority ruling elite to a truly popular paper that spoke the language of the people and carried their views and opinions. While the majority of previously marginalised Africans had construed inheriting the political kingdom and the coming of Uhuru as signifying a reversal of the oppressive colonial system, the political leadership understood attainment of independence as not marking the start of a return to a lost glorious pre-colonial past because such past if it existed, was no longer accessible in its virgin state. The only legacy that was available and thus 'worth' of preserving at least in the nationalist leader's mind, was the colonial legacy, hence Mugabe's call to restore 'order' in the cities using the same coercive measures reminiscent of those used by the colonial regime he replaced. By instituting Operation Murambatsvina/ Restore Order, Mugabe may have done so in the true spirit of heeding an elder African statesman's advice to preserve intact what he had inherited at independence. At independence in 1980, the former President of Tanzania, Mwalimu Julius Nyerere congratulated the newly elected Prime Minister of Zimbabwe, Robert Mugabe, saying 'you have inherited a jewel in Africa, you must preserve it'. But some critics question Nyerere's judgement as very problematic. If Zimbabwe was a jewel of Africa at independence in 1980 whose jewel was it for? Implied in Nyerere's judgement, is an unspoken acknowledgement that colonialism must have been good for Zimbabwe, for it produced a jewel out of her. Instead of problematising this old colonial myth and challenging Mugabe to initiate a new history, he embraces it as a premise upon which to inaugurate the new postcolonial situation (Said, 1995). What would 'preserving it' mean for the new government? Was this an injunction to not hurriedly dismantle colonial structures which had consigned majority Africans to penury in the process of turning Zimbabwe into the economic miracle it had become – the jewel of Africa? Kanyenze cited in Mazingi and Kamidza (2011: 326) went on to argue that:

> If Zimbabwe was a jewel of Africa then it must have been a flawed one indeed. The inherited economy had been moulded on a philosophy of white supremacy that resulted in the evolution of a relatively well-developed and modern formal sector, which co-existed with an underdeveloped and backward rural economy, the home to 70% of the black population. Thus the "jewel" was the enclave part of the economy, which was developed on the basis of ruthless dispossession of indigenous sources of livelihood.

To the above argument may be added the view that the press was an important gem in that jewel Mugabe inherited on 18 April 1980 and preservation of the whole necessarily entailed preservation of the press in its colonial form and function in the service of the new political class against the interests of the same people whose support was instrumental in catapulting it into power. The naivety that had led the oppressed class under colonial rule to repose their confidence in the black-educated class to lead the struggle for their emancipation had been aptly capture and immortalised in the character of old Chege in Ngugi's 'The River Between', who had thought that to fight the white man it was necessary to send his son Wayiyaki to the Mission School to learn the white man's ways so that they would use that knowledge to fight and defeat the white man and work for the good of their people. The disillusionment of the oppressed majority in Ngugi's fictional world had its real life equivalent in independent Zimbabwe when the former colonised saw those they had entrusted with leadership betraying the liberation cause, abandon the war time rhetoric of radicalised change and embracing a 'new civilised' pragmatism to preserve the colonial institutional arrangements that would serve the interests that their newly assumed roles thrust upon them at independence. This is the more generous view of the political elite that took over government at independence in Africa. A more pessimistic view, which evidence marshalled in this study appears to support, is the thesis that the nationalist leaders' seeming volte-face was not betrayal of some egalitarian ethos that they once espoused during the liberation struggle, but rather that their actions were consistent with intentions they had always secretly harboured, to take the white man's place in the management of our common affairs. For the black political class that inherits government at independence, Fanon (1970: 4) had warned us in *Black skin, white masks* 'there is only one destiny. And it is white'. What then goes on to compound the problem for the emancipation project is news media's unquestioning acceptance of a culture and ideology of news production that privileges elite interpretations ahead of those of the subaltern groups in society. In Zimbabwe's case and in particular with reference to how Zimbabwe's clean-up campaign was covered in the press, the victims of those demolitions and forced evictions were caught in a bind with the partisan polarised media, holed up in their respective elite camps, fighting a war of words at the expense of serving as purveyors of the views of those who were directly affected in the unfortunate situation of losing homes and livelihoods.

Systemic exclusion of subaltern definitions of reality

Given the fact that unlike during colonial times, *The Herald* at the time this study, save for only one staffer, is run by black editors and journalists throughout, one would have hoped that there now existed greater cultural, physical, racial and geographical congruency and proximity between reporters at *The Herald* and the urban/rural black poor people most of whom the Operation Restore Order targeted. If race alone were the factor behind exclusion of ordinary African victims' voices on forced evictions in colonial Rhodesia, then there would have been very significant presence of subaltern views in stories on forced eviction under Operation Murambatsvina. The dominance of officialdom in *The Herald*'s coverage of Operation Murambatsvina tends to be in line with Zvi Reich's (2015) findings in a recent study on why ordinary citizens still rarely serve as news sources in spite of the technological promise for greater participation by ordinary people in the production of news. He concludes that:

> findings suggest that not every human agent who opens his or her mouth and contributes a sound bite is treated by journalists as a full-fledged news source ... news is not simply "what someone says has happened" but is what someone with minimal authority, status, institutional affiliation, expertise, and regular contact says. In other words, journalists are still not in the business of information but in the business of institutionally certified information. Therefore, equipped and motivated as they may be, citizen sources don't count as full-blown news sources. While regular sources represent ongoing relationships, citizens represent one-time transactions of information, lacking not only mutual rapport with journalists but also a track record of reliability. This has severe epistemic ramifications because the more regular sources receive not only privileged access to news coverage but also the status of 'primary definers' (Hall et al., 1978) of social reality. (Reich, 2015: 789)

Thus, the domain of news production in postcolonial settings follows a logic that transcends transitions from colonial to postcolonial or from one regime to another. News, by design, in every epoch has tended to embed itself with power and becomes the most definitive text of power. It is better suited to a concern with power reporting rather than to reporting truth to power. This affinity between mainstream news and centres of power becomes more evident when one maps the locations of Zimbabwe's main national papers on the geopolitical map of the country. It is not by accident but by design that all three main newspaper organisations operate and ply their trade from Harare, the country's capital.

The renaming of Cecil Square to Africa Unity Square without changing its landscape, illustrates how the postcolonial present is just a toponymic overlay on the colonial soul and heart of the national power structure. The topographic landscape of the Africa Unity Square, former Cecil Square remains a ground replica of the British flag stretched out there as a constant reminder of the unity of power in the service of a departed empire. *The Herald* House in particular representing the

Operation Restore (colonial) Order 235

pliant Fourth Estate of the realm was from the very beginning sited closest to the heartbeat of governmental power. Its six storey building overlooks Africa Unity Square along the southern bank of Sam Nujoma Avenue. Directly opposite it across the Square stands Barclays Bank's Hurudza House and the Old Mutual Centre, symbols of the core of Zimbabwe's financial capital with its roots deep in the colonial history of the country. The Parliament building which stands flanked by the Anglican Church's Cathedral of St. Mary and All Saints on one side, and the Defence House on the other, along the northern flank of the Square. Meikles Hotel, the symbol of Zimbabwe's tourism and hospitality industry stands aloft to the south of the square. Radiating from this centre in different directions are other institutions of state power such as the Munhumutapa building, a few blocks down Nelson Mandela Avenue which houses the offices of the President and the Ministry of Information responsible for directing state propaganda, the Supreme Court, the Reserve Bank are all within the vicinity of *The Herald* House. *The Herald* and the other two national newspapers (The Alpha Media Holdings (AMH) and the Associated Newspapers of Zimbabwe (ANZ)) all operate from Harare, and taken together, they spread out thinly meshed newsnets around the institutions of elite power in the capital city daily. In this way they rake in a sufficient haul of news at the least cost to their newspaper organisations. Such news was unfaultable on points of news values or any other journalism criteria. The news values present the journalists schooled in them, with a grammar by which certain events and certain people are unintelligible as news (Traber, 1987).

The content of the newspapers on a topical issue like Operation Murambatsvina presented above bears testimony to the fact that the diet of news that the Zimbabwean citizen is fed on is sourced from no farther than the corridors of power with the stamp of authority of those who occupy these buildings. In white-ruled colonial Rhodesia the occupants of these corridors of power were exclusively white and the opinions and views which *The Herald* carried were therefore largely white views on issues of the day. After independence, *The Herald* continued to carry views of the new occupants of these houses of power who were now, of course, black. Thus, while the difference between the new black elite and their white predecessors in attitudes towards subjects of their (mis)rule was only skin deep, there was at least no change in *The Herald*'s news orientation towards power holders. Frantz Fanon had long predicted the cultural asphyxiation and the colonial unchanging in newly independent states in Africa:

> At the very moment when the native intellectual is anxiously trying to create a cultural work he fails to realise that he is utilising techniques and language which are borrowed from the stranger in his country. He contents himself with stamping these instruments with a hall-mark which he wishes to be national, but which is strangely reminiscent of exoticism. (Fanon et al., 1963: 180)

In many respects Fanons' comment above was prescient of the elite who took over the running of the people's common affairs in the post-colony together with their journalist intellectuals did not have the courage to alter a thing to

236 *Operation Restore (colonial) Order*

make the media work for their own people. They would not be expected to work differently by dint of their location relative to power as the map above clearly shows. This is less a government thing than it is a journalism thing to locate itself close to other centres of power. Any privately owned national newspaper that ever decides to set itself up for failure, in post-independent Zimbabwe must of necessity locate its operational offices far away from the seat of power – the capital city. This physical proximity then goes on to replicate itself in the domain of news content. *The Herald* continued to be just as alienated from the masses as ever and the way it covered Operation Murambatsvina is an illustrative case of this. If *The Rhodesia Herald* was guilty of thingifying Africans to justify their forced mass evictions by whites in colonial Rhodesia, *The Herald* of the postcolonial era was no less guilty of doing the same on largely African descendants of the colonised with the only difference being that, this time around, it was the thingification of blacks by fellow blacks.

> A good part of the psychical complexes that Africans evince in our relation-ship to ourselves, to one another, and to the rest of the world, ever since the end of slavery is easily traceable to the ideational structures fostered under slavery and reinforced by colonialism. (Táíwò, 2015: 57)

On a point of comparison, the annihilation of subaltern voices has largely remained the defining feature of the images of the dominated others in the news. These others may be defined by the colour of their skin, under settler colonialism or by a nexus of class, gender and ethnicity in post-independence Zimbabwe. If under colonialism the news imposed a total blackout of information on how forced evictions and resultant displacements affected whole communities of indigenous peoples, a blanket information embargo was no longer possible or sustainable, but the media was nearly as effective in denying the world, information on how, under the black nationalist government, the same colonial logic continued to inform the spatial displacement and ideological erasure of mostly black poor people's voices from elite spaces geographically and ideationally in the news.

Conclusion

This chapter has demonstrated the resilience of the colonial legacy of many news production processes and how they continue to discursively reproduce the inequalities of power that structured the relations of the governed to those who govern them. In reporting Operation Murambatsvina the usual excuses that journalism uses to justify selective coverage, sourcing practices and exclusions such as, for example, the news values of proximity and prominence have often come unstuck and exploded as myths. The urban poor people whose homes and shelter were demolished as illegal structures inhabited the same equi-proximate physical and geographical spaces with the journalism elites, to the newsroom and to the city as elite centres, but their voices were marginalised in the discursive constructions of the realities of Murambatsvina. A simplistic and dichotomous categorisation of news media in Zimbabwe as 'state-bad' and 'private good' also proved untenable. Evidence seemed to show strong similarity in elite orientation by location, choice of language and information sourcing practices of the press in Zimbabwe. *The Standard*'s story did not necessarily give a better, more accurate reflection of events under Operation Murambatsvina, only a different construction. There was no ideologically neutral venue from which to report on the events of Operation Murambatsvina. Each newspaper became vulnerable to the political spin given by the political elites they relied on as reliable and credible news sources. At the level of geographical spaces, Operation Murambatsvina represents an attempt to re-inscribe a colonial reordering of urban social spaces. It would be plausible to surmise that OM can be taken as a useful metaphor for a similar colonial re-structuring at work in the press as institutions of knowledge production discursively subordinated subaltern views under an 'authorised version' of Operation Murambatsvina from the top. Considering evidence presented in this chapter in can reasonably be argued that practices both in government and in the press trace their genealogy to a common colonial ancestry.

References

Ake, C., 2000. *Feasibility of democracy in Africa*. Council for the Development of Social Science Research in Africa, Dakar, SN.

Bird, S.E., 2010. *The anthropology of news & journalism: Global perspectives*. Indiana University Press.

Chabal, P., 2013. *Africa: The politics of suffering and smiling*. Zed Books.

Chennells, A., 2015. Doris Lessing's versions of Zimbabwe from The Golden Notebook to Alfred and Emily. *Engl. Acad. Rev.* 32, 53–69.

Fanon, F., 1970. *Black skin, white masks*. Paladin.

Fanon, F., Sartre, J.-P., Farrington, C., 1963. *The wretched of the earth*. Grove Press.

Mazingi, L., Kamidza, R., 2011. Inequality in Zimbabwe, in: H. Jauch & D. Muchena (eds), *Tearing us apart: Inequalities in Southern Africa*. Open Society for Southern Arica, pp. 322–382. Accessed 11 May 2019 from: https://pdfs.semanticscholar.org/add0/7b0f804ffff84771fcfee20fef8aaa9c035a.pdf.

Mignolo, W., 2000. *Local histories/global designs: Coloniality, subaltern knowledges, and border thinking*. Princeton University Press.

Nyamanhindi, R., 2008. Cartooning Murambatsvina: representation of Operation Murambatsvina through press cartoons, in: M.T. Vambe (ed.), *Hidden dimensions of Operation Murambatsvina*. African Books Collective.

Potts, D., 2011. 'We have a tiger by the tail': Continuities and discontinuities in Zimbabwean city planning and politics. *Crit. Afr. Stud.* 4, 15–46.

Raftopoulos, B., 2009. The crisis in Zimbabwe, 1998–2008, in: B. Raftopoulos and A.S. Mlambo (eds.), *Becoming Zimbabwe: A history from the pre-colonial period to 2008*. African Books Collective.

Reich, Z., 2015. Why citizens still rarely serve as news sources: Validating a tripartite model of circumstantial, logistical, and evaluative barriers. *Int. J. Commun.* 9, 22.

Rifkind, M., 1968. The politics of land in Rhodesia: A study of land and politics in Southern Rhodesia with special reference to the period 1930–1968 (Doctoral dissertation). University of Edinburgh).

238 *Operation Restore (colonial) Order*

Said, E.W., 1995. *Orientalism: Western conceptions of the Orient.* Penguin.

Táíwo, O., 2015. Looking back, facing Forward: (Re)-imagining a global Africa. *Black Sch.* 45, 51–69.

Tibaijuka, A.K., 2005. Report of the fact-finding mission to Zimbabwe to assess the scope and impact of Operation Murambatsvina. United Nations Settlements Programme. (UN_HABITAT). Accessed from: http://hrlibrary.umn.edu/research/ZIM%20UN%20Special%20Env%20Report.pdf.

Traber, M., 1987. Towards the democratization of public communication: A critique of the current criteria of news. Afr. Media Rev. 2, 66–75.

8 'Operation Restore Legacy' in post-Mugabe era

Introduction

On 15 November 2017, just two days after the commander of the Zimbabwe Defence Forces Major General Constantino Guvheya Nyikadzino Chiwenga had addressed a press conference warning that the military would not stand by and allow factional fighting destroy the ruling party and plunge the nation into chaos, the military took control of institutions of state power including state television and an army general made an announcement that the army had launched an operation to remove criminals around the President. The military intervention, codenamed Operation Restore Order, was to last until the 27 November and culminated with the ousting of President Mugabe and the inauguration of a 'new' political dispensation under a new operation: 'Operation Restore Legacy'. There was a ring of irony and contradiction of terms in an operation meant to 'restore legacy' which does so by inaugurating a 'new dispensation'. The present chapter focuses on media silences to assess any structural changes in the media as a barometer for a broader social transformation programme in the country. Zimbabwe is spoilt for choice when it comes to which legacy to restore both in the media and the larger society. These may include among others the colonial legacies in the organisation of state/media relations, legacies in the form of re-inscribing a sense of entitlement among a class of veterans of the liberation war evident in such self-referencing as stockholders of the country. The very threat of military intervention was justified by the army General as having been necessitated by perceived purging of those with liberation war credentials by the Mugabe government. There are traditions both hegemonic and counter hegemonic; traditions of brutal suppression and of popular resistance against oppression; traditions of co-optation and willing cooperation with dominant forces; traditions tangential to as well as complicit with forces of oppression and domination through the history of Zimbabwe.

The culture of brutal suppression of voices of dissent and forms of popular mobilisation of resistance against oppression has a long tradition that has been wired into the national psyche since the suppression of the 1896–1897 revolt against colonial occupation. From time to time organic communicators, those who fall outside the establishment media loop, through chain letter messaging, through music and art and through socialite platforms of communication and entertainment, have risen to champion and articulate popular 'truths' resonant with ordinary people's lived experiences, that often challenged official versions of reality. There is also a deeply rooted legacy of aloof silence by those who chose to aid and abate systems of injustice for selfish personal gain. Of these, the establishment press probably played the foremost role. There were those who were called 'friendly natives' or simply 'friendlies' who contributed so significantly to the victory of the colonists' campaign against the instigators of the 1896–1897 uprising against colonial dispossession and exploitation in the early years of colonial history in Zimbabwe. The role of the military wing in shaping politics has a long history in the ruling ZANU-PF with tacit encouragement by the political leadership, itself a beneficiary of that tradition dating back to the Mgagao Declaration of 1975 which deposed Ndabaningi Sithole and catapulted Robert Mugabe into the leadership of the then liberation movement, Zimbabwe African National Union (ZANU) (Chung, 2006). On 13 November 2017, history had come full circle, as some of the military leadership who were party to the Mgagao Declaration became, more than three decades later, the chief architects of the quasi-military/state and civil society supported intervention which precipitated Mugabe's ousting and his replacement by his former aide. Given the complex interpenetration and entanglement of societal forces and interests at this historical juncture the question to ask is: what was the 'Operation Restore Legacy' a celebration of? What legacy was being restored in the postcolony of Zimbabwe? Was it a celebration of the triumph of the human spirit against a long history of colonial and neo-colonial domination or the re-inscription of the old systemic suffocation of any voices of dissent in the public sphere under a new albeit ultra-repressive military-political state oligarchical order? As it turned out, developments a year after the transition, appear to affirm the latter as the vocation and trajectory of the new dispensation in Zimbabwe.

What is most disquieting, however, is not the fact of human suffering and poverty ordinary people of Zimbabwe have had to face and continue to endure through all these false transitions from Ian Smith's white colonial and racist regime in 1980 and from Mugabe's more than three decades-long despotic rule. It is the abject failure of news and historiography due to their obsessive focus on and preoccupation with the agency of 'Big Men' and extraordinary and dramatic irruptions, to capture and document what Obadare and Willems (2014: 8) term 'the more enduring everyday forms of resistance constantly present in the behaviours, traditions and consciousness of the subordinate'. The press will wait until the everyday forms of resistance have morphed and found expression through formally organised, large-scale protest marches through the streets and demonstrations against the state to pen it down as news. The protest has to be attributable to a prominent personality or a well-known organisation such as the main opposition political party, or preferably a civil society organisation like the Labour Union, and the more horrific and dramatic consequences the better for it to satisfy the news values of personalisation, prominence, proximity, negativity, etc., to merit the attention of the press as news. For the large part the press

'Operation Restore Legacy' in post-Mugabe era   241

is silent about the unorganised ordinary forms of resistance which are the real engine of societal irruptions which, from time to time, political demagogues and populists opportunistically harvest often for their own very parochial and selfish ends.

Some critics of the displacement of Mugabe by his former close aide Emmerson Mnangagwa at the helm of both the governing party and the state have expressed deep reservations and scepticism about the new dispensation's commitment to bringing about meaningful social transformation (Simpson and Hawkins, 2018). Others have derisively commented on the new dispensation's mantra 'Zimbabwe is open for business' as implying that Zimbabwe is now open and ready for recolonisation given the aggressive charm offensive the new regime embarked upon to endear itself with Western governments in an effort to attract new foreign direct investment from those countries it had always labelled as its enemies (Freeman, 2018). Others have highlighted the discrepancy between word and deed arguing that promises have not always been accompanied by the requisite change in action on the political and economic front. Basing on an analysis of press coverage of the euphoric marches in celebration of Mugabe's fall in November 2017, the brutal suppression of post-election protests at the beginning of August 2018, and government's equally brutal response to civic organised protests against general economic hardships sparked by the President's hiking of fuel prices in January 2019, the chapter discusses the potential of the new political dispensation charting new trajectories for news production in Zimbabwe. The chapter highlights the apparent inevitability of elite-centrism across time and circumstance in a news logic at the core of professional journalism in Zimbabwean press, re-affirming the truism which many scholars on the postcolonial situation in Zimbabwe have expressed, that somehow in Zimbabwe the cast in the newsroom as on the political stage, may change but not the colonial script (Harold-Barry, 2004; Moyo, 2004).

News of Mugabe's ousting

The period from Mnangagwa's dismissal as Vice President on 6 November 2017 followed by his subsequent expulsion from the party, to his inauguration as President of the second republic on 25 November was an eventful period of national anxiety, uncertainty mixed with euphoric expectation as the nation went through a political process that birthed the most unimaginable thing at the time the peaceful transfer of power from Mugabe to Mnangagwa, mediated by the military. During his 37 years reign as President of Zimbabwe, Mugabe had courted controversy and created as many sworn enemies as admirers and friends, both inside and outside Zimbabwe. It is not surprising then that, though the military staged what other observers would describe as a peaceful putsch, many commentators within as well as outside Zimbabwe were reluctant to describe it as a coup-de-état, partly because they just wanted the end of Mugabe's rule in Zimbabwe and cared less about how it was brought about.

242 *'Operation Restore Legacy' in post-Mugabe era*

In order to sanitise their military takeover of power, the army generals outmanoeuvred Mugabe into 'voluntarily' resigning as President on 22 November 2017. For that brief moment of the interregnum from Mugabe's resignation to Mnangagwa's investment with the presidency, Zimbabweans from all walks of life had a shared sense of ecstatic freedom probably only comparable to what happened at the transition from minority white rule to majority rule on the attainment of independence in 1980. The only difference between April 1980 and November 2017 was in the instantaneity of the news of political events as they unfolded. In the age of social media, the nation was literally able to break into jovial celebration as Jacob Mudenda, Speaker of Parliament, read Mugabe's letter of resignation to Parliament, all this happening in real time across the length and breadth of Zimbabwe. People just spontaneously started pouring onto the streets wherever they were, ululating, whistling, hooting and singing for joy on receiving the news of the President's resignation as it happened. People did not have to wait to hear it on the evening news bulletin or to read about it in the newspaper the following day. The traditional sources of news, newspapers and radio trailed far behind as they reported what the citizens already knew. In the section below we do a comparative analysis of how the three main national daily newspapers covered events leading up to and after the political transition that brought an end to Mugabe's rule and heralded the dawn of a new era in Zimbabwe.

The morning after the military leadership had issued a press statement warning that they were ready to intervene to restore legacy. *The Daily News* and *NewsDay* carried that story while *The Herald* and its sister paper *The Chronicle* completely ignored it. Instead, they focused on ZANU-PF and the government's response to the military's statement without reporting on the substance of the statement itself directly. This is a strategy the state media has used on many occasions to minimise the significant impact of actions by the state's 'adversaries' the outgroup, in the process of giving it coverage (Schudson, 2003). In a surprise television appearance to announce the military takeover of the state broadcaster, Major General Sibusiso Moyo in full military gab upbraided the national broadcaster and *The Herald* for not publicising the military's press statement stating that he was, however, aware that they had been directed to deny them coverage in the state-controlled media. It is important to underline the fact that the military man was not making a startling revelation here. On many occasions of serious political contestations, the government had never made it a secret that it expected the state-owned media entities to report in the 'national interest' narrowly understood to mean in the interest of power as personified in its ultimate sense in the person of the President. This has resulted in the persistence of a very predictable news template where the President is, except on rare occasions, always on the front page and leads in every story he is cited as a source. This phenomenon is not at all peculiar to the state-controlled press in Zimbabwe. Hasty, found this pattern also prevalent in the Ghanaian state press when Jerry Rawlings was President of Ghana. There are similar examples in African countries where the state directly owns a newspaper of its own such as Zambia (*The Times of Zambia*, and the *Zambia Daily Mail*), Uganda (*The New Vision*). Mozambique (*Noticias*, and *Diário de Moçambique*).

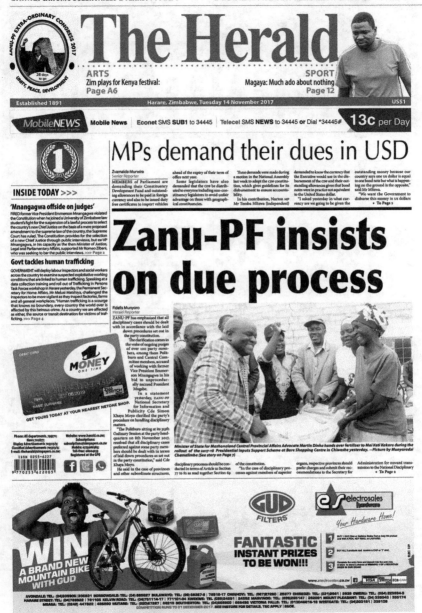

Figure 8.1a and b. *The Herald* front page and *The Daily News* front page on the 14 November 2017. Reprinted with permission.

Figure 8.1a and b Continued

On the next day after army generals issued a stern warning to ZANU-PF in a press statement, *The Herald*, just like the national broadcaster the ZBC the previous evening, totally blacked out any news about the military's treasonable threat to step in (Rogers 2019). The newspaper instead leads with a business-as-usual front page story headline: 'Zanu-PF insists on due process' accompanied by a stand-alone landscape picture of farmers happily receiving maize seed in preparation for the coming planting season. The imagery of planting and the growing season obviously connoting the regularity and rhythm of the cycle of life with one season seamlessly flowing into another. *The Daily News*, on the other hand, ran with the military press statement as its headline news (see the contrasting front pages of the two newspapers above). A reader from another planet with no alternative sources of information would have been unable to make out from the information made available in The Herald that a coup-de-état was in the making. With the advantage of hindsight, it is possible to look back and decide which one between the two newspapers 'lied' and which one reported the 'truth'. *The Herald* may be charged with bluffing its readers and in the process failing to measure up to its own standard as the 'newspaper of record'. *The Daily News*, on the other hand, may receive public approbation for living up to its billing, that of 'telling it as it is, without fear nor favour'. But to ask which one of the two papers lied and which one told the truth is to pose the wrong question in the first place because all news is ideological and it is for this reason that the libertarian philosophy of the press advocates a plurality of sources of information. 'Dominant media, whether commercial or state-sponsored, typically reinforce political understandings that reinforce the views of political elites' (Schudson, 2003: 253). The two newspapers worked with pieces of news cloth cut away from a fabric of Zimbabwean reality large enough to permit such variation in garment style and finish.

It was only after two days that *The Herald* dropped a hint that something untoward was in the offing in Zimbabwe's body politic when it leads with a front page official rebuttal of the army commander's statement, which its readers are supposedly still ignorant about. Its lead story on front page boldly announced: 'Zanu-PF unfazed by Chiwenga' with two bullet points that stated that the party 'raps him for treasonous statement' and 'reaffirms primacy of politics over gun'. A mugshot picture of Simon Kaya Moyo, the party spokesperson and Minister of Information accompanied the story. In an insert Kudzanai Chipanga, the firebrand leader of the Zanu-PF youth wing, weighed in, in a story headlined: 'We will defend President with our lives: Youths'. As it turned out Zimbabweans were not taken aback by this strongly worded reprimand of the army commander; they had kept themselves abreast with the latest information on the increasingly volatile political situation in the country, courtesy of the independent press and other alternative sources of information such as social media.

The period of uncertainty was, however, very short-lived as political developments escalated to a point where it became evident that Mugabe was losing grip on power and that the military was now in charge. Mugabe had somehow over

246 *'Operation Restore Legacy' in post-Mugabe era*

the years been allowed to monopolise headline news status in all state-owned and controlled news media. Now that the Mugabe figure was fading away from *The Herald* front page, an opportunity had presented itself for editors to self-introspect whether it was now time to truly democratise access to that coveted space or to simply await the political processes to yield a Mugabe replacement. That the state media was not yet ready for a paradigm shift as the news headlines of the week before Mugabe's resignation tended to show, the military as the caretaker authority before a political solution to the impasse was found, had been firmly slotted on front page as a place holder until a suitable replacement for Mugabe had come along. Below is the general pattern indicative of the crisis brought about by the uncertainties of the coup situation for *The Herald* editors as the battle for Mugabe's front page slot played itself out. On 22 November Mugabe tendered his resignation as President of Zimbabwe and literally exited Zimbabwean theatre of politics which he had dominated for the last 37 years he was the leader of the country. Quite telling was the spontaneous and instantaneous nationwide celebration in real time that greeted the announcement of Mugabe's resignation in Parliament. It was a telling example of how social media had literally drawn the rug from underneath the mainstream media when it comes to the breaking news function. People simply broke into wild jubilation wherever they were without having to wait for the main news bulletin to announce it nor for *The Herald* to publish it the following day.

The Herald's front page layout epitomised Mugabe's departure from the political limelight as well as from the news-frame. Only a silhouette of Mugabe walking away and stepping out of the front page news-frame as it were. On 24 November, *The Herald* inaugurates Mnangagwa as the worthy figure to take Mugabe's front page seat of power, even before his inauguration as President of the state. The headline 'EDenezer', is a clever play with Mnangagwa's initials combined with the word Ebenezer, a Hebrew name in the Bible translated 'the Lord has brought us this far' has the effect of investing the idea of Mnangagwa's rise to power as the work of God and therefore beyond contestation. Mnangagwa's figure posturing the ZANU-PF slogan of the raised clenched fist to signify revolutionary defiance against imperialist forces is superimposed on a collage of pictures authenticating his long history of participation in the liberation struggle – an important qualification of entitlement to rule. The military had long made it public that they were not ready to salute anyone with no liberation war credentials as the army Chief, the late Vitalis Zvenavashe had stated categorically in a televised press statement back then on 9 January 2002 that:

> Let it be known that the highest Office in the land is a straightjacket whose occupant is expected to observe the objectives of the liberation struggle. We will therefore not accept, let alone support or salute, anyone with a different agenda that threatens the very existence of our sovereignty, our country and our people. (*Daily News*, January 11, 2002)

At no time was that stance of the Zimbabwean military ever revoked. Mnangagwa, like his predecessor Mugabe, more than met the billing. But the above statement could have as well been made by the editor of *The Herald* with the phrase; 'the highest Office in the land' replaced by 'the front page of *The Herald*' and would still have made perfect sense.

The political changeover culminating with the replacement of Mugabe as both leader of the ruling party ZANU-PF and as state President by his former aide Emmerson Dambudzo Mnangagwa has been represented in the news as the dawn of a new era or the new dispensation. Little critical thought has been given to the ways in which the new era or new political dispensation would possibly wean itself from the past. As a nation, Zimbabwe has not been helped by its press to open up a serious debate on what ought to be the content of the change or transformation implied in the claim of instituting a new dispensation beyond getting rid of Robert Mugabe. Nowhere was the new dispensation's lack of substance more evident than in the domain of news media and the way the Zimbabwean press operated. If Mugabe morphed from a liberator to a tyrant, some of Mugabe's critics argue, he would not have got that far had the media not aided and abated him. In fact, the level of praise-singing in the press had grown so unreasonably shrill to a point where Mugabe was constructed as endowed with superhuman powers. The media were blamed for deifying Mugabe and developing a cult around his person. Given the way the state press has taken to priming Mnangagwa's presidency on their front pages, it would be quite surprising if he will not turnout in the mould of his predecessor. If media sycophantic infatuation with Mugabe plaid a not insignificant part in semiotically producing (Fowler, 2013) the absolutist leader that Mugabe became, it is logical to anticipate that, with little or no make-over in the media system, Mnangagwa's 'new dispensation' would become anything but new. By feeding the populace on a daily media fare of diversionary presidential spectacles and silences on matters of serious concern to the ordinary people, the media keeps them away from applying their minds to the task of imagining alternatives to the status quo. In the past the media did not only produce an autocratic monster in Mugabe but most importantly it also discursively produced a subject mindset in the reader which could put up with Mugabe's style of rule for more than 37 years. While the state-controlled press of which *The Herald* is the flagship boot-leaked and hero-worshipped Mugabe to a fault, the privately owned so called independent press went too far on the opposite extreme. They reduced the multifaceted Zimbabwean problem to a one-dimensional issue only intelligible through the prism of a Mugabe must go mantra. Give us anybody but Mugabe became the watchword. There was euphoric celebration when Mugabe was removed and replaced by Mnangagwa and one couldn't tell *The Daily News* and *The Herald* apart by looking at the headlines they carried to mark the end of the Mugabe era and *The Herald*ry that accompanied Mnangagwa's ascendance to the throne.

Figure 8.2a and b. Exit Mugabe; Enter Mnangagwa. Reprinted with permission from *The Herald*.

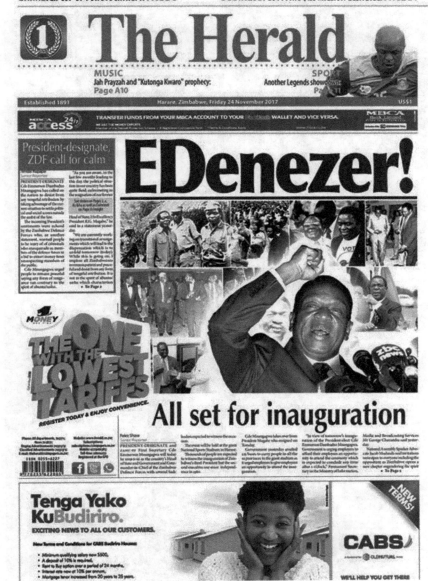

Figure 8.2a and b Continued

Figure 8.3a and b. *Daily News* headlines marking Mugabe's exit as the beginning of a new era in Zimbabwe. Reprinted with permission from *The Daily News*.

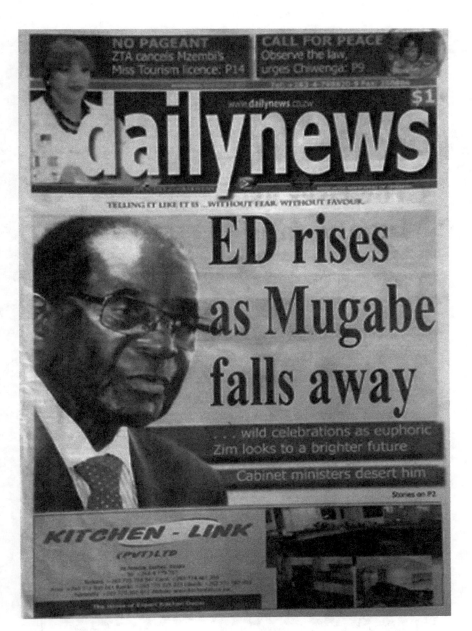

Figure 8.3a and b Continued

252 'Operation Restore Legacy' in post-Mugabe era

Covering the post-election violence

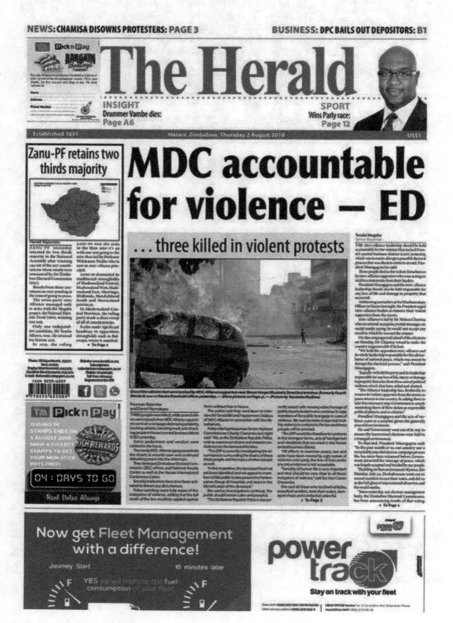

Figure 8.4a and b. Different headlines, the same event: *The Herald* implicates the MDC while *The Daily News* blames military heavy-handedness for the August 2018 post-election violence. Reproduced courtesy of *The Herald* and *The Daily News*.

Figure 8.4a and b Continued

Shrinking public sphere

The state's swift and decisive reaction to stop citizen protest action against government's decision to hike fuel prices by 150% is a textbook case but not the first of its kind to happen in the history of Zimbabwean media and communication. The Internet was shut down; Pastor Evan Mawarire of the #thisflag fame was picked up for questioning by the police. The editor of *The Herald* was fired for not giving Mnangagwa story due prominence in his paper. These state actions happening in the space of one week sent a chilling warning signal against 'abuse' of the newly opened space for democratic citizenship in Zimbabwe's new political dispensation. Citizens were never to take these freedoms for granted. Internet was only restored after the Supreme Court ruled its shutdown illegal. These repressive actions by the ZANU-PF new dispensation government hark back to similar actions against any liberal inclinations in the media in the period precedent to the then Prime Minister Ian Smith's Unilateral Declaration of Independence (UDI) back in 1965 Rhodesia. All progressive left-leaning newspapers sympathetic to the African nationalist cause were closed down by government action, the *African Daily News*, the *Central African Examiner, Moto* among others; editors of those publications were deported or forced into exile. Government censors were stationed at the remaining ones which were allowed to continue publishing. Those publications which were left to continue publishing were obviously the ones which were deemed 'innocent' and did not pose a security threat to the political establishment. That the minority white regime found all of the Rhodesia Printing and Publication Newspaper titles not to pose a security threat to warrant their closure remains a serious blot and indictment on those publications' claims that they were true proponents of a democratic politics in the country and remains a dent on their claims to a journalistic heroism in raising the standard of editorial independence and role to hold power to account. The true heroes of the struggle for social justice and against colonial repression were those publications which were targeted for closure by the colonial state. Their present-day equivalents will not be counted among the journalism that has sacrificed its conscience at the altar of neoliberal market fetishism so characteristic of mainstream independent press houses in present-day Zimbabwe but among the champions of guerrilla journalism operating on social media networks connecting and co-constructing a new politics of popular resistance against state repression. And it is this new brand of 'subversive journalism by the people' that the state was so afraid of and aimed to silence by its action of shutting down the Internet in the wake of a paralysing three-day strike called by some civic groups working with the main opposition party starting on 14 January 2019.

The demonstrations, which quickly turned violent, obviating a state response in which critics argue state repressive organs used force, out of all proportion to the simple task of mob control, resulted in the death of more than dozen people and destruction of property worth millions of dollars. The mainstream state press at best acknowledged the disruption to smooth running of business caused by the protests but were quick to blame it on social malcontents seeking political control

'Operation Restore Legacy' in post-Mugabe era   255

of the state by unconstitutional means – recycling the tired regime change conspiracy Mugabe always used to silence his critics. At worst the paper ignored the story and remained silent especially about the state's use of brute force, arbitrary arrests and use of unorthodox means to smoke out instigators and to suppress the protests. At least, due credit should be given to *The Herald* for remaining true to its founding template of 'reporting in support of the government of the day' to a fault. Where a choice had to be made between giving expression to ordinary peoples' voices on matters of public interest or circulating the government narrative then *The Herald* had consistently chosen the latter. The myth that Mugabe was the sole source of all problems affecting the country and that his removal from power by whatever means would automatically open a new page of economic plenty and prosperity for the country had been the oxygen of the opposition press ranged against Mugabe both local and foreign. So when Mnangagwa took over the reins of power from Mugabe the press was unanimous in orchestrating the belief that the end of Mugabe would be the end of Zimbabwe's problems, that the Western powers who had shunned Mugabe would fall over each other to embrace and bless Zimbabwe. The long yearned-for relief never came; if anything economic hardships worsened. Thus, when Mnangagwa announced oil price increases as a measure to stem the runaway parallel foreign exchange market speculations the story was lost to the public that this was necessary bitter medicine to address legacy economic challenges with their roots in protracted struggles for economic emancipation. Because journalism only sees and reports events and not structures behind those events, the national anger that expressed itself through violent demonstrations, is presented in the news as a spectacle with no logical explanation for its justification.

Many people including nationalist leaders in Mnangagwa's government today would express serious misapprehension at the fact that *The Rhodesia Herald* and other liberal sections of the white press uncritically reproduced the Edgar Whitehead government line on the brutal putting down of nationalist organised protests in African townships in July 1960. Below we reproduce *Rhodesia Herald* journalist John Parker's description of that slice of Zimbabwean history to illustrate the uncanny similarity with the way *The Herald* has continued to cover the state's response to popular acts of revolt against social injustice:

> That morning, 126 people were arrested for illegal assembly; the townships' streets were strewn with broken glass from police cars and the cars of other whites who had been stoned (we carried some hair raising stories); a bank had been broken into, a hotel badly damage, a post office van overturned and three people were taken to hospital with gunshot wounds. The next weekend, in parallel riots along Lobengula Street, Bulawayo, 11 Africans were shot dead by police and more than $100 000 ponds damage was caused. There were no white casualties. The newspapers, including ours, carried vivid accounts of police heroism in the face of African provocation. (Parker, 1972: 85)

256 'Operation Restore Legacy' in post-Mugabe era

Professional journalism purblindness prevented newspapers of Parker's time from finding the opposite story 'African heroism against police brutality' newsworthy. Such news stories would be impossible to write not only from a government censorship perspective but from a professional journalism point of view it was simply irrelevant (Smithson, 2015). That was then and such omissions on the part of the white Rhodesian press could possibly be accounted for in terms of what Melissa Steyn terms the racial ignorance contract which it would be expected such important institutions of white power like the press had signed-up to tacitly or explicitly. But on January 19, 2019, many decades after white colonial rule had ended a news headline; 'Police pursue looters countrywide' anchored *The Saturday Herald* front page, the tone of the story celebratory of police heroism in the face of provocation by riotous mobs 'looters' was not in any significant way different from the Rhodesian press archive. This media genuflection to political power is not something of an 'African eccentricity' an aberrant deviation from the norm in an essentialist sort of way. Stuart Hall and his colleagues at the Birmingham Centre for Contemporary Cultural Studies draw our attention to a much similar hegemonic pattern of reporting that ratcheted-up moral panics against rioting British citizens and celebrated the police valour in upholding law and order as clearly demonstrated by such news headlines as: "Police Win Battle of Grosvenor Square" "The Day The Police Were Wonderful" (Hall et al., 1978: 243).

Potential news stories that fell through the cracks of professional journalism's inbuilt filters were stories about the numbers of those who participated in the marches, how many had died, the circumstances of their deaths, the nationwide sites and scenes of clashes between demonstrators and the police, any noticeable differences between urban and rural areas. Stories such as these were not writable because journalists would not know how to source them with their limited number of credible, official and authorised sources in this particular case heads of government ministries relevant to the event and police officials all based in Harare, those in whose favour the uneven access to narrative resources is tilted those who have fought and 'won the battles of symbolic power' (Couldry, 2010: 117). What happens in Harare is often used metonymically as a shorthand gauge of the national mood in a 'Harare equals Zimbabwe and Zimbabwe equals Harare' simplistic sort of way. The news preference for urban to rural occurrences is problematic for two important reasons. Firstly, foreign relations policies towards Zimbabwe are often guided by and based on local national newspapers' elite and urban-centred news reports and not on what they are silent about. Just a few days after media publicity of Mnangagwa's military crackdown on protestors believed to have been partly responsible for the death of at least 17 people, the Washington Administration took the decision to renew its sanctions against Zimbabwe because, according to President Donald Trump: 'the actions and policies of these persons continue to pose an unusual and extraordinary threat to the foreign policy of the United States' (Hurungudo, 6 March 2019). Secondly, the urban orientation of professional journalism in a largely rural society such as Zimbabwe has introduced a distorted sense of which political party commands the largest national following and electoral outcomes continue to confound political leaders of both the winning and the losing parties as much as they do every opinion pollster who base their predictions on press reports of mass rallies often held in urban centres.

The front page of *The Herald* of Saturday 19 January 2019 read like a page plucked out of Zimbabwe's colonial past. The paper's denial of government responsibility for any negative impacts of its policies and the scapegoating in the stories about street protests was reminiscent of *The Rhodesia Herald*'s reportage on the Tangwena protests discussed in chapter 4 above. Then it was 'communists and their fellow travellers' like Guy Clutton-Brock who were the brains behind the Tangwena trouble. In the fuel protests above the newspaper was at pains to prove that it was not against fuel price hikes that people were protesting, rather that it was the work of some regime change conspirators.

The Herald editor's dismissal

Speculation and conspiracy theory formulation went into overdrive in the rumour machine in Zimbabwe to account for the unceremonious suspension or dismissal of Joram Nyathi from being editor of *The Herald*, one of Zimbabwe's leading daily national newspapers. One theory that seemed to gain traction judging by the volume and direction of commentary both on social media and in newspapers, was that Nyathi was a victim of factional fighting within the ruling party ZANU-PF. Below are some of the headlines reporting Nyathi's axing from the position of editor of *The Herald*:

Table 8.1 Reasons for the dismissal of *The Herald*'s editor

Headline	Source/Publication
Herald editor suspended for placing Mnangagwa return story inside paper	Zimlive.com
Chiwenga captures Herald?	bulawayo24.com
Herald Editor Joram Nyathi Suspended As Zanu-PF Factional Fights Intensify	news.pindula.co.zw
HERALD editor fired over Mnangagwa story; leaves after just one month on the job	NewZimbabwe.com
His Excellency, President @edmnangagwa's return only makes Page 2? Something cooking over at @HeraldZimbabwe. It'll all end with a lot of egg on some faces! What's going on Cdes @nickmangwana @energymutodi and where are you Editor at Large @caesarzvayi? January 22, 2019	□□ (@JusticeMayorW) | Twitter
Arrival Of ZUPCO Buses More Important Than ED's Arrival, New Herald Editor Fired	www.zimeye.net
Let me go cool home. I tried 9:18 AM - 22 Jan 2019	Joram Nyathi @JoramNyathi

The stories underneath the headlines above veered into speculations about political infighting within the party as the cause and gave a berth to considerations of the professional merits of the case. The social reflex to blame the state consistent with

258 *'Operation Restore Legacy' in post-Mugabe era*

the neoliberal mindset has become hegemonic and is often uncritically and unproblematically held and stated as the theory of everything in contemporary Zimbabwe. That attitude also feeds off entrenched colonial conceptions of Africa as the fount of everything that is aberrant and antithetical to progress and reason. However, it is important to consider all available evidence most of all the newspaper itself before jumping to conclusions. In publishing stories newspaper editors deploy commonly shared and accepted devices and standards of newspaper layout, design and story placement across the page (Damasceno and Gruszynski, 2014; Leckner, 2012; Došen and Lidija, 2018) among others as story-importance cues to signpost which stories are more significant than others, to create a clear hierarchy of stories in order to ease the reader's navigation through the mass of news reports and give them a sense of which stories merit their detailed and close attention and which ones merit less or ignoring altogether. Van Dijk also draws our attention to the discursive importance of graphical material accompanying text on the pages of a newspaper when he submits that:

> Whether a news report appears on the front page or on an inside page of the newspaper, high on the page or at the bottom, left or right, or whether it has a small or a banner headline, is long, short or broad, that is, printed over several columns, with or without a photograph, tables, drawings, colour and so on, are all properties of the graphical representation of just one genre that may have a serious impact on the readers' interpretation of the relevance or newsworthiness of news events ... Graphical structures may have several cognitive, social and ideological functions ... they control attention and interest during comprehension, and indicate what information is important or interesting, or should be focused on for other reasons. (Van Dijk, 1998: 201)

On the day in question, the newspaper had chosen to lead with a story on the return of Zupco buses instead of the story on the President's return from abroad as was 'expected'. The single column story on the President's return under a three-deck headline: 'President returns home' was placed on page 2. The headline was assigned the smallest font size and unbolded typeface as if to indicate to the reader the little significance attaching to the story on that page. The fact that it ran in the same column as the 'Matter of fact' headline announcing a correction of a previous editorial error has the effect of further depreciating the value of the 'President returns home' story. The headlining: 'President returns home' is equally problematic and rather flat in that it leaves out any indication why that return should be considered newsworthy and why the reader should bother to read the story. All these graphical facts contribute to the perception of the story's status as a filler on the page. The accompanying full-colour landscape picture of the President wearing his signature scarf and broad smile being welcomed home by his deputies at the airport, spreading across four columns on the top middle section of the page looks completely out of place and unrelated to the story with so small a headline running down a single column on its right. Regular followers of *The Herald* would have been accustomed to encountering a picture like this one, on the front page. The picture looks rather like an afterthought put there more to break the greyness of the page rather than for the importance of the persons and event it is meant to signify. The picture looks more like an accessory to the lead story on the page under the bold headline 'Zanu-PF applauds Govt interventions' from which it appears to hang. This reading is most consistent with standard principles of newspaper layout which suggest that a large picture on the page semantically operates to direct the reader's attention to the main story headline: 'Zanu-PF applauds Govt interventions'. In this particular case, although the picture is the most dominant feature on the page, its visual content seems to refocus the reader away from the main story and more towards the story with the least prominent headline: the 'President returns home' story. These factors alone give one the impression of a page either done hurriedly or by an armature sub-editor, for it throws all the signals on the page into total semantic dissonance. Such mishaps or gaffes can only be appreciated by those with an inkling on how and in what order news pages are filled with content. Because the front page of any newspaper happens to invariably be also one of the last pages to be laid out, the second page completed much earlier in the day often gets readjusted to accommodate the inflow or spill-over stories turning from the front page. One of the reasons for keeping the first page for last, being that of accommodating late-breaking stories, and the President's return home story was one such story which was written and filed late at night after the President's plane landed at the Robert Mugabe International Airport, as the accompanying photograph shows, and accordingly it had to be accommodated somehow in the newspaper.

It is not uncommon for a morning daily newspaper like *The Herald* to finalise the layout of its late pages in the wee hours of the next day. What complicates the editor's work is the fact that the editor does not have the final word on what *The Herald* front page should look like. He and his team have the responsibility of writing most of the stories, subbing and placing those stories on the pages, but as a matter of routine the editor as agent has to clear those pages with his principal, the owners of Zimpapers (Ltd), the government as the majority shareholder, through the Ministry of Information and Broadcasting Services before the paper goes to print (Napoli, 1997). For as long as an editor submits to the ministerial oversight he is normally safe even in the event that there is an error. But if for whatever reason he fails to observe this requirement he becomes seriously exposed and may face sanctions. Government's interest in the newspaper is above all as a political propaganda instrument. The commercial interests who have a minority stake in the newspaper have a profit maximisation interest but where these clash with the propaganda interests then the majority stockholder's interests always take precedence. A commonly shared joke among journalists at Herald House goes as follows: 'objecting to a ministerial directive to run a particular story on the front page of his paper, the Sunday Mail Editor said; "that story won't sell the paper" to which the minister on the other end of the telephone line retorted; "who ever said the Sunday Mail was for profit?"' (Abel Dzobo, *The Herald* sub-editor in an interview, December 2013).

260 *'Operation Restore Legacy' in post-Mugabe era*

The Herald front page often reflects the editor's creative attempts at balancing and resolving any conflict of interest between the political interests of government, the majority shareholder and the minority commercial interests in the media organisation's business. A political story publicising the good deeds of the President or government invariably leads and this is the case regardless of readership interests or tastes. Concerns about the story that sells the paper are of secondary importance to all Zimpapers publications and that status is reflected by how such stories always occupy the anchor position in the layout of *The Herald* front page. *The Herald* front pages below illustrate what has become a default layout design for the newspaper, where the ED story's designate position is 'above-the-fold Page one' (Cotter, 2010: 83).

In the two editions of *The Herald*, ED's return from state visits abroad is given leading story status thus placing the spotlight on the President whether that is the story the prospective reader would be interested to read or not is another matter. In both editions, ED (short form of the President's name) occupies the subject position in a way that makes him the centre of the story. The story 'ED returns to be with his people' diverts the reader's attention from focusing on the importance of that which precipitated the President's return in the first place, the cyclone tragedy. Even that tragedy is used to bring out some of the hitherto unknown qualities in the President who is presented as a caring president. The prominence given to this story has the rhetorical effect of shifting emphasis away from the tragedy to how the President bodily bears the full burden of the national grief occasioned by the cyclone and the hard decision he had to make, 'cutting short his visit to the United Arab Emirates to make sure he is directly involved with the national response to victims of cyclone Idai' as the lead makes clear. The humility, fortitude and courage the President demonstrates (hallmarks of great statesmanship and leadership) is the story not the magnitude of ordinary villagers' devastation. It is easy for analyses like the one engaged in here to fall into the extreme pitfall of essentialising the African experience with the media and tending to pathologise African media systems. Far from it being an African thing, it is a news values thing, nor is it more of a President Mnangagwa thing than it is the logical outcome of an application of a universalised 'news instinct' about prominence and proximity. Cotter (2010: 81) analysis of Western media operations suggests that editors in many Western newsrooms routinely make similar news judgements with no significantly different news outcomes for their readers. He cites a London newspaper editor's reaction to the charge that his paper had an obsession with covering the mayor at the expense of other locally relevant news as typical of how journalism rationalises its news selection decisions: 'First, the Standard is a metropolitan paper, not a local borough news sheet. Of what interest would the state of the streets in Battersea be to the people of Barking or Brent? Second, it is entirely appropriate for the paper of all London to be interested in the Mayor of all London'. It therefore stands to reason that *The Herald* being a national paper, it too must find it entirely legitimate for it to find the President of all the nation of Zimbabwe to be equally relevant and of news interest to its target readership.

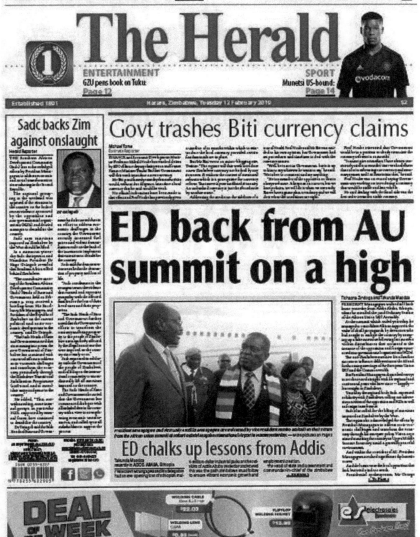

Figure 8.5a and b. *The Herald* front page increasingly becomes very predictable, carrying the President's picture or his name in the lead headline. Reprinted with permission from *The Herald*.

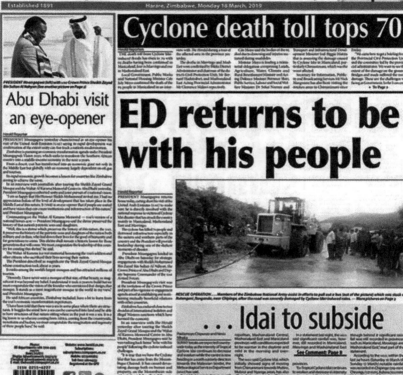

Figure 8.5a and b Continued

'Operation Restore Legacy' in post-Mugabe era   263

The propaganda interests of state legitimation take precedence at *The Herald*. The seller story alternatively called the top-strap in journalistic lingo because of its location across the top section of the page is placed there literally to sell the paper as its name suggests. To appreciate how and why editors accorded top-strap status to the story headlined: 'Govt trashes Biti currency claims' one would need to consider the story against the broader socio-economic context where availability and volatility of the local currency have become issues of public concern. Readers would also be drawn to the story by its reference to 'Biti currency claims'. Mr Tendai Biti, a prominent politician and a Member of Parliament on a main opposition political party ticket had successfully stewarded the economy onto a recovery path when he was Minister of Finance and Economic Planning during the tenure of the government of national unity (GNU) in Zimbabwe – 2009–2013. For its 18 March 2019 edition published under the circumstance where the nation was reeling under the devastating effects of cyclone Idai the front page seller headline: 'Cyclone death toll tops 70' was according to the editors' estimation the real reasons why readers might be persuaded to buy the paper that day. The shoulder-strap story text-boxed to augment its visibility is placed to run along the left column from top of the page down to the bottom. In both cases above, the story provides a window to Zimbabwe's international relations with other nations it may be strategically linked to in the wider world. The story that anchors the page and runs horizontally across the bottom part of the page may in certain instances be on a totally different subject but in most cases as in the examples above it is often on a subject closely related to the lead story to augment it, elaborate on it or give it a new angle. The bottom strap is dedicated to advertising and because it is on the front page, it is priced at prime rates and revenue earned from it is expected to more than cover for the costs of production for the editorial content on that page.

The intensity and regularity with which the ministry may provide guidance and suggestions to the editor is also a function of the speed with which the editor internalises the newspaper's house style. Under Mugabe's government, oversight on Zimpapers publications was helped by the fact that the Permanent Secretary in the Ministry of Information doubled up as the Presidential Spokesperson. Thus clearing the day's front page with the perm-sec was as good as obtaining government's as well as the President's nod on the paper. Under the new political dispensation, the functions of Permanent Secretary and Presidential Spokesperson have been separated and are no longer performed by one individual. This fact has complicated the agent/principal relationship by which *The Herald* editor as the agent is expected to submit to guidance and oversight of a unified principal (Chuma, 2018). The editor as the agent, now needed to submit to the monitorial oversight of a fractured principal. Before the paper hits the street the following morning the editor needed to clear it with the Presidential Spokesperson as well as with the Permanent Secretary, and consensus between the two offices cannot always be guaranteed.

Working from the facts made visible on the pages of the paper alone, it would appear an error was made from a journalistic point of view. A vigilant editor would have easily noted that the President story scored much more highly on most of the common news values (prominence, proximity, significance, conflict time-liness, etc.) applied in making critical gatekeeping decisions on which story leads. However, it is only when the stories are placed in the broader social milieu of stories suppressed and voices silenced that the case becomes a little more complex. The context was that the country had been plunged into social unrest since the President announced a 150% fuel price hike before he left on a state visit of four Eurasian countries of Russia, Belarus, Azerbaijan and Kazakhstan. The Labour Union together with other civic organisation supported by the main opposition party the MDC-A had organised nationwide demos in protest against the hiking of fuel prices. The demonstrations had turned violent and the state had responded by shutting down the Internet and unleashing the military, leading to the death of some protestors. The security situation was degenerating into anarchy, a situation which necessitated the President's cancellation of his planned trip to Davos and returning home to deal with the situation before it spiralled out of control. This whole story was conspicuous by its absence on *The Herald* news pages. If anything *The Herald* had deliberately tried to downplay, even deny, the existence of a crisis all along. It had tried to create the impression that all was normal and that everything was under control in the country. It downplayed the national appeal of the strike and gave prominence to government interventions meant to mitigate the immedi-ate hardships the fuel price hike had occasioned in people's lives. Such stories include 'Government offers civil servants $300m'; 'President talks up mega deals'; 'Zim, Kazakhstan deepen ties' among others. Thus reporting that the President had cut short his European tour of duty to come and quell the social disturbances would amount to making an admission that all was not well in the country. They chose to report that the President had returned but in a way that did not contradict the narrative of a stable country. Placing emphasis on the President's return by giving the story of his return front page status would tend to lend credence to the narrative of a society in turmoil. So the editor was caught between the rock and a hard place. They chose to publish the President's return story but in a way that allowed it to be drowned and eclipsed by the rhetoric of 'it is business as usual in Zimbabwe', in constructing the 'reality' of a country at peace with itself, engineer-ing solutions to people's fuel and transport challenges by retaining the 'Zupco buses return' story in the lead ahead of the 'President returns home' story. In fact, to reduce the editor's choice as between which of the two stories to use as the lead story, the President's return story or the Zupco story is to make a complex con-undrum rather a simple one. There is always a limitless list of occurrences which could have as easily qualified for front page apart from these two depending on the set of criteria being used.

Newsroom politics

Sometimes news story treatment becomes an artefact of the play of newsroom politics and management. Recognition and prestige that goes with a news story when it is assigned headline status also tends to attach to its byline. The reporter who produces the lead story of the day takes the credit. The more one accumulates these credits the more one is positioned for promotion. As a way of managing big egos, editors may from time to time deny or award front page story status as a system of distributing sanctions or rewards among reporters. Applying this principle to the facts surrounding editor Joram Nyathi's editorial mistake that led to his dismissal: the fact that the 'President returns home' story had been filed by Mabasa Sasa could most probably have a lot to do with its being assigned a non-front page status. Mabasa Sasa was the immediate former editor of *The Herald*'s sister paper *The Sunday Mail*. It was his removal from the editor's position together with Caesar Zvayi from the position of editor of *The Herald* that had paved way for Joram Nyathi's ascendance to the editor's position of *The Herald*. Social media sources commented that those changes in the editorships of Zimpapers' flagship newspapers did not enjoy the support of the former Permanent Secretary in the Ministry directly responsible for managing the media parastatal on behalf of the government. The duo of Mabasa Sasa and Caesar Zvayi had enjoyed a cosy working relationship with George Charamba during his long tenure as Permanent Secretary of the Ministry of Information and Broadcasting Services. It is also highly likely that Sasa's selection ahead of sitting editors of *The Herald* and *The Sunday Mail* to be part of the Presidential entourage on the Eurasia trip may have been directly influenced by George Charamba acting in his new capacity as the President' Spokesperson. The opportunity to travel with the President meant that Mabasa Sasa could potentially file front page stories daily for the duration of that foreign trip and in the process hog the limelight and give him a sense of self-importance out of proportion with his new station in the newsroom. So by assigning Mabasa's last instalment on the President's trip back, Joram may not necessarily have been motivated by any malicious intent to slight the President, he may have just intended by it to send an unmistakable signal to Mabasa and indirectly to his mentor, George Charamba that he was the man in charge now at *The Herald*.

Of importance in all this is the question of whether the editor deserved to be fired for such a mistake in the light of the chilling and spine breaking effect it was likely to have on those that remained in the newsroom. It obviously would have the effect of sending an unmistakable signal of how not to organise news pages at *The Herald* and in terms of which stories needed to be prioritised. The new template at *The Herald* henceforth was to always lead with the President. Anything the President did or said was to be given front page news treatment and stories about ordinary people's struggles were to be given short shrift at Herald House. Headline stories published in *The Herald* and its sister weekly *The Sunday Mail* after the incident confirm the shift of the editor's gaze away from ordinary people's concerns with hardships of life, to state-house and the President's person. ED's picture almost became a permanent feature on the front pages of *The Herald* and *The Sunday Mail*. Given that the main opposition party leader constantly calls ED's legitimacy as President into question, the government-owned newspapers take marketing ED's legitimacy as President as a matter of priority. The discursive repackaging, rebranding and reaffirmation of the President's legitimacy beyond

266 'Operation Restore Legacy' in post-Mugabe era

political contestation, has always been Herald House's unstated house style over time. State legitimation role has remained a cardinal principle of *The Herald*'s editorial charter from its inception (Gale, 1962). The variance between different regimes has been only in interpretation. At times when the President's hold on power is challenged and contested by one section of the citizenry, then publishing news in support of the government of the day has been narrowly construed to mean, in support of the President, and one media strategy of doing that has been to ensure that the President featured on the front page of the newspaper almost permanently. It is against this background that placing a people-centred story on front page ahead of the President story as did Joram Nyathi on 22 January was viewed as the equivalent of an act of displacing the President and therefore little short of treasonous. Placing the bus story on the front page and in the process 'displacing' the President's story to an inside page, was also treasonable in the way that it indirectly suggested to the reader that somebody had come up with an effective solution to a problem the President had somehow brought about with his hiking of fuel prices. Credit for engineering this intervention could not be attributed to the President since this was done when he was out of the country. It is important to note that the real debate should not have been about which one between the President or the bus story ought to have made it to the front page. Both these stories were poor sideshows meant to distract news readers away from the most urgent story on how the demonstrations had turned violent and how the law enforcement agents had used excessive force leading to the needless injury and loss of life by several unarmed protestors. The front page story which cost Joram his job was indeed a story so totally out of step with what had become the template lead story in *The Herald* that foregrounded the President. This particular story does not mention the President at all. It begins as follows:

> Commuter omnibus operators were yesterday forced to reduce their fares following the introduction of conventional buses mobilised by the Government to ferry passengers in and around Harare. Commuters in Harare and Bulawayo slammed kombi operators for exploiting them, with some people calling for their immediate ban.

The story's focus is on the event; the reduction of fares by commuter omnibus operators precipitated by the introduction of conventional buses by the government to ferry passengers. Commuter omnibus operators have been picked as the fall-guy of the ongoing social unrest between the government and its citizens. The second sentence goes on to displace and redirect citizens' anger, here represented by the commuters, away from fuel price hikes to Kombi operators who are themselves, victims, too. Either the reporter takes his readers to be very myopic and not sophisticated enough to logically join the dots and conclude that the minibus operators were just as much of victims as they were of the fuel price hikes initiated by the same government now being portrayed as their ally in the story. The story is accompanied with a landscape full-colour picture placed across three columns of the most attention-grabbing top centre spot of the front page, showing

'Operation Restore Legacy' in post-Mugabe era 267

supposedly grateful commuters boarding a bus in Harare. The caption further emphasises the government's 'benevolence and good deeds' in bringing back 'the conventional buses which will be managed by Zupco to cushion commuters from exorbitant fares being charged by kombi operators'. All the sources cited in the story, starting with the Zupco acting chief operating officer, the parastatal's former chief executive officer and the four named commuters have only positive things to say about government. Even the secretary general of the Greater Harare Association of Commuter Operators who would be most expected to express a view more sympathetic to the Kombi operators' plight in the situation also sees and says no evil in the unfolding situation. Below are the typical government praise-singing comments the story attributes to commuting passengers the reporter interviewed appropriately prefaced by: 'Passengers yesterday hailed the introduction of conventional buses by Government'.

1   'Zupco buses show that Government is alive to the challenges being faced by the population'.
2   'Government wants people to be happy but people are just panicking'.
3   'We thank government for the initiative. It has enabled us to come to work'.
4   'It is a good programme by Government'.
5   'Government has done well by introducing these buses'.

Through the use of lexical devices that connote positivity, the story discursively constructs government as caring and benevolent and in the same breadth delegitimating the ongoing civic protests as illogical even without having to mention them. This clearly demonstrates the link between what the paper chooses to report on and that about which it chooses to be silent. A critical and discerning reader would care to access that which the newspaper is silencing by reporting whatever it decides as worth reporting. Every news story is an index of its anti-story. Thus the debate about which story ought to have been placed where in the newspaper is beside the point, a distraction from engaging with the newspaper's broader discursive investments in the project of repair and maintenance of unequal power relations in society.

The writers pointed to explosive exchanges on social media by some prominent members of ZANU-PF and legislators following the military crackdown on nationwide civil society organised protests against fuel price hikes. The President had to cut short his trip to Switzerland for a Davos meeting to return home to deal with the national emergency. It was, on the face of it, the way *The Herald* handled the story of the President's abrupt return that caused Nyathi's sorrows. Nyathi had been promoted to the position of editor of *The Herald* in a recent reshuffle of top leadership at the parastatal media organisation as 'has become almost customary at Zimpapers that when a new minister is appointed, editors are changed. Zvayi and Sasa were seen as loyalists of the former Permanent Secretary in the Ministry of Information, George Charamba' (Vambe 18 December 2018), who had been given a new appointment as the Presidential Spokesperson. Charamba is said to not have been amused with the changes at the

268 *'Operation Restore Legacy' in post-Mugabe era*

government-controlled newspaper group and may have played a part in precipitating Nyathi's dismissal. While there may be substance in all these conspiracy theories very few of the commentators attempted a critical analysis of the merits of the case for Nyathi's dismissal based on an analysis of the particular edition of *The Herald* newspaper that was used as the basis for his suspension or dismissal. Could a prima facie case be established for Nyathi's dismissal on purely professional grounds? This is a question, observers seemed disinclined to pursue, for them state meddling in the editorial operations at *The Herald* was there for all to see. Chuma (2018) deploys the principal/agent theory to explain how the government of Zimbabwe has over the years, exercised influence and control through hiring and firing at its media parastatals.

Working with the opposition press

The Mugabe government had introduced a toxic form of politics that polarised the media into an us-and-them binary. The state-owned press was viewed as 'our press, the loyal ally' of the ruling party and government, while the privately owned press was characterised as enemies of the state, the adversarial other, Trojan horses of Western imperialism and agents of regime change who needed to be treated as such. Persistent persecution of journalists working for the privately owned press had increasingly become a defining feature of the last decade and half of Mugabe's rule. Where intimidation and persecution failed to work the Mugabe regime also instituted covert newspaper-buying projects in which previous owners were bought out of their newspapers and in the process tone down the adversarial slant of the paper or silence it altogether. The demise of Ibbo Mandaza's *The Mirror* newspaper in 2007 was one such example. The *Financial Gazette* (Fingaz) slowly lost its lustre after an outfit fronted by former Reserve Bank Governor acquired a controlling stake in its capital in 2005. The *Zimbabwe Independent* newspaper published a series of news reports between 2005 and 2007 in which it exposed what the paper dubbed 'Zimbabwe's mediagate', a scandal in which the government secret agency the Central Intelligence Organisation (CIO) pursued a deliberate policy of seeking to influence public opinion through acquisition of independent media entities in a war to win the hearts and minds of Zimbabwean newspaper-reading public. The media waters became even more muddied when the Fingaz went on to merge with the Associated Newspapers of Zimbabwe (ANZ) on the eve of the removal of Mugabe from power. It has remained a matter of conjecture which of the two merging entities swallowed and neutralised the other in the process, but basing on the resulting changes in the editorial structure it can be argued that the marriage tilted *The Daily News*'s editorial slant away from its earlier unequivocally anti-Zanu-Pf government line. Whatever the case might be, the editorial slant of both papers has since the merger been effectively steered towards the middle with a softly-softly approach to criticism of the government. The strategy of media emasculation through co-optation has been followed through with greater intensity in the post-Mugabe era.

‘Operation Restore Legacy’ in post-Mugabe era   269

Mugabe's fall created a renewed sense of hope and generated outpourings of goodwill from well-wishers across the political divide and from rank and file. Business leaders and captains of industry cautioned patience on the part of the long-suffering Zimbabweans arguing that Mnangagwa's new administration needed to be given a chance. Strive Masiiwa, renowned billionaire and owner of Zimbabwe's leading mobile service provider Econet, is famously quoted as saying:

> Concerning the change that has taken place, I believe it is real, I believe President Mnangagwa is sincere in the things he wants to do. It's going to be extremely challenging, everybody knows that. Anyone who understands economics knows it's going to be tough governing. But I think that Zimbabwe needs to be given a chance, we've got to stop the politicking and focus on rebuilding this country. I'm right up there. (*The Zimbabwe Mail*, 30 October 2018)

Masiiwa's remarks attracted very mixed reactions from many Zimbabweans as the following typical responses to Shingi Munyeza's tweet indicate:

> Shingi Munyeza @ShingiMunyeza ZIMBABWE HAS TO BE GIVEN A CHANCE 1. The change that has happened is real. 2. ED is sincere in what he wants to do but it's gonna be extremely challenging 3. We got to stop politicking and focus on rebuilding this country. 3. Sanctions must be removed @StriveMasiyiwa.
>   L Maware @l_maware 30 Oct 2018.Replying to @ShingiMunyeza I wonder how he measured ED's sincerity when ED has failed to reform the electoral process, failed to uproot corruption, let soldiers kill unarmed civilians. Are all these symbols of sincerity?
>   zanupf_patriots @zanupf_patriots 30 Oct 2018.Replying to @ShingiMunyeza This is a good story to tell. His message is clear, no politicking but putting Zimbabwe first.

Even Media mogul Trevor Ncube also weighed in with expressions of goodwill to the new dispensation. This made the government's charm offensive easier as what government needed to do was to reciprocate the good overtures. In due course Trevor Ncube, together with 16 other prominent citizens of the country got rewarded with an appointment onto the prestigious Presidential Advisory Council (PAC) tasked with providing the President with wise counsel on matters of the state. A few weeks after this appointment and a meeting held at the behest of the Minister of Information and Broadcasting Services to iron out differences between Trevor Ncube and the Deputy Minister at the ministry offices, Ncube went on to make a public apology to the nation of Zimbabwe on his Twitter handle for what he called 'our blind spots/ biases' contributing to unnecessary polarisation in the media. Below are some selected responses to Trevor Ncube's Tweeter post, illustrating the public outrage it occasioned:

270 *'Operation Restore Legacy' in post-Mugabe era*

Trevor NcubeVerified account @TrevorNcube. My heart breaks that @NewsDayzimbabwe got this story so wrong. This is example of our blind spots/biases colouring our world view contributing to polarisation. While l maintain my newspapers are not me/I am not my newspapers - I am embarrassed. Sincere apologies to Zimbabwe.

Don Chigumba @Donchigumba 15h15 hours ago. Replying to @TrevorNcube @NewsDayzimbabwe U are not the one who is supposed to apologise leave it to the newspaper management. That tendency is dictatorial. U have to be careful with the way u are running your media! They are slowly adopting herald and other state media's lies. U don't need to attack ur wokers in public.

Mbongeni Dube @mthembo12 14h14 hours ago. Replying to @TrevorNcube @NewsDayzimbabwe Poor Newsday editors, the owner is compromised and when they question stance of his papers he tells his papers they r wrong n apologise yet newspaper said truth!

BRIAN N. CHAWASARIRA @BRYANNCHAWASAR1 10h10 hours ago. Replying to @TrevorNcube @NewsDayzimbabwe This editorial interference is just pathetic. Is this the new normal for Newsday? If so, I am going to stop trusting it as a source of balanced and well researched news. It will soon join some other daily that I stopped buying a long time ago. Better to buy bread than propaganda.

Courage Gwena @CourageGwena 10h10 hours ago. Replying to @TrevorNcube @NewsDayzimbabwe I understand where you're coming from ... after all you have attained through bootlickinng then one small guy messes everything for you with a single headline.

M-Jay @M_Jay94 15h15 hours ago. Replying to @TrevorNcube @NewsDayzimbabwe Allow journalists to do their job independently without bullying them Mr Presidential Adviser. Thank you. #MediaFreedom.

Chisi @luckychisi 14h14 hours ago. Replying to @TrevorNcube @NewsDayzimbabwe A subtle way of intimidating @NewsDayzimbabwe journalists, presidential advisor is quite excitable these days.

Faith Silandulo Dube @silandulo247 2h2 hours ago. Replying to @TrevorNcube @NewsDayzimbabwe Mngagagwa's advisor you are in trouble in your dual role as Junta' s advisor & running an independent newspaper.

Dunmore Jamanda @dunniejays 4h4 hours ago. Replying to @TrevorNcube @NewsDayzimbabwe Mr Ncube your judgment is now blared because you are now part of the gravy train by way of being appointed to the advisory team.

Chitova wa Chitova @chitova_11 14h14 hours ago. Replying to @TrevorNcube @NewsDayzimbabwe You just took kunhanzva to a whole new level.

oscar chiwome @Oxid_08 9h9 hours ago. Replying to @TrevorNcube @NewsDayzimbabwe We know u, al of u. These biznesmen sapotin Ed r actually protectin their bizneses. Strive doesnt want vana @MTN kuti vauye, Now Trevor u dnt want @gvtadverts out of yo paper, Chanakira hopes that @MYCASH wil bchanged to Kingdom by Ed U r al, selfish selouts bt God is watching U.

'Operation Restore Legacy' in post-Mugabe era   271

The point that was not lost to most of Ncube's 266 tweeter followers who responded to his tweet, was the fat that Trevor Ncube had been recently favoured by Mnangagwa's government with an appointment to the PAC and that this could potentially alter his political opinions and views. They read his criticism of his own newspaper as representing some of the deleterious effects of his new appointment on his judgement. They interpreted his tweet as an attempt by Ncube as owner and publisher of the NewsDay at sending an unmistakable signal to the editors of his papers to change course and to begin toning down on their adversarial reporting of government policy. By simply offering a public apology on behalf of his newspaper, even if he may not have taken any further action against the editor of the *NewsDay* and the specific reporter who wrote the story, Trevor Ncube indirectly sanctioned the editorial staff on all of his newspaper titles against reporting differently from the way state media reported on political issues. Thus in spite of the protestations that there was a separation between him as owner and his newspapers, purporting that they do not take instructions from him that separation is only academic as the principal/agent model discussed above also equally applies even in the media section that prefers to call itself the independent press. Editors of privately owned newspapers do not enjoy unqualified editorial autonomy from owners and their owners from their political and commercial principals. But the debate about which one of the two newspapers got the story right on the exchange rate between the local currency (RTGS) against the United States dollar was really beside the point. The big story which both papers missed was the great heist by the state on ordinary citizens' bank balances as at the date when the state made it official that its original lie of a 1:1 equivalence between the country's own surrogate currency and the greenback was no longer sustainable. Ordinary bankers' balances were supposed to be automatically revised upwards by the same factor with which its value differed from the US dollar, the moment the market determined rate was announced as new policy, but they were not. All workers were the losers as salaries remained pegged at the same levels as when the value of the local currency maintained parity with the US dollar.

Trevor Ncube had for a long time been looked to as the last man standing in defence of a truly independent press in Zimbabwe but the recent developments under Mnangagwa's new dispensation, represent clear marker of a turning point in and a clean break with a polarising politics of the media environment of the past. Mnangagwa has not just charmed business and media owners, he has also extended an olive branch to civil society to complete his tripartite consensus-building project. Jenni Williams who had made a name for herself and her organisation the Women of Zimbabwe Arise (WOZA) as an unflinching critic of the Mugabe government has also been recruited as a government sympathiser. After being granted an audience with the new President Williams was all praise for Mnangagwa as reported by *The Herald* (26 March 2019), she is quoted as making the following positive remarks about Mnangagwa:

272 *'Operation Restore Legacy' in post-Mugabe era*

> "Most of my colleagues agreed that if the Head of State was still former President Robert Mugabe he would have never got onto the plane and flown to Bulawayo to meet us. That would have never happened. The contrast now is that for 37 years we have waited as people of this region to actually talk to Government. But on Thursday the President showed us that he wants a Zimbabwe where everyone feels included, so that is a contrast of the two leaders. (*The Herald*, 26 March 2019)

If leaders of big business and civic society have all been co-opted it is difficult to imagine the possibility of serious social cleavages and divergence of opinion finding expression in the media as these together form the bedrock of what is called credible news sources for the media. The Zimbabwean newspaper-reading public is likely to witness a convergence of opinion between state-owned and privately owned media on important political issues affecting the country like never before. Whether this will work for the better of the country's future or not remains a moot point. What is certain, however, is that the new political dispensation has set a framework for conciliatory discourse and for a broadly based consensus framework which will render media polarisation that had characterised the closing chapters of Mugabe rule virtually impossible.

Beyond just exposing the polarisation in the Zimbabwean press, the billboards above also vividly bring to light the constructed-ness of news as many sociology of news scholars have argued (Hall et al., 1978, Fowler, 2013; Philo, 2007; Schudson, 2003). It is not a question of which one, between *The Chronicle* and the *NewsDay*, got the story right on the intrinsic truth about the value of the RTGs currency. By alleging that his newspaper had got 'this story so wrong' and that it was caused by 'our blind spots/biases that colour our world view' Ncube is labouring under what Fowler (2013) describes as a 'drastically and dangerously false' assumption that his newspaper has all along been able to stand outside biasing factors to report unmediated 'truth'. The fact that two different newspapers could pick on the fluctuating value of the RTGS, illustrates that journalists draw on a common set of criteria to make judgements about which events are worth reporting on as news. How they then go on to turn the selected events into news stories depends on the journalists' worldview as alluded to in Ncube's tweet, but most importantly it also depends on which official news sources are readily available to the journalist. It is a mark of professional development for a journalist to have cultivated dependable sources – primary definers according to Hall et al. (2013) – from whom to obtain a comment on a news story when one is urgently needed. In this particular case the different main sources used by the two newspapers made all the difference. The Chronicle based its story on comments made by the Minister of Finance, Mthuli Ncube while the *NewsDay* on the other hand developed theirs on their interpretation of Reserve Bank Governor, John Mangudya's comments. Events in the world such as market driven fluctuations in the RTGS against the United States dollar, real or speculative, together with comments from official news sources constitute the raw materials the journalist has to produce the news confirming Philo's assertion cited in (Fowler, 2013: 13) that: 'news is not found or even gathered so much as made. It is a creation of a journalistic process'.

Possible futures for the press and for Zimbabwe

At a structural level, so far no deep changes can be anticipated in the mediascape as what has been witnessed since the end of Mugabe dispensation is the movement of chess pieces on the media chessboard without changing the game. A new minister heads the Ministry of Information now and George Charamba, former Mugabe spin doctor who doubled up as Permanent Secretary of the Ministry of Information, has been replaced at the ministry so he can give undivided attention to his new task as the spin doctor of the President in the new dispensation. Since the liquidation of the MMT George has been widely believed to micro-manage the state-owned media entities in the country to a point of turning them into mouthpieces of the Zanu-PF government over the years. He is likely to continue to exercise some considerable influence on the operations of both the ZBC and editorial activities at Herald House for the foreseeable future. Reasons for scepticism abound. If recent changes in the editorial line-up at *The Herald* are anything to go by, then the media are likely to remain the same the more they change. If under Mugabe *The Herald* was pro-first-family it was also decidedly pro-Zanu-PF, under Mnangagwa indications so far suggest that it has intensified this tendency rather than moving to become more national and pro-Zimbabwe in outlook.

The new Minister at the Ministry of Information and Broadcasting Services has given unmistakable signals about her determination to strike off the statute books the regime of repressive media laws of the Mugabe era. Be that as it may, as long as revival of the ZMMT and its mandate to protect state-owned media entities from undue influence and interference with their editorial independence, emanating from centres of political and economic power remains off the table for discussion then repealing the Access to Information and Protection of Privacy Act (AIPPA 2002) and the Public Order and Security Act (POSA 2001) may result in little change in the media status quo. The only change as evidence presented and discussed in the preceding chapters suggest, lie in that the current Zanu-PF government under Mnangagwa is intent on achieving by co-optation and cooperation, what Mugabe used to achieve by fiat – cross-media uni-vocality.

Press silences that come as a result of accepted norms and standards of journalistic production routines and received professional codes of practice will be much more difficult to deal with. Journalism is one profession that has no tradition of critical reflection on the taken-for-grantedness of its own methods as Wasserman argues with reference to the post-apartheid South African journalism that change in journalistic attitudes may not keep pace with structural transformation of the media industries in terms of change of ownership and the racial and gender composition of the editorial staff. He maintains that 'the continuities between the past and the present, as they play out in journalistic attitudes, routines and practices, call into question any glib notion of journalism in the democratic era as having made a clean break with the past' (Wasserman, 2018: 73). Far from its own claims of democracy facilitation and fourth estate monitorial role over state power, the press has set itself up as a power accountable only to itself. In countries where urbanisation has failed to take off, where the rural poor,

274 *'Operation Restore Legacy' in post-Mugabe era*

ever since colonisation, outnumbering their urban middle-class counterparts by a factor of more than 3:1 remains a demographic fact, then the establishment press or legacy media which caters for a fraction of that third of the national population – authorised news sources – has long lost its legitimacy. For the two thirds who have eked a precarious existence since colonialism, in the difficult to reach, tired white sands of rural Manyene, over-grazed, rocky and thirsty plains of Mhandamabwe, or in the former fly zone below the Charama plateau along the Zambezi escapement, or down in remote Checheche and Chibuwe villages along the eastern border, in the flood plains of Muzarabani or in Tsholotsho, the low-lying northwestern areas of the country, the idea that Uhuru came, let alone that a new political dispensation is upon us, remains a fiction so removed from the realities of their grinding poverty. They have never learned to tell the difference between a newspaper, the Bible or a children's storybook. They have one thing in common they speak in strange tongues about dramas and oddities of strange deities in faraway places. Rural Zimbabwe is a poverty structure where little happens and time passes almost imperceptibly, everything appears to stay the same except when a cyclone visits. They have learned to count time from one cyclone to the next, from cyclone Eline in 2000 to Dineo in 2017 to Idai most recently in 2019, in that order, the more devastating the impact, the more memorable. Cyclones are more remembered than 18 April 1980, the day independence came, or the day Mugabe resigned to mark the beginning of a new dispensation. At least cyclones touch their lives in more dramatic and transformative ways than one. They alone have the power to bring all of Harare home with the pressmen in tow. Cyclones are also known to sweep some fortunate villagers onto front pages of *The Herald*. So it stands to reason that in spite of their notoriety cyclones have this one good thing, they bring a photo opportunity for rural folk and affect to alter the content of the news once in a while. Otherwise as Golding and Eliot noted way back in 1979 as cited in (Manning, 2001: 52) 'news changes very little *even* when the individuals who make it are changed'.

References

Chuma, W., 2018. Journalism, politics and professionalism in Zimbabwe, in: *Newsmaking cultures in Africa*. Springer, pp. 251–267.

Chung, F., 2006. *Re-living the second Chimurenga: Memories from the liberation struggle in Zimbabwe*. African Books Collective.

Cotter, C., 2010. *News talk: Investigating the language of journalism*. Cambridge University Press.

Couldry, N., 2010. *Why voice matters: Culture and politics after neoliberalism*. Sage.

Damasceno, P.L., Gruszynski, A., 2014. Newspaper design–processes, routines and product: A study of Segundo Caderno, the Zero Hora cultural supplement. *Braz. Journal. Res.* 10, 102–121.

Došen, Đ.O., Lidija, B., 2018. Key design elements of Daily Newspapers: Impact on the reader's perception and visual impression. *KOME– Int. J. Pure Commun. Inq.* 6, 62.

Fowler, R., 2013. *Language in the news: Discourse and ideology in the press*. Routledge.

Freeman, N., 2018. Zimbabwe open for business, code for international finance capitalism. Race and History. Accessed 19 August 2019 from: http://www.raceandhistory.com/Zimbabwe/2018/1503.html.

'Operation Restore Legacy' in post-Mugabe era

Gale, W., 1962. *History of the Rhodesian printing and publishing company.* Madorn Print.

Hall, S., Critcher, C., Jefferson, T., Clarke, J., Roberts, B., 2013. *Policing the crisis: Mugging, the state and law and order.* Macmillan International Higher Education.

Hall, S., 1978. The social production of news, in: S. Hall, C. Critcher, T. Jefferson, J. Clarke and B. Roberts (eds), *Policing the crisis: Mugging, the state, and law and order.* Macmillan, pp. 53–75.

Harold-Barry, D. (ed.), 2004. *Zimbabwe: The past is the future.* Weaver Press.

Hurungudo, P., 6 March 2019. 'Trump cranks up heat on ED ... As Washington extends its Zim sanctions'. *Daily News.* wwwdailynews.co.zw/articles/2019/03/06/trump-cra nks-up-heat-on-ed-as-washington-extends-its-zim-sanctions.

Leckner, S., 2012. Presentation factors affecting reading behaviour in readers of newspaper media: An eye-tracking perspective. *Vis. Commun.* 11, 163–184.

Manning, P., 2001. *News and news sources: A critical introduction.* Sage.

Moyo, D., 2004. From Rhodesia to Zimbabwe: Change without change? Broadcasting policy reform and political control. *Media Public Discourse Polit. Contestation Zimb.* 27, 17.

Napoli, P.M., 1997. A principal-agent approach to the study of media organizations: Toward a theory of the media firm. *Polit. Commun.* 14, 207–219.

Obadare, E., Willems, W., 2014. *Civic agency in Africa: Arts of resistance in the 21st century.* Boydell & Brewer.

Parker, J., 1972. *Rhodesia: Little white island.* Pitman.

Philo, G., 2007. Can discourse analysis successfully explain the content of media and journalistic practice? *Journal. Stud.* 8, 175–196.

Rogers, D., 2019. *Two weeks in November: The astonishing untold story of the operation that toppled Mugabe.* Jonathan Ball Publishers.

Schudson, M., 2003. *The sociology of news.* Norton.

Simpson, M., Hawkins, T., 2018. *Primacy of regime survival.* Springer.

Smithson, M., 2015. Afterword: Ignorance studies: Interdisciplinary, multidisciplinary, and transdisciplinary, in: M. Gross and L. McGoey (eds), *Routledge international handbook of ignorance studies.* Routledge, pp. 403–417.

Van Dijk, T.A., 2013. Ideology and discourse, in M. Freeden, L.T. Sargent and M. Stears (eds), *The Oxford handbook of political ideologies.* Oxford University Press.

Van Dijk, T.A., 1998. *Ideology: A multidisciplinary approach.* Sage.

Wasserman, H., 2018. *Media, geopolitics, and power: A view from the global south.* University of Illinois Press.

Newspapers

The Daily News, 11 January 2002. Leader page, 'Army is attempting to blackmail voters'.

The Zimbabwe Mail, 30 October 2018. 'Strive Masiyiwa backs "sincere" Mnangagwa, wants US sanctions lifted'. wwwthezimbabwemail.com/zimbabwe/strive-masiyiwa-backs-sin cere-mnangagwa-wants-us-sanctions-lifted/.

9 Do-it-yourself (DIY) news and the emancipatory promise

Introduction

This chapter is a reflection on how ordinary people come by news (Nyamnjoh, 2012) in the light of a long and unbroken record of exclusion and silencing by a press system that has not shed its coloniality and that has acquiesced in its own capture and captivity to the political and commercial power block. It discusses how people against all odds have produced and shared their own alternative news accounts relevant to their own programme, first in the popular struggles for emancipation from colonial domination and more recently in their struggles to rid themselves of a narrow nationalism turned parasitic, self-serving and despotic against the same people it went to war to liberate. It teases out the possibility of evolving journalism along new trajectories away from the blind application of its time-honoured ideology of professional practice that produces news discourses that are predictably alienating and marginalising to the majority poor, as has been amply demonstrated in the few reportorial cases discussed in the preceding chapters; a journalism that has repudiated its democratic mandate. The chapter proposes an approach to reading the media that is critically sceptical and questioning of the opaque means by which journalism embeds strategic silences in that which they make manifest in ways that legitimate domination and social inequality along axes of difference and privilege. It builds an argument for developing a self-critical journalism practice that is capable of reflexively engaging with its own taken for granted conventional rules, norms and standards that structure and (mis)guide its practice in a way that firmly embeds it with oppressive systems. It discusses how modern journalism practice can adopt an approach 'of communication in solidarity with those whose freedom has been taken away, or seriously diminished, rendering them less than human' (Traber, 1999: 4), by borrowing from and extending the many strands of doing journalism otherwise than the mainstream way: Michael Traber's grassroots and advocacy journalism (Traber, 1989) irreverent journalism (Parker, 1972), guerrilla journalism (Frederikse, 1982) experimented with at different historical conjunctures in the making of Zimbabwe. The chapter maps these historical antecedents onto contemporary intersections between offline and online #tag movements, popular mojos and citizen journalism coalescing to provide a platform for shared resistances that subvert the oppressive neo-colonial system in

Zimbabwe. Both in history and at present, it was these participatory, often unin-stitutionalised, unorganised quasi do-it-yourself (DIY) models of news which were credited with upstaging oppressive dictatorial regimes' propaganda machinery and bringing about social change (Frederikse, 1982).

Proposals for a critical media literacy

The discussion of the various reportorial cases presented in the preceding chapters has consistently drawn attention to how mainstream news media, irre-spective of different historical conjunctures, actively produced silences in Zim-babwe even as they adhered to the dictates of their professional ethical conduct. The object of the analysis was not to demonstrate that the news as presented by the journalists were less 'true' than that which they were silent about, nor was it to cast aspersions at mainstream press generally. That would be irresponsible, given that inadequate though it may be its notional midwifery role in the emergence of democracy remains relevant. Rather, it served to debunk the myth that the news were objective proxies of some uncontestable truths (Popper, 1998) or reality out there and to illustrate that instead they are just as ideologically invested as any other instances of language in use, that news media discursively produce the world they report on in ways that entrench dominance, oppression and exploitation of the subordinated groups in society. A critical media literacy entails a reading of the media that is contextual, informed by a scepticism about the genre's claims of objectivity and self-pro-claimed ideological innocence and emptiness. Its primary concern like critical discourse analysis from which it draws its inspiration is with the role of news silencing in the discursive reproduction of dominance and social inequality (Van Dijk, 1993). But beyond a concern with manifest news (that which is published) perhaps a critical media literacy would need to draw on analytic methods and typologies proposed by Croissant (2014: 4) to engage with news silences, absences, omissions, in the 'structural production of ignorance'. Literature on the epistemology of ignorance (Proctor and Schiebinger, 2008; McGoey, 2012; Dossey, 2014; Gross and McGoey, 2015; Beddoes, 2019) awakens us to the fact that what is not there in media texts may be just as important in the critical appreciation of that which the media makes known because news absences make the foil upon which it is inscribed. The critical media literacy being pro-posed here approaches the news as a knowledge genre which is unavoidably implicated in the social manufacture of ignorance. What news neglects or voices and articulations it omits is acknowledged 'as a permanent structural phenom-enon that is produced in parallel with knowledge and therefore cannot be avoided or permanently eliminated' (Dorniok, 2013: 10). Every news story by the artefact of its visibility is an integer of the silence which feeds and nourishes it – a source of both ignorance and knowledge (Kourany, 2015). Hess's (2016) concept of 'undone science' which describes how a particular 'form of struc-tured ignorance rooted in systems of formal knowledge production, the weight of predominant theories, 'best' methodological practices, funding priorities, and

278 Do-it-yourself (DIY) news

other political matters can all work to generate undone science' may be germane to the task of unravelling the production processes by which news produces its own silences.

What would such a programme of study of the news entail? The problem with current news reading cultures even of a critical discourse analysis typology tend to take the saids of news as their departure point. Little attention is paid to reading that which is excluded from the news – the news' invisibilities. 'The African press', Michael Traber (1989: 92) contends, 'is too political in its obsession with the speeches and ceremonials of government ministers.' In postcolonial settings like Zimbabwe a news reading ought to focus its search light on the gaps, the blank spaces, the cracks in between the utterances to reconstruct from the saids, the missing, the muffled and unintelligible murmurs of the 70% poor subsistence farmers, vendors and hordes of unemployed or under-employed youths. Those silences are an important constitutive part of the work of ideologies and propaganda, and '… a necessity for the ever-oppressive state' (Croissant 2014: 12). In neo-colonial settings like Zimbabwe it behoves the reader well to direct their reading of newspapers mainly to the unsaids of news journalism. The geo and body politics and logics of silencing treats the poor as exteriorities of the 'mass communications' loop.

The Herald and all other metropolitan newspapers in the history of Zimbabwe have always been content to limit their affordances for voice to the elite fraction of the population with power and influence. This fact of Zimbabwean newspapers has remained immune to changes in the political realm from colonial to postcolonial and from the Mugabe era to the not so 'New Dispensation' at least in terms of news. The elitist, 'civil society good, state bad' empiricism that tends to narrowly frame the mainstream news discourse in Zimbabwe not only epistemically forecloses subaltern ways of knowing but also often obscures the role of exogenous constraints in the form of 'restrictions imposed by international financial institutions and global power relations more broadly – on the agency of individual Africans as well as on the sovereignty of the national state' (Obadare and Willems, 2014: 6). In the case of Zimbabwe both during the post-UDI colonial period (1965–1980) and most recently in the post-Fast Track Land Reform Programme since 2000, the externally imposed constraints on state sovereignty, have taken the more punitive form of regimes of economic sanctions and national isolation by powerful nations within the international system. It must be underscored that the nation state acts as the locus of explanation for any local occurrences for the local press. Thus when the economy screams the producers of news diagnose the problem and look for answers within the bounds of the state system. Economic mismanagement and corruption are presented as the usual culprits in an essentialist way in total abstraction from the state's global entanglements. The hand of the IMF or the World Bank or the operation of externally induced inflationary pressures are by their nature invisible to the local news net. It sees and reports the ineptness of the President and the Minister of Finance as the sovereign authors of an insular economic system of the nation, and civil society as the fount of the resistance and rioting directed against state rapacity. When

Do-it-yourself (DIY) news   279

disaster strikes whether of natural or anthropogenic causes, again comments and explanations are sought from local authorised commentators in a manner that often obfuscate the trans-frontier nature of such occurrences.

In this closing chapter it is meet for us to consider one more reportorial case to illustrate how an application of critical media literacy might operate to bring to the surface hidden ideological intentions in news stories. We make reference to news reports at the start of the cholera outbreak in Harare in early September 2018, and when the epidemic reportedly ended in October 2018. *The Herald* broke the story on 7 September 2018 with a news headline titled: 'Cholera outbreak claims five'. The first question is with the timing of the story. Did the story have to wait until five lives were lost for it to acquire newsworthy status? Its placement on the front page as a side bar gives it the status of a filler story on that page. The story is also accompanied with a mugshot picture of Dr Parirenyatwa, the then Minister of Health and Child Welfare. This obviously invests the story with the claim of official credibility. The headline itself actually hides more than what it reveals. For example, what would varying the headline to read: 'Five die in another case of cholera outbreak' or 'Cholera hits the slums of Harare suburbs again' have suggested to the reader about the culpability of government because of its inability to learn from past experience? Could the disaster not have been avoided? The use of the Minister's photograph is a marker of authenticity of the facts being presented in the story. The most important disclosure the minister who happens to be the sole source used in the story, makes is the acknowledgement that there is an outbreak of cholera affecting the high-density suburbs of Glen View and Budiriro, but that the magnitude of the problem is not that overwhelming, since only one death has so far been confirmed to have resulted from cholera. The other four cases remain unconfirmed as they were still under investigation. The problem is also very localised to just two high-density townships, not the whole city or the whole country. 'We believe this outbreak is in Glen View and Budiriro. There is nowhere else in Zimbabwe where we have cholera except those two places,' the minister is quoted as saying. The reader must derive solace, the story seems to suggest, in that government and the city council have responded 'expeditiously'. The story uncritically deploys the colonial metaphor of the unwashed black masses in the exhortation to the public to 'practice good personal hygiene' in a 'blame the victim' modernist accusation that the sufferers have no one else to blame for their condition but themselves. 'Wash your hands and make sure the water you are drinking is safe. If you do not have water that is clean then we have this problem that we are facing. It is usually a problem of water which is contaminated,' the minister is quoted as saying.

Drinking of unsafe and contaminated water is presented as a matter of personal choice on the part of the sufferers. The cause of the problem and therefore its solution as well is presented as lying squarely in the hands of the residents of Glenview and Budiriro. They just need to wash their hands a little more often and avoid drinking contaminated water. How the water got contaminated in the first place is a question the story does not go into. What also remains unsaid here is how urban residents ended up having to use borehole water instead of treated tap water supplied through the municipal water reticulation system. The story is

280 Do-it-yourself (DIY) news

silent on the phenomenon of burst sewer pipes that spew raw sewage that ends up contaminating underground water. The story is silent about the municipal failing water and sewer reticulation system, the municipality's failure to provide an efficient rubbish collection and waste disposal service to the growing urban population. The story is silent on the lack of fit between size of population and the carrying capacity of the municipality's aging infrastructure. The deeper meaning of this story is the construction of poor people as the problem to be solved. The silences then set the conceptual framework within which it becomes possible even imperative for government to prescribe behaviour change of the population at risk of contracting cholera as the solution.

To aid the reader's understanding, a well written news story would normally provide explanatory context to the story. This is often treated as a requirement of good news story craft (Cotter, 2010). The inverted pyramid is often taught as the default story format for a hard news story. Background detail comes at the tail-end of the story and is optional and can be cut out in the event that there is limited space for a longer story. This appears to have been the case in this particular story. Even when it is included, in certain instances, it may serve to occlude rather than add clarity to the subject being reported, as appears to be the case in this specific example.

The cause of the cholera disease (the bacterium) is conflated with the cause of the outbreak of the disease. The outbreak is connected with overcrowding, unhygienic conditions and the municipality's failure to provide sanitation and clean and safe drinking water. But the story explains:

> Cholera is caused by a bacteria called vibrio cholerae. It spreads by eating food or drinking water that is contaminated and is characterised by heavy watery diarrhoea. Its symptoms include among others thirst, little or no urine, dry skin and mouth, absence of tears.

That the bacterium vibrio cholerae causes cholera does not explain what caused the outbreak of the disease in Glen View and Budiriro and not in Borrowdale, or any other elite suburb in Harare or in any other place for that matter. By making the disease subject of the sentence in 'It spreads by …' the story absolves the state of any responsibility in this tragedy. The story keeps silent on the underlying structural duality of the economy inherited from the country's colonial town planning system, which the postcolonial state has done little to change, many decades after attainment of independence. How it so happens that the former white suburbs where the minister now lives are somehow not prone to these disease outbreaks is a question it does not occur for the reporter to ask. The story says nothing about the chronic state of disrepair of the water and sewerage reticulation system, urban over-population that puts a strain on a limited and ageing urban infrastructure. How much is the outbreak connected to the legacies of racist colonial town planning that had made sure that African townships were invariably located closest to the rubbish dumps and sewerage treatment plants of the city. Environmental pollution and foul air has remained a permanent feature of most former African townships, providing fertile conditions for occasional out-breaks of cholera and typhoid diseases. Former African townships were smart technologies of genocide in design and purpose, where Africans were destined to die slowly and sometimes suddenly in large numbers from anthropogenic disease outbreaks like cholera and typhoid. The news reporter is content to record the shocking statistics of the poor left dead by the pandemic and the emergency humanitarian measures put in place to address the symptoms and not structural causes of the problem. So, mainstream news in its surveillance role ensures it excludes from discussion such structural issues and steady states as falling outside of what it is reasonable to report as news. Focusing on these matters would expose the glorious liberation project for a monumental failure it has, for all intends and purposes, largely turned out to be in most ex-colonies in Africa.

The hypocrisy of the postcolonial state founding fathers is all too evident in that immediately on attainment of independence leaders like Mugabe and their political acolytes extracted from African townships (Memmi, 2006) such as Mbare, Mufakose and Highfields in Harare to the former whites-only enclaves of Borrowdale, Mandara, Chisipite and Gunhill. Mandela's house in Soweto had to be turned into a museum in memory of Mandela's odyssey from Soweto through Robben Island to the pinnacle of power as first black president of South Africa. Mugabe's house in Highfields has suffered the same fate. The new black elite now ensconced in power never looks back to see how those they left in the ghetto fared. They 'tend to forget the poverty and starvation in the back-country. In a kind of complicity of silence, by an irony of fate, they act as if their towns were contemporary with independence' (Fanon et al., 1963: 57).

A decolonial turn in journalism

The history of press silence across Zimbabwe's timeline does not quite confirm the old adage that says history repeats itself, instead it gives one to understand history as following a rather helical path in which each succeeding historical phase retains some and not all features of the past that birthed it, while intro-ducing new dimensions at one and the same time co-extensive with but also subversive of the status quo. The first time ever that I came across the idea that decolonisation could be applicable to anything other than the colonial political system itself was when our lecturer and mentor, Dr Rino Zhuwarara, at the University of Zimbabwe assigned us to read and write a critical review of three key texts viz; Ngugi's *Decolonising the mind*; Fanon's *The Wretched of the earth*; and Korten's *When corporations rule the world*, in what was meant to be the inaugural assignment for a course in media studies. I barely passed that reading and writing assignment. It sounded a very revolutionary idea, that the mind also needed decolonising. That was in 2001, and now at the time of writing this monograph, close to two decades have passed and a Google search for scholarly articles on 'Decolonisation' yields more than 80,000 results and most of them books beginning with the term 'Decolonizing …' in their titles. The range of things needful of decolonising has impressively expanded from the territory and

282   Do-it-yourself (DIY) news

the mind to include; the university, the curricula, knowledge, pedagogy, feminism, queer studies; the gaze; nature, anthropology, and so on and so forth. Nothing remains un-decolonised but decolonising itself. The press and news journalism, for some unknown reason has escaped the decolonial critique. Claims of commitment to facticity, accuracy and objectivity somehow made it insular. Scholarly critique on journalism, news media and the press emanating from Africa, and its diasporas has yet to seriously engage with a decolonial lenses in analysing media questions in former colonies. A neo-liberal concern with free speech which freedom of the press (narrowly defined in terms of the fourth estate watchdog role) supposedly guarantees has foreclosed debates about how its own value system, its practices and methodologies unconstrained by the state, may be complicit and co-extensive with interests of the power block. Contemporary critique of the news has failed to reveal how every news story is by its very nature and construction the story of power built out of the rubble and debris of the subaltern voices it silences and renders invisible, or what Mignolo (2011) termed the 'darker side of western modernity'. The object of such an analysis would be to lay bare and to unknot the interstitial connections between media and dominance beyond the end of formal colonialism.

The tragedy in decolonising everything though is that it then brackets off talk about how empire may still enforce its hegemon beyond decolonisation. Decolonisers are then left with nothing else to decolonise but decolonisation itself in the face of mounting poverty and the continuing misery of the poor. The contradiction in the persistence of the colonial condition begs the question; who is the coloniser now. Ramon Grosfoguel warned us against the naivety of unquestioningly accepting the myth that decolonisation is now history, that it has run its full course, was achieved and finished with (Grosfoguel, 2007).

'Historically and socially-speaking, what is the role of the [de]colonised in the process of decolonizing received forms of knowledge in the context of social and economic reconstruction in the ex-colonial world?' (Mafeje, 2001: 36) The question can be similarly posed regarding the coloniality of press silence as an episteme; when did it cease to be a colonial design? Where does the geo and body politics of the professional journalist as knowledge producer situate him/her along the spectra of power/marginality, dominance/subjugation or oppressor/oppressed?

The decolonised journalist like his intellectual counterpart or the writer may bear witness to the bloodletting of ethnic cleansing or the bleeding of the economy to support an increasingly predatory postcolonial nationalist politico-military elite that keeps invoicing the poor for its own economic profligacy but will remain silent on his/her own positionality in the power game. He may bear the brand of national suffering in his own flesh and blood but he dares not speak out on account of public opinion and for fear of offending the powers that be. He has become adept and practised at reporting only 'politically correct' news. 'The only writing that is tolerated is conformist, the praise of politicians and religious leaders, bland folkloric tales, reminders of a supposedly glorious past that will help the people forget the mediocrity of the present' (Memmi,

2006: 37). Is it any wonder, then, that Zimbabwe has muddled through and fumbled from the Gukurahundi of the early independence years, the violent suppression of opposition politics of the 2000s decade, the violent displacement of the urban poor through Operation Murambatsvina in 2005 and most recently violent suppression of civic protest against increasing economic hardships visited on the hapless citizens by the new dispensation government's often ill-conceived austerity measures? In each case, the decolonised journalist of the mainstream press neither saw nor heard any evil and reported no evil. It had to be left to commissions of enquiry to investigate and unearth the atrocities.

There is a long-standing tradition of a postcolonial critique of social anthropology's methods of knowledge production about the colonial other in the service of Europe's imperial project in the last three centuries (Edward, 1978; Loomba, 2007). The decolonial turn has extended this critique to include the entire edifice of Western epistemic and knowledge imperialism (Mignolo, 2011; Grosfoguel, 2007; Maldonado-Torres, 2004). Journalism emerged as a discipline early in the twentieth century (Nordenstreng, 2009) but did not introduce methods of its own rather it drew from already existing and well-established colonial science disciplinary methods already in wide use in linguistics, historiography, sociology and anthropology (Bird, 2010). Anthropology is accused of producing a discourse that objectifies the colonial as Europe's inferior other and therefore justifying his subjection. Instead of producing a discourse about the colonial subject, mainstream journalism's norms and standard news production practices are inherently productive of a systemic silence about the colonial other. There is a long tradition of scholarly critique of the hegemonic nature of mainstream journalism that renders it incapable of representing the poor and the powerless in society (Atton and Hamilton, 2008; Harcup, 2003; Downing, 2007; Couldry, 2008; Hamilton, 2000). Such scholarship has gone on to propose what they call alternative journalism or media which would be far more inclusive of diverse views and opinions including those of the segments of society often excluded by the mainstream. Their critique of the exclusionary practices of mainstream news production processes falls short of proposing an overhaul of the system or its replacement with alternative media/journalism. Rather their vision of society is where the mainstream operates side by side with alternative media. They thus eschew the conception of their more liberal approach to news gathering, processing and dissemination as decolonial. They do not conceive of their proposed alternative models of doing journalism as marking a decolonial turn. To ameliorate the deficiencies inherent in mainstream media's elitisim and urban-centricity as this study has established, the only hope according to the alternative media thesis, lies in socialising access to the means of communication and democratising news sourcing in the hope that this would create an opportunity for a diversity of opinions and views to be articulated. But there is a limit to the extent to which this may be a feasible option considering imperatives and constraints imposed by the market.

284 *Do-it-yourself (DIY) news*

A close analysis of journalistic news writing practices of the selected cases as well as the content analysis of selected stories, presented in this discussion helps one to arrive at conclusions not far different from those that Atton and Wickenden (2005) arrived at, in their own study in which they sought to establish whether really there existed meaningful differences in news sourcing practices between mainstream media and so-called alternative media. The difference consisted only in the elites that they preferred to source from but their sources were just as elite as those whom mainstream news organisations relied on. The alternative media did not escape the same imperatives which news deadlines and newsroom routines imposed on news production whose effect remains rendering the subaltern groups speechless on matters affecting them. The object of this study has been the bringing into question the normativity of professional news production processes and practices in postcolonial settings and their suitability in the service of the emancipatory promise of decolonisation. Whether under colonialism or its aftermath, irrespective of the colour of the skin of who is doing the reporting, the system of news values have consistently structured the news outcomes in ways that continue to lock the voices of those who inhabit the margins out. Alternative commercial media thus falls short on the claim of providing an egalitarian space for all voices including subaltern voices.

This book has tried to demonstrate how the much vaunted journalistic conventions of objectivity and processes of verification are fraught with serious challenges which institutionalise the most insidious forms of disinformation through silencing. This raises the question as to whether mainstream professional journalism remains the best tool to counter the rising wave of disinformation. Mainstream press may claim the credit recording the first draft of history of postcolonial Zimbabwe but the evidence presented and discussed in this book overwhelmingly supports the claim that the press has purveyed ignorance, disinformation and silence in equal measure leading to a serious deficit of public trust as sources of reliable information (Boyd-Barrett, 2007). The elitism of postcolonial news was alienating to the majority ordinal people, who have learned to live outside and in spite of the news. It taught them to devise what Frederikse describes as:

> a means of communication of their own which they had never conceived of as 'media', yet the message they received and communicated had a power and a relevance that the mass media never matched. The form as well as the content of that message unfolded in the telling ... As in the military struggle, it was the total involvement of the people that proved decisive in this psychological war of liberation. (Frederikse, 1982: ix)

The abiding spirit of popular uprising and resistance beginning with the uprisings of the first Chimuremga of 1896–1897 against the injustices of colonial domination has also left a legacy of distrust and rejection of a colonising mode of journalism of which *The Herald* has, through time, represented probably the foremost exemplar.

Irreverent grassroots journalism

Those whose voices the present mass media arrangements have muted:

> question whether it is fitting that he should have no word to say about the laws is required to obey, the taxes he must pay, the education he must receive and the share he must have of the public services of his country. "Am I never," he asks, "to take any part in determining matters that so vitally affect me and my people; shall I always remain, with folded arms, a mere amused spectator of this momentous drama. (Ranger, 1970)

When you have a medium that under the pretext of adherence to some news values pretends it has no means in its grasp to make you its addressee it is not only guilty of being silent about a section of society, what is worse, it is productive of a form of silencing that makes a nullity of that section of humanity's claim to existence. It makes of them the living dead. The short effervescence of a model of doing journalism that made of every citizen, in spite of their social standing, a potential addressee/speaker still holds the promise of drawing all social segments into a truly convivial imagined community in conversation with itself as Zimbabwe. That model can still draw on the strengths of various strands of what media critiques discussed earlier have invariably referred to as 'irreverent journalism' 'native journalism' or 'grassroots journalism'. These practices appeared from time to time in Zimbabwe's layered history of press silencing/unsilencing discussed in various sections of this book.

The editor of the *Central African Examiner*'s invitation to his readers to fill up all spaces left blank due to censorship in what he called 'A Special Christmas Do-It-Yourself Issue', readers were free to in those spaces the kind of news they would like to read (see cover page of the December 1965 edition of the *Central African Examiner* below).

This call, coming as it did more than two decades before the invention of the computer, was quite prescient and almost prophetic of the coming of the information age and the rise of citizen journalism and user generated content of the age of ubiquitous Internet. The question as to whether the readers of the *Central African Examiner* heeded the call and took the initiative to fill in the news gaps caused by government censorship with alternative news is a question media research has never really taken up in any meaningful way. A legacy that media silence on news that mattered to the ordinary reader, both acknowledged and unacknowledged, externally enforced or the more insidious type that is the artefact of professional journalism's own methods of verification has been an intergenerational deeply shared scepticism and mistrust of the mainstream media among Zimbabwe's poorer sections of society.

The main theme of press silence in postcolonial Zimbabwe which this book has explored through the history of the country since colonisation draws its inspiration from the rhetorical question Nyamnjoh poses: 'How similar to or different from the colonial state in reality are states and media institutions in post-colonial

Figure 9.1 Front page of the last edition of *The Central African Examiner* of December 1965. Courtesy of the National Archives of Zimbabwe.

Africa?' (2005: 33). This is one question, though often put differently, that has exercised the minds of many anti-colonial theorists and thinkers as well as their opposite number in the neo-liberal anti-postcolonial statist fold. It is a question about the enduring legacy of colonial power structures in ex-colonies. It is about the coloniality of news discourse and how it constructs media marginalities along the old axes of geography, gender, race, class and ethnicity. Through a multi-sited ethnographic engagement with news texts and participant observation of journalists at work for periods of one month apiece at two leading national newspaper organisations in Zimbabwe, the researcher gathered thick descriptions of a set of universalised norms and standards of doing journalism has spawned newsroom cultures which act as a constraint to journalistic agency and prevents reporting news from subaltern standpoints on issues in ways that reproduced and reinforced existing power hierarchies along race, class and gender lines. The national newspapers reify the use the former colonial master's language (English) as obviated by the inherent incapacity of local languages to carry weighty matters of the state and economy.

The so-called national press continued to cover the nation from the capital city, Harare, within convenient distance to their main sources of news subsidy, in the commanding heights of the nation's cultural, economic and political elite power. This study's findings support the conclusion that mainstream media in Zimbabwe, as in many parts of Africa, continue to be associated with a minority elite 'and for this reason enjoy minimal legitimacy among citizenries' (Willems, 2011: 50). But in spite of this being the case, media research on the continent, the present study is no exception, by focusing on mainstream news as insitutionalised forms of communication, seems to be caught up in the same vicious circle of overvaluing the elite discourses they circulate, at the expense of subaltern informal and unstructured spaces of communication (Obadare and Willems, 2014). This study, by engaging with what the mainstream press has been silent about as more important than the news it articulated, draws its inspiration from more recent scholarship that seeks to engage with hitherto neglected annihilations of discursive practices of the subaltern and their ways of knowing and communication, informed by the understanding that silence and ignorance are important by-products of visible news articulations and are just as essential to the ideological project of power and dominance as are news and knowledge (Proctor and Schiebinger, 2008). This book shares Obadare and Willems (2014) interest in 'understanding everyday forms of resistance (about which mainstream news is often silent) that are often implicated in, or positioned at, the nascent stage of processes of social change' (Obadare and Willems, 2014: 8). Mainstream news journalism is just as guilty for keeping the more enduring everyday forms of resistance, coping and getting-by characteristic of ordinary people's sometimes hopelessly heterogeneous ways of life, hidden from public view because of its infatuation with that which it narrowly defines as newsworthy.

This study has presented and discussed thick descriptions of empirical evidence drawn across a long stretch of Zimbabwe's media timeline as well as from diverse news production sites which extends the long established thesis that news is text

288 Do-it-yourself (DIY) news

produced in the service of power and is therefore ideological to include news silences (Van Dijk, 1997). This study therefore locates itself methodologically and theoretically at the nexus of long established traditions of critical constructivist approaches to the study of news, looked at through postcolonial lenses. Such media scholarship generally avers that mainstream news media, be they commercially owned or regime controlled, tend to construct versions of our life worlds from standpoints of dominant forces in society defined by race, class, or gender and that they tend to work in the interest of maintenance rather than subversion of systems of unjust and unequal power relations (Glasgow University Media Group, 1980; Hasty, 2010; Atton, 2002.; Nyamnjoh, 2012; Wasserman, 2010). The common thread that runs through the above scholarship is that; mainstream news offerings tend to under-serve and under-represent those in the margins, defined by race, class, gender or ethnicity. The news, throughout Zimbabwe's truncated history, has proved to be other than what it claims – a disinterested proxy for reality. To the extent that it denies its discursive nature and its silence about its silences, affects an air of facticity (Bird, 2010), news is far much more successful in its ideological purposes, than other genres that announce their fictionality and constructedness upfront. News is indeed, stranger than fiction.

The many news texts that were analysed and discussed in the preceding sections of this study across historical and political transitions from colonial to postcolonial Zimbabwe; from white minority ruled Rhodesia through Mugabe's 37-year autocratic rule to the post-2017 new political dispensation under Mnangagwa, were invariably located with power hierarchies they discursively constructed socially and geo-politically. In each of the cases studied, the subaltern voice was irretrievably lost in news translation and silence about oppression and intergenerational forced displacements. And this was not because of ineptitude on the part of news workers but a result of the application of accepted journalistic standards of practice of verification, application of universal, professionally accepted news values in news selection, news gathering and news sourcing practices. The brutal suppression of early resistance to colonial occupation (1896–97), to forced removals of the Tangwena people from Gayerezi in 1969, the Huchu people from Hunyani in 1970 were reported from a government perspective by *The Rhodesia Herald*. Competing interpretations of the events passed on through word of mouth, chain-letter messaging networks became the forerunners of modern day counter-hegemonic citizen media. Alternative media versions of events which the likes of Moto magazine reported in colonial Rhodesia, were articulations largely of a white counter-elite with a smattering, of course, of the affected Africans. In the post-independence era *The Herald*, true to its type, again gave a government perspective of events in the much publicised Fast Track Land Reform Programme which started in March 2000 resulting in the mass evictions of white farmers and their black employees. *The Daily News*, on the other hand, gave an account that was overly sympathetic to the white commercial farmer's plight and the subaltern former farm worker's point of view was marginalised in the stories. In 2005, those forcibly removed from urban areas under the government implemented campaign, code named Operation Murambatsvina, were denied voice in the many stories done by *The Herald* and by the privately owned weekly paper The Standard on the issues. The end of the Mugabe era and the inauguration of the new political dispensation under Mnangawa, dubbed in the press as the dawn of a new era, did not translate to a new and different way of doing news at the nation's oldest and leading national daily newspaper, *The Herald*. The same officialdom and sycophantic bootlicking of government officials has been continued with at *The Herald*.

The press came to Zimbabwe as part of the colonial state's imposition of an uncontested monopoly in the exercise of epistemic violence over the occupied territory it named Rhodesia. So news from the mainstream press, since the early years of colonial occupation in the then Rhodesia, was itself an occupying discourse in the service of empire (Gale, 1962). Postcolonial analytic lenses applied here expose how the colonised's ways of knowing and sharing that knowledge were inferioritised, displaced and replaced by professional news making as a discourse in a way that mirrored the spatial displacements and dispossessions of indigenous peoples to geographical margins through forced evictions. The study found a striking similarity between the symbolic annihilation and thingification of the Tangwena people and the Huchu people in The Rhodesia Herald under colonial rule and the marginalisation of the voices of displaced former farm workers during the Fast Track Land Reform Programme in 2000 and evictees under Operation Murambatsvina in *The Herald*. The evidence presented and discussed in the preceding chapters of this study suggests that *The Herald* as an institution has largely maintained rather than change a colonial news culture in postcolonial Zimbabwe. This has been largely achieved due to the way news production masks its ideological nature, first and foremost, to the journalists themselves and to the users as reflections of reality. Journalists often rationalised their editorial choices and news selections as well as news sourcing practices as inevitable outcomes of the application of 'universal' news values. The liquidation of the Zimbabwe Mass Media Trust, which had acted as a buffer to protect the newspaper from undue influence by government elites prior to its demise in 2001, resulted in the entrenchment of the colonial tradition of state interference at *The Herald*. The way African nationalist leaders used *The Herald* to suppress alternative views and interpretations of the way their policies affected marginalised groups (evicted ex-farm workers post-2000 and displaced shack dwellers in 2005) was reminiscent of the way the same newspaper was abused by the white settler government under colonial rule. Zimbabwe government leaders' use of the press they controlled, in particular *The Herald*, as discussed in Chapters 5, 6 and 7, exhibited an attitude which lends some credence to a critical scepticism about their commitment to the liberation ideals which they were wont to announce as their watch-word and slogan during the liberation struggle first intimated by Fanon in the chapter on 'The Pitfalls of National Consciousness' in *The wretched of the earth*, a book that almost became the bible for the liberation movements in Africa from the 1960s and as Mbeki and Ake also point out more recently:

> Nationalism in Africa has always paraded itself as a movement of the people fighting for their liberation. The reality is, in fact, rather different. African nationalism was a movement of the small, Westernised black elite that

emerged under colonialism. Its fight was always for inclusion in the colonial system so that it, too, could benefit from the spoils of colonialism. (Mbeki, 2009: 6)

With few exceptions, the elite who came to power decided to inherit and exploit the colonial system to their own benefit rather than transforming it democratically as had been expected. This alienated them from the masses whom they now had to contain with force. (Ake, 2000: 36)

In fact, evidence discussed in this study suggests that to argue as did Wasserman and de Beer (2009: 430) that: 'Journalism in Africa often displays an uneasy relationship between its colonial heritage and post-colonial appropriation' would be an understatement. What appears consistent with the facts is rather that news at *The Herald* changed very little with the attainment of political independence. Evidence based on the cases considered in this study support the conclusion that the press in postcolonial Zimbabwe did much to discursively manufacture acceptance of neo-colonial structures of domination by the subaltern groups. This, the media achieved mainly by producing silence over the need to take an audit of the nationalist government's achievements in bringing the much yearned for democratic transformation promised during the liberation struggle. This was all too evident in the silence over considerations of restitution as the basis for a fair and just Fast Track Land Redistribution Programme. None of the newspapers studied, broached the question of linking land reform with detribalisation and democratisation. That the TTLs were the centre-piece and kernel of colonial subjugation of the indigenous black population and that it was the linchpin of native administration escaped the memory of the nationalist political elite now in power. The press played a not insignificant role in aiding and abetting this amnesia in the national imaginary. The conflict over land was now recast as a struggle between veterans of the liberation struggle and white commercial farmers. Debates on the legitimacy of taking away land from whites without compensating them took precedence. The history of African dispossession and rights to the same land was simply written out of the story on land.

What underlines the institutional irrelevance of the press to the democratic aspirations is their uncritical blindness to which colonial structures such as the tribal organisation continues to produce colonial subjectivities across generations of indigenous people of Zimbabwe. The absences and one dimensional views of the realities reported on, realities such as forced evictions and displacement of marginalised groups following state sponsored programmes like the Fast Track Land Reform Programme and Operation Murambatsvina, were not accidents of a journalism gone wrong. This content outcome was according to the journalists themselves, the inevitable result of the application of what they defined as universal news values and normal newsroom routines requiring verification of facts with credible sources (read elite sources). Such news values were generally understood by the journalists as inhering in some events and occurrences just after the fashion of rain bearing clouds.

The idea of the subaltern like coloniality also does not end with the attainment of independence as was clearly demonstrated in news constructions of the same in the press post-2000 in Zimbabwe. The news only reconstitutes subaltern identities and subjectivities on newer axes other than along the old matrices of race and ethnicity. In the postcolonial state, subalternity is defined by lack of access to voice, lack of mobility along different axes of power and denial of political and economic agency. It is no longer solely and simplistically defined by skin colour as during the colonial period. In the postcolonial context; 'the condition of subalternity is that of not having any access to institutionalised structures of language and power—including structures of capital and culture' (Shome and Hegde, 2002: 181).

Thus throughout history subalternity has been an artefact of symbolic annihilation, through denial of speech in spaces of public discourse. Professionally produced news acts like the holy grail of reification and masking of the historicity of the very process by which the marginalised were silenced and denied voice. The attitudes of different sections of the press towards the political power establishment from colonial through post-independence period in Zimbabwe oscillated between the priestly and the prophetic roles. In playing the priestly role the press largely assumes a legitimating function for the hegemonic order. It may even take a mildly critical stance on government policy but always in a manner that accepts that power as legitimate and inevitable.

In Chapter 4 above, in reporting the forced evictions of the Tangwena people and the Hunyani people between 1969 and 1970 the white press represented by *The Rhodesia Herald* largely assumed the priestly role, while the church press led by *Moto* and *Umbowo* played the prophetic role of rebuking excesses in the colonial state, but also at the same time playing its pacification and civilising role within the framework were the colonial state was accepted as part of the natural order in God's scheme of things. The metaphor of priest and prophet would best describe the different roles that pro-state press like *The Herald* and press critical of the state represented by *Moto* in the pre-independence period and *The Daily News* and *The Standard* during the post-independence period played. While the priesthood in biblical times served to legitimate the hegemonic order best symbolised in the relationship between Moses and Aaron, the prophets on the other hand were the forerunners of mechanisms that challenged and spoke truth to power as exemplified by the prophet Nathaniel to King David and the prophet Daniel to the kings of Babylon. Sorcerers, on the other hand, the prototypes and forerunners of the subaltern fell completely outside the power block; they represented the 'insurrection of subjugated knowledges' (Shiva 2001) under the Judaic system. In a graveside speech at Nathan Shamhuyarira's funeral, when President Mugabe described *The Herald* and other news publications under the Zimpapers stable as 'our paper' he betrayed a long-standing tradition of the cosy relationship between *The Herald* and the political power establishment.

Nyamnjoh's (2012) critique of the resilience of a colonial legacy in education in postcolonial Africa is also relevant to the news. Mainstream media as public educators, have tended to be very conservative in the way they construct and

292 *Do-it-yourself (DIY) news*

communicate news as knowledge about changing African realities. The evidence provided by this study seems to suggest that *The Herald* has hardly broken with colonial tradition of silencing the poor. It has remained in its role as an appendage of the dominant power elite. In all these instances, and in particular in relation to the media, this duality is expressed by 'participation and alienation'. Local communities under colonialism found themselves unable to participate in the media that ostensibly reported on matters affecting their lives; they were alienated from the methods of production as well as from the nature of the reporting. They were not involved in the media, either as creators of stories or as actors within them. Instead there was the colonising journalism, described by David Spurr as 'placed either above or at the centre of things, yet apart from them' (Spurr, 1993: 16). Spurr argues that the power relations inherent in this relationship between observer and observed are grounded by standard narrative practices in journalism that, by adopting these perspectives, 'obviate the demand for concrete, practical action on the part of its audience' (Atton, 2002: 113).

The colonising journalism's unquestioning acceptance of a normative framework on what constitutes news and criteria for determining who is authorised to speak as source, has continued to repudiate voices of the subjugated and to reproduce colonial difference in Zimbabwe many decades after attainment of independence. Ewart et al. (2004) in a study of Australian news sourcing practices found out that little work had been done to change traditional news sourcing practices of journalists in Australia. That elite sources should be preferred as news sources is often treated as an inevitable, a given in the practice of professional journalism everywhere in the world. But in Zimbabwe, even that practice, is often practised in violation of basic journalism ethical requirements for balance and fairness because of partisanship and extreme polarisation. Conventions of best practice in mainstream journalism in Zimbabwe, it appears, enjoins reporters 'to report on, to speak at, to speak down to, to speak past, but hardly ever to speak with people (particularly those on the margins)'. Reporters trail the 'Big Men' not in order to ask hard questions about their public responsibilities and conduct but to curry favours with their respective official sources and to boot-lick. They door-step them as they leave their offices, at the airport as they fly out or into the country, or way-lay them at for-elite-only clubs like the Quill Club in Harare. In the routine of news gathering, reporters do not stray into the market place or stay long enough with the 'illegal' street vendors 'so as to create a relationship that brings out the issues with the necessary nuances and contradictions' (Wasserman, 2009: 8). With a press like that the prospects for another Operation Murambatsvina, or shooting of the poor on the streets of Harare in brutal suppression of dissent, remain palpable and it would still take a Catholic Commission for Justice and Peace or a UN Commission of Inquiry to bring out the near genocidal impacts of government policies on the lives of the poor under the press's watch.

What African journalism may need to unlearn

Africa first encounters the press and journalism as one of those institutional transplants that colonialism introduced generally designed to work for the colonial project. It introduced discursive practices and traditions of silencing the colonial under-classes. The old journalism that colonialism bequeathed to Africa as part of the colonial legacy actually stands in the way of reform and innovation. While new media technologies present an opportunity for devising a more dialogic journalism that is ecologically sound for the former marginalised groups, and provides scope for agentive interactions between journalists and the grassroots communities, the hierarchised professional journalism in modern newsrooms in Harare, has been content to adapt the new communication technologies to the preservation of an epistemically exclusive way of news as knowledge production in the service of power. Professional journalism would evidently need to unlearn much of what it regards as the canons of good journalism if it is to make itself relevant to the communication needs of those whom colonial structures have rendered and continue to render speechless.

African journalism lacks both the power of self-definition and the power to shape the universals that are deaf-and-dumb to the particularities of journalism in and on Africa. Because journalism has tended to be treated as an attribute of so-called 'modern' societies or of 'superior' others, it is only proper, so the reasoning goes, that African journalism and the societies it serves are taught the principles and professional practices by those who 'know' what it means to be civilised and to be relevant to civilisation' (Wasserman, 2009: 11). Nyamnjoh's comment above is borne out by many examples of stories cited and discussed in this study. The press was under colonial rule and in the postcolonial order indeed deaf-and dump to the concerns of the poor, those who inhabit marginality whom I refer to in this study as the subaltern. Journalism practice in postcolonial Zimbabwe lacks originality and authenticity; mainstream media are poor imitations and shadows of their colonial pasts completely out of touch with the realities and worlds inhabited by the majority African population. They have perfected the art of mimicry as they chant the loudest about the need to conform to universalist notions of what constitutes the news even where the outcome is continued exclusion and alienation of the vast majority of the national population.

Recent studies on Zimbabwean news production practices (Mano, 2005; Moyo, 2007) have noted political polarisation as a defining feature in news production processes including determining how journalists deploy new media technologies in ways that continue with rather than challenge a universalistic news sourcing practice that privileges elite world views largely unconnected to lived experiences of those on the margins. Mabweazara's ethnography of news production conducted between 2008 and 2010 concludes that the increase in the reliance on the Internet as a source of news and story ideas by journalists has had implications on news access and sourcing patterns. From observations and interviews it seemed clear that the Internet (and other ICTs) promoted the sourcing of stories from elite sections of society with access and the means to contribute content through the Internet. This scenario – coupled with the growing impact of online newspapers in 'setting the agenda' of news coverage – promotes an elite news culture, particularly in terms of political news (Mabweazara, 2010: 176).

294　*Do-it-yourself (DIY) news*

The elitist top-down tendency in mainstream media negates the media's normative role as a space for open rational deliberation of citizens on issues of the day. Its democratising function is seriously impaired due to its exclusion of mass participation. The advent of new communication technologies unfortunately placed in the hands of professional journalists cosily embedded with and debauched by the power elite, would tend to entrench a culture of national communication that is as Deuze (2010: 455) argues: 'anything but transparent, interactive or participatory'. The practice of journalism in the postcolony has continued on the old colonial paradigm, oblivious of calls by Africa's own leading lights (Nyamnjoh, 2005; Kareithi and Kariithi, 2005) on the role of the media in post-colonial Africa, for a paradigm shift. Kareithi, (2005: 14) urges African press to: 'show the greatest departure from Western traditions in the criteria used when selecting and evaluating news and other public information, and in the range and diversity of interests given voice in such news and public information'. This approach calls for a departure from the kind of news values common in the Western tradition which routinely privilege economic, political and intellectual elites. Evidence presented and discussed in the preceding chapters based on analysis of news content as well as observation of newsroom practices in the selected newspaper organisations does not give reason for optimism that Kareithi's call above will be heeded any time soon. Media elite construction of subaltern subjectivities continue unabated except that the bases may have changed from strictly racial to include class and gender, but the resultant exclusion, erasure and silencing is just as total as during the colonial era. In Fanon's characterisation of the national bourgeoisie class as the inheriting class of all privilege left behind by colonists, he was not so perceptive on how subordination and subalternity would be reproduced beyond colonial exploitation of blacks by whites. 'The production of subalternity in such nations', as Shome and Hegde (2002: 178) point out, cannot be coded merely as a matter of racial or national difference. The subaltern produced by such manoeuvres of nation states with global capital is not always caught between the 'West' and the 'rest,' or between nation and colonialism. Rather, the condition of subalternity in such situations is often constituted through, and located within, the contradictions produced by alliances (partial or otherwise) or collisions, or both, between sections of the national and the global.

And it can be added that internally within the postcolonial nation state, subalternity is produced at the interstices of collusion and collision, complicity and contradiction between the press and the political elite class. At its core, subalternity is characterised by voicelessness and lack of agency and invisibility in the press. The subaltern cannot speak, particularly so through the press, and this was consistently proved to be the case in the case studies examined in this study.

Pathways for possible further research

In light of this study's findings which expose how mainstream press in Zimbabwe has, over the years, continued with the colonial practices of undervaluing, subjugating and subalternising the masses' ways of knowing as the inferior 'other' of its own self-knowing, it becomes anachronistic for media scholars studying post-colonial communication settings, to continue investing in the scientific study of a mode of communication so alienating and irrelevant to the majority of the population's means of information and communication. While the present study was concerned with bringing postcolonial analysis to bear on the hegemonic nature of news content, and the newsroom cultural practices responsible for generating such content, and how these may still bear some resemblance with their colonial progenitors, it left the question of how the subaltern received and responded to the caricatured media images of themselves if indeed they had anything to do with it. Do they willingly and passively accept media imposed definitions and interpretations of reality or if not, what recourse do the socially, economically and politically marginalised have against such media imposed meanings and sense of their lived subordination? These very important questions were not addressed by this study and constitute a legitimate trajectory for future media research. A research agenda that trains its scholarly attention exclusively on the ideological nature of mainstream press and its offerings, as the present study has done, while it may have its own merits, becomes tainted and complicit, in a way, in re-emphasising and entrenching the same colonial condescension towards former colonial subjects and their knowledges as non-news and therefor unworthy of scholarly attention in postcolonial settings.

The question that this study finds ever so pertinent as a pointer for a research agenda on communication in Africa is a question which Nyamnjoh posed way back in 2010, when he opined: 'how do people on the margins come by information? How do they communicate with one another and with others over and above those margins'? (Nyamnjoh, 2010: 24). This is a question that redirects scholarly efforts and attention to the terra-incognita of mainstream journalism. Instead of continuing to pay unmerited scholarly attention to mainstream news offerings that speak across, above and in spite of the dominated majority, future communication research in postcolonial Africa may also need to refocus itself on those other forms of information exchange and communication processes and spaces which may make no pretences at a 'news' status and yet continue to animate the lives of the vast majority of Africans as they did during colonial times (Frederikse, 1982). It would be more productive for future research to heed the urgent call to refocus attention on popular media (Wasserman, 2010), citizen journalism (Allan and Thorsen, 2009), native reporting (Atton and Hamilton, 2008) and what other scholars elsewhere prefer to call alternative media or radical media (Atton, 2002; Pajnik and Downing, 2008; Couldry, 2008).

Using Zimbabwe as their case study, Leijendekker and Mutsvairo (2014) and Moyo (2015) have already started to chart tentative research pathways away from the mainstream media and into the uncharted terrain of alternative communicative ecologies and popular communication practices that are emerging everywhere in the wake of and enabled by new and social media technologies such as the mobile phone and the Internet. Such studies are beginning to ask different questions about media realities of the subaltern. Such research marks a scholarly attention shift away from the dominant research occupation with

296   *Do-it-yourself (DIY) news*

mainstream media and what it does or does not do for citizens and with or without them. Studies that shift attention to the new question of the possibilities of challenging, resisting and subverting existing hegemonic power relations between the governed and the elite ruling class through use of other journalisms such as citizen journalism and through other media platforms such as social media carry the promise of epistemic egalitarianism, inclusivity and greater democratic participation of those in the margins in the enterprise of self-definition.

Conclusion

A great deal of critical scholarly light has been shone on the processes of intellectual and scientific production of news knowledge/ignorance by which Western knowledge systems made so much store while tending to subordinate, provincialise and treat non-Western ways of knowing as the inferior Other of Euro-centred epistemologies (Willems, 2014; Grosfoguel, 2011; Mignolo, 2000). This study has extended this critical tradition by applying similar analytic lenses on a different domain of knowledge production, the epistemic production of news/silence and has clearly demonstrated how certain voices the voices of the subaltern, are systematically marginalised through an application of taken for granted assumptions about intrinsic newsworthiness of some events, actors and places rather than others. This study set out in search for an answer to the question Nyamnjoh (2005: 33) posed rhetorically 'How similar to or different from the colonial state in reality are states and media institutions in post-colonial Africa?' and this research comes to the conclusion concerning Zimbabwe's press that our mainstream news media, specifically the press, remain bastions of a lingering colonial discourse. In a critical reflection on the state of the press in postcolonial Africa, Nyamnjoh (2005) cautions us to abstain from premature celebrations of discontinuities while ignoring the continuities, so evident, with our colonial past. Nothing short of a paradigm shift in the uncritical, self-unconscious way mainstream journalism tends to produce silence can bring about any meaningful change to the colonial residues that stubbornly continue to colour news constructions of subalternity in Zimbabwe's postcolonial present. In ex-colonies like Zimbabwe, the press no longer follows the (British) flag, it follows the President. It does not toe government line on issues. It reports in the national interest as it is understood by the first family. Going forward, the only grounds for optimism lie on the subaltern's capacity for subversive use of the dominant discourse emanating from mainstream news discourses and their resourcefulness to engage in acts of epistemic resistance and practices of discursive self-emancipation through generation and dissemination of own counter-narratives and 'other' news.

References

Ake, C., 2000. *Feasibility of democracy in Africa*. Council for the Development of Social Science Research in Africa, Dakar, SN.

Allan, S., Thorsen, E., 2009. *Citizen journalism: Global perspectives*. Peter Lang.

Atton, C., 2002. *Alternative media*. Sage.

Atton, C., Hamilton, J.F., 2008. *Alternative journalism*. Sage.

Atton, C., Wickenden, E., 2005. Sourcing routines and representation in alternative journalism: A case study approach. *Journal. Stud.* 6, 347–359.

Beddoes, K., 2019. Agnotology, gender, and engineering: An emergent typology. *Soc. Epistemol.* 33, 124–136.

Bird, S.E., 2010. *The anthropology of news & journalism: Global perspectives*. Indiana University Press.

Boyd-Barrett, O., 2007. Alternative reframing of mainstream media frames, in: D.K. Thussu (ed), *Media on the move: Global flow and contra-flow*. Routledge, pp. 178–194.

Cotter, C., 2010. *News talk: Investigating the language of journalism*. Cambridge University Press.

Couldry, N., 2008. Media and the problem of voice, in: N. Carpentier and B. De Cleen (eds), *Participation and media production: Critical reflections on content creation*. Cambridge Scholars Publishing, pp. 15–26.

Croissant, J.L., 2014. Agnotology: Ignorance and absence or towards a sociology of things that aren't there. *Soc. Epistemol.* 28, 4–25.

Deuze, M., 2010. What is journalism?, in: D.A. Berkowitz (ed.), *Cultural meanings of news: A text-reader*. Sage.

Dorniok, D., 2013. What is ignorance?: A chronological overview of the discourse on ignorance in a historical context. Accessed from: https://pdfs.semanticscholar.org/b0a4/da8886594feaa5e832e19c2fe7d6ccee9db8.pdf.

Dossey, L., 2014. Agnotology: On the varieties of ignorance, criminal negligence, and crimes against humanity. *J. Sci. Heal.* 10, 331–344.

Downing, J., 2007. Grassroots media: Establishing priorities for the years ahead. *Glob. Media J. Aust. Ed.* 1, 1–16.

Edward, S., 1978. *Orientalism*. Pantheon.

Ewart, J., Cokley, J., Coats, P., 2004. Sourcing the news: Teaching journalism students different approaches to sourcing practices. *Asia Pac. Media Educ.* 33.

Fanon, F., Sartre, J.-P., Farrington, C., 1963. *The wretched of the earth*. Grove Press.

Frederikse, J., 1982. *None but ourselves: Masses vs. media in the making of Zimbabwe*. Heinemann.

Gale, W., 1962. *History of the Rhodesian printing and publishing company*. Madorn Print.

Glasgow University Media Group, 1980. *Bad news*. Routledge/Thoemms Press.

Grosfoguel, R., 2007. The epistemic decolonial turn: Beyond political-economy paradigms. *Cult. Stud.* 21, 211–223.

Grosfoguel, R., 2011. Decolonizing post-colonial studies and paradigms of political-economy: Transmodernity, decolonial thinking, and global coloniality. *Transmodernity: Journal of Peripheral Cultural Production of the Luso-Hispanic World* 1 no. 1.

Gross, M., McGoey, L., 2015. *Routledge international handbook of ignorance studies*. Routledge.

Hamilton, J., 2000. Alternative media: Conceptual difficulties, critical possibilities. *J. Commun. Inq.* 24, 357–378.

Harcup, T., 2003. 'The unspoken-said': The journalism of alternative media. *Journalism* 4, 356–376.

Hasty, J., 2010. Journalism as fieldwork: Propaganda, complicity, and the ethics of anthropology. *Anthropol. News Journal. Glob. Perspect.* 132–148.

Hess, D.J., 2016. *Undone science: Social movements, mobilized publics, and industrial transitions*. MIT Press.

Kareithi, P., 2005. Rethinking the African press: Journalism and the democratic process, in: P.M. Kareithi and N. Kariithi (eds), *Untold stories: Economics and business journalism in African media*. Witwatersrand University Press, pp. 2–15.

Kareithi, P.M., Kariithi, N., 2005. *Untold stories: Economics and business journalism in African media*. Witwatersrand University Press.

298   *Do-it-yourself (DIY) news*

Kourany, J.A., 2015. For better or worse, a source of ignorance as well as knowledge, in: M. Gross and L. McGoey (eds), *Routledge international handbook of ignorance studies*. Routledge, p. 155.

Leijendekker, I., Mutsvairo, B., 2014. On digitally networked technologies, hegemony and regime durability in authoritarian regimes: A Zimbabwean case study. *Inf. Commun. Soc.* 17, 1034–1047.

Loomba, A., 2007. *Colonialism/postcolonialism*. Routledge.

Mabweazara, H.M., 2010. 'New' technologies and journalism practice in Africa: Towards a critical sociological approach, in: N. Hyde-Clarke (ed.), *The citizen in communication: Revisiting traditional, new and community media practices in South Africa*. Juta & Co, pp. 11–30.

Mafeje, A., 2001. *Anthropology in Post Independence Africa: End of an Era and the Problem of Self-redefination* [sic] (Vol. 1). Heinrich Böll Foundation.

Maldonado-Torres, N., 2004. The topology of being and the geopolitics of knowledge: Modernity, empire, coloniality. *City* 8, 29–56.

Mano, W., 2005. Press freedom, professionalism and proprietorship: Behind the Zimbabwean media divide. Westminster papers in communication and culture, 2.

Mbeki, M., 2009. *Architects of poverty: Why African capitalism needs changing*. Picador.

McGoey, L., 2012. Strategic unknowns: Towards a sociology of ignorance. *Econ. Soc.* 41, 1–16.

Memmi, A., 2006. *Decolonization and the decolonized*. University of Minnesota Press.

Mignolo, W., 2011. *The darker side of western modernity: Global futures, decolonial options*. Duke University Press.

Mignolo, W., 2000. *Local histories/global designs: Coloniality, subaltern knowledges, and border thinking*. Princeton University Press.

Moyo, D., 2007. Alternative media, diasporas and the mediation of the Zimbabwe crisis. *Ecquid Novi*. 28, 81–105.

Moyo, L., 2015. Digital age as ethical maze: Citizen journalism ethics during crises in Zimbabwe and South Africa. *Afr. Journal. Stud.* 36, 125–144.

Nordenstreng, K., 2009. Media studies as an academic discipline, in: D.K. Thussu (ed.), *Internationalizing media studies*. Routledge, pp. 254–266.

Nyamnjoh, F.B., 2005. *Africa's media: Democracy and the politics of belonging*. Zed Books.

Nyamnjoh, F.B., 2010. De-westernizing media theory to make room for African experience, in: *Popular media, democracy and development in Africa*. Routledge, pp. 35–47.

Nyamnjoh, F.B., 2012. 'Potted plants in greenhouses': A critical reflection on the resilience of colonial education in Africa. *J. Asian Afr. Stud.* 47, 129–154.

Obadare, E., Willems, W., 2014. *Civic agency in Africa: Arts of resistance in the 21st century*. Boydell & Brewer.

Pajnik, M., Downing, J.D., 2008. Alternative media and the politics of resistance. Peace Institute. Accessed 19 August 2019 from: https://www.researchgate.net/publication/264242608_Alternative_Media_and_the_Politics_of_Resistance_Perspectives_and_Challenges.

Parker, J., 1972. *Rhodesia: Little white island*. Pitman.

Popper, K., 1998. *Des sources de la connaissance et de l'ignorance* (M.-I.-I. and M.B. de Launay, Trans.). Payot & Rivages[English original: 1960, *On the sources of knowledge and of ignorance*].

Proctor, R.N., Schiebinger, L., 2008. *Agnotology: The making and unmaking of ignorance*.

Ranger, T.O., 1970. *The African voice in Southern Rhodesia, 1898–1930*. Northwestern University Press.

Shiva, V., 2001. Monocultures of the mind, in J. Henry (ed.), *Creative management and development*. Sage, p. 199.

Shome, R., Hegde, R.S., 2002. Postcolonial approaches to communication: Charting the terrain, engaging the intersections. *Commun. Theory* 12, 249–270.

Spurr, D., 1993. *The rhetoric of empire: Colonial discourse in journalism, travel writing, and imperial administration*. Duke University Press.

Traber, M., 1989. African communication: Problems and prospects. *Africa Media Review* 3, 3, 86–97. Accessed 19 August 2019 from: http://pdfproc.lib.msu.edu/?file=/DMC/African%20Journals/pdfs/africa%20media%20review/vol3no3/jamr003003007.pdf.

Traber, M., 1999. Communication is inscribed in human nature: A philosophical enquiry into the right to communicate. WACC Communication for all. Accessed 19 August 2019 from: www.waccglobal.org/articles/communication-is-inscribed-in-human-nature.

Van Dijk, T.A., 1993. Principles of critical discourse analysis. *Discourse Soc.* 4, 249–283.

Van Dijk, T.A., 1997. Opinions and ideologies in the press. Accessed 13 June 2019 from: www.discourses.org/OldArticles/Opinions%20and%20Ideologies%20in%20the%20Press.pdf.

Wasserman, H., 2009. Extending the theoretical cloth to make room for African experience: An interview with Francis Nyamnjoh. *Journal. Stud.* 10, 281–293.

Wasserman, H., 2010. *Popular media, democracy and development in Africa*. Routledge.

Wasserman, H., de Beer, A.S., 2009. Towards de-westernizing journalism studies, in: *The Handbook of Journalism Studies*. Routledge, pp. 448–458.

Willems, W., 2011. Political jokes in Zimbabwe, in: J.D. Downing (ed.), *Encyclopaedia of social movement media*. Sage, pp. 410–412.

Willems, W., 2014. Provincializing hegemonic histories of media and communication studies: Toward a genealogy of epistemic resistance in Africa. *Commun. Theory* 24, 415–434.

Willems, W. and Obadare, E., 2014. Introduction African Resistance in an Age of Fractured Sovereignty, in: E. Obadare and W. Willems (eds), *Civic agency in Africa: Arts of resistance in the 21st century*. Boydell & Brewer, pp. 1–24.

Index

absence 22, 24, 27, 33, 50, 56, 63, 66, 123, 139, 140, 167, 180, 194, 195, 223, 264, 277, 280, 290, 297
Advertiser 9
Alexander, J. 111, 152, 155, 181, 204
anthropogenic 279, 281
Ashcroft, B. 79, 81, 108, 139, 155
Austin, R. 153,155

Bantu 17, 18, 24
Beach. D. N. 3–6, 21, 22, 25, 26, 39, 75, 108
Bednarek, M. 42, 63, 66, 143, 145, 155
Bird, S. E. 140, 155, 198, 199, 204, 205, 215, 237, 283, 288, 297
Brighton, p. and Foy, D. 53, 66
Brown, T. 198, 205
British South Africa Company, (BSAC) 1, 7
Buckle, C. 136, 146, 148–50
Bulawayo 8, 10, 11, 26, 44, 57, 58, 68, 104, 217, 225, 256, 266, 272
Byl, Van-der 48, 51, 95, 96

Caple, H. 42, 63, 66, 143, 145, 155
censorship; government censorship 41–5, 48, 50, 51, 67, 69, 87, 89, 93, 99, 101, 104, 159, 285
Cesaire, A. 69, 78, 108, 109, 155
Chakrabarty, D. 190, 205
Chamisa, N. 49
Charama 28–34, 37, 38, 75, 274
Charwe, *See* Nehanda
Chimurenga 3, 22, 131, 143, 177, 179, 187, 218, 274
ChiShona, *see* Shona
cholera 279–81
Chronicle 11, 16, 37, 44, 49, 57, 68, 104, 116, 159, 161, 228, 242, 272
Clutton-Brock, G. 76–80, 82, 83, 92, 257

colonialism 14, 25, 39, 60, 71, 106, 108, 113, 115, 131, 143, 145, 154–6, 183, 186, 196, 200, 203–5, 232, 236, 274, 282, 284, 290, 292, 293, 298
colonisation/decolonisation/recolonisation 7, 21, 27, 68, 106, 191, 204, 217, 223, 232, 241, 274, 281, 282, 284, 285
commercial farmers 119, 122, 128, 135, 136, 141–3, 146, 154, 156, 162, 166, 167, 171, 181, 183, 190, 191, 193, 195, 290
Commercial Farmers Union (CFU) 112, 135, 150, 162, 171
Conboy, M. Lugo-Ocando, J and Eldridge, S. 197, 205
concentration camps 24, 153, 201, 205
concession; Rudd Concession; Lippert Concession; concession hunters/seekers; treaty 25, 26, 39, 40
Cotter, C. 42, 52, 53, 58, 66, 260, 274, 280, 297
Cousins, A. 45, 51, 52, 66
credibility 2, 43, 63, 82, 120, 150, 195, 203, 220, 226, 230, 279
Criminalisation 141, 213

Dabengwa, D. 165, 166, 168, 169
Dahwye 137, 139
decolonial 67, 182, 190, 203, 205, 224, 281–3, 297, 298
decolonisation 21, 106, 191, 204, 217, 281, 282, 284
Desmond, C. 24, 39, 76, 108, 155, 185, 202, 205
Dombo, S. 8, 10, 12, 14, 15, 17, 22, 69, 108, 116, 156

editorial 2, 5, 10, 15, 18, 20, 21, 41–4, 49–51, 58, 66, 69, 90, 92, 99–101, 104,

105, 116, 120, 131, 135, 141, 146, 148, 149, 158–62, 166, 169, 172, 180, 182, 195, 224, 227, 254, 258, 263, 265, 266, 268, 270–3, 289
Economic Structural Adjustment Programme (ESAP) 117
embedded 10, 59, 60, 68, 71, 79, 201, 294
Erichsen, C. and Olusoga, D. 28, 39, 153, 156, 201, 205
euphemism 84, 86
exploitation 10, 27, 31, 114, 115, 207, 240, 294

Fairbridge, W. E. 2, 11, 56, 59
Fairclough, N. 121, 156
Fanon, F. 14, 22, 69, 108, 153, 156, 186, 194, 199, 205, 217, 233, 235, 237, 281, 289, 294, 297
farm invasions 109, 112, 117–20, 136, 151, 159, 161, 165–174, 177–81, 190–93, 200, 203, 204
Foucault, M. 105, 106, 180, 202, 205
Fowler, R. 52, 53, 58, 66, 247, 272, 274
Frederikse, J. 6, 7, 15, 19, 20, 22, 35–7, 39, 51, 63, 66, 71, 75, 77, 79, 80, 89, 108, 177, 205, 277, 284, 295, 297
Freire, P. 14, 15, 22
Fast Track Land Reform Programme (FTLRP) 109–11, 118, 182, 200, 207, 278, 288–90
Furedi, F. 70, 108

Gaeresi 74, 85, 86, 88, 90, 93, 94, 107; see also Gaerezi 74, 76–8, 83, 84, 90
Gale, W. D. 1, 2, 5, 6, 9–11, 22, 42, 50, 56, 67, 68, 104, 108, 266, 278, 289, 297
Galtung, J. & Ruge, H. 42, 53, 60, 67, 105, 145, 200
Glen Grey 26, 39, 79
Gobo 30, 74, 76, 94, 100–3
God See Mwari
Goronga 3
Grosfoguel, R. 57, 67, 282, 283, 296, 297
Guardian, 126, 150, 188, 189, 190
Gukurahundi 49, 128, 129, 283
Gumboreshumba See Kaguvi
Gweru 8, 44, 69, 94, 97, 217, 225; See also Gwelo 8, 97

Hall, S. 26, 28, 39, 123, 196, 202, 205, 234, 256, 272, 275
Hampshire Estates 112, 113
Hanlon, J., Manjengwa, J. and Smart, T. 110, 111, 139, 145, 156, 182, 197

Hanmer 80–82, 92
Harare 8, 9, 19, 24, 44, 55, 57–9, 64, 76, 108, 112, 113, 116, 122, 126, 132–4, 137, 142, 154, 159, 160, 166, 171–3, 179, 183, 208, 209, 213, 215–8, 220, 221, 225, 229, 234, 235, 256, 266, 267, 274, 279–81, 287, 292, 293
Harcup, T. and O'neill, D. 42, 53, 67, 283, 297
Hartley, J. 53, 63, 67
Hasty, J. 121, 122, 156, 202, 203, 205, 242, 288, 297
hegemonic 4, 85, 90, 104, 107, 116, 158, 180, 187, 196, 224, 227, 239, 258, 283, 288, 291, 295, 296, 299
Heise, N. 110, 156
Hochschild, A. 28, 39, 193, 194, 196, 198, 201, 205
Holdenby 81, 88
Huchu 28, 30, 32, 36, 74–6, 94, 101, 103, 288, 289
Huggins, Sir Godfrey 79, 210, 231
Hulley, C. M. 27, 39, 56, 57, 67
Hunyani 5, 15, 29–33, 69, 71, 73–6, 89, 94–103, 105, 107, 109, 288, 291, See also Whunyani 98
Hunzvi, C. 119, 122, 128, 129, 151, 165, 166, 171, 179, 195

independence 12, 14, 16, 18, 20–2, 33, 36, 39, 44, 56, 57, 61, 68, 74, 75, 106, 111–16, 124, 131, 151–4, 156, 158, 159, 161, 169, 181, 182, 187, 191, 194, 196, 199, 201, 202, 207, 211, 217, 231–3, 235, 236, 242, 254, 273, 274, 280, 281, 283, 288, 290–2, 298
Inyanga, see Nyanga

Jäger, S. 106, 108
Jahana 185
jewel of Africa 231–3
Jones, D. 16, 20–22, 44, 45, 49, 67
journalism 3, 7, 10, 16–19, 22–4, 39, 41–3, 49, 50, 52, 55, 57, 59, 63, 66, 67, 68, 110, 115, 117, 120, 149, 155, 156, 158, 159, 186, 190, 195, 198, 199, 202–7, 224, 226, 230, 235–7, 241, 254–6, 260, 273, 274, 276, 278, 281–5, 287, 290, 292–9, see Media; grassroots journalism 16, 18, 23, 285; native journalism 285; professional journalism 7, 23, 55, 149, 195, 202, 230, 241, 256, 285, 292, 293;
journalistic silencing 55
Jubane 36

302   *Index*

Kaguvi 3
Kalande, W. 70, 108
Kufakurinani, U. and Bamu, W.,185, 205

Lamont, D. 13, 97, 106, 107, 145
land acquisition policy 141, 146, 162, 165, 182, 191, 194
land issue 76, 83, 94, 103, 119, 128, 129, 131, 134, 140, 150, 162, 169, 174, 178, 187, 190
land story; ancestral lands 109, 119, 131, 145, 152, 183, 185; forced evictions 15, 109, 131, 144, 204, 212, 224, 227, 233, 234, 236, 289, 290, 291; land restitution 153, 181, 185, 193, 200
Lessing, D. 8, 22, 28, 29, 33, 39, 99, 108, 237
liberation 12, 19, 20, 37, 49, 74, 75, 111, 114, 122, 128, 131, 151–3, 155, 168, 172, 173, 180, 181, 186, 193, 200, 209, 211, 212, 217, 233, 239, 240, 246, 274, 281, 284, 289, 290, 294
Limehill 24, 76
Livingstone, D. 54, 139, 198, 205
Lobengula 11, 25, 68, 255
Loomba, A. 81, 108, 113, 156, 181, 205, 283, 298

Macdonald, M. 304, 205
MacShane, D. 53, 67
maggotisation 222
Maier, F. 106, 10837
Mail and Guardian 59
Makunike, E. 69, 76, 108
Mandela, N. 57, 235, 281
manipulation 4, 20, 37, 78, 80, 228
Manning, P. 158, 188, 203, 205, 274, 275
Manyene 112, 113, 274
Mapondera 25, 26, 39
Marongwe, N. 152, 156, 206
Mashayan'ombe (Chief) 3
Mashona, *see* Shona
Mashona rebellion/ rising, 2–6, 8, 9, 22, 25, 215, 216
Mashonaland Herald and the Zambezian Times 2
Masvingo 8, 58, 132, 134, 215, 216
Matadziseyi 85, 86
Mau Mau 70, 108
Mazoe 3, 5, 26
Mbembe, A. 116, 135, 156,
McNair, B. 53, 66, 67
Movement for Democratic Change (MDC) 117, 137, 139, 196, 226, 229

media 2, 6–9, 16–23, 25, 35, 37/9, 42, 48–50, 53, 57, 59, 60, 63–7, 69–71, 74–6, 94, 97, 106, 108, 109, 111, 115, 117, 120, 131, 132, 140, 145, 146, 148, 149, 151, 153, 156, 158, 161, 165, 173, 174, 177, 178, 180, 181, 183, 189–91, 194, 196–203, 205, 206, 208, 223–5, 227, 230, 233, 235–9, 242, 245–7, 254, 256, 257, 260, 265–77, 279, 281–5, 287–99
alternative media 21, 283, 284, 288, 295–298; mainstream media 48, 60. 151, 230, 246, 283, 285, 287, 291, 293–97
mediascapes 114, 161, 200, 273
Mhandamabwe 153, 274
Mignolo, W. 191, 203–05, 230, 237, 282, 283, 296, 298
Native Mirror 16, 17; Bantu Mirror 17; Mirror 65, 224, 268
Mkwati 3
Mnangagwa, E. D. 49, 66, 241, 242, 246, 247, 248, 254–7, 260, 269, 271, 273, 275, 288
Moretti, V. 111. 156
Moto, 13, 15, 16, 37, 44, 69, 76, 83, 89–94, 96, 97, 99–101, 103, 104, 106, 107, 181, 254, 188, 291
Moyo, Dumisani. 275, 293, 295, 298
Moyo, Jonathan. 160, 161, 172, 180, 203
Moyo, Kaya. 245,
Moyo, Last. 298
Moyo, Sam. 111, 156, 183, 205, 241
Moyo, Sibusiso. 242
Msika, J. 165, 169, 187
Msindo, E. 42, 51, 67
Mudimbe, V. Y. 116,156
Mufungwe hill 28, 32
Mugabe, R. G. 15, 48, 49, 74, 113, 121, 126, 127, 132–4, 137, 142, 143, 148, 151, 156, 159, 162, 165–9, 187–90, 194, 195, 208, 211, 216–18, 220, 231–3, 239–42, 245–8, 255, 259, 263, 268, 269, 271–5, 278, 281, 288, 289, 291
Mugari, Z. E. 112, 156
Mungoshi, C. 112, 113, 156
Mungoshi, R. 159, 160, 168
Mutare 8, 9, 13, 44, 58, 69, 217
Mutsvairo 295, 298
Muzarabani 121, 274
Muzorewa, A. T. 76
Mvuma 29, 75, 94, 100
Mvurwi 132, 137, 140, 143
Mwari 2–4, 21, 22,

Index 303

nationalism 18, 39, 42, 106, 107, 276, 289
native reserves 24, 28, 100, 111, 112,
153–155, 181, 183, 186, 193, 202; *see*
Tribal Trust Lands
Nault, D. M. 201, 205
Ndebele 4, 10, 16, 25, 26, 49, 68, 90, 95,
112, 126, 127, 129
Nehanda 3–5, 21
new dispensation 239–41, 247, 254, 269,
273, 274, 278, 283
news content 54, 58, 116, 122, 182, 204,
236, 294, 295
news silences 180, 277
news values 1, 16, 42, 50, 52–54, 60, 63,
66, 117, 121, 143, 145, 195, 200, 203,
235, 236, 240, 284, 288–90, 294
NewsDay 58, 66, 117, 242, 270–72
newspapers 2, 6–9, 12, 14, 17, 19, 20, 22,
34–37, 40–45, 48, 51, 52, 55, 57, 58,
61, 64, 67, 85, 93, 103, 105, 108–10,
116, 120–22, 150, 161–63, 173, 180–82,
186, 188, 190, 195, 199–204, 206, 207,
223, 227, 229, 230, 235, 242, 245,
254–57, 265, 268, 270–72, 274, 275,
278, 287, 290
newsroom 41, 48, 50–53, 55, 66, 116–118,
121, 158, 168, 188, 205, 212, 216, 236,
241, 260, 264, 265, 284, 287, 290,
293–5
newswork 50, 52
news diary meeting 50, 52, 65
newsworthiness 57, 59–61, 63, 99, 115,
124, 143, 145, 218, 230, 258, 296
Nkala, C. 128, 129
Nkomo J. 165, 187
Nkomo, J. M. 19, 38, 43
Norton 5, 27, 221
Noeton, L. 134, 136, 137, 139, 140,
143, 150
Nyafaru 76, 80
Nyambara, P. S. 29, 31, 39
Nyamnjoh, F. 276, 285, 288, 291, 293–6,
298, 299
Nyanga 85–8
Nyarota 60, 116, 159

O'Neill 18
Obadare, E. and Willems, W. 240, 275,
278, 287, 298, 299
Observer 150
Olusoga, D. 29, 39, 153, 156, 201, 205
Operation Murambatsvina (OM) 15, 49,
208, 210–14, 216, 219–24, 226–32, 234,
236–238, 288–90, 292

Palling, B. 44, 67
Palmer, R. 27, 31, 39, 70, 71, 108, 110,
112, 150, 152, 156
Parker, J. 18, 19, 22, 43, 48, 50, 67, 74, 89,
104, 105, 108, 110, 136, 156, 255, 256,
275, 276, 298
Patriot The 40, 185
patriotic journalism 159, 206
Phimister, I. R. 27, 39, 70, 108
Pilger, J. 183, 185, 202, 205
Pinto, M. 24, 39
Plangger, A. B. 13, 14, 22, 97, 106–8
postcolonial 7, 20, 24, 54, 59, 108, 109,
117, 122, 145, 155, 156, 158, 161, 185,
194, 199, 201, 202, 204, 205, 212, 223,
231, 232, 234, 236, 241, 278, 280–5,
287–91, 293, 296, 298, 299
prejudice 3–5, 11, 86, 97, 99, 111,
140, 196
Presidential Advisory Council (PAC) 269
propaganda 19, 20, 36, 37, 42, 45, 49, 66,
67, 99, 100, 159, 182, 188, 195, 205,
222, 230, 235, 259, 263, 270, 277, 297
proximity 37, 38, 53, 55, 57–9, 63, 115,
116, 121, 122, 124, 141, 230, 234, 236,
240, 260, 264
prominence 41, 53, 54, 63, 86, 90, 119,
121, 145, 173, 200, 230, 236, 240, 254,
260, 264

Que Que 95, 97, 101; *See also* Kwekwe 94

racial discrimination 40, 82, 108, 120,
182, 202
Raftopoulos 111, 155, 156, 204, 219, 237
Ranger, T. O. 3, 4, 6, 18, 21, 22, 27, 39,
150, 156, 159, 161, 203, 206, 285, 298
resistance 4, 18, 22, 25, 27, 48, 51, 56, 71,
74, 75, 78, 80, 90, 92, 94, 103, 107,
117, 187, 209, 218, 226, 239–41, 254,
275–78, 284, 287, 288, 296, 298, 299
Reuters 112, 131–5, 142, 143, 150
Rhodesian Front (RF) 11, 19, 20, 43, 45,
48, 50, 51, 74
Rhodes, C. J. 8, 11, 18, 20, 21, 34, 36, 50,
57, 58
Rhodesia 5, 6, 11–46, 49, 50, 53, 54,
59–62, 66–68, 70, 76, 77, 79, 82–84,
86–88, 90, 92, 94–97
Rhodesia Printing and Publishing
Company *see* RPP
Richardson, J. 103, 108, 181, 206
Riddell, R. 27, 28, 33, 39, 70, 71, 73, 108,
150, 156

304   *Index*

RPP 10–12, 16, 68, 69
Ruya 26, 30, 74, 94, 101–03

Saunders, R 158, 159, 206
Scarnecchia, T. 111, 156
Schoor, Van. 202, 206
Scoones 197, 206
segregation 10, 17, 23, 27, 38, 70–3, 89,
    97, 98, 103, 108, 110, 112, 151, 182,
    193, 206, 210, 211, 219
selective silence 6, 96
Shamhuyarira, N. 31, 70, 92
Shona 2–6, 10, 16, 21, 22, 25, 31, 34, 90,
    92, 103, 108, 126, 127, 129
silent majority 15, 19, 63, 169, 177, 190,
    191, 204
Silobela 30, 75, 76, 95, 96, 100–102
Sithole, B. 178, 206
Sithole M. 159, 206
Sithole N. 240
Smith, I. D. 20, 38, 41, 44, 48, 50, 67, 77,
    79–82, 89, 93, 102, 105, 135, 159, 205,
    240, 254
Smith, L,. 77, 81, 102
Smith, M. 44, 48, 50, 67
South Africa 1, 2, 7–9, 11, 12, 17, 20–2,
    24–6, 39, 70–2, 76, 108, 137, 153,
    161, 187, 198, 201, 201, 205, 206, 273,
    281, 298
Stanley, H. M. 54, 55, 67, 139, 198, 201
stereotype 4, 51, 79, 113, 197
Stevens, D. 137, 140
Sunday Mail 44, 159, 200, 228, 259, 265
Sunday News 44, 57, 116, 228

Tangwena, R. 6, 14, 23–26, 28–46, 67–70,
    72, 82
Terra incognita 137, 139, 295; *see also*
    Terra Nillius 139
The African Times 11, 13–16, 18, 19, 22, 34,
    62, 65, 81,102
The Argus Printing & Publishing Company
    Ltd 9
The Herald 5–9, 16, 43, 48, 49, 51, 57–61,
    63–6, 81, 116, 117, 119, 120, 121, 141,
    154, 155, 158–63, 165–72, 175, 177–92,
    195, 197, 199, 201, 203, 204, 213, 214,
    216–26, 228–32, 234–6, 242, 243,
    245–8, 252, 255, 257, 259–61, 263–8,
    2714, 278, 279, 284, 288–92
timeliness 53, 61, 63, 218

Traber, M. 16, 94, 97, 103, 235, 238, 276,
    278, 299
Tribal Trust Lands (TTL) 16, 17, 44, 84,
    85, see also communal areas 25, 112,
    154, 182, 193

Unilateral Declaration of Independence 66
Umbowo 15, 16, 44, 69, 104, 181, 191
Umtali, *see* Mutare
Umvuma *See* Mvuma
uprising 2–6, 22, 68, 75, 187, 198,
    240, 284

Van Dijk, T. A. 99, 105, 106, 108, 258,
    275, 277, 288, 299
visibility 23–25, 75, 145, 263, 277; *see also*
    invisibility 7, 294

Waldahl, R. 195, 197, 206
war veterans 118–20, 122–24, 126, 128,
    129, 131, 136, 140, 151, 154, 155, 161,
    162, 165–69, 171–75, 177–80, 182, 185,
    186, 190, 193, 195, 199, 200, 204
Wa Thiong'o, N. 199, 206
Wengraf, T. 159, 206
Whitehead, E. 52, 255
Whiteness 60, 61, 83, 108, 141, 186,
    209, 216
Wijnberg, R. 60, 67
Willems, W. 112, 140, 157, 180, 206, 240,
    287, 296, 299
Wilson and Reynolds 4, 21
Windrich, E. 13, 15, 16, 20–22

Yeros, P. 183, 205

Zimbabwe African National Union
    (ZANU-PF) 13, 14, 17, 21, 29, 33, 36,
    42, 46, 48, 56–58, 62, 69, 70, 77, 78,
    84, 88–92, 96, 100–107
Zapiro 6, 9, 24
Zimbabwe African People's Union (ZAPU)
    17, 21, 29, 96, 100
Zimbabwe Commercial Farmers Union
    (ZCFU), *see* Commercial Farmers Union
Zimbabwe Farmers' Union (ZFU) 187
Zimpapers 8, 25, 30, 38, 39, 42, 46, 47,
    55, 70, 83, 90–92, 94
Zimbabwe Tobacco Farmers Association
    (ZTFA) 150, 187
Zvitangwena 74, 209